The Work of the Holy Spirit In Redemption

by

Franklin Camp

© **Guardian of Truth Foundation 1972.** All rights reserved. No part of this book may be reproduced in any form without written permission from the publisher. Printed in the United States of America.

ISBN 1-58427-068-3

Guardian of Truth Foundation
P.O. Box 9670
Bowling Green, Kentucky 42102

DEDICATION

This book is dedicated to Jim and Jane Foster, Lester and Maxine Wright—whose Christian friendship, help and encouragement have made this book possible.

FOREWORD

Through the years I have counted brother Franklin Camp as one of the best, most trustworthy, and loyal friends of my entire lifetime. The two of us have spent many delightful hours in studying the riches of God's gospel—the good news that originated with the Father, centers in Jesus Christ his Son, and was faithfully revealed by the Holy Spirit. I have learned so much by listening to him preach and reading his gifted, deeply spiritual, and scholarly works in articles and books such as <u>Old Truths in New Robes</u>—both Volumes I and II. His name is a standing synonym for Christian humility, Bible scholarship, loyalty to truth, opposition to all error, and dedicated discipleship. I think I have been with him enough to know that he is one of the best and most sincere men I have ever known. Brother Camp is a good man, a great man, a godly man.

Brother Camp was born in Munford, Alabama, in 1915. He began to preach in 1935. His father and grandfather were both preachers of the ancient faith before him. Both would be deeply pleased to see the great work that their son and grandson has done and continues to do by word of mouth and by the prolific pen he wields so mightily and magnificently. Brother Camp attended David Lipscomb College and while there formed a lifelong friendship with brother Willard Collins. They were roommates in Lipscomb. He labored locally with the Munford, Alabama, church, his home congregation, for twelve years; Park Avenue in LaGrange, Georgia, for two years; the church in East Gadsden, Alabama, thirteen years; and served the Shades Mountain congregation in Birmingham for some ten years. Long ministries have steadfastly characterized his local ministries. His work of faith and labor of love among these churches have been fruitful and faithful. Since 1972 he has devoted his time to writing, lecturing, giving special lessons to Bible teachers, and holding gospel meetings throughout the country. "How to Study the Bible," "Evolution," "The Work of the Holy Spirit," and "Inspiration of the Bible" have been a few of the special themes on which he has lectured through the years.

He serves as co-editor of <u>First Century Christian.</u> Brother Roy J. Hearn is the other editor. It has been my pleasure to serve with them on the board of this great gospel monthly and as one of its staff writers for a number of years. Brother Camp is the editor of <u>The Word of Life</u>, a monthly, which has enjoyed phenomenal growth within recent months. He is a regular on such lectureships as Lipscomb's winter and spring lectures and the Memphis School of Preaching Lectures. He has spoken a number of times on the Freed-Hardeman College Lectureship.

Brother Camp is pre-eminently a student. For more than thirty-five years he has studied the Bible six hours daily. When he first began to preach he said something like this to himself, "If brother Gus Nichols needs to study the Bible five hours a day, then I need to study six hours each day." Thus brother Nichols, of whom brother Camp has been a lifelong admirer, helped inspire and mold the study habits of Franklin Camp from the 1930's to the present. For many years he has made it a point to arise at 4:00 a.m. to begin his day of scriptural study and Biblical meditation. This is why he is at home with the Bible and can speak intelligently on any scriptural theme on a moment's notice. He speaks and writes from the great overflow of many years of faithful and diligent study.

Brother Camp is eminently equipped to write a work on the Holy Spirit and the part he plays in the redemption of mankind. Early in his ministry he encountered the forces of Pentecostalism. He met their men upon the polemic platform. Such debates necessitated his deep study of the Holy Spirit and his work in the redemption of men. Brother Camp early became deeply skilled in meeting the errors of Pentecostalism. He was perhaps the first preacher among us that began to say we were going to have trouble in the church with the forces of Pentecostalism. He was sounding these warnings back in the mid-sixties. He recognized in some of the writings and lectures given by some of our preachers that they were leaning in the direction of Pentecostalism. As he has frequently stated, "One cannot be Pentecostal in argument without ending up in Pentecostalism." The decade of the seventies has witnessed the coming of what he saw eight or more years ago. Thus for more than thirty-five years brother Camp has studied the subject of the Holy Spirit. Even from that rich background he made the decision to spend an additional year of further concentrated study of the Spirit before he wrote the first syllable of this book. He took into this diligent consideration every passage in the Bible that touches the subject of the Holy Spirit. Brother Camp has done more study and preparation for the writing of this book than any other subject that has flowed from this fruitful pen.

It has been an appreciated honor and deeply enriching experience to read this book in manuscript form. Brother Camp is dealing with some of the most controversial themes currently existing among us. Not every one will agree with his conclusions. No one is more aware of this than the scholarly author of this book. But everyone can learn much relative to the Holy Spirit's work in human redemption by an open-minded perusal of this volume. Brother Camp has written with a kind and conciliatory approach in mind. Regarding passages about which there are strong differences among brethren he has tried to avoid dogmatism. Yet he has written his convictions with clarity and logical power. His premises have not been hastily formed nor his conclusions quickly reached. Everyone who reads this book will sense brother Camp's full trust in the all-sufficiency of the Bible. He truly believes the power of God unto salvation lies in the gospel. (Romans 1:16-17.) Those who read this book will have a far greater insight into the how of Pentecostalism and what its basic fallacies are. Those who read this book will have a greater insight into the differences between Judaism and Christianity. They will understand more relative to the real significance of Jerusalem's fall in A. D. 70. They will have a far greater insight into the work of the apostles. Brother Camp's material on the work of the Holy Spirit as outlined in John 14, 15, and 16 is worth far more than the initial price of the book. Even those who may disagree with his material on Acts 2:38, Romans 8, the Biblical use of manifestation, receiving of the Spirit, etc., will nevertheless reap profit by a careful study of the positions set forth. This book will no doubt prompt many to rethink again some of the positions that have been commonly accepted in regard to several of the familar Spirit passages. Serious students of the Holy Spirit will be appreciative of the manner in which he has tied in Joel 2 and Acts 2 with the work of the Holy Spirit in prophecy and fulfillment. These two chapters form the hub of this volume.

We predict this book will have a fine reading reception among all Bible students who desire a greater grasp of Biblical material relative to the third member of the Godhead and his far-reaching work in the realm of redemption. It has been a joy to write the Foreword to this scholarly work. An increasing number of people through the years will read with profit and interest this work of faith, labor of love, and patiently produced volume.

Robert R. Taylor, Jr.
Ripley, Mississippi
December 26, 1973.

INTRODUCTION

The subject of the Holy Spirit is one that I have been interested in from the time that I started preaching. One of the first errors that I had to meet when I began preaching was the denominational claim that the Holy Spirit worked directly and apart from the Word of truth. This is one of the basic doctrines of the denominational world. The teaching that the Spirit works directly and apart from the truth strikes at the very foundation of the authority of the Scriptures. This doctrine opens the door for the claims of all false teachers from Joseph Smith and Oral Roberts to Billy Graham. If one is led directly by the Spirit apart from the truth, then he does not need the Bible, nor indeed can he be expected to follow the Bible.

The question of how the Spirit works in conversion and sanctification is one that gospel preachers have debated with denominational preachers throughout the years. The proposition that the Holy Spirit works only through the Word is one that has stood the test on the polemic platform for more than a hundred and fifty years. It is my firm conviction that this proposition is as unshakable today as it has been in the past. The inroads of Pentecostalism into the church have not come as a result of brethren discovering something new about the Holy Spirit and His work, it has come about because of the neglect to teach on this subject.

The main theme of this book sets forth the proposition that the Holy Spirit works through the Word in conversion and sanctification. These lessons have been presented in numerous places by request, including college lectureships. They are now being put in print because of requests from numbers of people that asked for the material to be printed. The lessons were always presented in the spirit of love and good will, and without any desire to impugn the motives of those who might differ with me. In every place in which I have discussed the subject, there have been some who have disagreed with me on the gift of the Holy Spirit and on the indwelling of the Spirit. But I have always made it clear when these were discussed that I would not think any less of those who disagreed with me. I only asked that they not allow the differences to affect our relationship in the least. As far as I know, this has been true wherever the lessons have been presented.

While the things set forth in the book are, of course, my convictions on the subject, one thing I want to make crystal clear is that I do not believe that any differences about the gift of the Holy

Spirit and the indwelling of the Spirit should ever be made a test of fellowship. I do not have the slightest problem in my relationship with those who may differ with me on these questions. I have enough confidence in brethren that may not agree with me to believe that they in turn would not want to make their position a test of fellowship. I have always refused to allow any difference which I may have had with any brethren over these things not to cause any rupture of my relationship with them, and shall always continue this practice.

Let me say to all that may read this book that as long as we agree that the Holy Spirit convicts, leads, directs, and edifies only through the Word, whatever other differences there may be on the subject ought not to have the least effect on the question of our fellowship.

I am deeply indebted to the following people who have contributed to making this book possible: Dot Perry, who has transcribed the material for the book, Winifred Cooper has read all the material and helped in sentence construction and grammar. Dot, Winifred, Vera McKim, and Hazel Camp have all helped with proofreading. Robert Taylor, Jr. has read the entire manuscript and written the Foreword. Guy N. Woods has read some of the chapters and offered suggestions as to how to improve some sections. I am grateful to all who have contributed in any way in helping to get the book in print. It is my sincere prayer that the book may be an aid in a better understanding of the work of the Holy Spirit in redemption, and that Christ our Saviour may be glorified. The following books have been sources of help in the preparation of the material that is found in this book. All quotations in the book are taken from these books and periodicals: The Campbell-Rice Debate; The Christian Baptist; The Millenial Harbinger, Volume II and Volume V; Questions and Answers by Lipscomb; Bole's Commentary on Acts; The Firm Foundation; The Gospel Advocate; McClintock and Strong; History of the Christian Church; Macknight's Commentary on the Epistles.

Franklin Camp

PREFACE TO THE SECOND EDITION

I am grateful for the reception of the first edition. The second edition is sent forth with the prayer that it may encourage a deeper study of the Bible which must be the measure of all books.

Some features have been added to this edition which I hope will increase its usefulness. There is a scripture index that will aid in checking any passage. There is an added chapter on Pentecostalism. Four charts are included that will help in studying the book.

I want to express my thanks to Lyn Pulley for typing the manuscript on Pentecostalism and Tongues. I am indebted to Dan Jenkins for working up the index to the passages. I am grateful to Joe Nichols for permission to use the four charts.

Joe was a commercial artist before becoming a preacher. The charts may be ordered from him.

I want to add one final word. Occasionally I see where some one that has accepted Max King's teaching quotes from my book along with other brethren. Any attempt to use anything in my book as though it lends any support to their teaching is a perversion and must take the quote out of context. Such tactics are unworthy of any that understand Christian principles and fair play.

It is a misrepresentation to quote anyone out of context. One can appear to prove anything by this method. Suppose that I should quote one of these brethren and say that they teach that baptism is only for believers. Then show that Baptist doctrine also teaches this same thing and leave the implication that they believe Baptist doctrine on Baptism. Yet this would be as near the truth and any quotation from my book that implies that I agree with their theory.

As evidence that my book does not give the slightest support to their position I want to quote from a personal letter that I received from Mr. C. Vanderwaal. He is a church historian in The Republic Of South Africa. He is the author of an excellent book that repudiates the folly of some of Hal Lindsey's teaching. Here is the statement from Mr. Vanderwaal. "I am glad that you do not agree with Max King in his rejection of the second coming of Christ." This should be sufficient from an impartial reader of both books.

J.F.C.

TABLE OF CONTENTS

	Page
The Holy Spirit The Restoration in the Past	1
Objections Considered	13
Locating the Source of our Problem	24
Moral and Miraculous Influence of the Holy Spirit	35
Joel's Prophecy — The Key to Understanding The Holy Spirit in the New Testament	43
I — The Holy Spirit in Matthew	77
The Gift of the Holy Spirit	130
A Word Study	157
Romans 8	214
Some Final Thoughts	258
Pentecostalism & Tongues	275
Index	314
Charts	324

THE HOLY SPIRIT
THE RESTORATION IN THE PAST

The Restoration Movement has made numerous contributions to the religious world. One of the greatest contributions has been the insistence that the Holy Spirit operates only through the Word in conversion and sanctification. Calvinistic teaching of total depravity was the mother of the direct operation of the Holy Spirit. Calvinists' teaching that the sinner was dead and could do nothing, called for the direct operation of the Spirit in conversion. This laid the groundwork for the foolish claim of the Protestant world of the direct operation of the Spirit. The claim of the direct operation of the Spirit led men in all directions. Their feelings and moods became the evidence of pardon. Emotional experiences were offered as proof that the Holy Spirit was working in conversion and sanctification. Thus, each one was led by his feelings, not the Bible. Indeed his feelings were often in direct contradiction to the Bible. Since his feelings were the evidence of the Holy Spirit working, he paid no attention to the Bible and followed his feelings. This produced contradictory teaching, while each one claimed to be led by the Spirit. This resulted in a divided religious world.

The Bible was a neglected book. The sinner was told that he could not understand the Bible when he read it. The Christian was told that he was being guided directly by the Spirit, so he had no need to study. If one read the Bible, the Holy Spirit gave him his understanding and thus all rules of Bible study and interpretation were ignored.

It was against this background that the Restoration Movement began. Its emphasis was upon the Bible. The Bible was held up as man's only infallible guide. People were encouraged to study their Bibles and measure every man's teaching by it. The cry of the Restoration was "Back to the Bible." This plea was heard in open-air meetings, schoolhouses, and in every nook and corner of this country. There was a return to Bible teaching. The Holy Spirit operated through the Word. Bibles were dusted off and a period of dedicated Bible study was underway. There was a new day in the religious world. The Bible had replaced the emotionalism that was supposed to be the direct leading of the Holy Spirit.

THE PRESENT

Since the emphasis of the Restoration Movement was to turn men from emotional experiences back to the Bible, one would never have thought the day would come when the false teaching of the direct operation of the Holy Spirit would become a matter of controversy in the church. But it is here, and unless we can stop it, we are headed the same way that the Protestant world has gone. It is later than many think. The Bible study that has characterized us in the past will cease unless the claim of the direct leading of the Holy Spirit is repudiated—lock, stock, and barrel. The claim of the direct leading of the Holy Spirit has no place in the church. Any attempt to justify it by passages of Scripture is a misapplication of the Scriptures. It is to this end that this book is being written, to show the fallacy of all such claims, and establish the proposition that the Holy Spirit operates in conversion and sanctification only through the Word. This proposition has stood the test of debate after debate in the past. It will stand the test of all who may try to attack it. It is unshakable because it is the truth of the gospel of Christ.

SEEDS OF TODAY'S HARVEST

In order that the reader may see that I am not fighting a straw man, I now give some proof of the false teaching that we have on this subject. In 1966, I wrote a series of articles in reply to some articles in a bulletin. I pointed out at the time that the very claim that was made in these articles could only lead to the Pentecostalism which we have in the church today. It is true that the editor did not believe in the Pentecostalism that is being practiced today, but the arguments that were made in his articles could only lead to the present emotionalism and Pentecostalism with which we are confronted today. The warning that I gave in these articles was largely ignored and we are now reaping the harvest of this false teaching. It is impossible to make Pentecostal arguments, find people to accept them, and not end up in the Pentecostal camp. I cut my teeth preaching on meeting Pentecostal arguments. I knew they were wrong then; I knew they were Pentecostal arguments when they were made by brethren as far back as 1964, and stated publicly that unless this teaching was stopped, we would have some claiming the baptism of the Holy Spirit and being able to work miracles. The record now speaks for itself. We have not yet reached the end unless there is return to the simple Bible proposition that the Holy Spirit operates in conversion and sanctification only through the Word. Following are the three articles that I wrote in reply to the articles in the bulletin:

> Brother Curtis Dowdy sent me three issues of a bulletin. The editor has joined with brother Dwain Evans in an effort to defend the idea of some special operation of the Spirit in

relation to the Christian. It is to be regretted that these and other brethren are teaching this old worn-out denominational doctrine about the Holy Spirit. Since it is being taught, those that love the church and the truth cannot sit by and ignore it. The results of such teaching will lead to Pentecostalism unless it is opposed and stopped.

In spite of the editor's learning and ability, a "Holiness preacher" could have done a better job in proving his position. At least the "Holiness preacher" would have been consistent in his position of claiming a special operation of the Spirit as he would have insisted that miracles continue today. I take it that the editor does not believe that miracles can be performed today, but if his arguments prove anything, they prove that miracles have not ceased. There is not a single argument in the articles that proves that the Spirit operates on the Christian apart from the Word. The basis of every argument is in relation to miraculous operations of the Spirit.

The article is titled "The Acts of the Holy Spirit." He says that he learned from Dr. Erdman that the book of Acts should be called "The Acts of the Holy Spirit." I have a strong feeling that he did not stop with just getting the idea of changing the name of the book from Dr. Erdman. His contention of a special operation of the Spirit on the Christian today came from Dr. Erdman or some other denominational source. He did not find it in the book of Acts.

Note the fallacy of the editor's reasoning, if it can be called reasoning. Here is the way he reasons to reach his conclusion that the Holy Spirit operates in the Christian apart from the Word.

Major Premise: There was a special operation of the Spirit in the books of Acts.

Minor Premise: The Spirit operates today.

Conclusion: Therefore there is a special operation of the Spirit in the Christian.

Is it possible that he does not know that a special operation of the Spirit was needed in Acts because the gospel had to be revealed and confirmed through the apostles? Let me give him a parallel argument.

Major Premise: There were living apostles in the book of Acts.

Minor Premise: The apostles function today.

Conclusion: Therefore we need living apostles.

Were there not living apostles in Acts? Do the apostles not function today? Yes. Shall we conclude that we need living apostles today? No. The apostles that lived in Acts now function through the Word. The Mormons are wrong in claiming living apostles just because they find them in the book of Acts. But they are no further from the truth than this editor is in his claim for a special operation of the Spirit just because he reads of such in the book of Acts.

Let us look again at the editor's reasoning. Remember that his position is that there were special acts of the Holy Spirit in Acts and this proves a special operation today. One of the special acts of the Holy Spirit in Acts was speaking in tongues (Acts 2:1-4; 10:46; 19:6). Will he claim this power also? Surely he will not deny that this was one of "The Acts of the Holy Spirit." In Acts 3 there is the healing of the lame man. In Acts 9 there is the account of Peter healing a man and of raising Dorcas from the dead. Were these "Acts of the Holy Spirit"? Since the editor claims to have the Spirit as it was in "The Acts of the Holy Spirit," can he heal or raise the dead? If not, then he rejects the conclusion of his whole article. If yes, then he ought not to oppose Oral Roberts.

The article says that the "rushing mighty wind not only filled the whole house where they were sitting, the Holy Spirit filled the heart of every Christian with the motive and source for spiritual action." Does he believe in the baptism of the Holy Spirit today? If not, why refer to Luke's account of the coming of the Spirit upon the apostles and then conclude that, "The Holy Spirit filled the heart of every Christian"? I do not deny that a Christian can be filled with the Spirit, but I deny that it is done apart from the Word. He states further,

THE WORK OF THE HOLY SPIRIT 5

"Perhaps our lack of action can be traced to our failure to make full use of the Person of God's Spirit dwelling personally within our hearts." Why hedge by saying "perhaps"? If we are failing to "make full use of the Spirit dwelling personally within" us, why not tell how to do it? If the Spirit operates apart from the Word, why does he not do his work? WHAT ARE THE CONDITIONS OF HIS OPERATION? If this is the "motive and source for spiritual action," and the Christian has it, then how can one account for the lack of action?

He also says, "That we have taken the Spirit out." This is a false charge and is the same accusation made by denominational preachers when we deny the operation of the Spirit on the sinner apart from the Word. He then states that, "Through the Spirit, fear came upon every soul." There is no such statement. Acts 2:43 says, "And fear came upon every soul: AND MANY WONDERS AND SIGNS WERE DONE BY THE APOSTLES." Why did he not quote the last part of the verse? It would have ruined his pet theory. It is careless handling of the Word of God to put in words that are not there and then leave out parts of a verse to try to prove something. As is usual with those who attempt to defend false teaching, he meets himself going in one paragraph and coming in the next one. He thinks the gospel is complete, but insists that the Holy Spirit must indwell within the Christian apart from the Word.

The editor seeks to avoid anyone questioning his theory by saying that, "The indwelling of God's Spirit within our hearts is a great mystery." If he can get the indwelling of the Spirit in the realm of mystery, he is safe, as the word "mystery" indicates that he knows neither the "how" nor the "what." It is in this very area that this position of the Holy Spirit presents its dangers. When men claim to have the Holy Spirit in some mysterious way, then everyone is left to his own guess as to when the Holy Spirit is doing what. The ultimate end of this teaching is to reject the Scriptures as our guide.

In an effort to establish this indwelling, he states, "We cannot explain how Satan's spirit can enter into the hearts of men, but the Bible plainly declares that he does." If this statement refers to men that were possessed by demons in the days of Christ and the apostles, he will prove more than he intended to. The ones that were possessed by demons were controlled by them. Is this the kind of operation of the Spirit that he is claiming for the Christian? In the second place, it took a miracle to free the ones possessed by demons. Does he believe it takes a miracle to convert the sinner and free him from Satan's spirit? If he does not refer to demons, then he ought not to say, "We cannot explain how Satan's spirit can enter into the hearts of men..." for he is not speaking for me. I happened to have read the third chapter of Genesis and I learned from this chapter how Satan entered Eve's heart. My Bible makes it plain that he lied to her and deceived her—that he used words and not some mysterious influence. "For such are false apostles, deceitful workers, transforming themselves into the apostles of Christ. And no marvel; for Satan himself is transformed into an angel of light. Therefore it is no great thing if his ministers also be transformed as the ministers of righteousness; whose end shall be according to their works," (II Corinthians 11:13-15). "But I fear, lest by any means, as the serpent beguiled Eve through his subtilty, **so your minds** should be corrupted from **the simplicty that is in Christ**," (II Corinthians 11:3). Will he find where the Bible declares plainly that Satan enters the hearts of men in some other way?

The articles further state, "We must not reduce Christianity to pat formulas and sterilize faith into simple steps." I just wonder if he believes that the gospel is God's formula for sin. It is the only formula that I know of for sin. Paul said, "For I am not ashamed of the gospel of Christ: for it is the power of God unto salvation to every one that believeth; to the Jew first, and also to the Greek," (Romans 1:16). Does the editor have some other formula for sin? I have also been under the impression that the gospel as given by Christ was to stand pat. If not, what is the meaning of this statement by Paul? "But though we, or an angel from heaven, preach any other gospel unto you than that which we have preached unto you, let him be accursed. As we said before, so say I now again, If any man preach any other gospel unto you than that ye have received, let him be accursed," (Galatians 1:8-9). If (and there is no "if") the gospel is God's formula for sin and Galatians 1:8 and 9 means anything, it is a formula that is pat. I preach the gospel as God's only formula for sin and I preach it pat without apology.

Would the editor explain how denying the operation of the Spirit apart from the Word sterilizes faith? Is this why he insists on an operation of the Spirit apart from the Word? Does he think that the Word is a dead letter? Does he believe that the Spirit must operate apart from the Word to give it life? If not, what is the meaning of his statement? The Bible teaches that faith comes by hearing the Word (Romans 10:17). Is this the kind of sterile faith that he is talking about? The Bible also teaches that there are "steps" in connection with this faith. "And the father of circumcision to them who are not of the circumcision only, but who also walk IN THE STEPS OF THAT FAITH of our father Abraham, which he had being yet uncircumcised," (Romans 4:12). The sterile faith that I read of in the Scriptures is "faith without works," (James 2:26). Furthermore, the Bible teaches that this faith is to work by love (Galatians 5:6), not by some special operation of the Spirit.

Again, he says, "Refusal to acknowledge the mysterious is to negate the very premise of real religion." I know of no one that denies the mysterious. Life is filled with it, but what does this have to do with our believing and obeying the gospel? The gospel is a revelation of Christ given for the very purpose of delivering us from the mysterious and enabling us to know the "why and how" of salvation. It would be interesting to hear him explain how he follows the mysterious.

Notice carefully the following statement in his editorial. "Maurice Eagen has suggested that if the modern church ever dies, the dagger in its heart will be the Sunday morning sermon. The twentieth century church is definitely in danger of being talked to death. Through lectures and business meetings, workshops, and bull sessions — so much of our religion is lived in terms of talk. So much of our action has been reduced to mere words. The making of speeches has become an ecclesiastical art — an end within itself. The time has come to quit the conversation and stand with Peter: "And we are his witnesses of these things; and so is also the Holy Ghost, whom God hath given to them that obey him," (Acts 5:32).

He begins his editorial with "The Acts of the Holy Spirit" and concludes it with a comment on preaching, and attempts to support it by a quotation in reference to inspired preachers. He reasons (?) from the miraculous operation of the Holy Spirit in Acts to the kind of preaching needed today. Does he think we need inspired preachers today? We do not need inspired preachers today unless we need a new revelation. We have inspired sermons and the New Testament is full of them. We do not need a direct operation of the Spirit to preach these sermons. Less reading of modern, liberal, denominational preachers, and more genuine study of the Scriptures will get the job done. I agree with him that in many instances the "pulpit is sick," but our diagnosis is not the same. Mine would be a "book burning" (denominational books) like the one they had at Ephesus (Acts 19:19). Follow this with a good "old-fashioned dose" of dedicated Bible study, and watch the results. "So mightily grew the word of God and PREVAILED," (Acts 19:20). His diagnosis would be to ask, "... Have ye received the Holy Spirit since ye believed?" (Acts 19:2). Remember he says that the book of Acts is "The Acts of the Holy Spirit." Would he then lay hands on us and have the Holy Spirit come upon us? (Acts 19:6). I do not charge him with believing this, but the end of his reasoning would be just this. Of course, it is possible that his diagnosis is correct and mine wrong since he has some special operation of the Spirit and I only have the Bible.

Mr. Eagen refers to the "modern church." What does he have reference to? If it is to the modern denominational church, I agree that it is sick. Their claim to some direct operation of the Spirit, liberalism in their schools, and their loss of faith in the integrity of the Scriptures are some of the things that produced the "illness." Their illness today is "nigh unto death" because they have humanized and modernized the Bible, which amounts to a complete rejection of it. I have grave fears that the editor has associated with them until he at least has the first symptoms of their disease. I recommend an innoculation of, "Let the word of Christ dwell in you richly," (Colossians 3:16), and thus be "filled with the Spirit," (Ephesians 5:18).

Mr. Eagen also talks of the "twentieth century church." What about the first century church? I doubt that he knows much about the Restoration plea. Herein lies the crux of the whole matter. Back of all this talk about the Holy Spirit is a concerted effort to sidetrack the continued plea for New Testament Christianity. The great ado that some are making about some special operation of the Holy Spirit is just a smoke screen to hide their rejection of the Restoration Movement. The pioneer preachers that blazed the trail through sacrifice and tears to get back to the Bible are sneered at. Their type of preaching and sermons are supposed to be outdated. I make no claim that the pioneers were infallible. My faith is not based on what they taught, but upon my personal study of the Scriptures. But there are some things of which I am sure. When they started back toward Jerusalem, they started in the right direction. When they took their stand on the Bible as their only guide, they reached solid ground. The ones that would betray it today have not even made a crack in this solid ground. When they have gone the way of others that have preceded them, and left the church, the clarion call of simple Bible-based sermons will still be heard from men whose voices will not be stilled and whose faith in God's infallible Word cannot be shaken.

I do not deny that there are things in the church that need to be corrected. BUT I DENY WITH EVERY FIBER OF MY BEING THAT THE GREAT FUNDAMENTALS OF OUR SALVATION HAVE NOT BEEN RESTORED. *Mission Magazine* will not discover nor produce one single fundamental truth that is essential to the restoration of New Testament Christianity. If it succeeds in anything, it will be producing a liberal faction within the church. THE HOLY SPIRIT WILL NOT BE THE AUTHOR.

My purpose in reviewing these articles is two-fold. First, I wanted to show the fallacy of his arguments, and second, to point out the connection between what is being claimed about the Holy Spirit and the liberal thinking that is widespread in the church. The editor is one of the many young preachers that have attended liberal schools and have become infested with their thinking. If his articles were only an isolated instance, it would not deserve notice, but it is a sample of a widespread element within the church.

DEFINING THE ISSUE

I. GOD'S WAY IS THE ONLY WAY

Careless thinking has led many to think that any way is acceptable to God. It is sometimes said, "We are all trying to go to heaven. We're just traveling different roads." But God's way is one, not many. It's a fatal mistake to try to make God's way the ways of man (Isaiah 55:8-9). The fact that God planned man's salvation and made it possible should indicate that it is the only way. If the way was not important, then there would have been no use in God's coming to man's assistance. If the way was not important, God would have left every man to figure out his own way, and everyone could have made it to heaven. Casual reading of the Bible shows that this is not true.

II. GOD'S WAY IS ONE OF REVELATION

The only way that man could know the mind of God was by revelation. That is the reason we have the Bible. The natural world tells all, except fools, that God IS, but man cannot find the answer to his deepest needs by reading nature (Psalms 19). The answer to the problem of sin and redemption can only be found in the Bible. It would be just as sensible to deny the need of redemption as to deny the need of revelation to know how to be redeemed. The need of revelation is shown by the fact that God warns about changing His Word (Galatians 1:7-9). Man does not know enough to get along without revelation, nor does he know enough to get along with partial revelation. If we were dependent upon revelation only in part, then God would have given only a partial revelation. A world without revelation is a world lost forever. But the world that rejects revelation is just as lost as the world without revelation.

III. THE WAY OF REVELATION IS ONE OF INSPIRATION

Revelation without inspiration would be nonsense. The Bible is inspired or it is not a revelation. How would it be possible for the Bible to be a revelation of God without inspiration? "But I certify you, brethren, that the gospel which was preached of me is not after man. For I neither received it of man, neither was I taught it, but by the revelation of Jesus Christ," (Galatians 1:11-12). "... But holy men of God spake as they were moved by the Holy Ghost," (II Peter 1:21). Revelation implies inspiration, and

THE WORK OF THE HOLY SPIRIT

inspiration implies verbal inspiration. Some claim that only the idea is inspired, not the words. The Bible denies this. "Which things also we speak, not in the words which man's wisdom teacheth, but which the Holy Ghost teacheth; comparing spiritual things with spiritual," (I Corinthians 2:13). Words are the signs of ideas. The Holy Spirit selected the words. While translations are not inspired, this does not alter the inspiration of words when originally given. If translations are an argument against verbal inspiration, they would also be an argument against inspiration. The purpose of inspiration was to get the exact thought of God to man, and words are essential to the expression of thought. If we cannot be sure about the right word, how do we know that it is the exact thought of God? David said, "The spirit of the Lord spake by me [that is inspiration] and his word was in my tongue [verbal inspiration]." David did not say that his idea or thought was in my tongue. "If any man think himself to be a prophet, or spiritual, let him acknowledge that the things that I write unto you are the commandments of the Lord. But if any man be ignorant, let him be ignorant," (I Corinthians 14:37-38).

IV. GOD'S WAY IS ONE OF REVELATION, INSPIRATION, AND CONFIRMATION

These three things always go together. What good would inspiration and revelation be without confirmation? If God inspired men to reveal His Word, how can I know it is His Word and not theirs? How can I determine whether they were inspired or not? Shall I just accept their claim for inspiration? Joseph Smith claimed inspiration, and he claimed that the Book of Mormon is a revelation from God. How do I know that the Bible is inspired, and the Book of Mormon is uninspired? The difference is that the inspiration of the Bible is confirmed by miracles, while the claim of Joseph Smith is unconfirmed. Neither Smith, nor his witnesses, ever offered any proof of inspiration except their word. It has always been the procedure of God to give evidence of the inspiration of His revelation. God knew that any man could come along and say, "God told me this."

When God was about to send Moses to stand before Pharaoh and demand that he let the children of Israel go, Moses was concerned about this very question. "And Moses answered and said, But, behold, they will not believe me, nor hearken unto my voice: for they will say, The Lord hath not appeared unto thee," (Exodus 4:1). Moses knew that the Israelites and Pharaoh would have been fools to have depended solely upon his claim to have been sent by God. How would they have known whether Moses was telling the truth or not? Moses was not alone when God appeared to him in the burning bush, and he was not alone when he stood before Pharaoh and the Israelites. The same God that was in the burning bush accompanied Moses into Egypt. God's answer to Moses was, "I do not expect them to take your word that I have sent you." "And it shall come to pass, if they will not believe thee, neither hearken to the voice of the first sign, that they will believe the voice of the latter sign," (Exodus 4:8). Note that there were two voices speaking: the voice of Moses and the voice of miracles, or signs, telling the Israelites and Pharaoh in no unmistakable terms what Moses said was not from his imagination, but from God. The miracles recorded in the Bible are God's evidence of inspiration. But when inspiration and revelation ceased, so did miracles. So-called miracle healers of today are in the same class with Joseph Smith. The only difference is that he claimed inspiration and they claim confirmation.

Let me now summarize the work of the Holy Spirit as set forth in the preceding.

1. The work of the Holy Spirit is to take the mind of God and make it known to man. This proposition is set forth in I Corinthians 2:7-16; I Peter 1:10-12; II Peter 1:21. This we now have in the written Word.

2. It was the work of the Holy Spirit to take the mind of God, give it to man unmixed with error. It was the work of the Holy Spirit to give man the truth of God, and only the truth. It was the work of the Holy Spirit to assure us that the Bible is the Word of truth.

3. It was the work of the Holy Spirit to confirm the truth as a divine revelation. Revelation without confirmation would have made it impossible to distinguish between a genuine revelation and a counterfeit one; therefore, confirmation was essential with revelation. Miracles to confirm the Word are the means of furnishing supernatural evidence to a supernatural revelation. Confirmation of the Word by miracles assures us of the integrity of the Bible and its claim to be from God.

OBJECTIONS CONSIDERED

Before I begin a discussion of passages that deal with the Holy Spirit, it is necessary to clear up some objections. When I insist the Holy Spirit operates in conversion and sanctification only through the Word, some try to answer by raising a smoke screen. In order to allow for proper consideration of the Scriptures to be discussed, it is necessary to consider these objections.

THE ISSUE

What is the question under consideration in the work of the Holy Spirit? This is vital to a proper understanding of this discussion. The question is not, Does the Holy Spirit operate in conversion and sanctification; but, How does He work? I have never denied that the Spirit operates in conversion. I take the position that the Holy Spirit operates in every conversion. There has never been a conversion that the Holy Spirit has not had a part in. My disagreement with some of our brethren is not a question of the operation of the Spirit, but how does He operate? What means does the Holy Spirit use? Does He operate directly and without means? This is the issue and the only issue.

OBJECTION NO. 1

Brethren that contend for the operation of the Spirit apart from the Word try to dodge the question by saying that the Holy Spirit is not the Word. They attempt to show that if the Holy Spirit operates only through the Word, the Holy Spirit is the Word. No one believes this. The position of the Holy Spirit operating only through the Word does not lead to this conclusion.

"God, who at sundry times and in divers manners spake in time past unto the fathers by the prophets, Hath in these last days spoken unto us by his Son . . ." (Hebrews 1:1-2). Note that, among other means, God used the prophets in speaking to people in Old Testament times. Question: When God spoke through the prophets, did that mean that God became the prophet? If God could speak through the prophet, without God becoming the prophet, why may not the Holy Spirit use the Word as a means in conversion and sanctification, without the Holy Spirit becoming the Word? God speaks to us today through Christ. Does that mean that God the Father is Christ the Son? If God the

Father could speak through the Son without becoming Christ the Son, why may not the Holy Spirit speak to us through the Word without the Holy Spirit becoming the Word? The Holy Spirit operated by inspiration. Surely, no one except Modernists would deny this. But did the Holy Spirit operating by inspiration result in the Holy Spirit being only inspiration? Inspiration was the means used by the Spirit in giving us the Word. If inspiration can be the means of giving us the Word without the Holy Spirit becoming inspiration, why cannot the Holy Spirit use the Word as a means in conversion and sanctification and not become the Word?

The Holy Spirit operated by miracle. The miracles were the means used by the Spirit in confirmation of the Word. But does the Holy Spirit operating by means of miracles in the confirmation of the Word mean that the Holy Spirit is only a miracle? If the Holy Spirit could operate by means of a miracle and not become a miracle, why cannot the Holy Spirit operate through the Word and not become the Word?

Christ operates in our redemption through His blood. He certainly does not operate in our redemption apart from His blood. Does the fact that Christ operates in redemption only through His blood mean that Christ becomes only blood? If Christ can operate in redemption only through His blood and not be only blood, why cannot the Holy Spirit operate only through the Word and not become the Word?

The use of these means does not change the one acting into the agent used. I preach the gospel and use the gospel as means of converting the lost and in edifying the church. Would anyone contend that because I use the gospel as a means in converting people that I become the gospel? I am a person, but using means, and only means, to convert people does not change me from a person into the means used. The Holy Spirit is a person, but the Holy Spirit using means in conversion and sanctification does not change the Holy Spirit from a person into the means used.

From these considerations, you can see that the proposition that the Holy Spirit operating in conversion and sanctification only through the Word does not lead to the conclusion that the Holy Spirit becomes the Word.

OBJECTION NO. 2

A second objection which is offered to the proposition that the Holy Spirit operates only through the Word is that this makes the Bible take

THE WORK OF THE HOLY SPIRIT   15

the place of the Holy Spirit. The following is taken from the Christian Chronicle in an editorial by James Nichols: "Our view of the Bible must be considered in this discussion. Did the Bible take the Holy Spirit's place after the completion of the New Testament canon? Are we living in the age of the Spirit, the age of the Bible, or both? Is the Bible our only contact with God? Have we succumbed to the very extremes that honest study always eliminates legalism and bibliolatry? We must investigate more seriously our view of the Bible." The first sentence of this paragraph is of some encouragement in that the writer says that the Bible must also be considered in this discussion. The truth is that the consideration of the Bible is the very heart of the discussion. Either the Bible is a complete and sufficient revelation from God and meets all of our needs, or it's not. If the Bible is not our one and only guide, then it's not true, since it claims to be (II Timothy 3:15-16).

Consider now this question: Did the Bible take the Holy Spirit's place after the completion of the New Testament canon? As far as I know, there are none who claim that the Bible took the place of the Holy Spirit after the canon was completed. The question is not, Does the Holy Spirit work today; but, Does the Holy Spirit work apart from the Word? The question is not, Is the Holy Spirit working today; but, Is He working directly and without means, or is He working by means of the Word? Did the Holy Spirit write the Bible and retire? If brother Nichols had considered the question, he would never have asked such foolish things. The proposition is: The Holy Spirit operates (works) in conversion and sanctification through the Word. Does not the word "operate" indicate action? How can the Holy Spirit work through the Word and be retired? As far as I know, no one denies that the Holy Spirit works today. The question is not, Does the Holy Spirit work; but, How does He accomplish His work? The Holy Spirit has retired from miraculous operation. "Whether there be prophecies, they shall be done away," (I Corinthians 13:8). "The Authorized Version 'shall fail' misses the distinction between the former verb and this word **katargeo**, rendered 'done away.' This verb more literally means to reduce to inactivity (**kata**, down; **argos**, idle). This meaning might be assigned to every occurrence of the word. There would come a time when prophecies would be put out of action, would cease to function," I Corinthians, W. E. Vine, p. 183. The Holy Spirit has retired from this field of action. As Vines says, His miraculous operations have been reduced to inactivity. He is now idle in miraculous operations. It is a failure to make this distinction that is causing all of this false teaching today. Herein lies the very heart of the controversy.

Any claim for any influence of the Holy Spirit apart from the Word would be a miraculous operation. If the Holy Spirit influences apart from the Word, it would have to be a direct influence, and a direct influence would be a miraculous operation. To deny that the Holy Spirit is operating miraculously today is not to deny that the Holy Spirit operates. Before the New Testament was written, the Holy Spirit operated through inspired men. Now He operates through the inspired Book. Even when the Holy Spirit operated miraculously through inspired men, He did not operate in conversion and sanctification apart from the Word. The miraculous operation was to reveal the Word, by which the sinner was converted and the saint edified. Even the apostles who received the baptism of the Holy Spirit were dependent upon the revelation received in their living and conduct. Peter was an apostle and the gospel he preached was infallible, but his conduct was not. The Holy Spirit guided his preaching, but it was up to Peter to put into practice what the Spirit revealed. A miracle revealed to Peter that the gospel was for the Gentiles as well as the Jews. But the baptism of the Holy Spirit did not make Peter practice what the miracle revealed to him (Galatians 2:11-14).

Perhaps another question would help to clear up the misunderstanding that has developed as suggested in brother Nichols' question. Has inspiration ceased? Answer: Yes, inspiration has ceased in the sense of there being direct inspiration of men. But inspiration has not ceased in the sense that we do not have inspiration today. We have an inspired Book. Inspiration now works through this Book, but not directly as it did when the revelation was being given directly through inspired men. If inspiration at one time worked directly in giving the revelation through men, but now operates through the Book, why can brethren not see that though the Holy Spirit operated directly, and worked directly through men at one time, the Holy Spirit now works and operates through the Bible. The direct operation of the Holy Spirit in inspiration has ceased. But that does not mean that inspiration has retired in the sense that there is no inspiration in the world today. Inspiration now works through the Bible and in this sense, it has not retired. What is true of inspiration is also true in reference to the question that brother James Nichols raised concerning the work of the Holy Spirit when he asked the question, "Has the Holy Spirit retired today?" Just as the Holy Spirit has retired from direct inspiration and now furnishes this inspiration through the Word, so the Holy Spirit has retired from miraculous operation and now these miracles are contained within the Word (John 20:30-31; Mark 16:20).

OBJECTION NO. 3

Some claim that it is the personal indwelling of the Holy Spirit that keeps religion from being ritualistic and legalistic. One of the fallacies in the thinking of those who claim some operation of the Spirit on the Christian apart from the Word is a failure to see the difference in Judaism and Christianity. They think that it is the operation of the Spirit in the Christian that makes the difference between the legalism of Judaism and the spiritual nature of Christianity. Judaism was primarily fleshly and ceremonial. The blood of bulls and goats could not take away sin (Hebrews 10:4). Consider the following statement: "The Holy Ghost this signifying, that the way into the holiest of all was not yet made manifest, while as the first tabernacle was yet standing: Which was a figure for the time then present, in which were offered both gifts and sacrifices, that could not make him that did the service perfect, as pertaining to the conscience; Which stood only in meats and drinks, and divers washings, and carnal ordinances, imposed on them until the time of reformation. But Christ being come an high priest of good things to come, by a greater and more perfect tabernacle, not made with hands, that is to say, not of this building; Neither by the blood of goats and calves, but by his own blood he entered in once into the holy place, having obtained eternal redemption for us. For if the blood of bulls and of goats, and the ashes of an heifer sprinkling the unclean, sanctifieth to the purifying of the flesh: How much more shall the blood of Christ, who through the eternal Spirit offered himself without spot to God, purge your conscience from dead works to serve the living God?" (Hebrews 9:8-14).

The difference between the Old and the New Covenants is the provisions made. Here is the spiritual basis of the New Covenant. The atonement of Christ made possible the full remission of sin. There is nothing ceremonial in the New Covenant. It is spiritual from beginning to end. There is not the first command or action of the New Covenant that is ceremonial. This is not because of some peculiar operation of the Spirit apart from the Word, but from the very nature of the gospel made possible by the death of Christ. If there is any legalism in the church today, it is not because of a failure to teach the Christian about the Holy Spirit, but ignorance of the nature and the provisions of the gospel. The solution to any legalism in the church will come from preaching the gospel and not from warmed-up denominational error on the Holy Spirit.

Those who insist that it is the Holy Spirit that does away with legalism, meet themselves coming back. As far as I know, they all believe that the Holy Spirit operates only through the Word in conversion. It would be interesting to hear one of them explain how one can become a Christian in obedience to the demands of the gospel, and still have their obedience not be legalistic. If one's obedience in becoming a Christian can be spiritual and not legalistic without some direct operation of the Holy Spirit, why cannot a Christian's obedience and service to God be spiritual and non-legalistic without some direct operation of the Spirit?

Faith is commanded (Acts 16:31). Repentance is commanded (Acts 2:38). Confession is commanded (Matthew 10:32-33). Baptism is commanded (Acts 10:48). Here are four commands that have to be obeyed to become a Christian. Are these spiritual acts or legalistic commands? Does one obey legalistic commands in becoming a Christian and then the Holy Spirit take over and turn his service into spiritual service? If a Christian cannot be approved by God through legalistic service, and he cannot, can one please God in his primary obedience by legalistic obedience? Romans 1:5 states that our obedience is the obedience of faith. It is this that makes our primary obedience spiritual and not legalistic. It is this same obedience of faith that makes our Christian service spiritual and not legalistic.

Those who claim that it is the indwelling of the Holy Spirit in some mysterious way that warms Christianity and keeps it from being legalistic, would do well to study the Corinthian letter. We are told that a non-miraculous indwelling of the Holy Spirit makes us spiritual. Consider the church at Corinth. It had an abundance of miraculous gifts. Surely a non-miraculous gift will not do more than a miraculous gift. The church at Corinth was divided. This was not spiritual. They were carnal (I Corinthians 1:10-17; 3:1-4). They had turned the Lord's Supper into a feast (I Corinthians 11). Surely this was not spiritual. These are but samples of their lack of spirituality. If there was ever a time and a place for the Holy Spirit to take over and turn a worldly church into a spiritual one, this was the place. It is certainly significant that in I Corinthians 12 and 14 Paul discusses these miraculous gifts. They are even called spiritual gifts (I Corinthians 14:1). What solution did Paul offer to the lack of spirituality in the church at Corinth? It is enlightening to see that Chapter 13 comes between the two chapters that deal with spiritual gifts. After discussing the importance of love and the temporary nature of spiritual gifts, Paul concludes the thirteenth chapter by saying, "And now abideth faith, hope, charity, these three; but the greatest of these is charity." Evidently Paul thought that the answer to the lack of spirituality in Corinth would be corrected by these three basic principles. The direct operation of the Holy Spirit in the Corinthians had not accomplished this. If it is the work of the Holy Spirit apart from the Word, to do things of this nature, I ask again, why had He not done it in Corinth? If the miraculous operation of the Holy Spirit in Corinth would not, and did not accomplish this, how can a non-miraculous operation apart from the Word do it today?

The truth is that the problem in Corinth was a misunderstanding and a refusal to let the gospel, revealed by the miraculous operation by the Holy Spirit, do what God intended. Faith, hope, and love are the three pillars of Christianity. Each one of these is spiritual in its nature. All acceptable service to God must be undergirded by these three. When our service is motivated by these, it is spiritual. What promotes these three principles in our lives? It is the gospel understood and believed. There is nothing else to do it. Our faith must rest on the testimony of the Scriptures (Romans 10:17). Our response to God's love revealed in the gospel brings about loving obedience and service. Our hope based on God's revealed will inspires and fires our souls with enthusiasm. These are the principles that keep our service from being legalistic and ritualistic. Where these are, there is spirituality. Where they are not, there is carnality and a lack of spirituality. Each one of these three is prompted, motivated, and cultivated through the gospel. Warmed-over denominational teaching on the Holy Spirit will not take the place of simple, plain gospel preaching.

OBJECTION NO. 4

When the proposition is stated that the Holy Spirit operates only through the Word, some ask the question, "What about prayer?" Is the operation apart from the Word essential to prayers being answered? If so, where is the Scripture that teaches this? I know that Romans 8:26 is sometimes used, but this passage does not prove that the Holy Spirit must operate apart from the Word in order for God to hear and answer prayer. (This passage will be discussed in detail later on. Therefore, I am not entering into a discussion of this passage at this time.)

Those who insist that the personal indwelling of the Holy Spirit and the Holy Spirit operating apart from the Word are essential to God's hearing and answering prayers, have a problem that they have not considered. Those who take this position say that the Holy Spirit sustains a relationship to the Christian that He did not have prior to the Christian Age. Their position is that the Christian Age and the personal indwelling of the Holy Spirit go together. If the personal indwelling and the operation of the Spirit apart from the Word are necessary for God to answer prayers, then the following difficulty needs to be explained. Did God hear and answer prayer before the Christian Age? If yes, then the personal indwelling and operation of the Spirit apart from the Word is not essential to God's hearing and answering prayers.

In Genesis 18 Abraham prayed and God heard his prayer. God was willing to answer his prayer as long as the conditions could be met. Did Abraham have the personal indwelling as brethren claim that Christians have today? If God could hear the prayer of Abraham without the Spirit operating apart from the Word, or his having the personal indwelling, why can God not do the same today? Other examples of God's hearing and answering prayer in the Patriarchal and Jewish Age could be given, but this is unnecessary. God answered prayer in the Old Testament. The children of God in the Old Testament did not have the personal indwelling of the Holy Spirit. The personal indwelling of the Holy Spirit is not essential to God's hearing and answering prayer.

If the position that the personal indwelling of the Spirit is essential to God's hearing and answering prayer, then one of two things must follow: 1) The saints of the Old Testament had the personal indwelling (as claimed by some today) just as the Christians do today. 2) God did not hear and answer prayer until the Christian Age. If God heard and answered prayer in the Old Testament without the personal indwelling and the Spirit operating apart from the Word, then the argument that the personal indwelling and the operation of the Spirit apart from the Word does not prove that God cannot answer prayer, if the Holy Spirit operates only through the Word today.

OBJECTION NO. 5

If the Holy Spirit operates only through the Word, then what about providence? Is the personal indwelling and the operation of the Holy Spirit apart from the Word necessary for the working of providence? If so, where are the passages that teach it? I have read several articles that have made this argument. What were the Scriptures used to prove it? The eighth chapter of Acts is the prime passage appealed to. Does the example of Philip and the eunuch prove the operation of the Holy Spirit apart from the Word in providence? If this example proves the operation of the Holy Spirit apart from the Word in providence today, then it also proves the direct intervention of angels in providence. "And the ANGEL of the Lord spake unto Philip, saying, Arise, and go toward the south unto the way that goeth down from Jerusalem unto Gaza,

THE WORK OF THE HOLY SPIRIT

which is desert," (Acts 8:26). Does this verse prove the direct intervention of angels in providence today? Who has had an angel to personally appear and arrange a meeting between him and the sinner? If the account of Philip and the eunuch could be used today as an example of the Holy Spirit operating in the realm of providence, it also would prove the direct intervention of angels in providence today.

Does the example of Philip and the eunuch prove the necessity of the Spirit operating apart from the Word in order for providence to work today? If it does, then it also proves the direct and supernatural operation of the Spirit today. "Then the Spirit said unto Philip, Go near, and join thyself to this chariot," (Acts 8:29). Was this not a direct revelation of the Spirit to Philip? Does the Holy Spirit directly send the preacher to the specific sinner today? Surely it is clear that this is an example of the direct and miraculous operation of the Holy Spirit and does not prove the necessity of the Spirit operating apart from the Word today.

A second problem arises concerning the claim that it is necessary for the personal indwelling of the operation of the Spirit apart from the Word. The position is that the Holy Spirit sustains a peculiar relationship to the Christian. This relationship began at the first Pentecost after the resurrection of Christ. Thus, the claim is that the Holy Spirit sustains a relationship to the Christian today that He did not during the Patriarchal and the Jewish Age. Question: Did providence operate before the Christian Age? If no, what about Joseph? If no, what about the book of Esther? Both of these are examples of the providential operation of God. But if these examples in the Old Testament prove the providential operation of God, then providence is not dependent upon the Holy Spirit operating apart from the Word today.

There is still a third problem for those who claim the personal indwelling of the operation of the Holy Spirit apart from the Word as being essential to providence. Is providence limited to Christians? Does God's providential work include sinners? Looking back at the example of Esther, one can see that God's providence may work for the good of His people, while defeating those who oppose Him. Providence brought about the saving of the Jews through Esther. But it also brought Haman his reward for his evil deeds.

Haman's defeat and death were just as much providence working to this end, as it worked for the benefit of the Jews. While this is an example of providence working in relation to evil men to defeat their purpose, providence may work for the lost to bring about their salvation, if their hearts and minds are seeking it. I simply use the example of Haman to show that providence is not limited to the Christian. It is true that providence works for particular blessings for Christians, but this is not because of the operation of the Spirit apart from the Word, but because these blessings are the peculiar heritage of the Christian. God loves the sinner and the saint. Even so, He has a special love for the Christian. Thus, there may be special blessings reserved for the Christian and providence works to bring these to pass, but it is not any different in the principle of providence in working either for or against the sinner. Certainly it is not the Holy Spirit indwelling the sinner or working apart from the Word in providence. If providence is not limited to Christians, and it's not, then the proof that the Holy Spirit operates only through the Word, does not affect God's providential operation.

OBJECTION NO. 6

Some try to answer the fact that the Holy Spirit operates only through the Word by saying that an infidel can memorize the Scriptures. This objection fails to take into consideration that the proposition that the Holy Spirit operates only through the Word does not say that it is an irresistible operation. Those who offer this objection meet themselves coming back again. First, they say the Holy Spirit operates only through the Word in conversion. An infidel surely needs converting. Is an operation apart from the Word necessary in conversion? If not, then let them answer their own question, in saying that an infidel can memorize the Scriptures and this proves that the Holy Spirit must operate apart from the Word. Their position is that the Holy Spirit operates only through the Word in conversion. The infidel can memorize the Scriptures. Their conclusion from this is that this proves the Holy Spirit must operate in addition to the Word. Now then, let them deal with converting the infidel. Are they going to insist that the Holy Spirit must operate apart from the Word in conversion? If their example concerning the infidel memorizing the Scriptures proves that the Holy Spirit must operate apart from the Word in sanctification, then it even more definitely proves that the Holy Spirit must operate apart from the Word in conversion, for the infidel is not a Christian.

But not only is this true in reference to the sinner, they have the same problem with the Christian. Can a Christian backslide? Can a backsliding Christian memorize the Scriptures? The position of the

Holy Spirit operating apart from the Word does not keep the Christian from backsliding, nor does it keep him from memorizing the Scriptures. I have known any number of backsliding Christians that could quote Scripture as well as the preacher. But even still further, a Christian can apostatize (Galatians 5:1-4). Can an apostate memorize the Scriptures? I have known some who could quote the Scriptures as well as a preacher could. Thus, this does not prove that the Holy Spirit must operate apart from the Word simply because one can memorize the Scriptures.

Using the claim that a sinner can memorize the Scriptures as proof that the Holy Spirit must operate apart from the Word, fails to take into consideration the fact that it involves man's cooperation and will. The parable of the sower teaches this. The seed is planted in the heart. But the results depend upon the kind of heart receiving it. The reason the Holy Spirit does not operate on the heart of the infidel through the Word is because of the condition of his heart. The reason that the Holy Spirit does not operate on the heart of the Christian, one that is a backslider or an apostate, is because of his attitude toward God and his attitude toward truth. It is not that there is a lack of power in the Word, or that it is essential for the Holy Spirit to operate apart from the Word, in order to bring about either conversion or sanctification. Whenever the gospel is preached to sinners, whether they are converted or not depends upon their attitude of heart. It is not merely a matter of their memorizing the Scriptures, it depends upon whether or not they are willing to receive the Word and submit to it. Acts 2:41 says, "Then they that gladly received his word were baptized: and the same day there were added unto them about three thousand souls." This indicates the welcome reception of the Word. It is with this type of person that the Holy Spirit works through the Word. Even an operation of the Holy Spirit apart from the Word would not convert one who had the wrong attitude, who was prejudiced, who despised God, who doubted His Word, or who refused to obey it. So the statement that an infidel can memorize the Scriptures does not prove that the Holy Spirit must operate apart from the Word.

Not one of these six objections proves the fact that the Spirit must operate apart from the Word. The proposition still stands: In conversion and sanctification the Holy Spirit operates only through the Word.

LOCATING THE SOURCE OF OUR PROBLEM

The heart of the controversy over the work of the Holy Spirit today is: How does the Holy Spirit work in conversion and sanctification? Does the Holy Spirit work directly and without means, or does the Holy Spirit work by means of the Word? The question is not, Did the Holy Spirit work directly during the time the revelation was being given; but now that revelation has been completed, Does the Holy Spirit work through the Word and only through the Word in conversion and sanctification.

In order to make it clear, let me state it in another way. Whatever the Holy Spirit does today in either conversion or sanctification, He does it by means, not directly, and the means used by the Holy Spirit is the Word. Name anything you want to that the Holy Spirit does, and the Word is the means. Does the Holy Spirit convert the sinner? The Word is the means (Psalms 19:7). Does the Holy Spirit edify? The Word is the means (Acts 20:32). Let me emphasize this fact, whatever the Holy Spirit does in conversion or sancitification, He does by means of the Word.

THE SOURCE OF MISUNDERSTANDING

Any position that leads to the conclusion that the Holy Spirit works apart from the Word grows out of either one of two things, or a combination of both. One of these things is confusing passages that deal with the miraculous operation of the Spirit when the Word was being revealed and confirmed. In the study of the Holy Spirit and His work, it is vital to remember that at one time there was no written revelation. The Spirit revealed the Word directly to the apostles and others that had received miraculous gifts. It is easy for one to read passages that belong to this period of time and equate these passages with the time after revelation had been completely revealed and confirmed. This is obviously a fatal mistake because now we have a complete, written revelation. It is difficult for us to think in terms of a time when there was no written revelation. When passages that have to do with this preceding period are confused with the time afterwards when revelation was completed, it results in a complete misunderstanding of the work of the Holy Spirit in conversion and sanctification.

For example, denominational preachers use John 14, 15, and 16, to support the direct leading of the Spirit, which was to the apostles, and

THE WORK OF THE HOLY SPIRIT

had to do with the revelation of the gospel. When denominational preachers use these passages as applying to preachers today, they confuse a period when there was no written revelation with a period when revelation is completed and confirmed. The same thing results when we take passages which were written to Christians who had miraculous gifts during this preceding period of time, and apply them to Christians today who do not have miraculous gifts, but have written revelation. It is absolutely necessary to keep clearly in mind passages and their contexts which have to do with the miraculous while revelation was being given, and not apply them to present-day when we have a written revelation.

THE INFLUENCE OF CALVINISM

The Calvinistic false doctrine of total depravity is the basis of the teaching of the direct operation of the Holy Spirit on the sinner. The false doctrine of total depravity calls for a direct operation of the Holy Spirit in conversion. This false doctrine of total depravity and the direct operation of the Spirit in conversion was repudiated by the pioneers of the Restoration and is rejected by the majority of the church today. I say the majority, for I have seen a few articles in which brethren are teaching that there must be a direct operation of the Spirit in conversion.

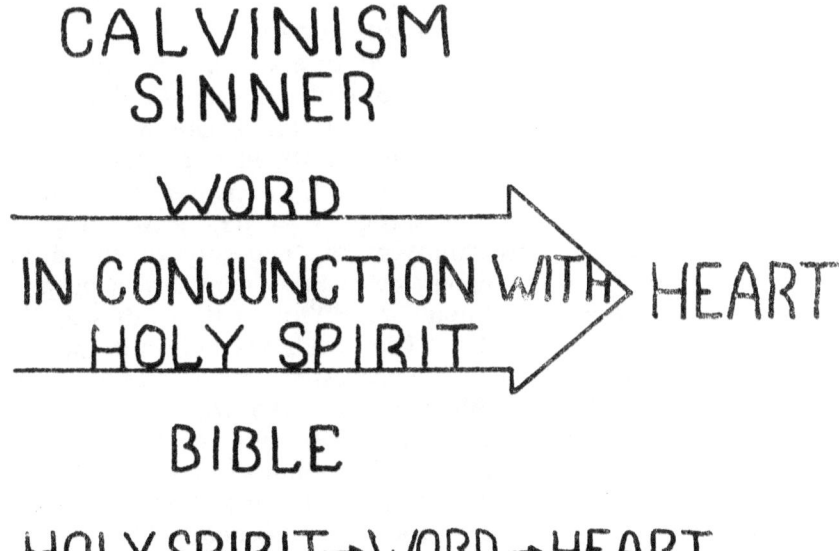

Calvinists do not deny that the Holy Spirit uses the Word in conversion, but contend that the Holy Spirit must operate directly and in addition to the Word in conversion. In order to establish this point, let me give some quotations by Mr. Rice in the Campbell-Rice Debate. Mr. Rice was one of the most able exponents of Calvinism that lived during the period of the Restoration Movement. Calvinism is presented in all of its phases and aspects in the Campbell-Rice Debate. The following are quotations taken from the Campbell-Rice Debate. Mr. Rice made the following statements: "The difference between us, so far as this subject is concerned, is in general terms this: Mr. Campbell believes that in the work of conversion and sanctification, the Spirit operates only through the truth. I believe that the Holy Spirit operates through the truth, where in the nature of the case the truth can be employed, but I deny that the Spirit operates only through the truth. I would not have consented to discuss the proposition if the Word only had been admitted for we believe and teach that the Holy Spirit operates ordinarily through the truth, but not only through the truth," (page 626). Again, Mr. Rice says, "We believe and teach that in conversion and sanctification, there is an influence of the Spirit in addition to that of the Word and distinct from it. An influence without which the arguments and motives of the gospel would never convert and sanctify one of Adam's ruined race," (page 628). Again, "In further elucidation of this subject, I remark that the modus operandi, the manner in which the Spirit operates on the human heart, we do not pretend to comprehend, nor is the mysteriousness of the influence as to the mode of it an objection against this doctrine," (page 629). Still further Mr. Rice states, "Why then, it will be asked, is it necessary that there should be an influence of the Spirit in addition to that of the Word and distinct from it? The necessity arises simply from the depravity of the human heart; its pride, its love of sin, and its deep-rooted aversion to the character of God, to His pure law and His soul-humbling gospel." In another statement made by Mr. Rice, in trying to emphasize the importance of the necessity of the direct influence of the Spirit on the sinner, he makes a comparison between men and angels. Here are his statements: "Why do they not see, feel, and act alike? The answer is plain. The angels are holy and men are sinful, deeply deprived; hence, the necessity of a special divine influence in addition to, and distinct from, the Word. Motives are sufficient to secure the obedience of angels, for they are holy. They are disposed to do their whole duty. Motives will not secure the obedience of men for they are sinful. They are disposed to rebel. Consequently, if any of the human family love and serve God, it is because He worketh in them to will and to do of His good pleasure. If those who have

THE WORK OF THE HOLY SPIRIT   27

entered upon His good service persevere to the end, it is because he who began the good work in them will perform it unto the day of Jesus Christ." Another statement from Mr. Rice: "It is then perfectly clear that every individual experiences a radical change in his moral character before he will ever love God or embrace the gospel of Christ. But are the truths of revelation sufficient to effect this change? They are not," (page 633). Another statement by Mr. Rice: "As the light is absolutely necessary to vision, though it cannot cause the blind to see, so is the gospel necessary, though alone it cannot purify the depraved heart," (page 649).

In an attempt to try to answer Campbell's argument that if the Holy Spirit operated directly, it would involve a miracle in conversion, Mr. Rice answered in the following way: "So the Holy Spirit operates, though invisibly, on the hearts of all who are renewed. The change is wrought by supernatural power, but it's not a miracle because it is invisible, nor is it a suspension of the fixed laws of nature. The effects of the divine influence we do see," (page 658). In an attempt to make distinct the difference between Campbell and himself, Rice makes the following statement: "I have been proving that in the conversion and sanctification of adults, there is: first, the instrumentality of the Word; second, a distinct agency of the Holy Spirit for which the pious are accustomed to pray, and influence effectually renewing and sanctifying the soul," (page 702). Again, Rice says, "How the Spirit operates on the heart in conversion and sanctification, I profess not to understand."

Note carefully the following: Rice makes no distinction between the direct operation in conversion and the direct operation in sanctification. He states that in sanctification there is an influence of the Spirit in addition to the Word and distinct from it. An influence, without which arguments and motives of the gospel never convert and sanctify one of Adam's ruined race (page 628). Other statements could be given to show that Rice believed that the Word was used in conversion, but there had to be a direct and distinct influence of the Spirit in addition to the Word in conversion. Let me summarize Rice's position as stated in the preceding quotes: 1) Rice says that the Word is used in conversion, but that there is an influence of the Spirit distinct from the Word and in addition to the Word that is necessary for conversion; 2) Rice claimed that the Spirit worked in connection and conjunction with the Word in sanctification, but that also there was a direct and distinct influence just as there was in conversion; 3) Rice maintained that the influence of the Spirit in addition to the Word was not a miracle. But in order to try to defend this, he explained that this operation was invisible and mysterious.

CHRISTIAN

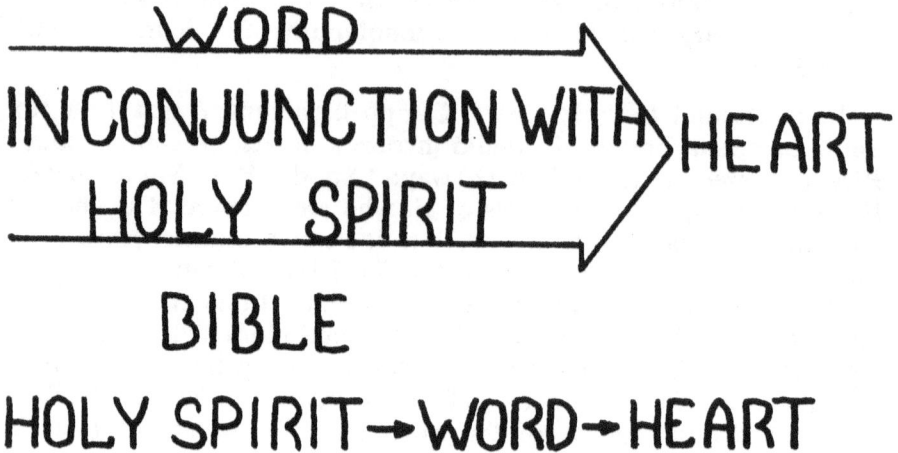

BIBLE

HOLY SPIRIT→WORD→HEART

Thus, what has happened in the church today is that some brethren have simply adopted the Calvinistic doctrine of the direct, invisible, and mysterious influence of the Spirit on the Christian, rather than teaching what the Bible teaches. The direct operation of the Spirit on the Christian, in addition to the Word and distinct from the Word, is Calvinistic teaching purely and simply. To show that this is true, I want to give some statements and arguments given by brethren trying to establish that the indwelling of the Holy Spirit operates distinct and apart from the Word.

The following is taken from a chapel speech given by one of the teachers in one of our Christian schools September 27, 1966. As part of the speech, under the general statement, "I do not believe . . . ," he said the following: "The Holy Spirit operates only through the Word of God in the life of a Christian."

THE WORK OF THE HOLY SPIRIT

Here you have the statement that he does not believe the Holy Spirit operates only through the Word of God in the life of a Christian. Take this now and compare it with statements made by Rice in his debate with Campbell.

Then the teacher gave the following summary: "a) The Spirit does operate through the Word (Ephesians 6:17); b) The Spirit operates only through the Word in conviction and the conversion of sinners (there are no Christians where the Word has not gone); c) However, the Holy Spirit actually dwells in Christians (Romans 8:9). If He does nothing as the indwelling Spirit, there is no advantage in having Him in us."

While it is true that he does not say what, nor how, the Spirit works in the Christian, it is evident that he thinks the Spirit does something in addition to the Word. It would be interesting to see this preacher discuss the operation of the Spirit with some Presbyterian or Baptist preacher. It would be of interest to see how he would prove that the Spirit operates on the sinner only through the Word, but that the Spirit operates on the Christian in addition to the Word. Furthermore, I'd like to hear him explain what, and how, the Spirit operates in the Christian, apart from the Word, the exact claim made by Mr. Rice in his debate with Campbell.

I have before me a book written by one of the prominent young preachers of the church today. The following claims are made by this young preacher in reference to the indwelling of the Holy Spirit in the Christians: 1) He calls the Christian Age the dispensation of the Holy Spirit. It is significant that he gave no passage to establish this. 2) He says that when Jesus said, "The least in the kingdom would be greater than John the Baptist," this was because John did not have the indwelling of the Holy Spirit. What a strange comparison. Luke 1:15 states that John would be filled with the Holy Spirit from his mother's womb. What an unusual development. The non-miraculous indwelling of the Holy Spirit in the Christian is the reason that he is greater than John, even though John was miraculously endowed. If his argument proves anything, it would prove that the non-miraculous indwelling of the Holy Spirit in the Christian would do more than a miraculous endowment. If this is the case, then Christians having a non-miraculous endowment are superior to the prophets, apostles, and those who had miraculous gifts. (He missed the whole point in reference to John.) Is it any wonder that we have some today that are claiming to do more than the prophets of old? 3) He states that Peter's sermon at Pentecost offered not only the means of justification, but POWER FOR SANCTIFICATION. Compare this statement with some of the statements made by Rice. In other words, the gospel is insufficient, and it's the indwelling of the Holy Spirit, directly, immediately, and apart from the Word that empowers the Christian for sanctification. 4) He states that our refusal to use this power provided by the indwelling accounts for the difference between us and the early church. He insists that when we allow the Holy Spirit within us to operate, we will again turn the world upside down. 5) He refers to Zechariah 4:6, "Not by might, nor by power, but by my Spirit." This is the very argument made by denominational preachers who accept the doctrine of total depravity, thus claiming the Word as a dead letter, and that the Spirit must operate directly in conversion. What is the difference in principle in the argument made by a gospel preacher, and the denominational claim in conversion? Here it is: The denominational people claim this passage teaches the direct operation in conversion. Our brother simply shifts it from the sinner to the Christian. What is it when the denominational preachers use this passage to prove the direct operation of the Spirit in conversion? It is Calvinism. What is it when a gospel preacher uses it to prove a direct operation of the Spirit on the Christian? It is still Calvinism. He just shifted from first gear to high gear. The principle is identical. Only the subjects are different. Denominational preachers have the direct operation on the sinner, and this young preacher has it on the Christian. 6) He states that because we have not preached what Peter did, that we have so-called Christians like the ones that Paul found at Ephesus in Acts 19. If this is the case, I would suppose that he would lay hands on us and then we could speak in tongues. If not, why use the example in Acts 19? 7) He states that the personal indwelling is a great mystery. This is exactly what Rice said in his debate with Campbell. 8) He affirms that the Word furnished the Christian unto every good work, but that the main thing the Word furnishes is the indwelling of the Holy Spirit. 9) He insists that taking the position that the Spirit does not work separately and apart from the Word, is contrary to the Scriptures. He did not prove this from the Bible. 10) He insists that the position that the Holy Spirit dwells only through the Word is the device of the Devil. 11) He says that to reject the personal indwelling is to reject supernaturalism. He maintains that the indwelling of the Holy Spirit and supernaturalism must stand or fall together. Again, is it any wonder with such teaching as this that we have those who claim to be able to perform miracles today? 12) He says that the indwelling of the Spirit is proof of Sonship. Question: How does the non-miraculous indwelling of the Holy Spirit prove one's Sonship? Where is the evidence? Right in exactly the same place where

THE WORK OF THE HOLY SPIRIT

denominational people claim—it's based upon feeling. 13) He states that the Spirit empowers with courage. If this is the case, I wonder why Peter lost his courage and then influenced Barnabas to the degree that he lost his (Galatians 2). 14) He contends that it is the indwelling of the Spirit that provides power to overcome the flesh. 15) He states that God provides a way of escape to every temptation and that the agency which God uses is the indwelling of the Holy Spirit. If this is true, then it's difficult to see how a Christian could apostatize. 16) The statement is made that it is the indwelling Spirit who gives power to become Christ-like. 17) He says that one cannot achieve spirituality without the indwelling of the Spirit, thus it is the Spirit who empowers for spirituality. 18) He states that the indwelling of the Spirit provides power for worship; that God has put the Spirit in us to help us find Him in worship. Thus, the Bible is no longer a guide. We do not walk by faith (II Corinthians 5:7); the Holy Spirit takes over and takes care of the situation, helping us find God when we come to worship. 19) He asserts that power comes from knowing that the indwelling Spirit controls all events and affairs of life and one's spiritual welfare. Where are all of these claims found to prove that the personal indwelling of the Spirit accomplishes these things in the Christian? They are all based on Calvinism. There's not a single claim that is based on a correct interpretation of the Bible passages used. There's not the slightest difference in these claims and the position of Rice in his debate with Campbell. The only difference is that the young preacher confined his claim to the Christian, while Rice applied them to the sinner and the Christian. Rice argued that the operation of the Spirit, as distinct from the Word, was because the Word was a dead letter. While the young preacher denies this claim (the idea that the Word of God is a dead letter), if his statements prove anything, they prove no more or less than the Bible is a dead letter. If this is not the case, then I would like the proof of what his claims establish.

Here is the evidence in black and white that the source of our trouble today is the teaching of Calvinism instead of the Scriptures. It is time that we not only reject Calvin's teaching on the operation of the Holy Spirit and the sinner, but that we also reject his teaching of the Holy Spirit empowering the Christian and enabling him to obey the commands of the gospel.

PROBLEMS TO CONSIDER

If the Holy Spirit operates separately and distinctly from the Word in the Christian, there are multiplied problems. 1) If the Holy Spirit operates directly and apart from the Word, then it must follow that the Word is insufficient. I realize that those who claim a direct operation deny this, but their denial does not prove it. The operation of the Spirit apart from the Word, and the insufficiency of the Word, are handmaidens. If the Spirit operates directly, He must supply something not supplied by the Word. If He supplies something not furnished by the Word, then the Word is insufficient. This is a direct contradiction of what the Bible teaches (II Timothy 3:16-17; Romans 1:16).

2) If the Holy Spirit operates directly and apart from the Word, but in a non-miraculous way, then how does one know when the Spirit is operating? This was no problem when the Spirit operated directly and miraculously. There was tangible evidence to establish that it was the Holy Spirit working. "He hath shed forth this which ye now see and hear," (Acts 2:33). But a non-miraculous operation of the Spirit would not provide any tangible evidence. If there's nothing that can be seen or heard, how do those who claim the direct operation of the Spirit establish that the Spirit is working? They do it by their feelings. Again, this is the exact parallel used by Calvinists to prove the Spirit works directly in converting the sinner. The claim of the direct operation of the Spirit on the Christian is the taproot of the practice of such things as turning out lights and holding hands while praying. These practices provide the atmosphere for emotions to run high, and these emotional feelings become the so-called evidence of the Spirit working directly.

The recent upsurge of all the talk about the direct operation of the Spirit, and the recent practices of turning out lights and holding hands developing at the same time, shows the connection between the two. The practice of holding hands and turning out lights was conceived for the very purpose of providing the needed emotional excitement and feelings to have some proof that the Spirit was working directly. Such things were never dreamed of among churches of Christ until all of this false teaching slipped into the church.

The claim of the Spirit working directly on the Christian, with emotionally packed gatherings, is also the taproot of the so-called testimony meetings and witnessing. Indeed, if it is the Holy Spirit working directly, why not give the testimony produced by the Spirit? What could be wrong with such? If it is the Spirit working, then the testimony is inspired testimony. Whoever heard of the Spirit working and producing uninspired testimony? All of the testimony meetings and witnessing sessions taking place in the church are denominational practices based on Calvin's teaching of the direct operation of the

THE WORK OF THE HOLY SPIRIT

Spirit. The denominational practice of the sinner relating some experience of grace was based on the claim of the Spirit working directly and in addition to the Word. The testimony meetings and witnessing today taking place in the church are just these old denominational practices that some have tried to palm off on young people. Feelings have never been the evidence of the Spirit working. Signs and miracles were the proof of the Spirit working directly (Mark 16:20; Hebrews 2:3-4; II Corinthians 12:12).

3) The direct operation of the Spirit apart from the Word demands a miraculous operation. There is no such thing in the Bible as a direct, non-miraculous operation of the Holy Spirit. If so, where is the passage? To operate directly means to operate apart from means, without means. How can there be an operation direct and apart from means, and not be a miraculous operation? This is the very thing that has led to the claim in the church today for some to be able to perform miracles. There is a positive relationship between this claim of the Holy Spirit operating directly and apart from the Word, and the claim of those today who say that miracles continue.

4) If the Spirit operates directly and apart from the Word, what does the Spirit do? Consider the following: a) The Spirit could not lead contrary to the Word. In II Corinthians 13:8 Paul says, "For we can do nothing against the truth, but for the truth." This simply means that as the Spirit directed Paul in inspiration, it was not possible for him to contradict any truth. Indeed, how could the Holy Spirit contradict Himself? This is one of the very arguments that we have made against denominational preachers who have claimed to be led by the Holy Spirit. They contradict each other and contradict the Bible as well. So if the Holy Spirit operated directly, He could not lead anyone contrary to what the Bible teaches. b) If the Holy Spirit operated directly, He could not add any new revelation. Jude 3 says, "Earnestly contend for the faith which was once delivered unto the saints." This simply means that revelation is complete. Thus, if the Holy Spirit operated directly today, He would not add any new revelation. c) If the Holy Spirit operates directly today, it would be to interpret the Word, for if the sinner can understand the Word without the Holy Spirit interpreting it for him, why could not the Christian? There would be no point in giving revelation if it was impossible to understand the revelation when it was given. In Acts, Chapter 2, the Spirit guided the apostles to reveal the truth. The audience did not receive the Holy Spirit to enable them to understand it. In Ephesians, Chapter 3, verses 3 to 6, Paul states that he received the mystery by direct revelation, and he was writing it to

the Ephesians. When the Ephesians read what he had written, they would know as much about it as he did. d) The direct operation of the Holy Spirit in the Christian strikes at the free moral agency in man. The claim is that the direct operation of the Holy Spirit empowers man and makes it possible for him to obey. If this is the case, then man's responsibility is eliminated. The Holy Spirit has taken over for him and is doing for him what he is unable to do. The direct operation of the Holy Spirit was never simply for the benefit of the individual, but for people in general. In I Corinthians 12, Paul says in verse 7, "But the manifestation of the Spirit is given to every man to profit withal." That is, the manifestation of the Spirit is given for the benefit of others, not the individual. It was to be used for the benefit of the church. This is also evident as he discusses miraculous manifestations of the Spirit in Chapter 14. If one spoke in a tongue and there was no interpreter, he was to remain silent, for the simple reason that it would not benefit the church. These problems cannot simply be passed off by ignoring them. They are vital to a discussion of this question.

MORAL AND MIRACULOUS INFLUENCE OF THE HOLY SPIRIT

God has always influenced man in two ways. First, He has used His Word and works to influence man's reason, conscience, emotions, and will. This was always done by the Word, for it involved an appeal to man through teaching. Since man has a free will and must choose which way he will go, it is necessary that God use the method of teaching as a means of trying to influence man. Any other method would have ignored man's responsibility to choose and would have violated man's free moral agency. This is the reason we have God's will revealed, and this is the reason that Christians must continue to be taught. Christianity is not forced on either sinner or saint. Thus, Matthew's account of the Great Commission requires teaching to convert the sinner and further teaching after he is converted. This is God's way and harmonizes with man's moral nature and being. Any work of the Spirit that does not conform to God's way of teaching His Word, or that would destroy or set aside man's free moral agency, is a misconception of how the Spirit works.

MIRACULOUS INFLUENCE

Second, God has exercised miraculous influence by inspiration and confirmation of His revelation. This has always been a direct influence as it was necessary in giving His Word and confirming it as a divine revelation. Since this influence is direct and involves revelation, it does not necessarily affect man's moral character.

BALAAM

The account of Balaam is an example of inspiration and direct influence. But the direct influence did not change Balaam's character. Notice the direct influence and inspiration of Balaam. "And Balaam said unto Balak, Lo, I am come unto thee: have I now any power at all to say any thing? the word that God putteth in my mouth, that shall I speak," (Numbers 22:38). "If Balak would give me his house full of silver and gold, I cannot go beyond the commandment of the Lord, to do either good or bad OF MINE OWN MIND; but what the Lord saith, that will I speak," (Numbers 24:13). The reason Balaam could not say anything else was not because he did not want to, but under the direct influence and inspiration of the Spirit, he could not. This direct influence of the Spirit did not change or influence Balaam's character in the least. The reason that he did not curse the children of Israel was not because he changed and did not want to do so, but being under the direct influence of the Spirit, he could not. "But I have a few things against thee, because thou hast there them that hold the doctrine of Balaam, WHO TAUGHT BALAK TO CAST A STUMBLINGBLOCK BEFORE THE CHILDREN OF ISRAEL, TO EAT THINGS SACRIFICED UNTO IDOLS, AND TO COMMIT FORNICATION," (Revelation 2:14). Balaam did this after the direct operation of the Spirit on him. The direct operation of the Spirit that inspired him to speak did not affect any change in his character.

EXAMPLE IN THE NEW TESTAMENT

Let me give an example from the New Testament of a Christian. "Then Peter opened his mouth, and said, Of a truth I perceive that God is no respecter of persons," (Acts 10:34). Peter said this by a direct operation of the Spirit. The sermon to Cornelius was inspired just as his sermon that is recorded in Acts 2. The truth of this revelation influenced Peter to accept the Gentiles as is shown from the rest of Acts 10 and the first part of Acts 11. But it was necessary for Peter to allow the teaching of revelation to influence him as to his future actions. When he failed to allow the teaching of revelation, that was given to him directly, to control his character, he slipped. Thus, Paul had to rebuke him before all because he departed from the teaching that he had received by direct revelation. The direct operation of the Spirit on Peter did not change his character. The content of the revelation did direct his actions as long as Peter permitted it to do so. It is important to keep this distinction in mind, or passages will be misapplied that have to do with inspiration by which the revelation was given, and those passages in which miracles occurred by which the revelation was confirmed (Galatians 2:11-14). The direct operation of the Spirit was always for revelation or confirmation, and the teaching of the Spirit through the revelation was, and is, the means to convert the sinner and edify the saint.

MORAL AND MIRACULOUS

I hesitate to use the phrase "moral influence and miraculous influence," but I cannot think of other ways that better express the distinction.

First, consider what I shall call the "moral influence" of the Spirit. I do not use the word "influence" in some mystic sense, but refer to the

THE WORK OF THE HOLY SPIRIT

method that the Spirit used for His influence by teaching to change men. The moral influence has always been by means of teaching. This influence has always been through the appeal of truth to man's reason and moral nature. The moral influence has been common to every age. The Spirit, through the preaching of Noah, was God's means of appeal by the truth revealed to Noah and proclaimed by him to the people of that day (Genesis 6:3; II Peter 2:5). The Spirit revealed the truth to Noah (I Peter 3:19, 20). Noah preached this truth to the world of his day (II Peter 2:5). It was up to the men of Noah's day to either accept or reject the truth he proclaimed. Genesis 6:3 makes it clear that it was the Spirit working. I Peter 3:19, 20 show the inspiration of Noah. II Peter 2:5 shows that the Spirit's appeal to the world was by Noah's preaching. Here we have the moral influence of the Spirit in the Patriarchal Age. What is the difference in this moral influence through the proclamation of the Word, and that which the Spirit exerted through the inspired preaching of Peter on Pentecost? The Spirit gave the Word to Noah and he preached it to the world. The Spirit gave the Word to Peter and he preached it to the Pentecostians. In both instances, it was the Spirit striving with men to convert them. It failed to convert any in Noah's day except his wife, his sons, and their wives. The rest rejected it and God left them to the judgment of the flood. The Spirit, through Peter, proclaimed the truth on Pentecost. Three thousand were moved by the appeal of truth and were converted. The rest, like the world of Noah's day, rejected the appeal of the truth given by the Spirit through Peter's preaching and remained in their sins.

Genesis 6 is the first reference to the Spirit after Adam sinned and was cast out of the Garden of Eden. This first mention of the Spirit in connection with His work in redemption, sets the stage for His work to redeem man in every age. This is the method: The Spirit reveals the truth to select men; they then proclaim or teach the truth to turn men from sin. If this fails, men are left in their sins without God and without hope. It must be evident then that the moral influence of the Spirit has been common to every age. The only difference has been the content of the truth revealed, as revelation has been progressive. A realization of this simple truth will avoid some conclusions that are reached concerning the work of the Spirit in conversion and sanctification today.

Before I leave this, let me give one other example to show that the Spirit's method of influence upon man has been teaching revealed truth, and that this has always been His method.

Genesis 6 gives the method of the Spirit's working in His appealing to sinners through truth. Nehemiah 9 presents an example of the Spirit's method of instructing children of God. The Israelites were a type. Look carefully at the ninth chapter of Nehemiah. Nehemiah 9:13 mentions the giving of the law. Nehemiah 9:16 and 17 show how the Israelites rejected the instruction of the law and refused to follow it. Now watch the method of the Spirit in His appealing to them. It was not a direct operation on each Israelite, but through chosen men, the prophets, that the Spirit sought to bring about the proper conduct in them.

THE SPIRIT AND THE ISRAELITE

"Thou gavest also thy good spirit to INSTRUCT THEM, and withheldest not thy manna from their mouth, and gavest them water for their thirst," (Nehemiah 9:20).

"Nevertheless they were disobedient, and rebelled against thee, and cast thy law behind their backs, and slew thy prophets WHICH TESTIFIED AGAINST THEM TO TURN THEM TO THEE, and they wrought great provocations," (Nehemiah 9:26).

Again, "Yet many years didst thou forbear them, and testifiedst against them BY THY SPIRIT IN THY PROPHETS: yet would they not give ear: therefore gavest thou them into the hand of the people of the lands," (Nehemiah 9:30).

Consider the following:

1. The Israelites were a type of Christian.

2. The Spirit was given to instruct them (Nehemiah 9:20).

3. The Spirit inspired the prophets who testified against the Israelites.

4. When the Israelites refused to hear the appeal of the Spirit through the prophets, God left them to His judgments.

5. The Spirit worked to edify the saints of old through the Word that was revealed to the prophets.

6. The method of the Spirit's teaching was in revealing the truth to the prophet, who in turn presented this truth to the Israelites and this

THE WORK OF THE HOLY SPIRIT

truth was to be accepted or rejected by them. If they accepted it and walked in harmony with it, they were blessed. If they rejected it, the Spirit had no other alternative but to leave them to the consequences of judgment.

THE SPIRIT AND THE CHRISTIAN

Consider just one example in the New Testament:

> For this cause I Paul, the prisoner of Jesus Christ for you Gentiles,
>
> If ye have heard of the dispensation of the grace of God which is given me to you-ward:
>
> How that by revelation he made known unto me the mystery; (as I wrote afore in few words,
>
> Whereby, when ye read, ye may understand my knowledge in the mystery of Christ)
>
> Which in other ages was not made known unto the sons of men, as it is now revealed unto his Holy Apostles and prophets by the Spirit;
>
> That the Gentiles should be followheirs, and of the same body, and partakers of his promise in Christ by the gospel:
>
> Whereof I was made a minister, according to the gift of the grace of God given unto me by the effectual working of his power.
>
> Unto me, who am less than the least of all saints, is this grace given, that I should preach among the Gentiles the unsearchable riches of Christ, (Ephesians 3:1-8).

Consider the following:

1. The Ephesians are children of God.

2. The Spirit made the truth known to Paul.

3. Paul wrote this truth to the Ephesians.

4. When they received the truth as revealed by the Spirit to Paul, and written to them, they would know as much about the truth as Paul.

5. It was up to the Ephesians then to take this truth and follow it.

6. When they did this, they would be instructed and edified by the Word given by the Spirit.

7. This is the method of the Spirit in edifying the saint in the Christian Age.

What is the difference in the method used by the Spirit of edifying the Ephesians, and the method used by the Spirit of instructing the Israelites? The Spirit, through the prophet, taught the Jew. The Spirit, through the apostle Paul, taught the Ephesians. Is this not evidence that the moral influence of the Spirit has been common to all ages? None, except denominational preachers, have any difficulty in understanding how the Spirit worked in the Old Testament. Why is it so simple in the Old Testament, but confusing in the New Testament? The method used was the same in each instance.

SUMMARY

THE OLD TESTAMENT

1. In the Old Testament, the Spirit revealed the Word.

2. In the Old Testament, the Word was the means by which sinners were instructed and the saints edified.

3. The influence of the Spirit in the Old Testament to convert or to build up was through the Word of truth.

THE NEW TESTAMENT

1. In the New Testament, the Spirit revealed the Word.

2. In the New Testament, the Word is the means by which the sinner is taught and the Christian is taught.

3. The influence of the Spirit in the New Testament to convert the sinner or influence the saint is through the Word of truth.

Thus, the method of the Spirit's working to reach the sinner, or instructing and edifying the saint, has been the same in every age. The scheme of redemption is adapted to man as he is. It is adapted to man's moral nature. Since man is a free moral agent, the Spirit's method of instructing must be in harmony with man's moral nature. This makes it necessary for the Spirit to use revelation in words that appeal to man's intellect; to make known in language and action God's love that appeals to man's motives or affections; to reveal God's will contained in commands and instructions that appeal to and challenge man's will. Any teaching concerning the Spirit's work that would override man's free moral agency, or teach that the Spirit directly works on the sinner

THE WORK OF THE HOLY SPIRIT

or Christian to enlighten, motivate, or to empower his will to obey the commands, violates the free moral agency of man, and is without any support in the Scriptures.

This has been common to all ages where God's revealed Word has been presented to people, either through inspired servants, or the record of what was revealed. This method of the Spirit's working has never been the subject of special promise. The introduction of the Spirit's work in this manner, as introduced in Genesis 6, shows that it is not the subject of special promise. The record is given to show the nature of this work, and the very nature of it shows that it was unnecessary to be a subject of promise.

THE MIRACULOUS INFLUENCE

The miraculous influence of the Spirit has always been direct. The miraculous influence of the Spirit was given for a special purpose. The special purpose was revelation and confirmation. This purpose of being special to provide revelation and confirmation, ceased when that purpose was accomplished in a completed and confirmed revelation.

The miraculous influence of the Spirit was always a direct, immediate operation of the Spirit on selected men. In this miraculous operation of the Spirit, He used the faculties of men in giving revelation. The miraculous power of the Spirit guided the minds, tongues, and pens of men in giving the revelation of truth. Thus, the miraculous influence of the Spirit belonged to the period of revelation and confirmation. When revelation ceased, so did these miraculous influences of the Spirit cease. We might as well claim continued revelation as to claim these miraculous influences of the Spirit today.

SUMMARY OF MIRACULOUS INFLUENCE

The miraculous manifestations of the Spirit may be considered under the following:

1. The inspiration of men until Pentecost to reveal God's will and provide prophecy concerning Christ and the Gospel Age. The Spirit confirmed these by miracles when necessary.

2. The baptism of the Holy Spirit at Pentecost and the outpouring of the Holy Spirit on the household of Cornelius. The apostles received

the Holy Spirit to qualify them for their work as apostles. Cornelius received the Holy Spirit to convince the Jews that the Gentiles stood upon the same level as recipients of the gospel.

3. The spiritual gifts that early Christians received by the laying on of the apostles' hands.

These will be discussed in detail later in the book, but I give the summary here to establish the nature and purpose of the miraculous manifestations of the Spirit. It is these miraculous manifestations of the Spirit that are the subject of promise. These were involved in special works and therefore the subject of special promise. When this special work for a special purpose is confused with the moral influence of the Spirit, confusion is the result. The ultimate end of this position is for these miraculous manifestations to continue today. This is exactly what has happened.

THE WORK OF THE HOLY SPIRIT

JOEL'S PROPHECY—THE KEY TO UNDERSTANDING THE HOLY SPIRIT IN THE NEW TESTAMENT

The Old Testament is the background of the New Testament. The foundation of the New Testament is the promise that God made to Abraham. The promise finds its fulfillment in Christ. The seed from which the whole New Testament develops is the promise of God to Abraham. The Old Testament from Genesis 12 through Malachi is but the progressive development of this promise. In order to understand Christ and His work, it is necessary to begin in the Old Testament. If this is true of Christ, why should it be strange that the same thing applies to the study of the Holy Spirit. The principles of redemption are found in the promises, prophecies, and types of the Old Testament. While I have already mentioned Genesis 6, let me call attention to it again. A careful reading of this chapter shows the following:

1. That salvation is by grace. Noah found favor in the eyes of the Lord. This is the first time that this is mentioned in the Bible.

2. Noah's salvation was by the obedience of faith (Hebrews 11:7; Genesis 6:22).

3. Noah's salvation was by water (I Peter 3:18-21). It is clear that Peter makes the salvation of Noah the type of baptism.

4. The Spirit inspired Noah (I Peter 3:19-20). Noah preached by inspiration (II Peter 2:5). Thus, the Spirit worked through the Word in striving with men. Those that responded were saved—Noah and his family. Those that rejected it were lost.

5. Noah's salvation was physical, which is a type of our salvation which is spiritual. Abraham was justified by faith. It was an obedient faith (James 2:21-22). We are saved by the obedience of faith (Romans 1:5). We are to walk in the steps of the faith of Abraham (Romans 4:12).

The promise was not through the law but through the righteousness of faith, or the righteousness provided by Christ through the gospel (Romans 4:13). The law was but a fleshly, temporary arrangement to bring the Messiah into the world so that the spiritual part of the promise to Abraham could be fulfilled. The New Testament is the development of this promise and the means of showing its fulfillment and meaning. Due to the misunderstanding of this promise by the Jews, much of the New Testament is written to show the distinction between the law and the gospel—to separate the gospel from the law, and to show that the law was fulfilled in Christ, the gospel, and the church (Matthew 5:17; Romans 1:16,17, and the entire book of Ephesians).

The variety and breadth of spiritual gifts in the church were to edify the church, while the gospel was being revealed, and to confirm the gospel as a divine revelation, and to emphasize the spiritual nature of Christianity in contrast with the fleshly, temporal nature of Judaism. This is the significance of the last part of John 4:24. The spirit here does not refer to the Holy Spirit, but man's spirit. It is man's spirit that engages in worship and his spirit must be directed according to the truth of the gospel. Paul's statement in Romans 1:9 is a divine commentary on the last part of John 4:24, "For God is my witness, whom I serve with [literally IN] my spirit in the gospel of his Son." A failure to make this distinction between the flesh of Judaism and a religion adapted to this fleshly system in contrast with the gospel, spiritual in nature and adapted to spiritual worship and service, is one of the basic causes of misunderstanding the work of the Holy Spirit in the New Testament. The ultimate aim in the New Testament is not the Spirit and His indwelling. The miraculous or spiritual endowments were the means used by God to give the gospel, which is spiritual in nature, and to confirm it, and to point to man's own spirit in worship and service through the gospel.

UNDERSTANDING JOEL'S PROPHECY TODAY

Joel's prophecy is the key to understanding what the New Testament teaches about the Holy Spirit. Due to the failure of the religious world to understand the purpose of the miraculous operation of the Holy Spirit, multiplied errors have developed around the subject. The religious world makes no distinction between the miraculous operation of the Spirit and the Spirit working through the Word. The miraculous operations of the Spirit are applied to sinner and saint without any reference to the purpose and the temporary nature of these miraculous gifts. While we have recognized, to some degree, the purpose of miraculous gifts and their duration, we have, at the same time, taken passages that deal with the miraculous and ignored the background, the context, and read into these passages a direct, but non-miraculous, operation. This is what has caused the confusion we're having today. When passages that have to do with miraculous operation

THE WORK OF THE HOLY SPIRIT   45

are interpreted to mean a non-miraculous indwelling, it results in a situation that none can explain. It necessitates an operation apart from the Word. Passages are quoted to sustain this position, but if called upon to explain how this operation works, no answer can be given. Since miracles have ceased, no man can establish when this non-miraculous indwelling works. But if it does something in addition to the Word, then people are searching for it, and the only thing left to rely on are feelings, moods, experiences, and similar things. Feelings as evidence allow every man to decide how, what, and where the Spirit leads. In spite of what its adherents say about the Spirit not leading contrary to the Word, the theory does not work out that way. The evidence of what is taking place in the church today is proof of this. While some would not follow those who are using their feelings and moods as promptings of the indwelling of the Holy Spirit, the results are the conclusion of this position.

Joel's prophecy is a summary of the miraculous operation of the Spirit by which the gospel was given and confirmed. Joel's prophecy is never out of sight when reference is made to the Holy Spirit in the New Testament. There are two reasons that Joel's prophecy is not understood: 1) Denominational people think Joel indicates that a direct and miraculous operation of the Spirit would continue after revelation was completed and confirmed. They miss the entire meaning and purpose of the prophecy and its fulfillment. 2) A second reason that Joel's prophecy is not understood, is that some in the church conclude that if it is allowed its full meaning, then miracles will have to continue today. In an attempt to avoid what they think is a difficulty, passages are read and explained without any reference to Joel's prophecy. This is the basis of the non-miraculous, personal indwelling. But the conclusion of having to make a choice between the continuous, direct, miraculous operation, and the non-miraculous operation and personal indwelling does not follow. The prophecy of Joel can be, and is, the basis and background of what the New Testament teaches about the Holy Spirit, and this does not lead to the conclusion that we have the direct operation of the Spirit today.

JOEL'S PROPHECY LIMITS THE BEGINNING AND THE END OF THE DIRECT AND MIRACULOUS OPERATION OF THE SPIRIT

Joel's prophecy is among the first of the prophets. Some think that he may be the earliest. Thus, his prophecy becomes the key to understanding what the other prophets say about the Spirit in the Christian Age. There is no such thing as a prophecy of a non-miraculous, personal indwelling in the Old Testament. Any prophet that refers to the Spirit and points to the Christian Age has reference to the same thing as Joel. When one reads the other prophets and sees the non-miraculous, personal indwelling, he is simply reading into the prophets what is not there. Acts 2 gives the beginning of the fulfillment of Joel's prophecy (Acts 2:16). There is no argument about its beginning. Does Joel also indicate the ending of the miraculous operation of the Spirit? I think so. The prophecy of Joel involves not only Pentecost, but also the fall of Jerusalem in A.D. 70; thus, his prophecy is placed between these two events. I am conscious of the questions that will be raised by this statement, but let us weigh the evidence and see if there is proof to sustain the proposition.

THE FALL OF JERUSALEM PROPHESIED IN THE OLD TESTAMENT

The Old Testament points to the destruction of Jerusalem. It is referred to in several of the prophets: Zechariah 14; Malachi, Chapters 3 and 4; as well as Joel and Daniel. Note Daniel's prophecy of the fall of Jerusalem (Daniel 9:20-27). Whatever may be the difficulty in figuring the seventy weeks in relation to the fall of Jerusalem, there cannot be any doubt that it is included. Christ settles this. Matthew 24 is a prophecy concerning the fall of Jerusalem. In the midst of the prophecy, Christ said, "When ye therefore shall see the abomination of desolation, spoken of by Daniel the prophet, stand in the holy place," (Matthew 24:15). Jesus identifies the prophecy of Daniel so as to include the fall of Jerusalem. Luke 21:20 makes it clear that the reference is to the Roman army. If we can accept the words of Christ, Daniel, by inspiration, saw Jerusalem fall. This takes on added significance when it is remembered that Daniel was in Babylonian captivity when this prophecy was made. Jeremiah had prophesied of the Babylonian captivity and the return. Daniel knew the nation would return from captivity, yet he prophesied of a future fall of the nation and city in contrast with the return from Babylonian captivity. The return from the Babylonian captivity was necessary for the fulfillment of the promise to Abraham. If the nation had been destroyed in Babylonian captivity, the promised seed could never have come. The fall of the nation in A.D. 70 is in direct contrast with, and answers some questions, as we will see later. Matthew, Mark, and Luke all give Christ's discourse on the fall of Jerusalem. It is also of interest that Daniel prophesied of the establishment of the kingdom, the setting up

THE WORK OF THE HOLY SPIRIT

of another kingdom, spiritual in nature. In Daniel, Chapters 2, 7, and 9, we have the prophecy of the establishment of the kingdom, or the church. Daniel sees the end of Judaism, as well as the beginning of the spiritual kingdom which would have its beginning on the first Pentecost after the resurrection of Christ. By inspiration, Daniel saw the tremendous struggle that would go on between Judaism and its attempt to destroy the church. It is for this reason that Daniel saw not only the setting up of a kingdom that would not ever be destroyed, but he also saw the fall of Judaism when Jerusalem fell in A.D. 70. The fall of Jerusalem in A.D. 70 answers a number of Bible questions, and it is for this reason that the significance is given to it in the New Testament. Christ points to the unusual significance of the fall of Jerusalem in Matthew 24:21: "For then shall be great tribulation, such as was not since the beginning of the world to this time, no, nor ever shall be." Surely, Christ would not have used language like this in referring to the fall of Jerusalem unless there was some special meaning attached to its fall. Jesus indicates that neither the judgment of the flood, nor the Babylonian captivity were equal to the fall of Jerusalem. Why the importance of this event? It was because of its relationship to some important Bible questions.

I. **IMPORTANT BIBLE QUESTIONS ANSWERED BY THE FALL OF JERUSALEM**

Judaism was a fleshly, physical, and temporal system. As a system, apart from its fulfillment in the New Testament, it could not save man. Since it was a fleshly, physical, and temporal system, its blessings were primarily temporal. When the Jews were obedient, they were blessed with abundant crops (Malachi 3:8-12). It also included the civil as well as the religious. While it existed, it was the kingdom of God expressed through this system. Judaism was a typical system. What better way was there to express in symbol the destruction of the physical universe than through the destruction of this system by the judicial judgment that God brought on this system. The passing of Judaism, its complete disintegration through God's vengeance, brought on the nation for its unbelief, is a fitting symbol of the final destruction of this world. In Matthew 23:36 through Matthew 24:34, Christ foretells the fall of Jerusalem. In Matthew 24:35, Christ says, "Heaven and earth shall pass away, but my words shall not pass away." This is a transitional statement from the preceding concerning the fall of Jerusalem to the verses that follow that deal with His second appearance. There is a contrast between the signs concerning the fall of Jerusalem and the absence of signs in reference to His second appearance. From this, Matthew passes on then to the final judgment in Chapter 25. The arrangement by Matthew shows that Christ intended by verse 35 to let His prophecy on the fall of Jerusalem stand as the certainty of the final end of the world. Will this world finally come to an end as mentioned in many other passages in the New Testament? Did Jerusalem fall as foretold by Christ? The answer is yes. Christ let the fall of Jerusalem stand as proof that this world will just as surely be destroyed as Jerusalem fell under the judgment of God.

II. ANSWER THE QUESTION, "WHAT THINK YE OF CHRIST?"

The fall of Jerusalem is an additional answer to the question, "What think ye of Christ? whose son is he?" (Matthew 22:42). Christ is the prophet promised by God through Moses in Deuteronomy 18:18, 19. His prophecy of the fall of Jerusalem in Matthew 24, Mark 13, and Luke 21, with its fulfillment in the "nth" degree, qualifies Him as a true prophet. But if He is the prophet foreseen by Moses, He is God's Son as foreseen by Isaiah (Isaiah 7:14; Isaiah 9:6). In addition to all the other proofs given in the New Testament to the Deity of Christ, the fall of Jerusalem is God's final answer to the question, "What think ye of Christ? whose son is he?" The fall of Jerusalem says, "Yes, He is David's Son, but He is also David's Lord."

III. PROOF OF THE INSPIRATION OF THE NEW TESTAMENT

The fall of Jerusalem is proof of the inspiration of the New Testament. There is no surer proof of the inspiration of the Bible than fulfilled prophecy (II Peter 1:19). Just as the prophecies of the Old Testament and their fulfillment by Christ are proof of the inspiration of the Old Testament, in like manner, the fulfillment of the prophecy of Christ of the fall of Jerusalem is God's final appeal and argument of the acceptance of the inspiration of the New Testament. The fall of Jerusalem settles this question for all people and all times as to the inspiration of the New Testament. The inspiration of the apostles is interwoven into the accounts of both Mark and Luke. It is a record of the prophecy of the fall of Jerusalem (Mark 13:9-11; Luke 21:13-15). There are many arguments to sustain the inspiration of the New Testament, but the last and final argument is the fulfillment of Christ's prophecy of the doom of Judaism in the fall of Jerusalem.

THE WORK OF THE HOLY SPIRIT

IV. CLOSED THE QUESTION OF THE MESSIAH

The fall of Jerusalem closed the question of the promised Messiah. In Matthew 24, verses 5 and 24, Christ points out that there would be false Messiahs following His rejection and crucifixion. It is not strange that when the Jews rejected Christ, the promised Messiah, that there were false Messiahs who used the false expectation of the Jews to deceive them. In rejecting Christ as the Messiah, the Jews would surely still look for one as long as the temple stood, which was the heart of Judaism. There would be the means of deceiving the Jews about the Messiah. It is of interest to note that until Christ came, there were no false Messiahs. His coming and His rejection left the door open to blinded Jews to still look for one. When Jerusalem fell, this forever closed the door on the question. The temple and the records were destroyed. The Messiah was the promised seed (Genesis 12:3; Genesis 22:18). This promise was renewed to Isaac and to Jacob. In Genesis 49:10, it is limited to the tribe of Judah. Then in II Samuel, Chapter 7, verses 10 to 13, it is limited in Judah to the house of David. This accounts for Matthew's introduction in Matthew 1:1. Abraham and David sum up the promised line. Then Matthew gives the genealogy from Abraham through David to Christ. If the babe born in Bethlehem is not the promised Messiah, then we can never know whether this promise will be fulfilled. When the temple was destroyed, it took with it the record of the line of descendants from Abraham. There is no way that a Jew can establish that he is of the line of Abraham and David. If the Christ that was born in Bethlehem is not the Messiah, there will never be one. God's judgment on the Jewish Nation and the fall of Jerusalem closed the door on the question of the Messiah. It is also well to remember that if Jesus is not the Messiah, the whole Bible collapses. Christ, the Messiah, is the heart of the Old and the New Testament. If He has not come, it would be impossible to determine it since A.D. 70, and the promise of God is left hanging without ever being fulfilled. But if God's promise to Abraham falls, down goes the integrity of the entire Bible. Is it any wonder that God closed the doors on the question of the Messiah when Jerusalem fell. We either have the Messiah and the Bible stands firm, or we can forget about the Bible and walk in darkness forever.

V. AN ARGUMENT FOR HIS CORONATION

The fall of Jerusalem in A.D. 70 is Christ's final argument for His coronation. The apostles saw a cloud receive Christ out of their sight. The Holy Spirit came on Pentecost as a witness of His coronation (Acts 2:1-37). But Christ had one final proof to give to all ages and for all time: "And then shall appear the sign of the Son of man in heaven: and then shall all the tribes of the earth mourn, and they shall see the Son of man coming in the clouds of heaven with power and great glory," (Matthew 24:30). This verse is often thought to refer to Christ's final and personal return. But the very language used guards against this. The verse says, "Then shall appear the SIGN of the Son of man in HEAVEN." Notice it says "in heaven," not "on earth." There were signs that preceded the fall of Jerusalem. These are given in the preceding verses. Verse 30 shows that when Jerusalem fell, it also became a sign. The fall of Jerusalem was, and is, a sign for all ages and time that Christ left this earth and was crowned King of Kings and Lord of Lords. Do you ask, "Did Christ really return to the Father and is He now at God's right hand"? The fall of Jerusalem answers, "Yes." Christ gave a detailed account of the events leading up to and including the fall of Jerusalem. In view of the prophetic nature of Christ's description of this event, He used it as one final argument to establish His coronation. Just as surely as Jerusalem fell, as foretold by Christ, it is that certain that He is at God's right hand today. When Jerusalem fell, it was a sign that He was in heaven at God's right hand.

VI. A PICTURE OF THE DEFEAT OF THE WICKED

The fall of Jerusalem is a symbol of the final defeat of the wicked and the overthrow of Satan. The woes of Matthew 23 are Christ's pronouncement of the judgment on an unbelieving nation. In Romans 16:20, Paul foresees the fall of Judaism and pictures it as the defeat of Satan: "And the God of peace shall bruise Satan under your feet shortly." Notice that Paul says that this will happen "shortly." If Paul was inspired, and there is no "if" about his inspiration, this statement cannot refer to Christ's final and personal return. He said God would bruise Satan shortly. The word "shortly" means "with haste, speedily." The word "bruise" means "to break, to shatter." Thus, Judaism as an agent of Satan in trying to defeat the church would be defeated in spite of Judaism's vain efforts to keep alive and claim to be a God-ordained religion. It went down to defeat in the fall of Jerusalem. It was defeated to rise no more. Yes, there are Jews still living. But Judaism is dead and buried. It was buried when

Jerusalem fell in A.D. 70. The defeat of Judaism is a symbol of the final defeat of the wicked when time shall be no more. Just as surely as Judaism went down to rise no more, when Jerusalem fell, just that certain, the wicked will end in defeat to rise no more when Christ returns. The bruising of Satan and the fall of Jerusalem are the picture of his final doom when Christ returns.

VII. THE FALL OF JERUSALEM IS A SYMBOL OF THE FINAL JUDGMENT

The fall of Jerusalem was God's judicial sentence on the unbelief of the Jewish Nation. Peter refers to the fall of Jerusalem and uses the word "judgment" in reference to it: "For the time is come that JUDGMENT must begin at the house of God: and if it first begin at us, what shall the end be of them that obey not the gospel of God? And if the righteous scarcely be saved, where shall the ungodly and the sinner appear?" (I Peter 4:17-18). The fall of Jerusalem was God's judgment on the nation for its rejection of Christ. The fall of the nation under God's sentence of judgment is a small symbol of the final judgment on all who are not faithful Christians. Will there be a final judgment? Did God's judgment fall on the Jewish Nation? The final judgment and the punishment of the wicked is just as certain as Christ and the apostles' announcement of judgment on Judaism that came to pass. The fall of Jerusalem is a warning to all unbelievers and impenitents that they will face God in judgment and be lost forever.

VIII. A PICTURE OF THE VICTORY OF THE FAITHFUL

The fall of Jerusalem is a symbol of the certainty, the security, and the victory of the faithful. In Matthew 24:13 Jesus said, "But he that shall endure unto the end, the same shall be saved." The context shows that this salvation was a physical salvation from the destruction of Jerusalem. Christ's admonition that they pray that their flight be not in winter, neither on the Sabbath day, shows that the salvation of verse 13 was a physical salvation. What would winter or the Sabbath have to do with salvation from sin at the return of Christ? Again, in verse 22 Christ uses the word "flesh." "And except those days should be shortened, there should no flesh be saved: but for the elect's sake those days shall be shortened." Luke's account says, "But there shall not an hair of your head perish," (Luke 21:18). According to historians, not a single, faithful Christian lost his life when Jerusalem fell. In spite of the seeming difficulties that would surround the fall of Jerusalem, Christ promised that not one faithful Christian would lose his life when it fell. Numbers of Christians suffered martyrdom before it fell, but not one died in the fall. What a fitting symbol of the certainty of the final and the eternal salvation of every faithful Christian. What an encouragement to every Christian to be faithful. Thus, the physical salvation of the faithful Christian during the time before the fall of Jerusalem becomes the symbol of assurance of the final victory of every faithful Christian in the final judgment. Christians faced their trials and difficulties through the persecution that preceded the fall of Jerusalem, but of those that remained faithful, none lost their lives in the fall itself. Even so, in the midst of the difficulties of life, the Christian that continues faithful is assured of heaven. Not a single, faithful Christian will miss his eternal reward. Will every faithful Christian receive the crown of life? Did every faithful Christian escape with his life when Jerusalem fell? In like manner, every faithful Christian will pass through the judgment victorious. It is well to keep in mind and underscore the word "faithful." I did not say, nor does the Bible teach, that every Christian will be assured of heaven, but the Bible does clearly teach that every "faithful" Christian has an assurance of the final victory when this life is over. The victory of the Christians who were delivered from Jerusalem when it fell, without the loss of a single life, is a symbol of the Christian's assurance of his final victory when this life is over.

IX. THE POLITICAL SIGNIFICANCE

The fall of Jerusalem had a political significance as well as religious. Judaism was both religious and civil. The civil part of Judaism is often overlooked in the New Testament. It is always important in the study of the Bible to keep in mind the Old Testament. The nature of Judaism made possible the combination of the religious and civil. Judaism was fleshly, temporal, national, and confined to one geographical location. Thus, the religious and the civil could be tied together. Christianity is none of these. It is spiritual, not fleshly. It is universal, not national. This is one of the reasons for the separation of the religious and the civil under the gospel. The religious side of Judaism ended at Pentecost. Christ fulfilled the types and shadows of the Old Testament. His death made null and void the ceremonies of Judaism (Colossians 2:14; Hebrews 9:16-17). While God no longer recognized the civil authority of Judaism after Pentecost, it didn't cease to function and was an instrument in opposition to the church. When the church began in A.D. 33, the Roman Government granted religious freedom. This accounts for the inability of the ecclesiasticism of Judaism to be successful in its attempt to use the Roman civil authority in opposing the church. Read carefully the book of Acts and you will see that this accounts for the protection of the church by the Roman Government. The opposition of the Jews to Paul was on religious grounds. The Jews could not find any legal grounds against Paul. This is summarized in Acts 26. Acts 26 gives Paul's defense before Agrippa. Notice Agrippa's decision,. "And when they were gone aside, they talked between themselves, saying, This man doeth nothing worthy of death or of bonds. Then said Agrippa unto Festus, This man might have been set at liberty, if he had not appealed unto Caesar," (Acts 26:31-32). The only charge the Jews could offer against Paul was his preaching the gospel and showing that Judaism found its fulfillment in Christ. This situation did not last. The time came when the powers of Rome no longer offered religious freedom. When this developed, it gave the ecclesiasticism of Judaism an opportunity to join with pagans in opposing the church. This enables one to see the significance of the political and the ecclesiastical system of Judaism from Pentecost until the fall of the nation. This explains some passages that point to the fall of the nation as being the end of Judaism. When Jerusalem fell, it ended Judaism's ability to use its claim of civil authority in opposing the church. The religious part of Judaism stopped at Pentecost. The civil authority ceased at the fall of the nation. Technically one may say both the religious and the civil authority ceased at Pentecost, but practically one may say that the civil authority continued until the fall of the nation, since it continued to function as an instrument in trying to destroy the church. Of course, the Jews continued to worship at the temple, but the separation of the worship of Judaism and the church started at Pentecost. The fact that some of the apostles did not understand this, in no way affects the reality of the end of the religious side of Judaism from ending at Pentecost. The Jews worshipping in the temple could not affect the separation of the worship of the church. A denomination with its false worship and opposition to the church today cannot have any effect on the worship of the church. In the same way, the Jews worshipping in the temple and teaching against the gospel did not hurt the church. But this was not true in connection with the civil and ecclesiastical part of Judaism. They were able to use this as an instrument in trying to kill the church. When Jerusalem fell, it put an end to the persecuting power of Judaism. The church was left free to preach the gospel without this kind of opposition. Passages that seem to indicate a continuance of Judaism after Pentecost and point to its future end, are in connection with the fall of Jerusalem when all functions of Judaism, including its claim as a civil authority cease. This also accounts for some of the language in the New Testament as to "the end of the age" or "consummation of the age," meaning the end of Judaism in relation to its civil and ecclesiastical function.

X. SEPARATED JUDAISM FROM THE CHURCH

The fall of Jerusalem separated Judaism from Christianity. Judaism was a God-ordained religion. This made it possible for Judaizing teachers to deceive and confuse people as long as the temple existed. It was one thing to appeal to people to give up paganism with its religion as it was never approved by God. It was still another thing to call on the Jews to lay aside Judaism which was given by God and at one time acceptable to God. It is easy to see how Judaizing teachers used this in opposing the church. But when Jerusalem fell, the temple was destroyed, and they could no longer use this as a means of trying to confuse people. While the temple stood, many thought of the church as only a sect of Judaism. Christianity had its roots in Judaism. The types and shadows of Judaism pointed to the church. The prophecies of the Old Testament foretold of the establishment of another kingdom (Daniel 2, 7, 9; Isaiah 2:1-4). The fact that Christianity had its roots in Judaism did not mean that it was a continuance of it, or just an advancement within it. The gospel was an entirely different system from Judaism. The sacrifice of Christ was not just another sacrifice, it was a different kind of sacrifice (Hebrews 9 & 10). When Paul went to Rome, they asked to hear "concerning this sect that was everywhere spoken against," (Acts 28:22). This indicates that many considered the church as just another sect of Judaism like the Pharisees and the Sadducees. When Jerusalem fell, it ended any thoughts of the church being only a sect of Judaism. The fall of the nation left neither root nor branch: "For, behold, the day cometh, that shall burn as an oven; and all the proud, yea, and all that do wickedly, shall be stubble: and the day that cometh shall burn them up, saith the Lord of hosts, that it shall leave them neither root nor branch," (Malachi 4:1). When Jerusalem fell, God pulled up Judaism by the roots and burned the branches. Nothing was left but the ashes of Judaism. One might as well expect to use the ashes of a house that has burned down to rebuild it as to expect to put life back into Judaism. Thus, when Jerusalem fell, Judaism was plucked up by the roots and burned. This left nothing but the church. The fall of Jerusalem forever separated Judaism and the church. Notice carefully these verses: "And this word, Yet once more, signifieth the removing of those things that are shaken, as of things that are made, that those things which cannot be shaken may remain. Wherefore we receiving a kingdom which cannot be moved, let us have grace, whereby we may serve God acceptably with reverence and godly fear: For our God is a consuming fire," (Hebrews 12:27-29). When Jerusalem fell, Judaism went down to rise no more, leaving only the kingdom that Daniel saw remaining, and one that could not be moved. The fall of Jerusalem closed the door of Judaism and left only the church remaining.

XI. SETTLED THE QUESTION OF SONS OF GOD

The fall of Jerusalem settled the question as to who are the sons of God. The struggle between the Jews, Judaizing teachers, and the apostles, and especially the apostle Paul, runs through all the Epistles. The attempt of Judaizing teachers to bind circumcision on the Gentiles and obligate them to keep the law is evident in the Galatian letter. Chapters 3, 4, and 5 of Galatians deal with this question. In Chapter 3 Paul shows that the promise to Abraham includes the Gentiles (Galatians 3:8); that the law was temporary (Galatians 3:19); that the law pointed to Christ (Galatians 3:23-25). Then in verses 26 to 29 Paul draws his conclusion: "For ye are all the children of God by faith in Christ Jesus," (Galatians 3:26). Notice the word "all"—Jew and Gentile. "By faith"—not flesh. They were children of God by faith, not flesh. "In Christ"—and not in Abraham. "For as many of you as have been baptized into Christ have put on Christ," (Galatians 3:27). "As many"—that is, without distinction, whether Jew or Gentile. Those "baptized into Christ"—not those baptized and then circumcised. Thus, the one baptized into Christ, whether Jew or Greek, bond or free, male or female, were one in Christ and Abraham's seed and heirs according to the promise (Galatians 3:28-29). This shows the attempt of false teachers to try to maintain that in order for a Gentile to be a son of God, it was necessary for him not only to be baptized, but also to be circumcised and keep the law. Of course, the apostles, and especially Paul, denied this claim, and this Epistle shows that it was false. But God had one final argument in answer to these false teachers. When Jerusalem fell, that was God's way of saying, "I will show you once and for all who the sons of God are." Consider this passage, "But in the days of the voice of the seventh angel, when he shall begin to sound, the mystery of God should be finished, as he hath declared to his servants the prophets," (Revelation 10:7). What was the mystery declared by the prophet? Paul leaves no doubt about this. "How that by revelation he made known unto me the mystery; (as I wrote afore in few words, Whereby, when ye read, ye may understand my knowledge in the mystery of Christ) Which in other ages was not made known unto the sons of men, as it is now revealed unto his holy apostles and prophets by the Spirit; That the Gentiles should be fellowheirs, and of the same body, and partakers of his promise in Christ by the gospel," (Ephesians 3:3-6). The mystery was that Jew and Gentile would be heirs in Christ by the gospel. John sees this question settled when Jerusalem fell. Notice the connection between the mystery and the fall of Jerusalem in Romans 16. In Romans 16:25 Paul ties together the gospel and the preaching of Jesus Christ. Then he states that it was "according to the revelation of the mystery, which was kept secret since the world began." Back in verse 20, Paul points to the fall of Jerusalem. Is there no connection between his reference to the mystery and the fall of Jerusalem? While the teaching of the New Testament makes plain that both Jew and Gentile stood on equality before God in one body, God had one last and final answer to settle the question. When Jerusalem fell, the mystery had its concluding answer and proof that all baptized into Christ were sons of God whether Jews or Gentiles. The outpouring of the Holy Spirit on Cornelius and his household was God's first argument that he was no respecter of persons. The Epistles insist on this all the way through them. The fall of Jerusalem clenches the argument once and for all, and, thus, the fall of Jerusalem answers another Bible question as to who are the sons of God. The fall of Jerusalem and the end of Judaism was God's way of saying, "Sons of God are those who are obedient to the faith and are added to the church by the Lord."

XII. ANSWERS THE QUESTION OF THE PROMISE TO ABRAHAM

The fall of Jerusalem answers the question as to the meaning of God's promise to Abraham. In Genesis 12 God made three promises to Abraham: 1) "I will make of thee a great nation," (Genesis 12:2). 2) "Unto thy seed will I give this land," (Genesis 12:7). 3) "In thee shall all families of the earth be blessed," (Genesis 12:3). In order for a nation to develop from Abraham, they needed a land. The nation and the land belonged together. The reason back of the nation and the land was the spiritual promise—the Messiah, the Son of God, and the Saviour of the world. The entire Old Testament from Genesis 12 through Malachi develops around the land of Canaan. The birth, life, death, and resurrection of Christ are in the land of Canaan. The church had its beginning in Jerusalem. A careful reading of the book of Acts shows the shift from the city of Jerusalem. The church was scattered out of Jerusalem (Acts 8:4). The gospel was preached to the Samaritans (Acts 8). The conversion of Saul is recorded in Acts 9. This is placed here because Saul was to be the apostle to the Gentile world. In Acts 10 and 11 is recorded the conversion of Cornelius, the first Gentile. The purpose is to show that the gospel is for the Gentiles as well as the Jews. In the last part of Acts 11 is the beginning of the church in Antioch. Here is the first Gentile congregation. It is from here, not Jerusalem, that Paul goes on his missionary journey. Antioch becomes the center from which the gospel radiates world-wide. This is not by accident. It is according to God's purpose. This change from Jerusalem to Antioch, as the center of the spread of the gospel, is in keeping with the change from national and fleshly Israel to the universal and spiritual church. The church is now the Israel of God (Galatians 6:16). The church is the nation, but it is spiritual, not fleshly (1 Peter 2:8-9). When the nation went into Babylonian captivity, God brought it back to the land. This was necessary for the spiritual promise to be fulfilled in Christ. But Christ has come. He has fulfilled the spiritual promise. There is no more place for the mission of the nation. Since the nation has fulfilled its mission in the coming of Christ, there is no further need for the land. When Jerusalem fell, this was God's way of saying that the promise to Abraham had found its fulfillment in Christ. When Jerusalem fell, it left nothing but the spiritual promise and the gospel as man's only hope. Any future for the Jews will be found in the gospel and as an individual, not as a nation. The fall of Jerusalem crowns the promise that God made to Abraham. The fulfillment of the promise began at Pentecost. When God brought judicial sentence on the nation in the fall of Jerusalem, it was His way of saying, "The gospel is the answer to the promise to Abraham." The only hope for Jews or Gentiles is to be found in the gospel of Christ.

The fall of Jerusalem is a warning to all men and for all times that God is through with the Jews as a nation. The fall of Jerusalem is a warning to all men and for all times that their only hope is the gospel of Christ.

FALL OF JERUSALEM AND THE END OF THE MIRACULOUS AGE

Joel's prophecy of the coming of the Spirit comprehends the beginning and the ending of the miraculous operation of the Spirit. The miraculous age of the Spirit in Joel's prophecy is placed between Pentecost and the fall of Jerusalem. During this period, revelation was completed and confirmed. During this period, the church grew from its infancy to its maturity. I realize that there are some that claim that part of the New Testament was not written until after the fall of Jerusalem, but I have not seen anything but speculation as proof. It is generally claimed that Revelation was written in A.D. 95 or 96. Is there evidence to show that it was written before the fall of Jerusalem? The internal evidence shows without question that it was written before the fall of Jerusalem in A.D. 70. Before I offer some evidence that I think proves that the book was written before A.D. 70, let me give a quotation from Schaff's History Of The Christian Church: "On two points I have changed my opinion. The second Roman captivity of Paul which I am disposed to admit in the interest of the pastoral Epistles and the date of the Apocalypse which I now assign with the majority of modern critics to the year 68 or 69, instead of 95 as before," (Preface to Revised Edition, page 6). Schaff admits that the internal evidence in the book demands an earlier period than A.D. 95. What better evidence can be offered than internal evidence? This is Bible evidence and not based on speculation as to what some uninspired man says.

Consider some of the internal evidence in the book of Revelation that indicates that it was written before A.D. 70:

1. "The Revelation of Jesus Christ, which God gave unto him, to shew unto his servants things which must shortly come to pass; and he sent and signified it by his angel unto his servant John," (Revelation 1:1). Notice three words in this verse. Note carefully the words "things," "must," and "shortly." The verse does not say "some of these things," but "things." Look at the word "things." This word is like an arrow pointing to Matthew 23:36 and 24:34. The "things" of Revelation 1:1 are "the things" of Matthew 23:36 and 24:34. The very first verse of the book of Revelation is tied to the fall of Jerusalem in Matthew 23:36 and 24:34 by the word

THE WORK OF THE HOLY SPIRIT 59

"things." Then the verse says "must" and limits it to "shortly." Shortly does not mean "longly." Young's Concordance gives four instances where the Greek word translated "shortly" is found in the New Testament. Here are the passages: Acts 25:4, Romans 16:20, Revelation 1:1, and Revelation 22:6. The first reference is to Festus going to Caesarea "shortly." There is no question as to the word here meaning a short period of time: "And when he had tarried among them more than ten days," (Acts 25:6). If the word "shortly" in Revelation 1:1 means what it says, it cannot refer to more than nineteen hundred years. The only thing that it can point to is the persecution leading up to and the fall of Jerusalem. This did shortly come to pass. The book is introduced in such a way as to show the near events as symbolized in it.

2. The book closes as it begins: "And he said unto me, These sayings are faithful and true: and the Lord God of the holy prophets sent his angel to shew unto his servants the things which must shortly be done," (Revelation 22:6). This is the same word used in Revelation 1:1. This was done to avoid the mistake made by many in stretching out the things in the book over the entire Christian Age. The book begins by saying, "These things must shortly come to pass," and closes with the statement, "These things must shortly be done." The content of the book is limited by the word "shortly." There is still further evidence that the book is related to the fall of Jerusalem and the end of Judaism. The fall of Jerusalem buried the lifeless body of Judaism. In Romans 16:20 Paul uses the same term translated "shortly" used by John. Romans 16:20 points to the fall of Jerusalem, as I have already shown in commenting on this verse.

3. There is still additional evidence in the first chapter of the book pointing to near events. "The time is at hand," (Revelation 1:3). Verse 2 states, ". . . and of all things that he saw." This refers to the whole of the book. Again, verse 3 says, "For the time is at hand." When Mark 1:15 says, "The kingdom is at hand," this does not mean nineteen hundred years later. If "at hand" in Mark 1:15 means "near," or "soon," why does the phrase not mean the same thing in Revelation 1:3? When Paul said, "The time of my departure is at hand," did he mean it was near, or could it have been nineteen hundred years later?

4. Finally, Revelation 10:7 states in the connection with the voice of the seventh angel that the mystery was finished. The mystery is defined in Ephesians 3:3-6. Also, Paul mentions this mystery in Romans 16, where he points to the fall of Jerusalem. The fall of Jerusalem settled the question with the destruction of the temple, leaving only the church, with both Jew and Gentile in this one body.

The Old Testament is filled with prophecy. These prophecies point to the New Testament for their fulfillment. If one begins only with the prophecies during Judaism, he will have a period of fifteen hundred years. Study these prophecies and you will not find such language as John used, but if "shortly" can cover nineteen hundred years, why should such language not be used in the Old Testament even though the fulfillment of these prophecies would be found some fifteen hundred years later in the New Testament? The very absence of such language in connection with Old Testament prophecy is an indication that the word "shortly" in Revelation means just that.

Since the book of Revelation deals with the particular problems of the church in relation to the events leading up to and the fall of Jerusalem, it certainly was written before A.D. 70.

Someone may ask, "If that's true, then what value is the book to us?" The book was written to the seven churches of Asia and directed toward their particular need, but this does not mean that it has no value to us today. The book of Galatians was written to the churches of Galatia, and dealt with the special problems they faced. But it does not follow that the book has no value to us. The book of Galatians was directed toward the problem created by Judaizing teachers. We do not have any Judaizing teachers today, but the principles in the book apply to various problems which we may face today. In the same manner, the principles of the book of Revelation have their application for us today. The previous points already discussed in this chapter show its relevance for today. The struggle between truth and error, evil and good, righteousness and sin, will last until Christ's personal return. The exhortations, encouragement, and warnings for the seven churches of Asia offer the same for us in our trials and difficulties. The problems that beset these churches through economic pressure, false religion, and political opposition will continue in principle throughout all ages. Just as the seven churches were to overcome through faith, patience, and the blood of the Lamb, we are to do the same. Every principle within the book has its application today. The particular event, the fall of

THE WORK OF THE HOLY SPIRIT

Jerusalem, for which the principle applied then, is not the event for us. This leaves the book to offer hope and encouragement for us today. We do not have any problem in understanding that the particular thing stated in reference to the flood in Genesis 6 is to be understood in that light, but it does not follow that there are not lessons that may apply to us today in the account of the flood in Genesis 6. What is true of the flood is also true of the book of Revelation, even though it points directly to the problems and the difficulties of these churches facing the trials leading up to, and in, the fall of Jerusalem.

JOEL'S PROPHECY AND THE FALL OF JERUSALEM

The prophecy of Joel points not only to Pentecost, with the beginning of the miraculous operation of the Spirit, but also the fall of Jerusalem and the cessation of miraculous operations of the Spirit. There is no question of Joel pointing to Pentecost, but does it also foresee the fall of Jerusalem and the burial of the dead body of Judaism in that fall? Christ quotes Joel 2:30-31 in Matthew 24:29 and Mark 13:24-25. There is no doubt as to what Christ means by this language. It is used in reference to the fall of Jerusalem. These quotations in the New Testament give a New Testament interpretation of Joel 2:30-31. Not only do we have a New Testament interpretation of Joel 2:30-31, but this interpretation is given by Christ. This should settle the question as to whether Joel foresaw the fall of Jerusalem. A New Testament interpretation of Old Testament prophecy cannot be mistaken.

If Joel's prophecy was all one had pointing to Pentecost and the fall of Jerusalem, it might not be definite proof that the miraculous operation of the Spirit was placed between these two events, but there are some passages in the New Testament that cannot be explained in any other way. These passages, as we shall see, make no sense unless they are understood in this light.

A WORD STUDY

Matthew 24, Mark 13, Luke 21

Christ's prophecy of the fall of Jerusalem is recorded in Matthew 24, Mark 13, and Luke 21. These chapters must be studied with the fall of Jerusalem in mind, or confusion will be the result. Some simple things will help in understanding these chapters. The place to begin the study is Matthew 23:36: "All these things shall come upon this generation." First, it is important for one to identify and define the meaning of the phrase, "all these things." Christ explains the meaning of the phrase in Matthew 24:2: "See ye not all these things?" He then shows the meaning of the phrase by referring to the destruction of the temple: "There shall not be left here one stone upon another, that shall not be thrown down." Thus, there is no question as to the meaning of "all these things" in Matthew 23:36. The phrase points to the fall of Jerusalem, the destruction of the temple, and the end of Judaism. Now trace the phrase down through Matthew 24:34: 1) The disciples asked the question, "When shall these things be?" (Matthew 24:3). 2) "For all these things must come to pass," (Matthew 24:6). 3) "All these [things] are the beginning of sorrows," (Matthew 24:8). 4) "When ye shall see all these things, know that it is near, even at the doors," (Matthew 24:33). 5) "This generation shall not pass, till all these things be fulfilled," (Matthew 24:34). There can be no mistaking the meaning of the phrase. It refers to the destruction of the temple. Notice also that Jesus used the word "all" and said, "**ALL** these things shall come upon this generation." The discussion was introduced in Matthew 23:36 with "all these things." "All these things" point to the fall of Jerusalem, not some to the fall and some to the personal return of Christ. Then Matthew 24:34 closes the discussion with "all these things." The very language used by Christ was designed to keep one from confusing the signs of the fall of Jerusalem with the discussion of His personal return in Chapter 24:36 forward.

In the second place, it is important to understand the meaning of the word "come," (Matthew 23:36). Christ said, "All these things shall COME." Is there anything in the chapter to help determine the meaning of this word? The answer is yes. The phrase, "all these things," separates this coming from Christ's personal return. Verse 34 of Chapter 24 further explains the meaning of the word "come" in 23:36. Verse 23:36 is quoted again in 24:34 with a variation that explains the "come" in 23:36. The "come" of 23:36 becomes "be fulfilled" in 24:34. If one lets the chapter interpret itself, one can see that "come" refers to the coming in judgment on Jerusalem and not to Christ's personal return. Christ explains what He means by "come." He even hemmed it in so there could be no mistake.

Now consider the "coming" in Matthew 24:3: "Tell us, when shall these things be?" The context shows that "these things" refer to the the destruction of the temple: "And what shall be the sign of thy coming?" What coming? The one introduced in 23:36, and fulfilled in these signs and events leading up to, and the destruction of, Jerusalem

THE WORK OF THE HOLY SPIRIT

in Matthew 24:34. The "coming" of 24:3 is the same as 23:36 and 24:34. Thus, the "coming" of 24:3 is His coming in judgment on Jerusalem.

The third thing to determine is the meaning of the phrase, "this generation." Remember that Matthew wrote especially for Jews. Consider just one of the instances where Matthew uses the word "generation": "O generation of vipers, who hath warned you to flee from the wrath to come," (Matthew 3:7). Note John's description of the Pharisees and Sadducees and also the warning. Christ uses the same language in Matthew 23:33. Then in Matthew 23:36 Christ said, "All these things shall come upon this generation." In the next verse He calls Jerusalem by name (23:37). In the next verse He mentions specifically the temple (23:38). Put all these together and "this generation" equals Judaism. "This generation" is just another way of describing Judaism and its final fall.

The fourth phrase to study is, "the end of the world." Some think that this phrase has reference to the last part of Chapter 24 rather than the fall of Jerusalem. Thus, they divide the question of 24:3 into two parts. Here is the way that some divide it: 1) When shall these things be? 2) What shall be the sign of thy coming and the end of the world? But a careful study of the verse will show that there are not two questions, but one. Divide the verse into phrases: 1) When shall these things be? 2) What shall be the sign of thy coming? 3) And the end of the world? All three phrases point to the same thing—the destruction of Jerusalem. I have already shown that the "coming" points to the fall of Jerusalem, so there can be no question about the first two phrases. Also, the word "sign" in connection with "coming" shows that this refers to the fall of Jerusalem. Neither Mark nor Luke used the phrase, "the end of the world." Mark says, "And what shall be the sign when all these things shall be fulfilled?" (Mark 13:4). Luke has, "And what sign will there be when these things shall come to pass?" (Luke 21:7). If one keeps in mind that Matthew wrote for the Jews, and Mark and Luke wrote for the Gentiles, he can understand why Matthew uses the phrase, "the end of the world," while Mark and Luke do not. "The end of the world" in Matthew does not refer to Christ's personal return, but to the same thing as "all these things" and "the sign of thy coming." It is just another way of referring to the same event, the fall of Jerusalem.

The word "world" in Matthew 24:3 means "age." So the question is: "When shall these things be?"; "What is the sign of thy coming?"; and, "The end of the age?" This is further established by the use of the word "end" in the chapter. Look at it: "The end is not yet," (Matthew 24:6). What end? There is no doubt that the "end" here is used in connection with the fall of Jerusalem. The word "end" is used again in 24:13. What end? Again it refers to the fall of Jerusalem. Finally, the word "end" is used in verse 14," . . . then cometh the end." What end? The fall of Jerusalem. The fall of Jerusalem is considered as the consummation or end of the age. The margin of the American Standard Version gives this rendering. I have already pointed out that the religious aspect of Judaism ended at Pentecost, but the civil and the ecclesiastical aspect continued until the temple was destroyed. Judaism from Pentecost to the destruction of Jerusalem in A.D. 70 was nothing but a dead carcass (Matthew 24:28), but since the fall of Jerusalem buried forever the dead carcass of Judaism, this is described as the consummation of the age or the end of the age.

Fifth, it is important to consider the word "saved" in Matthew 24. While the word "saved" may have a double significance in Matthew 24, since the salvation from the destruction of Jerusalem is symbolic of our final and eternal salvation, its primary meaning is the physical salvation in the destruction of Jerusalem. Look at some things that establish this fact: 1) "When ye shall see Jerusalem compassed with armies," (Luke 21:20)—there is no doubt as to what this refers to. 2) "Then let them which be in Judaea flee into the mountains," (Matthew 24:16)—it must be evident to anyone that this cannot refer to Christ's personal return. 3) "Woe unto them that are with child," (Matthew 24:19)—this likewise points to the fall of Jerusalem. 4) "Pray ye that your flight be not in the winter, neither on the sabbath day," (Matthew 24:20)—the fact that the gates of Jerusalem could be closed on the Sabbath is the reason for this statement, and therefore would hinder their flight from the city. 5) "Except those days should be shortened, there should no flesh be saved," (Matthew 24:22)—surely this language cannot be mistaken. It points to a physical salvation. Matthew 24:22 makes this clear as it uses the words "flesh" and "saved" together. Further evidence is also found in Luke: "But there shall not an hair of your head perish," (Luke 21:18). Surely this language cannot be misunderstood; it could have no reference to salvation from sin, or our final and eternal salvation. The word "saved" in Matthew 24 refers to the physical salvation when Jerusalem fell. This should surprise no one, as the physical salvation of Noah, and the deliverance of the nation of Israel from Egyptian bondage, have a typical significance in relation to our spiritual salvation, and the same is true of the physical salvation in Matthew 24. It is necessary to get these things clearly in mind as they become the keys to understanding the passages in the Epistles.

THE WORK OF THE HOLY SPIRIT

I have taken a long journey to establish my point in relation to Joel's prophecy, but this was essential to get the whole subject before us. This evidence will help one to see that Joel's prophecy places the miraculous operation of the Spirit between Pentecost and the fall of Jerusalem. We are now ready to look at some of the passages that further establish this, and, in my judgment, cannot be explained any other way.

THE FALL OF JERUSALEM IN THE EPISTLES

There are some passages in the Epistles that can only be interpreted in reference to the fall of Jerusalem. If these passages are not considered in this light, the result will be that the apostles were mistaken. If the apostles were mistaken in their preaching and writing, then one has a problem with inspiration. There is no way to reconcile inspiration with the apostles being mistaken about the coming of Christ. Matthew 24, Mark 13, and Luke 21 give an inspired account of Christ's promise to come in judgment on the Jewish Nation. When the passages in the Epistles are understood in this light, there is no problem. The coming of Christ in judgment on the Jewish Nation was near, or at hand, when the apostles wrote. Surely it will not be difficult for one to interpret these passages against the background of what both the Old and the New Testaments teach concerning Christ's coming in judgment on Jerusalem, when the only other alternative will be an interpretation that must reject the inspiration of the apostles.

> And that, knowing the time, that now it is high time to awake out of sleep: for now is our salvation nearer than when we believed.
> The night is far spent, the day is at hand: let us therefore cast off the works of darkness, and let us put on the armour of light. (Romans 13: 11-12).

I realize that Romans 13:11 has been used as an argument against impossibility of apostasy, but the context shows that the salvation mentioned here is not salvation from sin, but the salvation mentioned in Matthew 24 from the destruction of Jerusalem. Notice some of these things in these verses:

1. "... knowing the time"—what time? The time for the fall of Jerusalem as the signs of Matthew 24 pointed toward. "So likewise ye, when ye shall see all these things, KNOW that IT is NEAR, even at the doors," (Matthew 24:33). The time of Romans 13:11 is the same time of Matthew 24.

2. "... for now is our salvation nearer than when we believed"—what salvation? The salvation mentioned in Matthew 24:13 and 22. Consider also the word "near" of Romans 13:11. What salvation is near? The deliverance from the fall of Jerusalem. Matthew 24:33 says, "When ye shall see all these things, know that it is near." What was near? The whole discussion in Matthew 24 down through verse 34 is with reference to the fall of Jerusalem. The salvation of Romans 13:11 that was near is the salvation of Matthew 24 and not the final and eternal salvation of the soul when time shall be no more.

3. "... the day is at hand"—what day? This cannot refer to Christ's personal return since His personal return was not at hand when Paul wrote this letter. Shall we conclude, as some do, that Paul was mistaken about Christ's personal return? We cannot accept this conclusion if we accept the verbal inspiration of the Bible. I accept its verbal inspiration. The day of the fall of Jerusalem was at hand. This harmonizes with other scripture, with the background teaching of Matthew 24, and the inspiration of the apostle Paul. Revelation 1:3 says, "The time is at hand"—what time? The time of Romans 13:11. "But exhorting one another: and so much the more, as ye see the day approaching," (Hebrews 10:25). What day approaching? "... when ye shall see all these things," (Matthew 24:33). When they saw these things, they saw the day approaching. The day of Hebrews 10:25 was the day of Romans 13:12—the fall of Jerusalem. Romans 16:20 is another passage in this Epistle that points to the fall of Jerusalem. I will not comment on this passage as I have already discussed it in a previous part of this chapter.

4. "I suppose therefore that this is good for the present distress, I say, that it is good for a man so to be," (I Corinthians 7:26). The word "distress" refers to that which arises from the pressure of external circumstances. The verb translated "present" denotes that which is about to begin. In verse 29 Paul says, "The time is short." The word "time" denotes a season. The Corinthian letter includes the fall of Jerusalem in it. The Hebrew letter was written against the background of the sore trials which Christians were facing. These trials were causing some to fall away (Hebrews 6:6). The fact that pressures were rising from persecution by the Jews and Judaizing teachers is evident from the content of the letter. Christians were being pressured to give up Christ and the church and return to the dead works of the carcass of Judaism and the

temple. The letter is written to encourage them to remain faithful in spite of the suffering and to hold out the hope that these would be over when judgment was brought upon their enemies.

Look at the passages in the Hebrew letter that point to the fall of Jerusalem:

1. "... the day approaching," (Hebrews 10:25).

2. "... Vengeance belongeth unto me," (Hebrews 10:30). "For these be the days of vengeance, that all things which are written may be fulfilled," (Luke 21:22). This verse in Luke is a divine commentary on Hebrews 10:30.

3. "... The Lord shall judge his people," (Hebrews 10:30). Compare I Peter 4:16-18.

4. "For yet a little while, and he that shall come will come, and will not tarry," (Hebrews 10:37).

5. Hebrews 12:26-29 also points to the fall of Jerusalem. Hebrews 12:27 signifies the removing of the temple and Judaism, once and for all leaving the kingdom remaining and unshakable. The fall of Jerusalem, in its being sacked and burned, was God's way of consuming Judaism by fire and leaving only the ashes behind.

"Be ye also patient; stablish your hearts: for the coming of the Lord draweth nigh," (James 5:8). The coming of the Lord is mentioned in verse 7. Verse 9 says, "... the judge standeth before the door." These verses must be understood in the light of Matthew 24. There is no way to reconcile the inspiration of James any other way. The coming mentioned in Matthew 24 was nigh. The judge standing before the door is a reminder of Matthew 24:33: "... it [the margin says "he"] is near, even at the door."

Finally, Peter sees the fall of Jerusalem when he says, "But the end of all things is at hand," (I Peter 4:7). What end? The end foretold by Christ in Matthew 24. Furthermore, verses 17 and 18 of the chapter show that this is what Peter refers to: "For the TIME is COME that JUDGMENT must begin at the house of God: and if it first begin at us, what shall the END be of them that obey not the gospel of God?" These passages, and others, show that the fall of Jerusalem was foreseen by the inspired writers. This harmonizes with Matthew 24, Mark 13, and Luke 21. It also establishes the inspiration of these writers. They saw by inspiration what Christ foretold concerning the fall of Jerusalem and the ending forever of Judaism.

I have selected these instances of passages on the fall of Jerusalem in the Epistles as a foundation to establish the fact that the miraculous endowments beginning at Pentecost are also related to the fall of Jerusalem. When Jerusalem fell, revelation had been completed and confirmed. The miraculous ceased.

PASSAGES ON THE MIRACULOUS AND THE FALL OF JERUSALEM

The prophecy of Joel 2:28-32 is the background of the miraculous operation of the Holy Spirit in the New Testament. Joel's prophecy of the coming of the Spirit also points to the fall of Jerusalem (Joel 2:30-32). The quotation of these verses by Christ in Matthew 24:29, Mark 13:24, and Luke 21:11 is proof that Joel's prophecy of the coming of the Holy Spirit also included the fall of Jerusalem. This background provides the key to a number of passages in the New Testament in relation to the miraculous operation of the Holy Spirit.

Matthew wrote especially for the Jews. The first reference to Joel's prophecy is in Matthew 3:11. It is not necessary to give the passages which show that Matthew 3:11 points to Pentecost, but what about the fall of Jerusalem? Matthew 3:10 is a direct reference to the destruction of Jerusalem. The symbolism of the fall of Jerusalem as a judgment on unbelievers passes into the final and eternal judgment in Matthew 3:12. In other words, the fall of Jerusalem in verse 10 is a symbol of the final judgment of unquenchable fire in verse 12.

MATTHEW 10:16-42

The first part of Matthew 10 deals with the limited commission, but beginning in verse 16 Christ passes beyond the limited commission to Pentecost and what followed. Compare Matthew 10:5-6 with Matthew 10:17-18 and one can see that the latter verses follow Pentecost. Matthew 10:17 is a reference to the persecution of the apostles by the Jews. Matthew 10:18 is a reference to the combined persecution of Jews and Gentiles after the Roman Government no longer provided religious freedom, but persecuted Christians. Beginning in verse 19, Christ promises inspiration for the apostles. This statement by Christ has Joel as its background. The inspiration promised the apostles here, came with their being baptized in the Holy Spirit at Pentecost. Is there anything else in the chapter that would tie the miraculous operation of the Spirit to Joel's prophecy between Pentecost and the fall of the Jewish Nation? Careful study of the context will establish this truth. Matthew 10:19-20 points to Pentecost and what follows. Matthew 10:21-23 foretells the persecution which the apostles would receive. Matthew 10:22 indicates the persecution would spread beyond the Jews and also include the Gentiles. Last, but not least, Christ says, "Ye shall not have gone [the margin says 'end or finish'] over the cities of Israel, till the Son of man be come," (Matthew 10:23). What "coming" is under consideration? It cannot be the coming of the Spirit on Pentecost because the context shows that this coming follows after Pentecost. It cannot be Christ's final and personal return, for then Christ was mistaken as the reference is made to the cities of Israel. This happened during the lifetime of the apostles, and if the "coming" here refers to His final and personal return, Christ was wrong. Thus, we are left with only one possibility—His coming in judgment on the Jewish Nation. An analysis of Joel 2:28-32 includes Pentecost and the fall of Jerusalem. A study of Matthew 10 promises the inspiration of the apostles, but it follows this promise with a reminder of the persecution that would come on them, and includes the coming of Christ in judgment on the Jewish Nation. Does not this arrangement suggest that the miraculous would begin at Pentecost and cease by the fall of the Jewish Nation? Why would Christ place it in this connection unless the miraculous belongs between these two events—1) the coming of the Holy Spirit on Pentecost; 2) the persecution that would follow; 3) with a promise that the persecution would be judged by His coming in judgment.

MATTHEW 28:18-20

It is important to keep in mind Matthew 24 in connection with the Commission as given by Matthew. The Commission was given originally to the apostles. It was necessary for them to receive the gospel by direct revelation. This needs to be kept in mind in studying the Commission. The fact that the Commission was originally given to the apostles, who received the gospel by direct revelation, does not mean that we have no responsibility to preach the gospel to the world, because the church has the responsibility to preach the gospel to the whole world just as the apostles did. The difference is that the apostles received the revelation of the gospel directly, and we now have it in written form. It is the same gospel which the apostles preached and it must be carried to the world. When the Commission was given to the apostles, there was no written gospel as of then. It was yet to be revealed to them. It is necessary to keep this fact in mind.

"LO, I AM WITH YOU ALWAY"

The last part of Matthew 28:20 is Matthew's account of the promise of inspiration to the apostles. A careful reading of the verses shows this: "Go ye therefore, and teach all nations, baptizing them in the name of the Father, and of the Son, and of the Holy Ghost: Teaching them to observe all things whatsoever I have commanded you: and, lo, I am with you alway, even unto the end of the world." Look carefully at the pronouns and you will see the promise of inspiration to the apostles: "teach all nations," "baptize THEM," "teaching THEM," "whatsoever I have commanded YOU," "I am with YOU." The change in pronoun from "them" to "you" makes it clear that the promise, according to Matthew, was to the apostles. The phrase, "Lo, I am with you," is simply the promise of inspiration to the apostles. But now consider the last part of verse 20: "... even unto the end of the world." Matthew 24:3 explains the meaning of this phrase—"the end of the age" or "the consummation of the age." "The consummation of the age" looks toward the fall of the Jewish Nation as Christ foretold in detail in Matthew 24. Matthew's account of the Great Commission promises inspiration to the apostles, which would come through their receiving the baptism of the Holy Spirit at Pentecost. This harmonizes with Joel's prophecy. If the phrase, "I am with you," refers to the inspiration of the apostles, and it seems evident that this is its meaning, then how long did Christ promise the miraculous to the apostles? He promised the miraculous to the apostles to "the end of the age"; "the consummation of the age," which has reference to the fall of the Jewish Nation according to Matthew 24. This makes the entire Commission harmonize with Joel's prophecy as to the beginning of the miraculous age and its ending. Someone may ask, "Is there no promise that the Lord will be with us?" The answer is yes. The Lord has promised in both the Old and New Testaments to be with His people in providential care, but not miraculously as promised to the apostles. "For the eyes of the Lord are over the righteous, and his ears are open unto their prayers: but the face of the Lord is against them that do evil," (I Peter 3:12). Here is but one sample of the promise of God's providential care for His people.

ACTS 2

In Acts 2 we have a record of the coming of the Spirit as promised by Joel. Peter quotes Joel's prophecy and includes verses 30 and 31 in

THE WORK OF THE HOLY SPIRIT

the quotation. After quoting Joel's prophecy, Luke records Peter's sermon. Included in Peter's sermon is a reference to Matthew 24. This is indicated by Peter's call to the Jews to save themselves from "this crooked generation," (Acts 2:40). What generation? Does not the phrase, "this generation," refer to Matthew 23:36 and Matthew 24:34? Peter's exhortation to the Jews to obey the gospel would not only save them from sin and bring the remission of sin, but if they continued to serve the Lord faithfully, it would save them from the judgment of God upon the Jewish Nation (Matthew 24:22). In the very first sermon recorded in connection with the coming of the Spirit and the quotation of Joel's prophecy, there is the reminder of the prophecy of Christ as to the fate of the nation. Thus, in Acts 2 there is an intimation of the miraculous between Pentecost and the fall of the nation.

I CORINTHIANS 1:4-8

The church at Corinth was plagued by many problems, but one of the major problems of the church was with miraculous gifts. This is evident from the amount of discussion that is given in the letter to this problem. A second, and related problem, was the Judaizing teachers who were trying to undermine Paul's work by denying his apostleship (I Corinthians 9:1-2). The teaching of these Judaizing teachers must be considered in the study of the problems at Corinth.

> I thank my God always on your behalf, for the grace of God which is given you by Jesus Christ;
> That in every thing ye are enriched by him, in all utterance, and in all knowledge;
> Even as the testimony of Christ was confirmed in you:
> So that ye come behind in no gift; waiting for the coming of our Lord Jesus Christ:
> Who shall also confirm you unto the end that ye may be blameless in the day of our Lord Jesus Christ. (I Corinthians 1:4-8).

These verses solve some of the problems that have developed around the thirteenth chapter. The first thing that Paul mentions following the introduction of the letter is spiritual gifts. Here is the key to unlocking Chapter 13 of I Corinthians as to the duration of miraculous gifts. Consider several important points in these verses:

1. The word "utterance" in I Corinthians 1:5 is not the same word translated "utterance" in Acts 2:4. The word in I Corinthians 1:5 is a reference to all kinds of inspired utterances. Paul purposely selected another word to indicate inspired utterance here because

of the problem and the abuse of tongues in Corinth. He selected a word that included tongues, but was broader so as to also cover all kinds of inspired utterance as a rebuke to the Corinthians for the priority they gave to tongues. Then Paul adds "knowledge," which is inspired knowledge. Compare I Corinthians 12:8. This is also a hint toward the abuse of tongues in the Corinthian church. Tongues, or languages that people did not understand, would not provide knowledge (inspired knowledge), and therefore would not edify. Almost with the first stroke of his pen, Paul strikes at one of the major problems in Corinth and sets the stage for understanding what he will later discuss in Chapters 12 to 14. In I Corinthians 1:5 Paul is already laying the ax to the root of the tongue problem in the church at Corinth. His method is simple, and he uses two phrases to do it: "ALL UTTERANCE" and "ALL KNOWLEDGE." The word "utterance" is to call attention to all kinds of inspired speaking, and the word "knowledge" to indicate the importance of the speaking being understood so as to be called "knowledge" and therefore edify.

A second thing is also indicated in this verse. The very fact that Paul used a word to cover all inspired revelation shows that tongues cannot be isolated. The tongues, inspired speaking in other languages, belonged in the group of miraculous operations of that period. Paul puts the miraculous in a package plan in this verse and the claim of tongues today demands a claim for the whole package that belongs with these miraculous gifts. One of the essentials of the miraculous gifts in the Corinthian church was an apostle to impart the gifts (I Corinthians 9:1-2). Thus, the claim for tongues of I Corinthians 14 is to be placed in the position of having to have living apostles. Tongue speakers can now join the Mormons and the Catholics. The Mormons claim to have living apostles and the Catholics claim that the Popes are successors of the apostles. The Mormons repudiate the Catholics. The Catholics repudiate the Mormons. But I suppose the compromising tongue speakers in the church will accept both. As for me, I reject the claims of both Mormons and Catholics and with them all claims for any miraculous operations of the Holy Spirit today. The written Word is sufficient.

2. The words "testimony" and "confirm" point unmistakably to miraculous endowments. The word "testimony" is the testimony concerning Christ, the inspired revelation of the gospel. The word "confirm" also points to the relationship between inspired

THE WORK OF THE HOLY SPIRIT

revelation and miraculous confirmation. Vines lists the following passages as other instances of the word translated "confirm" in this verse: Mark 16:20, Romans 15:8, Hebrews 2:3, Hebrews 13:9. The testimony of Christ was confirmed in the Corinthians through the miraculous gifts given to them by the laying on of Paul's hands (I Corinthians 9:1-2; II Corinthians 12:12). The gospel which the Corinthians had received, I Corinthians 15:1-4, was a genuine gospel, and attested by the miraculous endowments which they had received from the laying on of Paul's hands. Their miraculous endowments were the guarantee of the validity of the gospel that Paul preached and the genuineness of Paul's apostleship.

3. "That ye come behind in no gift," (I Corinthians 1:7). While this verse indicates the abundance of miraculous endowments in the Corinthian church, it is stated to show that Paul was indeed an apostle of Christ (I Corinthians 9:1-2). Is there evidence that some denied Paul's apostleship? If not, why did Paul ask the question, "Am I not an apostle?" and in the next verse appeal to the miraculous endowments in the church as proof of his apostleship? This verse shows that Paul "was not a whit behind the very chiefest apostles," (II Corinthians 11:5). No church had more miraculous endowments than the church at Corinth, and this was proof that Paul was truly an apostle of Christ. If the Judaizing teachers could have established that Paul was not an apostle of Christ, then his gospel would have been counterfeit and the church at Corinth a counterfeit church. This is at the very heart of the Corinthian letter. When Paul refers to the abundance of the gifts in the Corinthian church, it is to show that no church had more gifts than the Corinthian church and that Paul was equal to any of the other apostles.

4. Finally, the word "gift" means miraculous gift. The reference to miraculous gifts in the very first part of the Corinthian letter accounts for this letter having a more detailed discussion of miraculous gifts than any other letter.

5. "Waiting for the coming of our Lord Jesus Christ," (I Corinthians 1:7)—waiting for what coming of the Lord? Is this a reference to Christ's final and personal return? The context indicates otherwise. The next verse says, "Who shall also confirm you unto the end." The word "confirm" is a reference to miracles. The "end" indicates the duration. What "end" will harmonize with

what the Bible teaches about the miraculous? The end of life will not for that would mean miracles would continue beyond the period of revelation and confirmation. This cannot be true because revelation has been completed and confirmed and there are no latter-day revelations (Mark 16:20). If the coming is a reference to Christ's final and personal appearance, then you have the same problem with the continuance of miracles down until today. In fact, this is one of the arguments used by Pentecostals to try to prove that miracles did continue beyond the period of revelation, or the first century. Is there an explanation that will harmonize with what the Bible teaches about miracles belonging only to the period while revelation was being given? The answer is yes. The "coming" under consideration here is the "coming" of Matthew 24. The "end" in verse 8 is the end of Judaism foretold by Christ in Matthew 24. Christ did come in judgment on Jerusalem and the miraculous did continue until then. Revelation had been completed by then and the miraculous ceased, for there was no further need for it. This harmonizes with what the Bible teaches about the cessation of miracles. It harmonizes with what the Bible teaches about Christ coming in judgment on Jerusalem. It seems to me that there are insurmountable difficulties with any other interpretation of this passage.

6. There is still additional evidence to support this interpretation. The word "confirm" is sometimes used in another way; that is, it includes the passing of some event as foretold in the Scriptures, or the fulfillment of a promise. "Now I say that Jesus Christ was a minister of the circumcision for the truth of God, to confirm the promises made unto the fathers," (Romans 15:8). In this passage an event is appealed to as confirmation of a promise made to the patriarchs. The passing of the event, the fulfillment of the prophecies concerning Christ, confirmed the promises to the fathers. The fall of Jerusalem as foretold by Christ confirmed everything He said. Thus, the event itself was a confirmation. A prophecy is a miracle in words. When the event is fulfilled, it furnishes the same confirmation as a miracle of healing, or raising one from the dead. The prophecy of the fall of Jerusalem was just such a miracle—a word miracle. When the event happened as given in detail by Christ, it had the same tangible evidence of the miraculous as any miracle performed by Christ. Since a prophecy is a word miracle, it can be a miraculous confirmation for all ages and time. The fall of Jerusalem is just as much a word miracle for us today as it was for those who lived to see the city fall as

foretold by Christ. The fulfillment of Matthew 24 was God's last miracle (a prophecy or word miracle) of confirmation. It furnishes miraculous evidence for all time.

The Corinthian letter is the first of Paul's letters that strikes at the problem created by Judaizing teachers. This question is not dealt with as extensively in this letter as later in other letters such as Galatians, but it is a part of the problem in this letter. The II Corinthian letter makes it abundantly clear that the Judaizing teachers were troubling the Corinthians. See II Corinthians 3. If this is kept in mind, then I Corinthians 1:5-8 is clear. The miraculous endowments in the Corinthian church were proof of Paul's apostleship, the integrity of the gospel that he had preached to them, and the assurance that the Corinthian church was a genuine church of God. The miraculous endowments of the Corinthians would continue to confirm the church as a true church until, with one final stroke, God would forever remove the arguments of Judaizing teachers by the judgment on Judaism in the fall of Jerusalem. This event would be one final confirmation in answer to the question. Revelation being completed by this time, the miraculous would no longer be needed and God would leave this event as confirmation for all ages. This is one of the reasons that this subject is dealt with at length in the book of Revelation. No single event in all history is discussed as extensively and in such a detailed way in the Bible as the fall of Jerusalem, (the end of Judaism), in the book of Revelation. Now one can see why the peculiar nature of the book of Revelation. From the time of the fall of man, God had gradually revealed Himself unto man. This involved direct revelation, but with the coming of Christ, the proclamation of the gospel, and the establishment of the church, revelation would finally be completed. The direct operation of the Spirit would cease, leaving behind a written, inspired revelation. Christ foretold the event of the fall of Jerusalem. Prophecy and inspiration go hand in hand. Prophecy is a miracle in words. This method of a miracle can furnish confirmation throughout all times without there being a continuous direct operation of the Spirit. This is the case. The fall of Jerusalem and the end of Judaism remain for each generation as a confirmation of the entire New Testament. The fulfillment of the prophecy gives assurance that every promise is genuine and trustworthy. Just as this prophecy was fulfilled as a confirmation of the New Testament, we may look forward to the resurrection, the judgment, and to the eternal reward promised to the faithful. In view of the multiplied counterfeit claims of latter-day revelations, the direct operation of the Spirit, is it not reasonable to think that God would give some specific reference to the completion of revelation and the cessation of the direct and miraculous operation of the Spirit? I believe that He did just that, and these verses supply this fact. I Corinthians 1:5-8 nail down Paul's statement in I Corinthians 13:10: "But when that which is perfect is come [completed revelation], then that which is in part [the gifts of I Corinthians 1:7] shall be done away." The very first chapter of the Corinthian letter makes it plain that the meaning of I Corinthians 13:10 points to the completion of revelation. Revelation would be completed, gifts would cease, and, with one final event, God would confirm by the fulfillment of prophecy, a miracle in word—the New Testament—for all time and for all ages.

I – THE HOLY SPIRIT IN MATTHEW

There are some important principles in the study of the Bible to keep in mind at all times: 1) To whom was the book written? 2) What was the purpose of the book? 3) What is the general theme of the book? 4) What is the book's relationship to the other books of the Bible? These are simple truths to consider in the study of any book of the Bible. These principles should also be kept in mind in the study of any subject in any book of the Bible. These are guidelines that enable one to see a subject in relation to the whole. Truth always harmonizes, and this method of Bible study will aid one in putting together the portions of truths so that the parts equal the whole. I am convinced that this has been a part of the problem in studying the subject of the Holy Spirit.

The book of Matthew is a transitional book. It is at the right place in the New Testament. Its design is to make the transition from the Old to the New Testament. The work of John the Baptist was to prepare the way for Christ. The book of Matthew prepares the way for the passing of Judaism and the beginning of the church. This accounts for the portrait that Matthew gives of Christ: His birth, His life, His miracles, and teaching. Even the language in Matthew is adapted toward making the transition from Judaism to Christianity. The phrase "kingdom of heaven" used by Matthew is to help the Jew make the transition in his understanding of the contrast between the temporal, earthly kingdom of Judaism and the spiritual nature of the kingdom beginning at Pentecost. This is why Matthew selects certain instances in the life of Christ and adds that "this was done that it might be fulfilled." The quotations in the book of Matthew from the Old Testament tie it back to the Old Testament, and the phrase "that it might be fulfilled" shows the passing of the Old and the preparation for the beginning of the New. The book of Matthew was written for the Jew, and its purpose was to guide him from the Old Testament to the New Testament. The book was to show that the shadows of the Old Testament led to Christ, and culminated at Pentecost and what was to follow. Thus, Matthew has the Old Testament as its background and the book of Acts in the foreground. These are simple truths, but they are essential for understanding the book of Matthew.

MATTHEW 3:1-12

Matthew's introduction to the coming of the Spirit sets the stage for the study of the Holy Spirit and His work. Note carefully the following truths as given by Matthew: "I indeed baptize you with water unto repentance: but he that cometh after me is mightier than I, whose shoes I am not worthy to bear: he shall baptize you with the Holy Ghost, and with fire," (Matthew 3:11). This verse looks toward Pentecost in Acts 2. As far as I know, there are none that deny that the baptism of the Holy Spirit took place at Pentecost. When the apostles were baptized in the Holy Spirit at Pentecost and were asked to explain the meaning of it (Acts 2:12), Peter quoted Joel 2:28 to 32. The quotation of Joel by Peter shows that Joel's prophecy is the background of the outpouring of the Holy Spirit at Pentecost. Since Matthew 3:11 points to Pentecost, and Peter quotes Joel as an explanation of the outpouring of the Spirit, we can establish two truths: First, Matthew 3:11 has Joel as its background, and Pentecost and what followed in the foreground. This must be kept in mind at all times in the study of the Holy Spirit in Matthew, Mark, Luke, and John. This fact is essential for one to understand the references to the Holy Spirit in these books. Joel's prophecy is the background of every mention of the Spirit in Matthew, Mark, Luke, and John, with Pentecost in view.

Second, the third chapter of Matthew is an introduction to Matthew's plan to present Christ to the Jew and is a forecast of the outcome. Matthew begins his account of the life of Christ with the line of descent from Abraham to David to Joseph, and then states that He was born of a virgin. The last part of Chapter 3 tells of John baptizing Christ as preparation for His personal ministry. Verses 1 to 12 of Chapter 3 prepare the way for His ministry, the miracles, and the teaching of Christ, with the indication of the opposition of the Jewish leaders which would lead to the death of Christ, the promise of the Spirit as foretold by Joel, and the fall of the Jewish Nation, as a consequence of its unbelief. The first verse of Matthew 3 prepares the way for Christ with the introduction of John and his preaching. John's preaching was to the Jews and it was an announcement of the coming kingdom (Matthew 3:1, 2, 5). Matthew quotes from Isaiah to show that the Old Testament announced the work of John in preparing the way for Christ. John's clothes and food were not just some peculiarity of his, but God's way of contrasting the material blessings of Judaism with the spiritual blessings of the kingdom, which John preached as being at hand. The simple clothes and food of John underscored the value and the superiority of the spiritual blessings that would be in the kingdom. The rejection of John's baptism by the Pharisees and Sadducees is a forecast of their rejection of Christ (Matthew 3:7). Verse 9 is a forecast of their attempt to hold on to the fleshly, temporal Judaism, resulting in their rejection of Christ and their continuing and

THE WORK OF THE HOLY SPIRIT

intense opposition of the church following Pentecost. John's calling them a generation of vipers is a forerunner of the language of Christ in Matthew 23:33. Matthew 3:10 is a direct statement pointing toward the fall of the nation. The Holy Spirit is introduced in the New Testament in a way that indicates the following points to remember:
1. It points backward to Joel's prophecy.
2. It points forward to Pentecost.
3. The context of the passage forecasts the rejection of Christ.
4. The rejection of Christ by the Jewish leaders would not cease following Pentecost, but would continue by opposing the preaching of the apostles and persecuting the church.

The Pharisees and Sadducees formed the Jewish Sanhedrin, which was the heart of the ecclesiasticism of Judaism. This was the civil and the political aspect of Judaism that was the main instrument in crucifying Christ and in opposing the church. This was the prime element that formed the leadership in seeking to destroy the church and leave Judaism as a God-ordained religion. If one stops and considers what would have been the fate of the world if Judaism had succeeded in wiping out the church, and continued to remain in Jerusalem with the temple still standing, he can see still another reason why the fall of the nation is so prominent in the New Testament. Even with God's judgment bringing an end to Judaism with the destruction of the temple, the majority of the religious world thinks that God will restore this old dead carcass when Christ returns. If this is true, then it almost defies the imagination to think what would have happened if God had left the temple standing and Judaism continuing to function. In view of the misunderstanding of the nature of the kingdom of Christ today, if the temple had been left standing, Judaism would be converting more than one could convert with the gospel. Billy Graham, Ted Armstrong, and their like would be hovering over the temple in Jerusalem like martins in a gourd. Divine wisdom knew this. God anticipated the problem, and settled it once and for all with men who are willing to look at the fact that the temple is gone and with it every jot and tittle of Judaism.

The miraculous endowment of the Holy Spirit is put in this context as the Holy Spirit revealed the gospel. When revelation was completed, God used one final argument to establish for all time that He was through with the Jewish Nation, and He was leaving the world a divine, inspired gospel as its only hope. The Jewish Nation was of divine origin, but a temporary arrangement to bring the Messiah into the world that provided the gospel and the church for man's salvation.

Combine the misconception of the Jews with the misconception of the gospel in premillennial teaching today, and the false teaching on the Holy Spirit, and the miraculous operation of the Holy Spirit, and one can see why God arranged it as He did. God had been working directly through miraculous manifestations in giving and confirming revelation for more than fifteen hundred years, but revelation would be completed, and all direct and miraculous manifestation would cease. What could be more reasonable than for God to select a time and occasion to make this clear? It is my conviction that this is the case. Revelation, having been completed, eliminating any further need for the direct and miraculous operation of the Spirit of God, signaled the end of revelation and Judaism with one of the most unusual providential acts in all the Bible. This not only harmonizes with numerous passages, which in my judgment cannot be explained in any other way, but also seems to me to be in harmony with God's method of not leaving important facts hanging in the air. If one keeps in mind that written revelation began with Moses, then it becomes significant that revelation closes with God's judgment and the end of the Jewish Nation in the destruction of the temple. Written revelation had a beginning point with Moses and ended with the fall of the nation. This fall of the nation marked the completion of revelation, as foretold by Christ, making the fall of the nation a final confirmation of the New Testament. The nature of this event marked the transition from direct revelation to a completed, written revelation and the cessation of the miraculous.

MATTHEW–CHAPTER 10

Matthew 10 is an expansion of Matthew 3 and a further development of Joel 2:28-32. The background of this chapter is Matthew 3. The promise of the Holy Spirit in Matthew 3:11 is rather indefinite. This chapter will help to clarify the meaning of Matthew 3:11. Christ selected the twelve apostles. The selection of the twelve apostles gives a further suggestion of the status of the apostles. The selection of the apostles is a forerunner of Acts 2 and what grows out of Acts 2. Later in the study there will be a more detailed discussion of the place of the apostles and their function in the New Testament church.

Following the selection of the apostles, Christ gave the apostles instructions for their work under the limited commission. This commission may be divided as follows: 1) the commission, 2) the equipment for the commission, 3) directions for their conduct on this

THE WORK OF THE HOLY SPIRIT 81

mission. The limited commission was preparatory work and training for their future work as apostles. The limited commission not only was a call to Israel that the kingdom was at hand, but it was training for the apostles for their future work, which would begin at Pentecost. Matthew 10:14-15 is a reminder of the reception of the apostles under the limited commission. There would be some in Israel that would not heed their appeal to repent in view of the coming kingdom. The consequences of the rejection of their message would leave the rejector to face judgment. Verse 15 points to the final judgment. This is done to distinguish the final judgment from the judgment on the nation when Jerusalem fell. There can be no question but what this judgment refers to the final judgment, because the men of Sodom and Gomorrah will be in the judgment referred to here. The only way this could be possible would be for this to be a reference to the final judgment, when all men of all time and ages stand before God when time shall be no more. Brother Max King would have difficulty showing how the men of Sodom and Gomorrah were included in the judgment upon the Jewish Nation when Jerusalem fell. In the verses that follow, the judgment on Jerusalem will be mentioned, but the Lord first called attention to the final judgment so that one would not conclude that the judgment on the Jewish Nation was the final judgment. Matthew 10:15 is an anticipation of Matthew 25:31-46, which is a reference to the final judgment.

Since the limited commission was in preparation for the work of the apostles beginning at Pentecost, Christ then discusses the nature of their work beginning at Pentecost. These verses anticipate the Great Commission in Matthew 28:18-20. Matthew 10:16 and the following look toward Pentecost and successive events. Matthew 10:17-18 was to prepare the apostles for the persecution they would face in preaching the gospel. The persecution would begin with opposition from Jewish leaders. Acts 2 and the following is a divine commentary on these verses. Matthew 10:19-20 is an explanation of Matthew 3:11. The baptism of the Holy Spirit in Matthew 3:11 is then shown to have reference to the inspiration of the apostles. These verses show that the apostles would be inspired and that inspiration includes not only the thoughts, but also the words. "Take no thought" is explained by the phrase, "What ye shall speak." Then verse 20 states, "For it is not ye that speak, but the Spirit of your Father which speaketh in you." Notice carefully the following: Speaking involves words. It was to be the Spirit in them speaking; thus, the Spirit provided the words which were used. This is verbal inspiration. Any denial of verbal inspiration must reject the evident meaning of these verses. Joel 2:28-32 is introduced in Matthew 3:11. Matthew, Chapter 10, expands both Joel and Matthew 3:11. Matthew 10 points to Pentecost, the coming of the Spirit, and the revelation of the gospel as recorded in Acts. Any proper understanding of the work of the Holy Spirit must take into consideration the apostles and their work in the revelation of the gospel. Here is where a great amount of misunderstanding develops in the study of the Holy Spirit and His work. The peculiar place of the apostles in the church must never be lost sight of, or one will never understand the work of the Holy Spirit. More will be said about the place of the apostles when we come to the book of John.

MATTHEW 28:18-20

And Jesus came and spake unto them, saying, All power is given unto me in heaven and in earth.

Go ye therefore, and teach all nations, baptizing them in the name of the Father, and of the Son, and of the Holy Ghost:

Teaching them to observe all things whatsoever I have commanded you: and, lo, I am with you alway, even unto the end of the world. Amen.

These verses climax Matthew's discussion of the work of the apostles. As already noticed, this commission was already anticipated in Matthew 3:11 and Matthew 10:19-20. But as Matthew 10 was an expansion of Joel 2:28-32 and Matthew 3:11, one can see the significance now of the Great Commission as given by Matthew. In a previous chapter, I have already discussed this commission in some detail. I have shown that the commission was given to the apostles. The apostles were to receive the gospel by revelation. Inspiration was necessary for the apostles to receive the revelation of the gospel. The gospel once received by the apostles and put into a written revelation, direct inspiration would cease. Matthew's account of the Great Commission foresees the completion of revelation and the cessation of the miraculous endowments by the end of the age or the Jewish state. Therefore, Christ promised to be with the apostles (inspiration) unto the end of the age. As I have already pointed out, the promise, "Lo, I am with you," was the promise of the inspiration to the apostles. See the discussion of this in detail in the chapter, "Joel's Prophecy — The Key to Understanding the Holy Spirit in the New Testament." When revelation was completed, the direct operation of the Spirit ceased, leaving behind a written revelation for all time and for all ages. "Go ye therefore, and teach all nations, baptizing them in the name of the Father, and of the Son, and of the Holy Spirit." "All nations" makes the transition from the Jewish Nation in the Old Testament to the universal offer of the gospel to all nations. In order to establish this truth, the Holy Spirit, through the inspiration of the apostles and miraculous endowments, given through the hands of the apostles, became the agent to prove this truth. While revealing the truth through the apostles, and furnishing the means of edification to the church by spiritual gifts, the Holy Spirit also established the genuineness of the gospel and its universal offer to all nations. The Jews denied the universal offer of the gospel and sought to bind circumcision on the Gentiles, and by this, to bind the law on the Gentiles. The Holy Spirit, through the apostles and spiritual gifts in the church, was a denial of the Jewish attempt to bind the law on the Gentiles. This struggle between Judaism trying to hold on to the past with its roots in Palestine and Jerusalem, and the gospel launching out to wider fields, including all men of all nations, is the background of the appeal to the Spirit in many passages in the Epistles. The reference to the Spirit in various passages is an appeal to recognize the genuineness and the integrity of the gospel proclaimed by the apostles.

Finally, consider the phrase, "Baptizing them into the name of the Father, and of the Son, and of the Holy Spirit," (American Standard Version). The preposition "into" denotes relationship. Baptism is the consummating act for the penitent believer that brings him into a saving relationship with the Godhead. But does not the wording here indicate that baptism brings the person into the same relationship with God the Father, Christ the Son, and the Holy Spirit? This language should help avoid thinking that the Christian sustains a peculiar relationship to the Holy Spirit. Yet the idea seems to be that when one is baptized, he receives the Holy Spirit in some way distinct and different from which he receives God or Christ. If one reads carefully the very language which is used when one is baptized into Christ, it seems to me that it would help him avoid reaching the conclusion that when one is baptized into Christ, he receives the Holy Spirit in some peculiar way, and that he sustains a relationship to the Holy Spirit different to the relationship that he sustains to God or Christ. The language here is designed to help us realize that when one is baptized into Christ, he is brought into the same relationship with God the Father, Christ the Son, and the Holy Spirit.

II – THE HOLY SPIRIT IN MARK

"And he said unto them, Verily I say unto you, that there be some of them that stand here, which shall not taste of death, till they have seen the kingdom of God come with power," (Mark 9:1).

The promise that the kingdom would come with power had as its background Joel 2:28-32 and looked toward Pentecost and what followed. The word "power" makes a reference to the miraculous manifestation of the Spirit that came at Pentecost. (Miraculous power usually by implication a miracle, Strong's Concordance.) Joel had foretold of the coming of the Spirit and miraculous power. John preached that the kingdom was at hand. He also said that the apostles would be baptized in the Holy Spirit (Matthew 3:2 and 11). Christ put the kingdom and the Spirit together to show the fulfillment of Joel's prophecy. The coming of the kingdom called for the revelation of the gospel. The revelation of the gospel called for inspiration to receive the revelation that it might be proclaimed. The beginning of the kingdom demanded a new revelation. The law would be set aside and the gospel would be given. The gospel was, and is, a different system from the law. Every new revelation was always accompanied with miraculous evidence to establish it as a divine revelation. The gospel in fact began at the same time that the kingdom did. Mark 9:1 simply points to the miraculous power that came on Pentecost with the beginning of the kingdom. "And as I began to speak, the Holy Ghost fell on them, as on us at the beginning," (Acts 11:15). Note Peter referred to Pentecost and the coming of the Spirit as the beginning. The power of Mark 9:1 is a reference to the miraculous power promised to the apostles: "And, behold, I send the promise of my Father upon you: but tarry ye in the city of Jerusalem, until ye be endued with power from on high," (Luke 24:49). Putting Luke 24:49 and Mark 9:1 together, we have the promise of Joel for the outpouring of the Spirit on the apostles at Pentecost. According to Luke's account, the apostles were to be in the city of Jerusalem. Luke then described the power on the apostles as being endued, or clothed, with power from on high. Thus the power of Mark 9:1 is the promise of the Father, which is a reference to Joel 2:28-32. The place of the fulfillment of Mark 9:1 was the city of Jerusalem. The power of Mark 9:1 was also the miraculous clothing of the apostles for their work as apostles. This put the power with the apostles in the city of Jerusalem. The kingdom came in the city of Jerusalem. The apostles received power when they were baptized in the Holy Spirit (Acts 2:1-4). Peter quoted Joel's promise, which was the promise of the Father in Luke 24:49. The kingdom came on the same day in the same city that the Holy Spirit came. Acts 1:8 is a divine commentary on Mark 9:1 and Luke 24:49. Mark 9:1, like the passages in Matthew, had Joel 2:28-32 as its background and pointed to Pentecost.

THE WORK OF THE HOLY SPIRIT

MARK 16:16-20

He that believeth and is baptized shall be saved; but he that believeth not shall be damned.

And these signs shall follow them that believe; In my name shall they cast out devils; they shall speak with new tongues;

They shall take up serpents; and if they drink any deadly thing, it shall not hurt them; they shall lay hands on the sick, and they shall recover.

So then after the Lord had spoken unto them, he was received up into heaven, and sat on the right hand of God.

And they went forth, and preached every where, the Lord working with them, and confirming the word with signs following.

These passages have been perverted by men who have completely misunderstood the work of the Holy Spirit in conversion and sanctification. Pentecostals have had trouble among themselves in trying to interpret these passages. Some limit them to tongues and miraculous healing. Others claim the passages authorize tongues, casting out demons, and healing today. A small number of Pentecostals attempt to practice everything mentioned in the passages, including handling snakes, and a still smaller number claim that these passages authorize the drinking of poison. Some have just recently tried this and ended up dead, which is proof that the passage does not have application for us today. The ones that are foolish enough to attempt to drink poison are indeed few and far between. These passages, like the others studied, have Joel as their background and then Pentecost and what followed Pentecost. The passages have no difficulties in being understood if one only lets the fulfillment of them, in the book of Acts, explain them. When the Commission was given, there was no written revelation of the gospel. The gospel was to be revealed by direct revelation and confirmed by miracles. This started at Pentecost when the gospel was preached and continued following Pentecost when congregations were established. When a congregation was established, there was no written revelation to leave with the congregation. What was left behind by the apostles was miraculous gifts given through the laying on of their hands. Acts 8 shows that while Philip had a miraculous gift, he could not impart the gift to others. Only the apostles could impart these miraculous endowments (Acts 8:17-18). These signs (Mark 16:20) followed believers when the gifts were given to those who had been baptized. Notice that Mark says, "...Go...preach...baptized...saved...these signs shall follow," (Mark 16:15-17). If one will consider the eighth chapter of Acts, he will be able to see an example of the signs following believers. Philip went down to Samaria and preached (Acts 8:5). The Samaritans believed the things that Philip preached and were baptized. Peter and John came down to Samaria and laid their hands on the ones that had believed and been baptized. The gifts that the Samaritans received were the signs that followed the believers. Acts 8 is a Bible interpretation and explanation of Mark 16:16-20. The attempt to make the signs of Mark 16:17-20 apply only to the apostles comes short of what took place under this Commission. The fear that this interpretation will allow miracles to continue today is without any basis. Mark 16:20 states that the purpose of miracles was to confirm the Word, showing that revelation and confirmation by miracles belong together. When revelation ceased, so did the signs of Mark 16:17-18. Matthew's account of the Great Commission promised inspiration to the apostles. Mark's account of the Great Commission added the fact that believers would receive miraculous gifts. This should not be considered strange as Joel's prophecy was a promise of the inspiration of the apostles and miraculous gifts for believers during the period in which revelation was being given. This is evident when one reads the prophecy of Joel. The part of the prophecy that says, "...your sons and your daughters shall prophesy, your old men shall dream dreams, your young men shall see visions: And also upon the servants and upon the handmaids in those days will I pour out my spirit," (Joel 2:28-29). And they "shall prophesy" can only be a reference to miraculous gifts received by believers. Since Joel's prophecy included miraculous gifts for believers, in addition to the inspiration of the apostles, why should there be any surprise that the Great Commission mentioned these gifts? Joel's prophecy included gifts that believers would receive while revelation was being given and confirmed. The book of Acts shows that believers did receive miraculous gifts through the laying on of the apostles' hands. Since Joel's prophecy promised miraculous gifts for believers and the book of Acts gives an account of believers receiving miraculous gifts from the apostles (Acts 8; Acts 19), I can see no difficulty in understanding Mark 16:17-20. The word "sign" in verse 17 shows the relationship of these gifts to the period of revelation. Verse 20 limits the duration of the gifts to the period of the confirmation and the completion of revelation. Following are four articles that discuss this passage. The first three articles are from the <u>Gospel Advocate</u> and were written by brother Frank Van Dyke, who at the time of the writing was head of the Bible Department at Freed-Hardeman College. The last article is by brother Roy H. Lanier, Sr., and is taken from the <u>Firm Foundation</u>. Read these articles carefully, and I think you can see the

THE WORK OF THE HOLY SPIRIT 87

proof that the signs that were promised to follow believers were simply the gifts that Christians received during the period that revelation was being given and confirmed.

ARTICLE NO. 1
THESE SIGNS SHALL FOLLOW
Frank Van Dyke

"Afterward he appeared unto the eleven as they sat at meat, and upbraided them with their unbelief and hardness of heart, because they believed not them which had seen him after he was risen. And he said unto them, Go ye into all the world, and preach the gospel to every creature. He that believeth and is baptized shall be saved; but he that believeth not shall be damned. And these signs shall follow them that believe; In my name shall they cast out devils; they shall speak with new tongues; they shall take up serpents; and if they drink any deadly thing, it shall not hurt them; they shall lay hands on the sick, and they shall recover. So then after the Lord had spoken unto them, he was received up into heaven, and sat on the right hand of God. And they went forth, and preached every where, the Lord working with them, and confirming the word with signs following" (Mark 16:14-20).

The promise of miraculous power (verses 17, 18), it seems to me, is to baptized believers, not to the apostles. Let us now give the reasons for this position.

THE CONTEXT

The context makes this the most natural and obvious reference. Two speeches are contemplated here—one, the upbraiding speech, is only mentioned (verse 14); the other, the giving of the commission, is recorded (verses 15-18). McGarvey, in his "Fourfold Gospel," has the two speeches delivered at different times and different places. He puts the upbraiding speech (verse 14) on Sunday evening (the day Christ arose), when Jesus appeared to the apostles the first time—the meeting recorded in Luke 24:36-43 and John 20:19-23. The commission (verses 15-18) was given on a mountain in Galilee not so long before Christ ascended. (Matt. 28:16-20) B. W. Johnson also takes this view.

There are good reasons to believe that McGarvey and Johnson are right.

1. Mark 16:9-13 records things that did occur on the day Christ arose. Verse 14 could well be a continuation of what happened on

that day. The "afterward," with which verse 14 begins, does not have to mean **on another day**; it may mean **later in the same day**—after the event in the preceding verses. This is the significance of "after" in verse 12, and so it may be with "afterward" in verse 14.

2. When had the apostles failed to believe "them which had seen him after he was risen"? On the day he arose, and verses 10-13 have just discussed this. So far as the record shows, that day is the only time they ever doubted such reports. And Christ did appear unto them immediately after this, on the evening of the same day. (Luke 24:33-36). It is only natural to suppose that it was then that Christ upbraided them for not believing those reports. Why would he wait nearly forty days later to do it?

3. Did the apostles doubt the resurrection when Christ gave them the commission? Hardly so. They had believed at the first appearance nearly forty days before this (John 20:20, 25, 28), and there is no conclusive evidence that they ever doubted the resurrection after that. From Matthew's account, many conclude that some of the apostles did doubt at the time the commission was given. Matthew just mentions the eleven in this connection; however, he does not say they were the only ones present. McGarvey and Johnson think this was the time Christ appeared to above five hundred, and that Matthew's meaning could be this: "And when they [the eleven] saw him, they worshipped him [the eleven believed]; but some [others] doubted." (Matt. 28:17).

4. The upbraiding in verse 14 was "because they believed not them which had seen him after he was risen." This sounds like his first appearance; for even if the apostles did doubt the resurrection after that first appearance, Christ should have upbraided them then for not believing their own eyes—not for failure to accept the report of others.

5. The appearance mentioned in Mark 16:14 was while the apostles sat at meat. This was not likely on the mountain in Galilee when Christ gave the commission. At that first appearance, however, the apostles were in a room. (John 20:19). And evidently they had been eating for Jesus asked for meat and got it—most likely a part of what the apostles had been eating. (Luke 24:41,42).

6. The appearance in verse 14 seems to have been sudden and unexpected. This fits the first appearance, but the meeting on the mountain in Galilee was by appointment (Matt. 28:16). The apostles went there expecting to see the Lord.

7. Verse 15, though it may seem to be relating something else that happened at the appearance in verse 14, may very properly begin

THE WORK OF THE HOLY SPIRIT

an account of a different incident—something that occured much later. Cases like this are common in the Gospels. An example is in Luke 24:36-48. Verses 36-43 record the appearance Christ made to the apostles on the day he arose. Verse 44, with no apparent break in the narrative, begins a discourse that was given much later. Reading Luke's account alone, one might get the idea that Jesus made this speech at that first appearance, immediately led the apostles out near Bethany, and ascended. Everybody knows, however, that such is not the case. So Mark 16:15 may begin a speech which was given a long time after the incident in verse 14.

For these reasons we are compelled to believe, with Johnson and McGarvey, that the upbraiding in verse 14 did not occur at the time and place of the speech in verses 15-18. The promise in Mark 16:17, therefore has no connection whatever with a speech in which Christ urged the apostles to believe. Christ had not just been telling the apostles to believe; so there is no basis for an interpretation like this: "Christ had just upbraided the apostles for not believing, and then told them if they believed, they could work wonders."

Such an interpretation would not be justified if all of this had happened at the same time. Even then, beginning with verse 15, Christ is no longer trying to get the apostles to believe; he is instructing them to make believers of somebody else. So the promise in verse 17 still would not be directly connected with the exhortation for the apostles to believe; it is part of the speech to the apostles about making believers of every creature in all the world.

Without some indication that he intended to switch the thought back to the apostles in verse 17, all rules of grammar, proper coherence, and smoothness of diction would demand that the "them" be from all the world, the last group under consideration. Even if we were to grant that all of these things in verses 14-18 happened at the same time, it would still take a strained effort to refer the promise to the apostles. To do so would at least make the Savior's statement ambiguous. His coherence would be poor, not showing the transition of thought from one group to another. Such a connection between verses 14 and 17, considering the grammar and sequence of thought, would be unnatural and awkward. The language would be subject (and that easily so) to a different interpretation.

THE GRAMMAR

Christ was addressing the apostles in the second person. If "them" refers to the apostles, then we have a pronoun in the third person with its antecedent in the second person, which is not permissible for a rule of grammar says that "a pronoun must agree with its antecedent in gender, number, and **person**." Another rule of grammar says that the second person indicates the one spoken to; the third person, the person or thing spoken about. Jesus said: "Go ye into all the world, and preach the gospel to every creature . . .And these signs shall follow them that believe." It is strange to me that anybody ever thought of referring "them" to anyone except the group (all the world) introduced in the beginning of the discourse—the ones spoken about.

It may be said that the ones spoken about may be among the ones spoken to, like this: "You believe, and these signs shall follow them [of you] that believe." Such is not the form, however, in Mark 16:17. There, as we have seen, Christ was not urging the apostles to believe when he made the promise. The event in verse 14 happened at a previous time. But even if all this had occurred at the same time, we still would not have a case like the example given above; for in that example no third party has been introduced to whom "them" could possibly refer. In Mark 16:15-18, however, a third party (every creature in all the world) has been introduced, and Christ is urging the apostles to make believers of them. Immediately following this, not immediately after urging the apostles to believe, the promise in verse 17 was given; and from the grammar and sequence it naturally seems to refer to the last group mentioned—the ones spoken about.

A very unfortunate example is sometimes used to justify making "them," a pronoun in the third person, refer to an antecedent in the second person. Jesus said: "Seek, and ye shall find;. . .for . . .he that seeketh findeth." (Matt. 7:7,8). It has been said that "the 'he' here is the 'ye' or 'you' of verse 7." No, no, no! The "he" is indefinite; it comprehends everybody, and is restricted only by the modifying clause. Turn the statement around: "He [anybody] that seeketh findeth; therefore, you [a particular person or group of persons] seek, and ye shall find." Anybody ought to see that the "he" is not the "ye."

This violation of grammar is sometimes dismissed this way: "The interpretation which says that the 'them' refers to the believers of verse 16 involves a violation of English with reference to number, for they make the 'them' of verse 17 have the antecedent 'he' of verse 16. Thus

THE WORK OF THE HOLY SPIRIT

the objection drawn from the rules of English grammar is as much against one position as another. Therefore, the question must be settled on other grounds than that of English grammar."

There are serious objections to this statement. First, the question cannot be settled on any grounds that will make Jesus wrong in his grammar. We have used faulty grammar as one argument against the claims for inspiration of Joseph Smith and others. Be careful—somebody will throw it back at you that Jesus was not divine! Second, "the interpretation which says that the 'them' refers to the believers of verse 16" does not "involve a violation of the rules of English grammar with reference to number." This does not "make the 'them' of verse 17 have the antecedent 'he' of verse 16." Take the "he" first. What is its antecedent? It is any person that will believe and be baptized. The "he" is indefinite except as restricted by the modifying clause. Likewise with the "them". Is its antecedent the "he"? No, it is all who will believe. The "them" is indefinite except as restricted by the modifying clause; its antecedent would be the same if the "he" were not in verse 16.

It may be said that "them that believe" must not be extended beyond the group under consideration—that if a particular group is contemplated, then it can only mean the ones in that number who believe. Exactly right! But a group—every creature in all the world—is introduced in verse 15. (The distributive form "every creature" does not alter the fact that a group, the whole world, is considered.) Now, consider verse 16. Since the passage contemplates the whole world, the meaning is obviously this: "He [in all the world] that believeth and is baptized shall be saved." Just so with verse 17. The whole world is still under consideration, so the meaning is this: "Them [in all the world] that believe." "The 'them,' like the 'he' of verse 16, finds its antecedent in the group mentioned in verse 15, and the modifying clause restricts the antecedent to certain ones in that group."

The relation between verses 16 and 17 is this: they both contemplate believers—believers made by the apostles in all the world. Verse 16 uses the distributive form: "He [every one in all the world] that believeth," etc. Verse 17 uses the collective, or aggregate, form: "Them [in all the world] that believe." It is perfectly in order to switch from the singular, or distributive, form to the plural, or collective, form. An example of this is in John 15:6: "If a man [any man in the world] abide not in me, he is cast forth as a branch, and is withered; and men gather them [all that are thus withered], and cast them into the fire, and they are burned." Would anybody argue that the "them" here has the singular "man" as its antecedent?

Verse 16, though it does not express the grammatical antecedent of the "them" in verse 17, does refer to a believer of the same class, and says he is a baptized believer. Let nobody quibble, therefore, that our explanation makes it impossible to tell whether or not the believers of verse 17 are baptized believers.

CONDITIONS AND TIME ELEMENT

Any other conditions, or means, stipulated elsewhere, necessary for baptized believers to receive miraculous power must be understood to prevail in the fulfillment of the promise in Mark 16:17. Christ did not state just **how** and **when** believers would receive this power. When we learn how baptized believers did come to possess miraculous gifts, then Mark 16:17, interpreted in the light of this, is simply a promise that believers would receive this power that way. When apostles laid hands upon baptized believers and gave them miraculous power, this could well be the way the promise of Mark 16:17 was fulfilled. Our position does not demand that believers possessed such gifts immediately after, nor as the direct result of, their baptism.

Is it objected that this is adding conditions that Jesus did not stipulate? Well, this same passage promises salvation to one who believes and is baptized. Another condition, repentance, is stipulated elsewhere; and nobody has any trouble interpreting this promise accordingly. And, too, I take it that those who apply the promise of verse 17 to the apostles will agree that something not mentioned here (the baptism of the Holy Spirit) actually occurred before the apostles had such powers, (not before they had any miraculous power, for they performed some miracles under the limited commission; but before they had the full measure of such powers—that which was theirs after Pentecost).

Neither did Christ state how long the signs would follow. Eph. 4:11-13; II Tim. 3:16, 17; and I Cor. 13:8-10, considered together, show that miraculous gifts continued in the early church only until the New Testament was revealed and recorded. Mark 16:17, interpreted in the light of this, is simply a promise that believers would have such powers—the signs would follow for that time only.

Some make a distinction between "signs following" and "working signs." They say that two things are found in the promise—first, that the signs could be done; second, that the signs would follow. The first, they agree, has ceased; but the second continues. The signs follow even now in the record of the work done by those who once performed them just as a person's deeds follow, or live on, after he is gone. It is true, of course, that the signs do continue to follow in this manner; but such an idea does not seem to me to be in the text. "These signs shall follow them that believe"—that is, "in my name shall they cast out devils," etc. The latter part, which says they shall do them, seems to tell what he meant by saying that the signs would follow.

But Christ did not say how long the signs would follow—no, he did not say they would follow until the end of the world. Attention will be given to that point in another article in which we shall discuss the objections offered against the explanation set forth herein. Keep this article for reference when the next one appears,—Gospel Advocate, Oct. 18, 1945.

ARTICLE NO. 2

In a previous article we set forth the view that the promise of miraculous power in Mark 16:17 was to baptized believers. That article was written with special emphasis upon the fact that grammatically the promise does not refer to the apostles—that it can, and does, refer to baptized believers. In strict grammatical analysis, "apostles" is not the antecedent of "them" in verse 17. Though our first article viewed the promise strictly from the standpoint of its reference to baptized believers, it may not be necessary to conclude that the apostles were excluded. Some refer the promise both to the apostles and to baptized believers. This is permissible.

We learned that the "them" of verse 17 finds its antecedent in the group—the whole world—introduced in verse 15, with the modifying clause restricting it to believers in that group. Well, the apostles were believers. Though in grammatical analysis "them" in verse 17 does not refer to the apostles, the promise made there, since it comprehends all believers in the world, may by projection of thought be made to include them, since they were believers. Speaking to the church today, one might say: "Make disciples of everybody in the community, and the Lord will bless those who do become Christians." Grammatically, "those who do become Christians" does not refer to the ones spoken to. The promise, however, is something God does for his people; hence, the thought, though expressed in specific reference to new converts, may be extended to those who were already such. Thus Mark 16:17, though a direct reference to those to be made believers, may be understood, by projection of thought, to **include** the apostles, who were already believers.

According to this, the promise would carry no indication of just **how** and **when** believers would receive its fulfillment—it would not even demand that all classes of believers (apostles and those not apostles) would have to receive it alike. Any conditions, or means, by which different classes of believers did actually come to possess such powers would have to be understood to prevail in the fulfillment of the promise. When the apostles were baptized with the Holy Spirit and received miraculous power, this might well be the way that the promise, insomuch as it refers to the apostles, was fulfilled. When baptized believers had these powers delegated to them by laying on of hands, this could very properly be the way the promise was fulfilled to them.

This explanation, we say, may be permissible. We have no objection to including the apostles in this manner. At the most, however, the apostles were **only included**. The promise most certainly was not restricted to them. It does refer to baptized believers (that which is denied by the other view), whether or not it refers to them exclusively. Let nobody object that we are just trying to work the apostles in by a "roundabout method" to escape difficulties presented by leaving the apostles out of this promise. **We are satisfied to leave the apostles entirely out of this particular promise. The supposed "difficulties" caused by so doing are easily explained.**

Let us consider some of those objections—objections to the whole explanation we have given, not merely to leaving the apostles out.

1. **"Why limit the time element in verses 17, 18, but not in verse 16?"** Answer: If other passages showed that, for a limited time only, people were saved by believing and being baptized, then Mark 16:15, 16 would have to be interpreted as a promise of salvation upon those conditions for that time only. Other passages limit the one, but not the other.
2. **"Jesus said: 'I am with you alway, even unto the end of the world.' (Matt. 28:20). This is parallel with Mark 16:17, so the signs are to continue until the end of the world."** Answer: The passages are parallel, but every item in one does not have to have its counterpart **expressed** in the other. We simply put the two passages together to get all items—this way:

"Gospel" and "believeth" are not synonymous with something in Matthew, but are other items given by Mark so with "signs shall follow" and "with you...unto the end of the world." These are two distinct promises—one stated by Mark, the other by Matthew. How long were the signs to follow? Christ did not say. How long was he to be "with you"? Until the end of the world.

If there is anything to this argument on parallel passages, it would ruin the position that applies the promise of Mark 16:17 to the apostles. The latter part of the promise, which says the signs would be done, seems to explain what was meant by saying the signs would follow, like this: "And these signs shall follow them that believe"—that is, "in my name shall they cast out devils," etc. The signs were to follow by being done—that is, signs following is the working of miracles. If the expression in Matt. 28:20 means the signs would follow until the end of the world, then it means they would be performed that long. But the apostles were not to live that long, so they could not be the only ones to work the signs.

To offset this and escape the conclusion that miracles can be worked today, some brethren, agreeing that Jesus did not say the signs would follow until the end of the world, make a distinction between "working signs" and "signs following." The first, they agree, has ceased; but the signs will follow (live on in the record of those deeds) until the end of the world. But if Matt. 28:20 qualifies one part of the promise, the part about signs following, by the same logic, would it not have to modify the part that says signs would be done? If not, why not? The Holiness could still argue, therefore, that Jesus promised that signs **could be done** until the end of the world. So if their argument on parallel passages is true, it forbids limiting the promise to the apostles, even if the promise has two parts.

Matt. 28:	Go	Teach		All Nations		Baptize			With you alway
Mark 16:	Go	Preach	Gospel	Every Creature	Believe	Baptize	Saved	Signs Follow	
	Go	Preach	Gospel	Every Creature	Believe	Baptized	Saved	Signs Follow	With you alway

This argument must be met, then, whether we apply the promise to baptized believers or restrict it to the apostles. Actually, there is nothing to it; for the statement in Matt. 28:20, as we have shown, has no bearing on the promise in Mark 16:17.

3. "If the ones promised, in verse 17, these powers were the believers mentioned in verse 16, the promise applied to all of these believers." Answer: Not necessarily so. Believers, as a group, did possess such powers; but each individual did not have to. It is common to speak of a number this way: "They sang, prayed, and preached." Every person present did not do all of these; some sang, others prayed, and another preached. Perhaps some in the group did none of these. John the Baptist said: "He that cometh after me...shall baptize you with the Holy Ghost and with fire." (Matt. 3:11). He was speaking to a group, but not all of them were to receive both of these. Some were to receive one; some, the other. Not all in that group were to receive even one of these.

Our position does not demand that every believer had to have even one of the gifts, much less all of them. Some did part of the signs; others, the rest. Some perhaps did none. Baptized believers who did not receive "laying on of hands" did not share in the promise of Mark 16:17; and the form used in the promise, as has been shown, allows for this. The objection that "all believers most assuredly did not have all the gifts" and that "there is no indication in the New Testament that all believers possessed the power to work even one of these wonders" simply goes for naught.

This way of referring to a group without demanding that each individual receive the things promised may account for the change from the singular "he that believeth" to the plural "them that believe." Each believer would have had to possess the gifts if Jesus had said: "These signs shall follow **Him** that believeth," etc. Not so, though, when he switches to the plural and refers to believers as a group.

4. "This passage contained no promise of miraculous powers to the apostles, if the promise referred to the baptized believers of verse 16." Answer: We have seen one way the apostles may be included. But even if they are not included, this is no objection; for it is admitted that "this would not mean, however, that the apostles were not elsewhere promised miraculous powers." (John

14:26; Acts 1:8; and Acts 2:1-4 show when and how the apostles did receive miraculous power, and "thus we do not need to go to Mark 16:17 in order to find how" the apostles received power to work miracles.)

Those who are excited about our leaving the apostles out might consider this: Our position does not leave the apostles without a promise of miraculous power; but their position, which restricts the promise to the apostles, does leave baptized believers without a promise of such powers as they actually received. They had miraculous powers (under the conditions already explained). When and where were they ever promised such, if not in Mark 16:17? No, they did not have to have a promise; they could have possessed these without a previous promise. But so could the apostles!

5. **"Since the apostles were the ones who possessed these powers, they must have been the ones who were the object of the promise."** Answer: Not unless the apostles were the only ones who ever possessed these powers. Even if this proves that the apostles were objects of the promise in Mark 16:17, it does not prove that they were the only objects of that promise. Others did have miraculous powers, so they could have been objects of the same promise, as already explained.

But the fact that the apostles possessed these powers does not even prove that they were objects at all of the promise in Mark 16:17. They were "elsewhere promised miraculous powers," so they could have possessed the gifts of fulfillment of this "elsewhere" promise only.

6. **"The list of special gifts possessed by early Christians does not include all the signs in Mark 16:17: therefore, we cannot say that baptized believers had the powers promised here, so they were not objects of this promise."** Answer: It cannot be shown that all of them were done by apostles, for there is no record of an apostle drinking poison. Apostles did the others, and it is inferred that they could do that one too. Well, baptized believers upon whom the apostles laid hands did some of these. Is it unsafe to infer, as our friends do with the apostles in the case of the poison, that they (some of them) could do the others too—that is, that the apostles could delegate all of these powers? Is there any reason to believe that the apostles could delegate only a part of these gifts?

Is it necessary to assume that the New Testament lists every miracle performed by early Christians?

7. **"Who was it, to whom the Lord was then speaking, who had not believed?"** Answer: Here it is assumed that the speech in verses 15-18 was given at the appearance in verse 14. It is said that Christ "upbraided them for their unbelief. He told them [at the same time] what to do, and he promised them that if they believed [verse 17], they would be able to perform wonders." Christ had not then been upbraiding the apostles. Verse 14 happened at evening on the day Christ arose; verses 15-18, nearly forty days later. (See previous article for full discussion of this point.) So Christ, when he made this promise, was not **talking to** anybody who had not believed; he was **talking about** somebody—every creature in all the world—who had not believed.

Even if we admit that the Lord had just upbraided the apostles for their unbelief, it is still begging the question to say that verse 17, therefore, refers to them. It would first have to be shown that "them that believe," in the light of the grammar and the sequence of thought, refers to the apostles. When that is done, then it could be said that he was telling the apostles that if they believed, they would be able to perform wonders.

Whether or not we separate verses 14 and 15 in point of time, the question to settle is this: Beginning with verse 15, whom is he **speaking about** that had not believed? He is speaking about every creature in the whole world, telling the apostles to make believers of them. He is not telling the apostles what will happen **if they** believe, but is telling them what will happen when they go and make believers of **others**.

8. **"If these miraculous powers were to be given to all believers, they would cease to be the 'signs of an apostle.'"** Answer: This may be an objection to the position of Holiness, who apply the promise to all believers of all times; but it is no complaint against our position. It is admitted that the fact that "these apostles could delegate by laying on of hands, some of these powers to one and some to another, does not make against these miraculous gifts being the specific badge of the apostles." Well, then, our explanation offers no difficulty; for the promise of Mark 16:17, according to our view, was fulfilled to baptized believers only when they had such powers delegated to them in the proper way.

THE WORK OF THE HOLY SPIRIT

9. "The apostles, in verse 20, performed signs which were the fulfillment of the promises of verses 17 and 18; therefore, the promise was to them." Answer: This would not prove that the apostles were the **only ones** who performed signs in fulfillment of that promise. Others, under conditions we have pointed out, did work such signs, so they might have done so in fulfillment of that promise too. This objection would mean nothing, even granting that what the apostles did in verse 20 was in fulfillment of verses 17 and 18, unless they were the only ones who ever had miraculous powers.

It is not necessary to say that the signs done by the apostles in verse 20 were in fulfillment of the promise in verse 17. The events of verses 19, 20 were not next in order after the commission was given—that is, they were not immediately after the speech in verses 15-18. Some time after the commission was given (just how long after, we do not know) Christ appeared again to the apostles, either in Jerusalem or on the Mount of Olives and gave the discourse in Acts 1: 6-9. This speech closes this way: "But ye shall receive power, after that the Holy Ghost is come upon you: and ye shall be witnesses unto me both in Jerusalem, and in all Judaea, and in Samaria, and unto the uttermost part of the earth." Immediately after this speech Christ ascended. (Acts 1:9.) So Mark 16:19, 20 must be read this way: "So then after the Lord had spoken unto them [the instructions and promise in Acts 1:6-8, not immediately after the commission in verses 15-18], he was received up into heaven...And they went forth [after they had tarried in Jerusalem ten days—that is, after Pentecost], and preached every where, the Lord working with them, and confirming the word with signs following."

The event in Mark 16:20 (working of signs by the apostles) was removed several days from the speech in verses 15-18. Another speech was made and another promise was given (Acts 1:6-8) before these signs were performed. The apostles did these signs after, and in fulfillment of, the promise of miraculous power in Acts 1:8, not immediately following, nor necessarily in fulfillment of, the promise in Mark 16:17. Some people mistake proximity of statements for proximity in time of occurrence.

WHY LIMIT THIS TO APOSTLES?

Why did anybody ever think of restricting this promise to the apostles? Obviously, to escape a promise of miraculous powers to baptized believers. Well, suppose their case is established, and Mark 16:17 is not a promise to baptized believers. The fact remains that early Christians did have miraculous powers, and we must still face the main issue: **Does the fact that miracles were done in the early church prove that they can be done now?**

It may be said that if we apply Mark 16:17 to baptized believers, the Holiness have a strong case in contending that it is a promise to believers for all time. To me, to show that the promise, even when applied to baptized believers, was not general and unlimited—that it is not a promise to believers today—is much easier than trying to prove that it refers exclusively to the apostles. About the strongest argument the Holiness can give to make it general and unlimited is the one on parallel passages (comparing Mark 16:17 with Matt. 28:20), but we have seen that this argument must be offset just the same if the promise is limited to the apostles.

Learn the facts as to how long, how, and when believers did possess miraculous powers. These facts must be explained, even if Mark 16:17 is restricted to the apostles. Having understood these facts, what could be plainer and simpler than to understand Mark 16:17 as a promise of such powers under all these conditions?

Of course, if the Holiness could establish the fact that the promise in Mark 16:17 must be, by its very nature and content, a promise for believers of all time, then nothing else could be interpreted to conflict with that. But the wording of that promise and the context, as already shown, do not **demand** that it be for all time—that is, as far as the wording of the promise is concerned, one cannot tell whether it was for all time or for a limited time. It could be either way, so far as the promise itself is concerned. But when other passages teach that such gifts **actually ended** at a certain time, then the promise cannot be interpreted as one for believers of all ages. The promise must be interpreted by the facts, but the facts cannot be twisted or ignored just to fit an interpretation that is arbitrarily placed upon the promise. The promise is subject to two interpretations, but the facts are stubborn and immovable. And in view of the facts, the promise becomes subject to only one interpretation, and that is that these signs were promised to believers for a limited time only.

THE WORK OF THE HOLY SPIRIT

ARTICLE NO. 3

Oftentimes some very interesting, even though unexpected, developments result from the discussion of main issues. Several months ago two articles by this scribe appeared in the Gospel Advocate, setting forth the idea that the promise of miraculous powers in Mark 16:17, 18 was to baptized believers. It was shown, of course, that this does not necessitate the conclusion that such miracles can be performed today.

Two points raised in reaction to these articles deserve some attention.

INTERVAL BETWEEN VERSES 14 AND 15

It was shown that there was an interval of nearly forty days between verse 14, when Jesus upbraided the apostles for their unbelief, and the giving of the commission, verse 15. Many brethren assume that Christ spoke the words in verses 15-18 at the time he upbraided the apostles in verse 14. They give an exegesis like this: "Christ rebuked the apostles for not believing and told them [at the same time] that if they would believe, then they could perform miracles." This connection between verse 14 and verses 15-18 is wholly unwarranted, and the explanation based upon it collapses, if it is true that two different events—events separated by nearly forty days—are here recorded; for this being true, it is easy to see that the faith of the apostles is not under consideration when Jesus says in verse 17: "These signs shall follow them that believe." One brother from Arkansas wrote: "To take your position and say that there was an interval of time between verse 14 and verse 15 of Mark is merely speculative and only serves to bolster your position." Well, the brother did feel the force of this point, if it is true!

It is in order to quote some scholars on this matter. Gray and Adam's Biblical Encyclopedia, commenting on "afterward" in verse 14, says, "Still later in the same day," putting the event on the evening of the day Christ arose. B. W. Johnson likewise identifies the incident of verse 14, and then on the quotation beginning in verse 15 he says: "Probably not at the time referred to in verse 14...These words may have been spoken at the great meeting in Galilee. (Verse 7; Matt. 28: 18-20)." McGarvey, in his commentary on Matthew and Mark, after identifying the event in verse 14 with the appearance on the evening of the resurrection day, says this about verse 15: "Here there is a silent transition from the interview on the evening after the day of the resurrection, which is the subject of verse 14, to one which occurred on the day of the ascension (verse 19), forty days later (Acts 1:3). From Mark's narrative alone we would not be able to discover this transition, but would suppose that the words of Jesus in verses 15-18 were spoken at the time of the appearance in verse 14, but this is only one among many instances in which details not essential to the understanding of the chief thought to be conveyed are omitted from one narrative, but found in another."

This "speculation" about an interval between verses 14 and 15 may not be as new to some people as it is to the brother from Arkansas!

WHEN WAS MARK 16:15-18 SPOKEN?

It was also stated that Mark 16:15-18 was spoken on a mountain in Galilee—the same time of Matt. 28:16-20. Word has come to me that some brother (I know not who he is) complained thus: "Van Dyke says that the three accounts of the commission—Matt. 28:19,20; Mark 16:15-18; Luke 24:46,47—are just different versions of the same speech; therefore, Van Dyke has denied verbal inspiration."

The brother should read more carefully. There is not a word in those articles about when Luke 24:46,47 was spoken. It was not put with Matt. 28:19, 20 and Mark 16:15-18. To put Mark 16: 15-18 at the time of Matt. 28:19, 20 and speak of that as the time the commission was given (when it was first and formally given) does not forbid the idea held by some scholars that Luke 24:44-47 is a record of a subsequent conversation. It was stated that some time after the commission was given—after the meeting in Galilee, with which we connected Mark 16:15-18—Jesus appeared again to the apostles and spoke the words in Acts 1:6-8. This was not intended to mean that Acts 1:6-8 was all that was spoken at this subsequent appearance. Luke 24:44-48 may have been spoken at this time. This was not under consideration, so no effort was made to place this passage. The brother just assumed something here that was not stated in the articles.

Furthermore, the brother has inadvertently put himself in the position of denying verbal inspiration. Regardless of whether or not the three accounts of the commission are different versions of the same speech, or give different parts of the same discourse, or are records of speeches given at three different times, there are variations in different quotations of certain speeches in the Bible. Take Acts 9:6 and Acts 22:10 for example. In Acts 9:6 Luke quotes Jesus as saying to Saul: "Arise, and go into the city, and it shall be told thee what thou must do." Acts 22:10, where Paul related the same thing, says: "Arise, and go into Damascus: and there it shall be told thee of all things which are appointed for thee to do." This is just one among several variations in the different accounts of this conversation. But our brother's premise is that if the same speech is quoted differently by two or more writers, this disproves verbal inspiration. Is he prepared to accept the consequences of his criticism? Verily, as he is reported to have said, one should watch things like this! (The purpose here is not to discuss how to harmonize, or explain, such variations in the light of verbal inspiration. Let the brother do this, and then he should see that his criticism would be groundless even if the three accounts of the commission were different records of the same speech.)

Scholars are not agreed on whether Mark 16:15-18 was spoken at the time of Matt. 28:19,20 or in the conversation immediately preceding the ascension. B. W. Johnson, as already quoted, says: "These words may have been spoken of the great meeting in Galilee." "The Fourfold Gospel," by McGarvey and Pendleton, also puts Mark 16:15-18 and Matt. 28:19,20 together on the mountain in Galilee. In his commentary on Matthew and Mark, an earlier work, McGarvey has Mark 16:15-18 as a part of the conversation just before the ascension with Luke 24:46-48 and Acts 1:4-9.

In the previous articles the chronological order of "The Fourfold Gospel" was followed, and this, to me, seems to be the more satisfactory arrangement. Anyway, if it is incorrect to put Mark 16:15-18 at the same time as Matt. 28:19,20, this is only an error in chronological arrangement—it most certainly is not a denial of verbal inspiration to do so.

Commenting on the promise of miraculous power in Mark 16:17, McGarvey says: "The promise is, not that these signs shall follow for any specified time, nor that they should follow each individual believer; but merely that they shall follow, and follow 'the believers' taken as a body. They did follow the believers during the apostolic age—not every individual believer, but all, or nearly all, the organized bodies of the believers. This was a complete fulfillment of what was promised. My ideas to a nicety! The exegesis given in the previous articles may not be as strange among reputable Bible scholars as some think it is.

ARTICLE NO. 4
MARK 16:17, 18
Roy H. Lanier, Sr.

"And these signs shall accompany them that believe: in my name shall they cast out demons; they shall speak with new tongues; they shall take up serpents, and if they drink any deadly thing, it shall in no wise hurt them; they shall lay hands on the sick, and they shall recover."

Various religious sects have long claimed the power to work miracles and men have become wealthy by praying upon gullible people who are seeking relief from some physical or mental malady. For some time untaught brethren among us have been disturbed by these wonder workers and some have been led to believe they can "speak with new tongues" mentioned in this passage. I have not heard of any of my brethren who think they can cast out demons, drink carbolic acid without injury, or let a rattlesnake bite them without harm, but consistency will drive them to believe they, or others, can do such things and we shall not be surprised to learn that they are attempting to do such things.

Our first inquiry is, To whom was this promise made? Some think the promise was made to the apostles only. This I believe to be a mistake. If the reader will turn to Mark 16 and begin reading with the 14th verse, he will find Mark relating a story of Jesus meeting with the eleven apostles. He upbraided **them**, and he said unto **them**. The word **"them"** is a personal pronoun, third person, plural and refers to the apostles. And when Jesus said to the apostles, "These signs shall accompany **them**" many good brethren think this word refers to the apostles. But go back to verse 15 and read, "And he said unto them, Go ye into all the world...He that believeth and is baptized shall be saved." Here the word **them**, third person, refers to the apostles, and the word **ye**, second person, refers to the apostles. Why the change from third person to second person? The answer is that the style of discourse has changed. Verse 14 and through the word **them** in verse 15 is what is called indirect discourse; this is Mark's language. Beginning with **Go ye** in verse 15 through all of verse 18 is the language of Jesus; it is direct discourse. In Mark's language the word **them** refers to the apostles, but in the language of Jesus to the apostles the word **them** refers to others than the apostles. In the language of Jesus directed to the apostles the word **ye**, second person, must refer to the apostles, and he cannot be expected to use the word **them**,third person, to refer to

THE WORK OF THE HOLY SPIRIT

the apostles. In direct discourse the word **you** is used of people spoken to, while **they**, or **them**, third person, is used of people spoken about. So when Jesus said to the apostles, "These signs shall accompany **them**," he must have been referring to people other than the apostles.

Again, when Jesus said, **He that believeth**, he was not speaking of the apostles, so why should we think he was speaking of the apostles when he said that signs should accompany **them that believe?** The word **them** in verse 17 is the plural of the word **he** in verse 16, and that Mark resumes indirect discourse at the beginning of verse 17. One would have to be hard pressed to prove his position to make such a statement as that, for there is obviously no break in the statement of Jesus until we reach the end of verse 18. But to put the matter beyond any possibility of argument we have only to point out that all these signs mentioned in verses 17 and 18 are said to be done "in my name." "In my name shall they cast out demons," etc. Is this the language of Mark? Is he saying that believers will cast out demons and do other miracles in his name? Certainly Mark would make no such claim. This must be the language of Jesus to the apostles and while addressing them he would not use the word **them** to refer to them. So "them that believe," being the plural of "he that believeth and is baptized," must refer to people who believed the gospel and were baptized.

But someone is ready to say that this proves that all believers for all time are promised the power to work miracles. If verse 16 applies today, why does not verse 17 apply to us today? Neither verse 16 or 17 tells the whole story and we must go elsewhere in the New Testament to learn the rest of the story. According to verse 16, belief and baptism are all that is essential to salvation; neither repentance nor confession of Christ is mentioned. We have to go to other verses of scripture to learn that these things are essential to salvation. So verses 17 and 18 do not tell the whole story and we have to go to Acts 8:12 to 18 to find the rest of the story. There we learn that Philip went to Samaria and preached the gospel. And verse 12 says that the people of Samaria believed what Philip preached and were baptized. Did the signs of Mark 16:17, 18 accompany all who believe in Samaria? They did not. But when the apostles, Peter and John, went to Samaria and prayed for believers and laid their hands on the believers they received the Holy Spirit in miraculous power. Verse 16 says the Holy Spirit had fallen on none of them, "only they had been baptized into the name of the Lord Jesus." This means that they had received the Holy Spirit as the indwelling, abiding presence of God, but they had not received the

Holy Spirit in his miraculous manifestation. This manifestation came to believers only when apostles prayed for them and laid their hand upon them.

This idea is clearly taught in Acts 19:1-7. Here we find Paul at Ephesus. He found disciples, learners, of Jesus who had not been properly baptized. He taught them the way of the Lord accurately and they were baptized into the name of the Lord Jesus. They were the kind of believers to whom the promise was made that they could exercise miraculous powers, but they were not yet ready to do so. Then Paul laid his hands upon them and they received the Holy Spirit in the miraculous manifestation and they proved it by speaking in tongues and prophesying (v. 6).

From this we reach two conclusions. First, these miraculous powers had to cease when the last man on whom the last apostle laid hands died. If these powers could be given through apostles only (Acts 8:18), it follows that when all the apostles died there was no one on earth to lay hands on people and give them this power; and upon the death of the last man on whom apostles laid hands there just was not anybody on earth who could work miracles. Second, our brethren who are claiming the power to speak in tongues are deceived or these scriptures we have studied do not teach the truth. Brethren, do you believe the scriptures are inspired? If so you must believe that you cannot speak in tongues by the power of the Holy Spirit unless and until an apostle lays hands on you as these scriptures teach. Paul wished to go to Rome that he might impart a spiritual gift (Rom. 1:11). What apostle has laid hands on you to impart this spiritual gift?

III — THE HOLY SPIRIT IN LUKE

"For he shall be great in the sight of the Lord, and shall drink neither wine nor strong drink; and he shall be filled with the Holy Ghost, even from his mother's womb," (Luke 1:15).

This verse is a part of the statement made by the angel to Zacharias. (See verse 13.) The fact that the angel told Zacharias that John would be filled with the Holy Spirit from his mother's womb, coupled with John 10:41 which states that John did no miracles, has been used by some to attempt to use Luke 1:15 to contend for a literal personal indwelling. The argument is this: John was filled with the Spirit; John did no miracles; therefore, one may be filled with the Spirit and not perform miracles. Now consider the fallacy of the reasoning:

THE WORK OF THE HOLY SPIRIT

1. John was a prophet: "And thou, child, shalt be called the prophet of the Highest: for thou shalt go before the face of the Lord to prepare his ways," (Luke 1:76). Is it not in view of John being a prophet that it is said of him that he would be filled with the Spirit? Do those who use this passage to prove the literal personal indwelling of the Spirit believe that Christians are filled with the Spirit as the prophets were?
2. Were there not prophets that were filled with the Spirit that did no miracles?
3. The phrase, "filled with the Spirit," is used three times in this chapter. Compare the verses:
    a) "He shall be filled with the Holy Spirit," (Luke 1:15).
    b) "And Elisabeth was filled with the Holy Spirit," (Luke 1:41).

This phrase in Luke 1:41 shows that when Elizabeth was filled with the Spirit, it refers to inspiration. Question: Since the same phrase is used for John (Luke 1:15) that is used for Elisabeth (then we have Elisabeth's inspired song), does not this phrase likewise refer to the inspiration of John as a prophet? Furthermore, did Elisabeth do any miracles?

    c) "And his father Zacharias was filled with the Holy Spirit and prophesied . . ." (Luke 1:67).

Lest anyone should want to quibble about Elisabeth's being inspired, there can be no question as to what verse 67 means. When it is said that Zacharias was "filled with the Spirit," and then adds that he "prophesied," we have an inspired definition of the phrase, "filled with the Spirit." Did Zacharias do any miracles? If Elisabeth and Zacharias could be filled with the Spirit—meaning inspiration—and do no miracles, since the same phrase is used in the same chapter in reference to John, why should it mean non-miraculous for John and miraculous for the two other times it is used in the chapter?

> In the scriptures, to be filled with the Holy Spirit commonly signifies that degree of inspiration by which the ancient prophets spoke. Accordingly, in this chapter it is applied to Elisabeth, to Mary, to Zacharias, in each case a reference to inspiration, (Macknight).

"If ye then, being evil, know how to give good gifts unto your children: how much more shall your heavenly Father give the Holy Spirit to them that ask him?" (Luke 11:13).

This passage is used by some to try to prove that Christians should pray for the Holy Spirit. The denominational world has followed the practice of praying for the Holy Spirit. The "mourners' bench" religion was based on praying through, and among other things, this included the reception of, the Holy Spirit. The basis of Pentecostalism is praying for the Holy Spirit. This is one of the fundamental tenets of Pentecostalism. It ought not to be difficult to see how Pentecostalism got into the church, when a teacher in a Christian college teaches young people to pray for the Holy Spirit. The results will be Pentecostalism. There is no way that young people can be encouraged to pray for the Holy Spirit without sooner or later looking for some kind of evidence that they are receiving the Spirit. The only evidence that it is possible for them to claim is feelings; thus, their feelings become proof that the Holy Spirit is working in them. All kinds of gimmicks are used to stir up emotions, such as turning out the lights, holding hands, and telling experiences. This kind of atmosphere sets the stage for the "Spirit" to start to work. This is the soil in which Pentecostalism has crept into the church of the Lord. Emotional excitement is not Christianity. Emotional excitement is not the Holy Spirit working. If emotional excitement is proof that the Holy Spirit is working, then false teachers and false religions of every type can claim the Holy Spirit. Their meetings are characterized by emotional excitement, death-bed tales, and anything else to stir up the emotions. Once the emotions are stirred, then they claim the Holy Spirit begins His work. Anyone that knows anything about the Bible knows that this is not true.

What is the significance of Christ's statement to His disciples to pray for the Holy Spirit? As in other passages in Matthew and Mark, which we have already studied, Joel 2:28-32 is the background of Luke 11:13, and Pentecost and what followed is in the foreground. First, let us consider the context of the verse. The chapter begins by the disciples of Christ asking Him to teach them how to pray as John taught his disciples. Verse 1 is the introduction and verse 13 is the conclusion. These verses belong together. We learn from verse 1 that John taught his disciples to pray. We do not have any account in the Scriptures of John doing this. We do not have a model prayer that John gave his disciples. We do have a record of John's preaching, and we may infer from this what he taught his disciples to pray for. Is it not reasonable to believe that what John taught his disciples to pray for was in harmony with his preaching? Surely, he did not preach one thing and teach his disciples to pray for something else. What was the content of his preaching? Primarily, two things: baptism of repentance for the remission of sins in view of the coming kingdom (Matthew 3:2; Mark

THE WORK OF THE HOLY SPIRIT 109

1:4), and the baptism of the Holy Spirit (Matthew 3:11). While it is not stated in Matthew 3 that John connected the coming of the kingdom and the coming of the Holy Spirit, the context indicates it. May we not, without doing any violence to the Scriptures, infer that the teaching of John to his disciples about prayer involved these two things. Christ started where John left off. His preaching was also about the coming kingdom and the Holy Spirit. He expanded what John had introduced. His first sermon was, "The time is fulfilled, and the kingdom of God is at hand: repent ye, and believe the gospel," (Mark 1:15). He also discussed the Holy Spirit. When Christ discussed the Holy Spirit, it was always in view of the coming of the Spirit on Pentecost. A failure to recognize this will end in confusion of the rankest sort. Now consider Luke 11 again. In the model prayer the first petition is, "Thy kingdom come," (Luke 11:2). Now consider two statements by Christ about the Holy Spirit. "...If I go not away, the Comforter will not COME unto you; but if I depart, I will SEND him unto you. And when he is COME..." (John 16:7-8). In view of these statements of Christ to His disciples, what would be the significance of Christ telling His disciples to pray for the Holy Spirit? Can anyone really think that Christ was not pointing toward Pentecost and the coming of the Holy Spirit? In order that there may be no doubt about Luke 11:13, look at another passage. Remember this is Christ's own statement: "And he said unto them, Verily I say unto you, That there be some of them that stand here, which shall not taste of death, till they have seen the kingdom of God come with power," (Mark 9:1). Compare Acts 1:8 with Mark 9:1 and there can be no doubt as to the meaning of the passage in Mark 9:1. In the study of Mark, I have already shown how Mark 9:1 points to the miraculous coming of the Spirit at Pentecost. I have also shown in the discussion of Mark 9:1 that the kingdom came at the same time that the Spirit did. If one puts these passages with Luke 11:13, they spell out in clear letters the meaning of the passage. Luke 11:13 is not any authority for a Christian today to pray that he might receive the Holy Spirit. This statement has Joel's prophecy as its background, and the prophecy in Joel was the promise of the miraculous operation of the Spirit which came at Pentecost and the miraculous gifts that believers received following Pentecost during the period in which revelation was being received. Thus, the passage in Luke 11:13 is simply another passage that points toward Pentecost. The statement made by Christ encouraging His disciples to pray for the Holy Spirit, was simply another way of encouraging them to pray for the kingdom to come as He had authorized and encouraged them to do in the model prayer which is in the context where this statement is found. When Christ made the statement in Luke 11:13 to encourage His disciples to pray for the Holy Spirit, it was entirely appropriate for them to do so. The Spirit had not come in the miraculous outpouring as prophesied by Joel. But the Spirit as promised in Joel's prophecy has now been fulfilled. The miraculous outpouring of the Spirit came at Pentecost. This was the fulfillment of Joel's prophecy. This was the event toward which Christ pointed, and the miraculous endowments which came through the laying on of the apostles' hands that followed Pentecost. There is a great deal of difference in studying the passage at the time Christ made the statement and in taking the passage and saying that it authorizes a Christian to pray for the Holy Spirit today. Since the passage has Joel as its background and Pentecost in the foreground, with a reference to the miraculous operations of the Spirit, and since the miraculous operations of the Spirit have now ceased, as we have a completed, written, confirmed revelation, it is no more appropriate for one to pray for the Holy Spirit today than it is for Pentecostals to pray to receive the baptism of the Holy Spirit, or to pray to receive some miraculous endowment of the Holy Spirit. It ought not to be difficult to see that there was a time when it was scriptural for the disciples of Christ to pray for the Holy Spirit. The time that it was scriptural for them to pray for the Holy Spirit was the time before the Holy Spirit came in the miraculous operations by which the gospel was revealed and confirmed. It was scriptural during the days of miracles for people to pray for the Holy Spirit. As I have already pointed out, Luke 11:13 points to Pentecost and the miraculous operation of the Spirit that followed Pentecost. There is only one passage that makes any reference of anyone praying for the Holy Spirit. An inspired example of one praying for the Holy Spirit ought to be a sufficient, divine commentary on the meaning of Luke 11:13. In the eighth chapter of the book of Acts, beginning in verse 14, I read the following: "Now when the apostles which were at Jerusalem heard that Samaria had received the word of God, they sent unto them Peter and John: Who, when they were come down, prayed for them, that they might receive the Holy Ghost." Here is an example of men praying that Christians might receive the Holy Ghost. When Peter and John prayed that the Samaritans might receive the Holy Ghost, in what sense were they praying for them to receive the Holy Ghost? Were they praying for them to receive the Holy Ghost as brethren would teach Christians to pray to receive the Holy Spirit today? Let Luke's account give the answer, Acts 8, verses 16-19:

(For as yet he was fallen upon none of them: only they were baptized in the name of the Lord Jesus.)

THE WORK OF THE HOLY SPIRIT

> Then laid they their hands on them, and they received the Holy Ghost.
> And when Simon saw that through laying on of the apostles' hands the Holy Ghost was given, he offered them money,
> Saying, Give me also this power, that on whomsoever I lay hands, he may receive the Holy Ghost.

As I have pointed out, Luke 11:13 has Joel 2:28-32 as its background and Pentecost, or Acts 2, in the foreground. The Holy Spirit came with miraculous endowments on the apostles on Pentecost. The eighth chapter of Acts gives an example of Christians receiving the Holy Spirit in a miraculous way through the laying on of the apostles' hands. Luke is careful to explain in verse 15 that in connection with the Christians receiving the Holy Spirit by the laying on of the apostles' hands, that the apostles prayed for them that they might receive the Holy Ghost. It seems to me that nothing could be clearer than the fact that Luke 11:13 points to the miraculous outpouring of the Holy Spirit and, at the time the statement was made, Christ was simply encouraging the apostles to pray for the coming of the kingdom and the Holy Spirit, which came at the same time the kingdom did. This points to the miraculous operation of the Holy Spirit and this is what Christ was speaking of when He told His disciples to pray for the Spirit. When you take Acts 8 and the example that is given there where the apostles prayed that the Samaritans might receive the Holy Spirit, and that their reception of the Spirit was evidenced with miraculous endowments through the hands of the apostles, it seems that it would be impossible not to understand Luke 11:13.

A verse of scripture that authorizes the disciples of Christ to pray for miraculous endowments of the Holy Spirit, during the period when there were miraculous operations of the Spirit, is in no way any authority for a Christian to pray for the reception of the Spirit in a non-miraculous way today.

LUKE 24:44-49

> And he said unto them, These are the words which I spake unto you, while I was yet with you, that all things must be fulfilled, which were written in the law of Moses, and in the prophets, and in the psalms, concerning me.
> Then opened he their understanding, that they might understand the Scriptures,

And said unto them, Thus it is written, and thus it behooved Christ to suffer, and to rise from the dead the third day:

And that repentance and remission of sins should be preached in his name among all nations, beginning at Jerusalem.

And ye are witnesses of these things.

And, behold, I send the promise of my Father upon you: but tarry ye in the city of Jerusalem, until ye be endued with power from on high.

Luke's account of the Great Commission differs from that of Matthew and Mark. There is no contradiction in these accounts. Matthew says, "Go teach. . .baptize. . .teach. . .and lo, I am with you alway." Mark says, ". . .Go preach. . .believe. . .baptized. . .saved. . .these signs shall follow." Luke says, "And that repentance and remission of sins should be preached in his name among all nations, beginning at Jerusalem," and, ". . .until ye be endued with power from on high." Peter's sermon in Acts 2 is a commentary on the Commission as given by Matthew, Mark, and Luke. In Acts 2 we have a record of Peter's sermon, thus the preaching of the Commission as given by Matthew, Mark, and Luke. Acts 2:36 says, "Therefore let all the house of Israel know assuredly, that God hath made that same Jesus, whom ye have crucified, both Lord and Christ." This verse points to the faith, or believing, of Mark 16:16. Acts 2:38 states, "Repent and be baptized . . .for the remission of sins, and ye shall receive the gift of the Holy Ghost." The repentance of Acts 2:38 is that which is authorized in the Commission as given by Luke. Baptism for the remission of sins is that which is authorized in the Commission as given by Matthew and Mark. When the Commission of all three is considered, and Peter's sermon under this Commission, it is easy to see that there is no contradiction. Luke 24:44 is a reminder that Christ has fulfilled the Old Testament and that it is soon to be set aside. Verse 47 is an announcement that the gospel will be for all nations, showing the transition from the fleshly, national, temporal Judaism to the universal and spiritual gospel. Verse 48 says that the apostles were witnesses of His life, His death, and resurrection, but the words of the apostles alone would not be sufficient. Therefore, they were told to tarry in Jerusalem until they were endued with power from on high (Luke 24:49). There are some things to notice carefully in connection with Luke 24:49:

1. This is the first time that the word "promise" is used in connection with the coming of the Holy Spirit on Pentecost. In what sense was the Spirit promised? This is a vital and important question. It needs to be kept in mind at all times in the study of

THE WORK OF THE HOLY SPIRIT

this subject. The qualifying phrase answered the question as to what sense the Holy Spirit was promised.

2. It is called the promise of the Father. The promise of the Father was a reference to Joel 2. This qualifying phrase enables one to understand that the promise of the Spirit was a reference to the miraculous endowments which the apostles received at Pentecost and for Christians that came through the laying on of the apostles' hands.

3. Luke, in referring to the coming of the Spirit upon the apostles, uses the phrase, "be endued with power from on high." A better translation of the word "endued" is "clothed." This word points to the authority of the apostles. It is equal to Matthew's phrase, "lo, I am with you," signifying the inspiration of the apostles. The apostles would receive their revelation of the gospel through their being clothed with power from on high. The power and the authority of the apostles (II Corinthians 10:8, 13:10) places the apostles in the same relationship to the church in the period when revelation was being given directly, as the written Word is our authority today. The Word was in the apostles by the inspiration of the Holy Spirit, and was the authority during this period. The apostles exercise that same authority through the written Word today. This is the reason that the apostles have no successors. They now function through the written Word. It would be as reasonable to expect to have another revelation to supplant the Bible as to claim the apostles have any successors. The Holy Spirit sustained a relationship to the apostles that was peculiar to them. This relationship of the Holy Spirit to the apostles was because of the nature of their work. The apostles completed their work when revelation was completed. The miraculous operation of the Spirit and the work of the apostles coincided. When the work of the apostles was completed, revelation was also completed and confirmed, and the miraculous operation of the Spirit ceased. The miraculous operation of the Holy Spirit and the apostles are joined together. It is impossible for one to claim the miraculous operation of the Spirit today without accepting the conclusion that we must have living apostles. Luke's account of the Great Commission sets the stage for the special work and the function of the apostles in the church. The book of Acts and the Epistles show the nature of the work of the apostles and their authority. The authority of the apostles is now contained in the New Testament. There is no place for any direct operation of the Spirit or latter-day revelations (Jude 3). The Commission in Luke, like the Commission in Matthew and Mark, has Joel as its background and points to Pentecost.

IV – THE HOLY SPIRIT IN JOHN

He that believeth on me, as the scripture hath said, out of his belly shall flow rivers of living water.
(But this spake he of the Spirit, which they that believe on him should receive: for the Holy Ghost was not yet given; because that Jesus was not yet glorified.) (John 7:38-39).

This passage has been a thorn for commentators. The phrase, "as the scripture hath said," has been a part of the problem. Commentators have been at a loss to find a Scripture in the Old Testament that says this. Some say that it is a reference to several passages and not a single passage.

The vital question concerning these verses is, What is the significance of the reference to the Holy Spirit and the believer? Is this a promise of a non-miraculous gift of the Spirit and a reference to a non-miraculous indwelling of the Holy Spirit? This is what some contend. This passage is used to claim a non-miraculous personal indwelling of the Spirit in the Christian. The following is taken from the Firm Foundation, September 20, 1966. The article is by brother J. D. Thomas. Here is his statement on John 7:38-39:

> In John 7:38-39 we read, "He that believeth on me, as the scripture hath said, from within him shall flow rivers of living water. But this spake he of the Spirit, which they that believe on him would receive: for the Spirit was not yet given; because Jesus was not yet glorified." This passage clearly indicates that with the coming of the Christian dispensation (after Jesus' glorification) there was to be a reception of the Spirit by them that believe which was to be different from any manifestation given in former dispensations. This gift (and seal) would of course also be different from the WORD of the gospel, which must be received BEFORE one could believe and in order to produce the faith. One must receive the Word and believe it before he can qualify to receive this special manifestation of the Spirit, which was inaugurated with the coming of the Christian dispensation. It was not to be limited to the apostles, since ALL WHO BELIEVE are to receive it.

THE WORK OF THE HOLY SPIRIT 115

Notice his comment: "This passage clearly indicates that with the coming of the Christian dispensation (after Jesus' glorification), there was to be a reception of the Spirit by them that believed which was to be different from any manifestation given in any former dispensation."

1. Brother Thomas recognizes that the passage points toward Pentecost and the Christian dispensation.
2. He also states that this passage is connected with the glorification of Christ.
3. He assumes that this passage promises a non-miraculous indwelling to believers. His basis for this argument is that the promise is to believers and is not limited to the apostles.

Do these arguments support the position that there is a promise of a non-miraculous indwelling? I don't believe so and shall now offer what I consider to be the proof.

1. I agree that the passage points to Pentecost.
2. I also agree that there is a connection between this promise and the glorification of Christ.
3. I also accept the fact that the passage indicates that there would be a difference in manifestations.

Let us now consider the first part. The first statement does not need any discussion. The passage points to Pentecost and the beginning of the church. Consideration of point No. 2: What is the relationship of the Spirit to the glorification of Christ? Another passage in the same book will help to clarify this point—John 16:7-16:

> Nevertheless I tell you the truth; It is expedient for you that I go away: for if I go not away, the Comforter will not come unto you; but if I depart, I will send him unto you.
> And when he is come, he will reprove the world of sin, and of righteousness, and of judgment:
> Of sin, because they believe not on me;
> Of righteouness, because I go to my father, and ye see me no more;
> Of judgment, because the prince of this world is judged.
> I have yet many things to say unto you, but ye cannot bear them now.
> Howbeit when he, the Spirit of truth, is come, he will guide you into all truth: for he shall not speak of himself; but whatsoever he shall hear, that shall he speak: and he will shew you things to come.

> He shall glorify me: for he shall receive of mine, and shall shew it unto you.
>
> All things that the Father hath are mine: therefore said I, that he shall take of mine, and shall shew it unto you.
>
> A little while, and ye shall not see me: and again, a little while, and ye shall see me, because I go to the Father.

Here Christ makes it plain as to the relationship of His glorification to the coming of the Spirit.

1. Christ says that it was expedient for Him to return to the Father in order that the Spirit might be sent (John 16:7). There is no question but what this passage points to the apostles and the outpouring of the Spirit at Pentecost.
2. The coming of the Spirit upon the apostles was to glorify Christ. This was done through the revelation of the gospel, which the apostles proclaimed (John 16:14-15). These verses show that the coming of the Spirit was related to the glorification of Christ. This coming of the Spirit is the miraculous coming on Pentecost. Now I have established by the Scriptures that the coming of the Spirit in connection with the glorification of Christ was the miraculous manifestations beginning at Pentecost. I have found the miraculous manifestation connected with the glorification of Christ. Where is the passage that teaches a non-miraculous indwelling that is connected to the glorification of Christ? I know that brother Thomas appeals to Acts 2:38 as proof, but that is another assumption on his part. I'll deal with Acts 2:38 in a separate chapter.
3. What about the difference in manifestations of the Spirit in contrast to the previous dispensation? Brother Thomas thinks this must refer to a non-miraculous indwelling, since it included more than the apostles, but again he assumes this.

As I have continually shown in these studies, the background of the references to the Holy Spirit in Matthew, Mark, Luke, and John is Joel 2. Pentecost and the book of Acts is in the foreground. Now consider Joel's prophecy and see if it throws any light on this question. Does the prophecy of Joel include more than the apostles? The answer is yes. Joel's statement that your "sons and your daughters shall prophesy, your young men shall see visions, your old men shall dream dreams, and on my servants and on my handmaidens I will pour out in those days of my Spirit and they shall prophesy," is a reference that is not limited to the apostles. There were no women apostles and women were included in the reference to miraculous gifts in Joel's prophecy,

THE WORK OF THE HOLY SPIRIT

but if it's not a reference to the apostles, what is it a reference to? The only answer that can harmonize with what the Bible teaches is that it's a reference to the miraculous endowment that believers received through the laying on of the apostles' hands. Thus, Joel's prophecy promised miraculous endowments to believers. (The book of Acts, as well as other passages, shows that these could only come through the laying on of the apostles' hands.) The book of Acts gives an account of believers receiving miraculous endowments through the hands of the apostles. See Acts, Chapters 8 and 19. This is the first difference between Pentecost and the period of direct revelation, and the previous dispensations. Miraculous endowments were not given in general to the Israelites in the period of Judaism as they were given to believers during the period when revelation was being given directly and confirmed. As added proof that John 7:38 and 39 points to Pentecost and the things that followed, look again at Mark 16:16-20:

He that believeth and is baptized shall be saved; but he that believeth not shall be damned.

And these signs shall follow them that believe; In my name shall they cast out devils; they shall speak with new tongues;

They shall take up serpents; and if they drink any deadly thing, it shall not hurt them; they shall lay hands on the sick, and they shall recover.

So then after the Lord had spoken unto them, he was received up into heaven, and sat on the right hand of God.

And they went forth, and preached every where, the Lord working with them, and confirming the word with signs following.

First, let us examine Mark. Mark says," . . .Go . . .preach . . .he that believeth and is baptized shall be saved . . .these signs shall follow them that believe."

Second, look at John 7:38-39: "He that believeth . . .out of his belly shall flow rivers of living water. (But this spake he of the Spirit. . . .)" The word "believeth" in John 7:38 is a generic term; a reference to the obedient believer. It is equal to the obedience of faith (Romans 1:5). The believer of John 7:38 is the same as the baptized believer of Mark 16:16. The reception of the Spirit by the believer of John 7:39 is equal to the signs that followed believers of Mark 16:17. The signs of Mark 16:17 are simply the miraculous endowments that believers received through the hands of the apostles.

Third, the statement in John is general, while the one in Mark is more specific. I am sure that brethren would agree that the believer in

John 7:38 is not the "faith only" kind of believer. I think that they would further agree that the believer of John 7:39 is the baptized believer of Mark 16:16. If this is true, then why does not the reception of the Spirit in John 7:38-39 mean the same thing as the signs that believers received in Mark 16:17-20? This is the truth about the matter. The promise of the Spirit in John 7:39 was the promise of miraculous endowments through the hands of the apostles to believers. Joel's prophecy promises it. Mark 16:16-18 promises miraculous endowments to believers. The book of Acts gives examples of believers receiving miraculous endowments, and the Epistles refer to believers having received miraculous endowments. This was an entirely distinct thing and had never characterized any previous period.

Fourth, (this is still not all the difference in the miraculous manifestation which began at Pentecost that came through the hands of the apostles, which believers received during this period while revelation was being given), look at the signs of Mark 16:17 and 18: "And these signs shall follow them that believe; In my name shall they cast out devils; they shall speak with new tongues; They shall take up serpents; and if they drink any deadly thing, it shall not hurt them; they shall lay hands on the sick, and they shall recover." Note the number of things that are mentioned, as signs in these verses which would characterize believers during this period that were distinct from any previous dispensation. For example, new tongues were something that characterized not only the apostles, but others as well. Acts 19:1-6 is proof that some spoke in tongues other than the apostles. Of course, the tongue here is a language. The figure of living water flowing from the belly of believers was the preaching of the gospel by direct revelation and the confirmation of the gospel by these miraculous manifestations. "Therefore they that were scattered abroad went every where preaching the word," (Acts 8:4). This preaching was done by the miraculous endowments that believers had received through the hands of an apostle. Philip is an example of this in Acts 8.

SUMMARY OF JOHN 7:38-39

1. The coming of the Spirit and the glorification of Christ is a reference to the miraculous operation of the Spirit beginning at Pentecost.

2. The believer of John 7:38 and 39 is the baptized believer of Mark 16:16.

THE WORK OF THE HOLY SPIRIT 119

3. The reception of the Spirit by believers of John 7:38-39 is the miraculous endowments of believers that came through the hands of apostles and is according to the promise of Joel 2 and the Commission as recorded by Mark 16:16-20.

JOHN 14, 15, 16

These chapters form a unit. In these three chapters are some special promises to the apostles. A failure to keep this in mind in the study of these chapters leads to endless confusion and misunderstanding of the Holy Spirit. When these promises of the Holy Spirit are applied to Christians in general, it is a complete misapplication of the promises. The misuse of these passages on the Holy Spirit is perhaps the taproot of the greatest misunderstanding in the religious world. When these passages are quoted and applied to Christians today, it prepares the groundwork for the misunderstanding of the Holy Spirit in relation to the Christian.

In the study of the Bible, it is necessary that attention be given to the questions, Who is doing the speaking? Who are the ones spoken to? Some promises are limited in their application, and a failure to note the limitation leads to false teaching. For example, when Peter's statement to Simon, a baptized believer, is applied to those who have not been baptized, it is false teaching. To use Peter's statement to attempt to justify the mourners' bench, or the alien praying for pardon, is to ignore one of the vital rules of Bible interpretation. Should someone tell a Christian who has sinned to repent and be baptized for the remission of sins, he would be telling that person to do something that is completely false and would be holding out to him a promise that would not apply. In the same manner, when a promise or promises that were made to the apostles are applied to Christians in general, the applications are completely false. I have mentioned in previous chapters the unique relationship the apostles had in the church. Before a further discussion of these chapters, it is appropriate to study in a more detailed way the work of the apostles.

THE WORK OF THE APOSTLES

Jesus said to Peter, "And I will give unto thee the keys of the kingdom of heaven: and whatsoever thou shalt bind on earth shall be bound in heaven: and whatsoever thou shalt loose on earth shall be loosed in heaven," (Matthew 16:19).

No one can properly understand the church of the New Testament without knowing the relation the apostles sustained to it. "And God hath set some in the church, first apostles..." (I Corinthians 12:28). In this passage, Paul shows that the apostles were first in the church. This is not a reference to the time of entrance, but rather to rank or order. The fact that the apostles sustained a relationship to the church that no others did, shows that there were some things peculiar to the apostles. Let us notice some of those things that were peculiar to the apostles.

1. The apostles were ambassadors. "Now then we are ambassadors for Christ, as though God did beseech you by us: we pray you in Christ's stead, be ye reconciled to God," (II Corinthians 5:20). The word "ambassador" is never used of any except the apostles. The word means "one clothed with authority and representing one government in another country." This is exactly what Paul said of the apostles: "We pray you in Christ's stead." This is the meaning of Christ's statement to Peter in Matthew 16:19. God has no living ambassadors today. No man, or set of men, can bind anything that the apostles did not bind; nor can they loose anything that the apostles bound. The apostles still function as ambassadors through the New Testament. Just suppose that an American citizen should visit London. While visiting there, he goes down to No. 10 Downing Street, and attempts to carry on business in the name of the U. S. Government. What would be the results? He would find himself in difficulty. This is an illustration of why Christians, or even preachers, are not ambassadors today. The apostles were Christ's embassy on earth. When Christ ascended back to heaven, He promised to send the Holy Spirit to the apostles to qualify them for this work. When the Holy Spirit came upon the apostles on Pentecost, then they began to function as the ambassadors of Christ. This was Christ's embassy on earth and clothed with all the authority that an official embassy could have. Thus when Paul wrote the Corinthians, he said, "...the things that I write unto you are the commandments of the Lord," (I Corinthians 14:37). It is a misapplication of Scripture for anyone to claim to be an ambassador of Christ. This was a function that was peculiar to the apostles.

2. The apostles had a special call. The apostles, being ambassadors, needed a special call: "Paul,...called to be an apostle," (Romans 1:1). For one to be an ambassador, he must be appointed by the government. He cannot just assume the responsibility. Because the apostles were ambassadors, clothed with authority, acting in behalf of the government of heaven, they had to be appointed.

Jesus said to the apostles in Luke 22:29: "And I appoint unto you a kingdom, as my Father hath appointed unto me." The apostles could not just assume that they were apostles. They became apostles only by the appointment of Christ. This is the reason for the special call of Christ to all of the apostles. No preacher today has any authority, as far as binding and loosing is concerned, and since no preacher today is in the same place as the apostles were, he needs no special call. Preachers would never claim to be called directly by God today if they knew the difference between an apostle and a preacher. Preachers cannot bind or loose anything. They are not ambassadors.

3. The apostles had special needs. The work of the apostles, being peculiar to them, meant that they had needs that were peculiar to their work. The very fact that the apostles had responsibilities that preachers do not have should suggest that they had needs that preachers do not have.

The apostles were to receive and reveal the truth. Paul said that he had received the gospel by revelation (Galatians 1:12). "How that by revelation he made known unto me the mystery," (Ephesians 3:3). We have the truth revealed today in the New Testament. The apostles wrote it. No man today can write any new revelation. This shows that we have no living apostles. In order for the apostles to reveal the truth, they needed a special guide. This accounts for the apostles receiving the baptism of the Holy Spirit (Acts 1:8; Acts 2:1-4). Because of the nature of the work and the needs of the apostles, the Holy Spirit sustained a relationship to them that He did not sustain to any others even in the period of direct revelation. The promises of the Holy Spirit in John 14, 15, and 16 are limited to the apostles. Christ was talking to the apostles when He made the promises in these chapters. After the church was established, we find many references to the Holy Spirit, but not one time is He referred to as "the Comforter." If the promise of the Comforter in John 14, 15, and 16 is not limited to the apostles, why is this word not used in connection with the Holy Spirit in others? It would indeed seem strange, since we have numerous references to the Holy Spirit in Christians, that if He were related to Christians as He was to the apostles, the same word is not used. If people could one time see that the apostles had a special need, and therefore a special manifestation of the Holy Spirit, because of a special work, then most of the confusion that exists about the Holy Spirit and His work would vanish.

4. The apostles had special credentials. The apostles needed something special to prove that their work was special; therefore, there were signs of an apostle. Consequently, Paul told the Corinthians, "Truly the SIGNS of an apostle were wrought among you . . ." (II Corinthians 12:12). These miracles were their credentials as ambassadors. The chief sign of an apostle was that of imparting miraculous endowments to others. Revelation and confirmation went together. When one ceased, the other ceased. Thus, we had apostles, their baptism in the Holy Spirit, revelation and confirmation. We have no living apostles, therefore, no revelation and no confirmation. All so-called miracle workers today are fakes (II Thessalonians 2:9).

THE COMFORTER

The Greek word that is translated "Comforter" has been a problem to translators. It is translated "Comforter" in the King James and the American Standard Version. The margin of the American Standard Version renders it "Advocate." There is no question in my mind but what the word "Comforter" is an unfortunate translation. There are two reasons for this: 1) The word **"Paraclete"** is broader than the word "Comforter." 2) The word "Comforter" leaves the wrong impression in these chapters, as these promises of the Comforter are limited to the apostles. The word "Comforter" is the reason for some using these promises and applying them to Christians in general. This is surely a mistake.

The Holy Spirit is called a Comforter only in these three chapters. The word is never used for the Holy Spirit anywhere else. The Greek word is used only one other time in the New Testament. The other time that it is used is also in the writings of John (I John 2:1). In this instance it is used for Christ and not the Holy Spirit and is translated "Advocate." Since the word "Comforter" is used for the Holy Spirit in John 14, 15, and 16, a study of the use of this word in these chapters should help to clear up the meaning. The Holy Spirit is called a Comforter four times in these four chapters. Let us examine the verses in which the Holy Spirit is called a Comforter.
1. "And I will pray the Father, and he shall give you another Comforter, that he may abide with you for ever," (John 14:16). Note carefully the word "another." The word "**allos**—**another**" indicates the significance of the word "Comforter" in this verse. "Christ was this to His disciples, by implication of His word 'another' (**allos**—another of the same sort, not **heteros**—different,"

THE WORK OF THE HOLY SPIRIT

W. E. Vine Expository Dictionary of New Testament Words. Christ promised the apostles that the Comforter would take His place with them. A consideration of the relationship of Christ to the apostles should help one see that the promise of the Comforter in John 14:16 must be limited to the apostles. While Christ was the Saviour of the apostles, He was also their personal teacher and guide while He was with them. When He returned to the Father, the Holy Spirit would take His place as their teacher and the guide. One might as well claim to have Christ back on earth, selecting him for a special work, and expecting Christ to personally train him for that work, as to claim the promise of the Holy Spirit in John 14:16. This promise of the Holy Spirit was only given to the apostles. Surely, anyone ought to be able to see that the relationship of the Holy Spirit in this verse was peculiar to the apostles, as was their selection and personal training by Christ while He was on earth. It would be just as scriptural to expect Christ to come back to earth to personally call, teach, and train one, as for one to claim the promise of the Holy Spirit in John 14:16. This was a promise of the Holy Spirit given to the apostles to take Christ's place as their teacher and guide. When this promise was made to the apostles, there was not a written New Testament. The promise of John 14:16 supplied their need in the absence of written revelation. If this promise applies to Christians in general today, we do not need a New Testament. The Holy Spirit would supply it by direct revelation.

What about the phrase, "that he may abide with you for ever"? Since the promise was made to the apostles, "abiding for ever" is limited to this. The duration of time is indicated in the very fact that the promise was given to the apostles. Christ had been with the apostles and would soon return to the Father. John 16 shows the reaction of the apostles to the announcement that Christ would not continue to be with them in person. The promise of the Holy Spirit to abide with them forever was a promise that the Holy Spirit would be with them until their work as apostles was completed. If this is not the case, since the word "Comforter" in this verse is a promise of miraculous guidance to the apostles, then it must follow that the miraculous operation of the Spirit continues today.

John 16:17 identifies the nature of the work the Spirit would do in the apostles. The phrase, "even the Spirit of truth," is proof that the promise of the Comforter in verse 16 was a reference to the inspiration of the apostle. Do those who claim these promises are to be applied to Christians in general today, also believe that inspiration and infallibility apply to Christians in general? If not, then it must be evident that the promise was limited to the period of miraculous operation of the Spirit.

2. "But the Comforter, which is the Holy Ghost, whom the Father will send in my name, he shall teach you all things, and bring all things to your remembrance, whatsoever I have said unto you," (John 14:26). The Comforter in John 14:26 was to equip the apostles with two things: a) "...He shall teach you all things..." Again, this is a promise of inspiration to the apostles. This was direct teaching and instruction. We have no need of this promise today since we have a completed, written revelation. This was not a promise to the apostles to enable them to be able to understand written revelation such as denominational preachers claim today. The promise was to provide, by inspiration, the revelation which the apostles were to teach. To hold up this promise to Christians today is to offer them the promise of inspiration and infallibility. b) "...He shall...bring all things to your remembrance..." Here the promise is to supply the apostles with a direct remembrance of the things Christ taught them while He was with them. Even though the apostles were with Christ personally, heard Him teach the multitudes, and also had Christ to teach them privately, this teaching was not to be left to their fallible memories. The Holy Spirit would supply directly the things that Christ had taught them personally. The promise of inspiration to the apostles reaches both ways, forward and backward. Inspiration reached back to guide the apostles' memories as to the teachings they had received personally from Christ. Christ, in person, has not taught me anything. I was not among the ones on earth when He instructed His apostles in person. Since the phrase, "Whatsoever I have said unto you," is descriptive of His personal and private teaching of the twelve, how can the promise of the Comforter be extended to include all Christians today? No person today has had Christ as a personal instructor. We now have the teachings of Christ and the apostles in a written revelation and this is the only method that either Christ or the Holy Spirit uses in teaching men today.

3. "But when the Comforter is come, whom I will send unto you from the Father, even the Spirit of truth, which proceedeth from the Father, he shall testify of me," (John 15:26). Here is the third reference to the Holy Spirit as a Comforter. Note the characteristics of the promise of the Comforter in this passage: a)

THE WORK OF THE HOLY SPIRIT

"...whom I will send...from the Father..." is evidence that Joel 2 is the background and points to Pentecost. b) "...even the Spirit of truth..." means inspiration and infallibility. c) "...he shall testify of me" means the Holy Spirit, through the apostles, would present Christ to the world as the Son of God and Saviour. The book of Acts and the Epistles furnish the examples of the Holy Spirit testifying of Christ through the apostles. d) John 15:27: "And ye also shall bear witness, because ye have been with me from the beginning." The apostles had been with Christ, seen His miracles, heard His teaching, and would also see Him following His resurrection. They had been with Him from the beginning. But the testimony of the apostles would be inspired testimony. The apostles were not left to simply tell some experiences they had and call this "witnessing" or "testifying." Even when an apostle gave some personal experience, it was inspired testimony. The Holy Spirit directed the apostles in giving even this type of testimony. There is as much difference in this type of testimony and witnessing and what denominational and Pentecostal people offer for witnessing for Christ today, as there is the difference between the apostles of Christ and a Christian. The apostles were Christians, but they were also Christ's ambassadors. As already shown, Christians are not ambassadors. "But when the Comforter is come, whom I will send unto you from the Father, even the Spirit of truth, which proceedeth from the Father, he shall testify of me," (John 15:26). John 15:26 is just as certainly a reference to the apostle receiving the baptism of the Holy Spirit as anything can be. For brethren in the church of the Lord to promise Christians today the Holy Spirit as a Comforter is equal to promising them the baptism of the Holy Spirit. A smattering knowledge of the Scriptures should be sufficient for one to know that the baptism of the Holy Spirit was not promised to Christians in general.

4. "Nevertheless I tell you the truth; It is expedient for you that I go away: for if I go not away, the Comforter will not come unto you; but if I depart, I will send him unto you," (John 16:7). This is the fourth and the last time the word "Comforter" is used in reference to the Holy Spirit. Jesus said that it was necessary for Him to go away so that the Spirit might be sent. Again, it is plain that the background of the passage is Joel 2 and points to Pentecost. As already shown, the Holy Spirit was to take Christ's place with the apostles. The Holy Spirit was to be the personal guide and instructor of the apostles: a) The Holy Spirit was to guide the apostles into all truth. This promise was in connection with

revealing the truth of the gospel to the apostles. When the apostles had completed their work, all truth necessary for redemption had been revealed. The Holy Spirit, through the apostles, revealed "the faith" once for all delivered to the saints. This leaves no place for the direct operation of the Spirit or latter-day revelation. The gospel is now completed and all-sufficient. b) The Holy Spirit was to show the apostles things to come. The books of Matthew, Mark, and Luke contain the historical facts that are the basis of redemption. These books present Christ in His mission into the world to save through His death, burial, resurrection, and ascension. The Holy Spirit, through the apostles, as recorded in the book of Acts, interpreted the meaning of the facts in Matthew, Mark, Luke, and John, and showed how these facts were to be understood and appropriated by the obedience of faith. If the Bible had ended with Matthew, Mark, Luke, and John, men would not have understood the means of appropriating the redemption that was made possible through the Christ presented in these books. Thus, the Holy Spirit, through the apostles' preaching and writing, explained how the redemption provided by the Christ can be obtained. The Holy Spirit, through Peter, presented Christ to the people on Pentecost, showing the meaning of His death, and explaining how men could appropriate this redemption through Christ by their obeying the gospel (Acts 2). Another example was Philip preaching to the eunuch in the eighth chapter of Acts. The eunuch was reading from the Old Testament, but he needed a man (inspired man) to help him understand the meaning of Isaiah 53. The Spirit, through Philip, interpreted the prophecy through the facts in the gospel, and then showed the eunuch how he could appropriate the redemption foreseen by Isaiah, fulfilled by Christ in Matthew, Mark, Luke, and John, and was now being preached by the inspiration of the apostles. One might as well expect to have the Spirit through the hands of the apostles and to have the Spirit speak directly to him, as the Spirit spoke to Philip, as to look for the Comforter of John 16:7 to come into his heart. The Holy Spirit as a Comforter was promised only to the apostles and in a secondary sense to believers that received miraculous endowments through the hands of the apostles.

A SUMMARY

1. The Holy Spirit as a Comforter was promised to the apostles to take the place of Christ. During the personal ministry of Christ, Christ was the teacher and guide of the apostles. When Christ

THE WORK OF THE HOLY SPIRIT

returned to the Father, the Holy Spirit came to the apostles to take Christ's place with them. It would be as reasonable to claim that Christ appeared personally to one and trained and instructed him personally, as to pretend that one has the Holy Spirit as a Comforter as promised in these verses.

2. The Holy Spirit as a Comforter was to equip the apostles for receiving the revelation of the gospel. If this promise of the Holy Spirit is to Christians in general, then there is no need for a written revelation. The Holy Spirit would furnish the revelation directly. The very fact that we have a completed, written revelation is proof that the promise of the Holy Spirit was not to Christians in general, nor to preachers of today in particular. One's knowledge of the will of God does not come by direct revelation, but through the revealed Word. One gains this knowledge by hearing the Word preached or by study.

3. If these promises of the Holy Spirit applied today, the one who had the Holy Spirit could write a New Testament. This promise qualified the apostles to write the New Testament. Since it enabled the apostles to write a New Testament, it must follow that if one has the Comforter as promised in these verses, he could do the same thing that the apostles did; that is, write a New Testament. If not, why not?

4. This promise of the Holy Spirit was made to the apostles before Pentecost. The promise of the Holy Spirit before Pentecost was the promise of Joel 2 and began at Pentecost. The promise of the Comforter is equal to the promise of the baptism of the Holy Spirit to the apostles. It would be just as scriptural today to promise one the baptism of the Holy Spirit as to hold out to him the idea that he could receive the Holy Spirit as a Comforter as based on these passages.

5. Finally, it is vital to realize that the gospel had to be revealed and confirmed. The gospel was a strange and new doctrine in the world. The enemies of the gospel were many in number. The apostles had to face, not only audiences that were angry and turned into mobs, they had to face courts. In the midst of the discussion of the Holy Spirit as a Comforter, Christ reminds His apostles of this opposition: "These things have I spoken unto you, that ye should not be offended. They shall put you out of the synagogues: yea, the time cometh, that whosoever killeth you will think that he doeth God service," (John 16:1-2). When the apostles were called before magistrates for preaching the gospel, far more than the lives of the apostles were at stake. The integrity of the gospel preached by the apostles was also being laid on the

line. The defense of the integrity of the gospel preached by the apostles is included in the promise of the Comforter. If the apostles could have been discredited, the gospel would have been discredited also. A careful study of the book of Acts and the Epistles will establish this truth. Paul's defense of his apostleship in the Galatian letter was a defense also of the integrity of the gospel that he proclaimed. It was this that was in Paul's mind—the integrity of the gospel—when as a prisoner in Rome he said, "I am set for the defense of the gospel," (Philippians 1:17). In view of this, notice carefully W. E. Vine's comment on the word "Comforter": "**Parakletos**, lit. called to one's side, i.e., to one's aid, is primarily a verbal adjective and suggests the capability or adaptability for giving aid. It is used in a court of justice to denote a legal assistant, counsel for defense, and advocate; then generally one who pleads another's cause, an intercessor, advocate as in I John 2:1 of the Lord Jesus." The Holy Spirit as a Comforter in the apostles furnished the counsel for the defense when the apostles were called into court by the opposition of the Jews. The apostles were not simply defending themselves, but the gospel they preached. Look at the promise of the Holy Spirit to the apostles in a few passages and notice the context:

> Behold, I send you forth as sheep in the midst of wolves: be ye therefore wise as serpents, and harmless as doves.
> But beware of men: for they will deliver you up to the councils, and they will scourge you in their synagogues;
> And ye shall be brought before governors and kings for my sake, for a testimony against them and the Gentiles.
> But when they deliver you up, take no thought how or what ye shall speak: for it shall be given you in that same hour what ye shall speak.
> For it is not ye that speak, but the Spirit of your Father which speaketh in you. (Matthew 10:16-20).

> But take heed to yourselves: for they shall deliver you up to councils; and in the synagogues ye shall be beaten: and ye shall be brought before rulers and kings for my sake, for a testimony against them.
> And the gospel must first be published among all nations.
> But when they shall lead you, and deliver you up, take no thought beforehand what ye shall speak, neither do ye

THE WORK OF THE HOLY SPIRIT

premeditate: but whatsoever shall be given you in that hour, that speak ye: for it is not ye that speak, but the Holy Ghost.

Now the brother shall betray the brother to death, and the father the son; and children shall rise up against their parents, and shall cause them to be put to death.

And ye shall be hated of all men for my name's sake: but he that shall endure unto the end, the same shall be saved. (Mark 13:9-13).

But before all these, they shall lay their hands on you, and persecute you, delivering you up to the synagogues, and into prisons, being brought before kings and rulers for my name's sake.

And it shall turn to you for a testimony.

Settle it therefore in your hearts, not to meditate before what ye shall answer:

For I will give you a mouth and wisdom, which all your adversaries shall not be able to gainsay nor resist. (Luke 21:12-15).

In these verses, the Holy Spirit supplied the answer for the apostles before courts and kings. Read Paul's defense before Felix and Agrippa. A careful study of these passages will show that Paul was not only defending himself from the false charges made against him, but he was also defending the gospel he proclaimed. The Holy Spirit as a Comforter to him was his legal assistant, counsel for defense, and his advocate. We now have the gospel. It carries within its bosom the defense of its integrity. Of course, if I should be called upon to defend the gospel, I would use the written Word in my defense. This was not the case with the apostles. The gospel was a new revelation and it had to be revealed to the apostles to be in its present written form. One might as well expect to get up in debate without study and preparation of any sort, depending upon the Holy Spirit to supply one's defense directly, as to claim the promise of the Holy Spirit as a Comforter today. It is a fatal blunder for preachers to read these passages that speak of the Holy Spirit as a Comforter and promise the Holy Spirit as a Comforter today. These promises were special promises made to the apostles who had a special work, and these special promises were to qualify the apostles for this special work. This was in a time when there was no written revelation, when revelation was being given directly. Surely, brethren ought to be able to see that a promise made to the apostles for the purpose of furnishing them the direct revelation of the gospel and the defense of the integrity of the gospel they proclaimed, is not a promise that should be applied to Christians in general.

THE GIFT OF THE HOLY SPIRIT

"Then Peter said unto them, Repent, and be baptized every one of you in the name of Jesus Christ for the remission of sins, and ye shall receive the gift of the Holy Ghost," (Acts 2:38).

The gift of the Holy Spirit in Acts 2:38 has been a source of difficulty and various answers have been given as to what this means. I am fully conscious of the differences that brethren have had over this question. In view of the differences that there have been on the subject of the Holy Spirit, I want to present some preliminary remarks. The position which I shall present on the Holy Spirit is the result of more than thirty-five years of study. I realize that this study does not mean that what I shall say must necessarily be correct, but the conclusions that I have reached on this question have not been hasty and without careful and diligent searching of the Scriptures. The things that I shall present in this chapter are presented in the spirit of good will and for the purpose of encouraging an honest study of the passage. I would like to make it abundantly clear that I have never sought to make this an issue with brethren that have disagreed with me. As will be seen in the study of the gift of the Holy Spirit, I do not believe that it is a reference to what is commonly called a non-miraculous indwelling. I shall set forth from the Scriptures what I believe that the gift of the Holy Spirit is, and seek to establish it upon a scriptural basis. In setting forth what I believe to be the meaning, I also want it clearly understood that I have never attempted to press this position on anyone, or indicate in any way that this question should be made a test of fellowship. While I do not believe that the gift of the Holy Spirit is a non-miraculous indwelling that one receives when he is baptized, there are many brethren that hold this position, who I consider in the highest esteem. The ones that generally hold this position believe that the Holy Spirit leads and directs one only through the Word. I have never made what I believe about the gift of the Holy Spirit an issue with the brethren that hold this position. I do reject the idea that some have that the gift of the Holy Spirit, which one receives when baptized, operates in him and leads and directs him separately and apart from the truth. This latter position can only end in one following his feelings and moods rather than the Word of God. This position would lead one in any direction and his subjective feelings become the standard, rather than the Bible. This position must be rejected by all that believe the Bible to be our rule of faith and practice. I only ask that those who read this book weigh the evidence presented and then draw their own conclusions as to whether or not I have proved the proposition that I shall set forth.

THE WORK OF THE HOLY SPIRIT

Alexander Campbell expressed my sentiments when he said, "Patience in the investigation, openness to conviction, and a freedom from dogmatism are, on all abstruse and difficult questions and especially on this cardinal matter of indispensable importance to the discovery of truth." Again, Campbell said, "For our own part, we are desirous to understand all that God has revealed, and receive the exact ideas which are couched in the words which the Holy Spirit used."

I believe that the Scriptures teach that the gift of the Holy Spirit refers to miraculous endowments that belonged to the period when these miraculous gifts were for the purpose of confirming the apostles of Christ as His apostles and providing the church with inspiration through these gifts that came through the laying on of the hands of an apostle. I am fully conscious of the questions that arise when I make this statement, but these questions will be dealt with later in the chapter. Let me appeal to you not to allow the questions that may be in your mind to keep you from weighing carefully the Scriptures that I shall present to establish the proposition that the gift of the Holy Spirit was miraculous.

WHAT OTHERS HAVE SAID

It is not my purpose to try to prove by other men that the gift of the Holy Spirit was miraculous. I shall offer what I consider to be proof from the Scriptures. I am giving these quotations simply to show that there were some able men of the Restoration Movement that understood the gift of the Holy Spirit to be miraculous. In instance after instance when I have discussed this question and presented the evidence to establish that the gift of the Holy Spirit was miraculous, many brethren seem to be surprised as though this was something new and had never been heard of in the Restoration Movement. This is the reason that I am giving these quotations from several men.

"The gift of the Holy Spirit (Acts 2:38) is the bestowal of the Spirit, possibly in His miraculous manifestations,"—David Lipscomb.

"Hence, we conclude that Peter promised the Spirit to such as would believe and obey the gospel therein as ample measure as he had power to impart it to them. Why should he not thus amply bestow it upon them, having the power to do so? And why should he not thus amply promise it to them? We are inclined to think that Peter intended to promise something more than the ordinary measure of the Spirit to those he addressed at the beginning,"—T. W. Brents.

"It seems that some of the early Christians' miraculous measure of the Holy Spirit, and that this is what Peter meant,"—H. Leo Boles.

"We have this phrase, the gift of the Holy Spirit, as has been said, but twice, in all the apostolic writings;—Acts 2:38 and 10:45. Both of which denote all that is comprehended in the promise of Joel, the Holy Spirit and all His miraculous powers,"—Alexander Campbell.

I do not believe that an interpretation should be based on what others have said. I have not given what these men said to prove the point under consideration, but to show that the idea of the gift of the Holy Spirit being miraculous is not as strange as some seem to think. Brother Guy N. Woods told me that this has been his understanding of the gift of the Holy Spirit for a number of years. He also told me that more than twenty-five years ago he set forth this position in an article in the <u>Firm Foundation.</u> Soon after the article appeared in the paper brother Joe Warlick wrote to him and said that he had set forth the truth on the gift of the Holy Spirit.

SOME IMPORTANT CONSIDERATIONS

In view of what is recorded in the book of Acts and the Epistles about miraculous endowments, what is more evident than the chief function of the Holy Spirit being the provision of miraculous endowments in relation to the apostles and churches? If one read carefully the New Testament, noticing what the Holy Spirit gave during the period of direct revelation and confirmation, would he not conclude that this was the main operation of the Spirit in the time when there was no written revelation? If I have read my New Testament correctly, and I think I have, this is exactly the case. During the time that there was no written revelation, the work of the apostles and the functioning of a congregation depended upon miraculous endowments. The most prominent work of the Holy Spirit, beginning at Pentecost and continuing until revelation was completed, was the miraculous manifestation of the Spirit to furnish revelation and confirmation. What other explanation of the gift of the Holy Spirit better explains the meaning of the gift of the Holy Spirit?

1. Consider the following and see if this is not true:
    a. Notice the abundance of references to the miraculous operation of the Holy Spirit beginning at Pentecost.
    b. The entire revelation of the gospel was to be given by the Spirit, which involved the miraculous operation of the Spirit.

THE WORK OF THE HOLY SPIRIT

    c. The gospel was not only revealed by the miraculous operation of the Spirit, but it was also confirmed by miraculous operation.

    d. Churches had miraculous endowments through the hands of the apostles. Indeed, they would have had nothing to direct them without these miraculous endowments, since the apostles could not leave them a New Testament. Now read your New Testament, beginning at Acts 2, and see if this is not what you find. Since the miraculous operation of the Spirit was necessary for the revelation of the gospel and its confirmation, what would be the most likely meaning of the gift of the Holy Spirit in Acts 2:38?

2. Consider a second question: Would it be impossible for the gift of the Holy Spirit to refer to miraculous endowments? The answer to this question is no. Acts 2 is the beginning of the Christian Age which was accompanied by miraculous endowments. The book of Acts (Chapters 8 and 19) shows that there were miraculous gifts beginning at Pentecost and continuing while revelation was being given and confirmed. The book of Acts is proof that it is possible for the gift of the Holy Spirit to be a reference to miraculous endowments through the hands of the apostles. The interpretation that the gift of the Holy Spirit was miraculous endowments cannot be rejected because it was impossible. It was an apostle that made the statement in Acts 2:38. Spiritual gifts were imparted by the apostles and so the explanation that it means the miraculous cannot be ruled out by saying that it was impossible.

3. Would the idea that the gift of the Holy Spirit was miraculous contradict anything the Bible teaches? Again, the answer is no. If one says that the gift of the Holy Spirit is miraculous, he is not contradicting a single passage of Scripture. Instead of contradicting any Scripture, this harmonizes with what the book of Acts and the Epistles both teach.

LET THE BIBLE INTERPRET ITSELF

I have always believed that the Bible is its own best interpreter. Shall we let the Bible explain what is meant by the gift of the Holy Spirit? It is my conviction that the Bible will make clear just what is meant by this phrase, if we will only let it do so. I know the questions that will be in the minds of many as they read this. Let me appeal to each one not to allow these questions to close his mind to the things that I am presenting. The objections that may be in your mind will be noticed at the close of the chapter.

THE WORD "GIFT"

According to Young's Concordance, the word translated "gift" is used six times in the New Testament in connection with the Holy Spirit. Is there any better way to determine the meaning of the word than to see its use in the Scriptures? It is my conviction that a careful analysis of these passages where this word is found will enable one to understand the meaning of the word.

ACTS 2:38

1. "Then Peter said unto them, Repent, and be baptized every one of you in the name of Jesus Christ for the remission of sins, and ye shall receive the gift of the Holy Ghost," (Acts 2:38). This passage is the first time the word is used. While I have already stated that I believe that this refers to the miraculous, I want to look at the other times that the word is used before I consider Acts 2:38 in detail.

ACTS 8:20

2. "But Peter said unto him, Thy money perish with thee, because thou hast thought that the gift of God may be purchased with money," (Acts 8:20). The second time the word is used is in Acts 8:20. Here it is called the "gift of God." But this should not be thought of as strange, since the prophecy of Joel is called the promise of the Father (Luke 24:49). The gift of God in Acts 8:20 is a reference to the miraculous apostolic power to impart spiritual gifts to believers. This is made clear by the conversation between Peter and Simon. Notice the context: a) The apostles imparted miraculous gifts to the Samaritans. b) Simon saw that through the laying on of the apostles' hands the Holy Spirit was given; i.e., spiritual gifts. c) Simon attempted to buy this power that the apostles had to impart spiritual gifts. d) Peter called that which Simon wanted to buy the "gift of God." e) The "gift of God" was the miraculous power that belonged to the apostles to impart spiritual gifts. It should not be difficult to see that the word "gift" in Acts 8:20 was: a) a reference to the Holy Spirit; b) a reference to the apostolic power to impart spiritual gifts; c) a reference to the miraculous.

THE WORK OF THE HOLY SPIRIT

ACTS 10:45

3. "And they of the circumcision which believed were astonished, as many as came with Peter, because that on the Gentiles also was poured out the gift of the Holy Ghost," (Acts 10:45). This is the third time the word "gift" is used in connection with the Holy Spirit. It is used by Peter, the same one that used it the first time in Acts 2:38. This verse has the identical phrase used in Acts 2:38. The phrase here is in reference to the household of Cornelius receiving the Holy Spirit: a) The "gift" of the Holy Spirit in Acts 10:45 was the miraculous outpouring of the Holy Spirit on Cornelius and his household. b) The miraculous reception of the Spirit on Cornelius and his household resulted in their speaking in tongues. c) The speaking in tongues was a spiritual gift. d) The third time the word "gift" is used is a reference to the miraculous. I think that all would agree that the gift of the Holy Spirit in Acts 10:45 means a miraculous gift. e) In Acts 10:45 we find not only the word "gift" of Acts 2:38, but the entire phrase that is in Acts 2:38.

ACTS 11:17

4. "Forasmuch then as God gave them the like gift as he did unto us, who believed on the Lord Jesus Christ; what was I, that I could withstand God?" The fourth time the word "gift" is found is in Acts 11:17. It is used here in reference to the same incident as in Acts 10 when the Spirit was poured out on Cornelius and his household. The use of the word here means miraculous just as in 10:45. This time it is called the "like gift." In Acts 11:17 the word "gift" is used for what the apostles received at Pentecost, as well as for what Cornelius and his household received. The reception of the Spirit by the apostles and by Cornelius and his household were both miraculous: a) In Acts 11:17 the word "gift" is used to describe the reception of the Spirit by the apostles. b) The word "gift" is used to describe the reception of the Holy Spirit by Cornelius and his household. c) The word "gift" is used in Acts 11:17 to equal the gift of the Holy Spirit in Acts 10:45. Acts 10:45 uses the phrase, "the gift of the Holy Spirit." Acts 11:17, in speaking of the same thing, uses only the word "gift." d) We now have additional proof that the word "gift" means the same as the gift of the Holy Spirit. e) All would agree that the word "gift" in Acts 11:17 means miraculous.

EPHESIANS 3:7

5. "Whereof I was made a minister, according to the gift of the grace of God given unto me by the effectual working of his power," (Ephesians 3:7). The fifth time the word "gift" is used is in Ephesians 3:7. Here it is spoken of as "the gift of grace." When Paul used the word "gift" here, he was referring to the apostolic gift which he received when he became an apostle. This is clear from the context in which Paul uses it: a) Ephesians 3:3 mentions revelation that Paul received. This could only be by direct miraculous power. b) He mentions that which he had written. That which Paul had written certainly means inspiration and inspiration means direct, miraculous power. c) Ephesians 3:5 states, "...it is now revealed unto his holy apostles and prophets by the Spirit." Here is a reference to: 1) revelation; 2) apostles and prophets; 3) by the Spirit. In Ephesians 3:7, the word "minister" is equal to Paul's apostleship. Thus, the gift of grace was the apostolic gift of the Spirit that Paul received as an apostle. Finally, the phrase, "the effectual working of his power," means the miraculous power that belonged to Paul as an apostle. The fifth time that the word "gift" is used in connection with the Spirit, it means miraculous.

EPHESIANS 4:7

6. "But unto every one of us is given grace according to the measure of the gift of Christ," (Ephesians 4:7). This is the sixth and the last time the word "gift" is used in connection with the Holy Spirit. Here the gift is called "the measure of the gift of Christ." In view of the context in which this phrase is found, it can only refer to the miraculous operation of the Spirit given by God through Christ and as is summarized in verse 11. Ephesians 4:10 says, "He that descended is the same also that ascended up far above all heavens, that he might fill all things." Christ had said to the apostles in John 16:7: "Nevertheless I tell you the truth; It is expedient for you that I go away: for if I go not away, the Comforter will not come unto you; but if I depart, I will send him unto you." The "going away" of Christ in John 16:7 is equal to His ascension in Ephesians 4:10. The promise that the Comforter would come of John 16:7 is equal to "that he might fill all things" of Ephesians 4:10.

Finally, the measure of the gift of Christ in verse 7 of Ephesians 4

THE WORK OF THE HOLY SPIRIT

is just another way of saying that He gave gifts unto men of verse 8. The gifts of verse 8 are summarized in verse 11. Thus, the word "gift" in Ephesians 4:7 is another reference to the miraculous.

We have now studied all the passages in the New Testament where we find the word "gift" of Acts 2:38 used. Let me put them all together:

Gift of the Holy Spirit	Acts 2:38	?
Gift of God	Acts 8:20	Miraculous
Gift of the Holy Spirit	Acts 10:45	Miraculous
Like Gift	Acts 11:17	Miraculous
The Gift of the Grace of God	Ephesians 3:7	Miraculous
The Measure of the Gift of Christ	Ephesians 4:7	Miraculous

I think that there would be complete agreement that the word "gift" in the last five passages is in reference to the miraculous operations of the Spirit. I do not believe that there would be a dissenting voice, nor would these last five passages cause any careful Bible student the least difficulty. It is simple to see that the word "gift" in these last five passages is in reference to the miraculous operations of the Spirit during the time when revelation was being given directly and confirmed. Does it not strike you as being strange that the word "gift" is used six times in the passages that refer to the Holy Spirit, and that five of them are miraculous and one non-miraculous? This was the first thing that caused me to re-study Acts 2:38, and it was then that I decided that the gift of the Holy Spirit in Acts 2:38 was miraculous. In view of the general problem that the religious world has had on this subject, it did not seem to me to be reasonable that God would use the word "gift" in speaking of the Holy Spirit five times meaning miraculous and one time non-miraculous.

Before I leave this part of the study, I want to call attention to another thought about the word "gift." Notice the variety of ways that the word "gift" is used, and for the sake of argument, I will not include Acts 2:38.
1. Acts 8:20—The apostolic power to impart spiritual gifts
2. Acts 10:45—The pouring out of the Holy Spirit on the household of Cornelius
3. Acts 11:17—Includes both Pentecost and the household of Cornelius
4. Ephesians 3:7—Miraculous endowment of the apostle Paul
5. Ephesians 4:7,11—Miraculous gifts for: a) apostles, b) prophets, c) evangelists, d) pastors, e) teachers — all miraculous

Now add to all of this the final passage where the word "gift" is used in Ephesians 4:7. Ephesians 4:7 points to the gifts of 4:8, and Ephesians 4:8 points to the gifts of 4:11. But now look at Ephesians 4:11. In this verse, one finds apostles, prophets, evangelists, pastors, and teachers. Each of these is mentioned in connection with the miraculous endowments that accompanied their work during the period of the miraculous. The phrase, "the measure of the gift of Christ," meaning the miraculous in verse 7, comprehends all that is in Ephesians 4:11. Ephesians 4:7 shows that the word "gift" used in connection with the Holy Spirit is a generic term that includes all the miraculous as foretold by Joel and fulfilled in the apostles, prophets, evangelists, pastors, and teachers. Thus, the words "gift of the Holy Spirit" may be used, and indeed are used, as a reference to the whole of the miraculous in the New Testament. In some places, it may be restricted to one particular thing, while in another it may be used to denote a different miraculous operation of the Spirit. Until recent years, we had no difficulty with what the New Testament taught about spiritual gifts. All understood that they were miraculous, temporary, and ceased when revelation was completed and confirmed. The difference between a spiritual gift and the gift of the Holy Spirit is that a spiritual gift referred to a particular manifestation, while the word "gift" is a general term that was used for the miraculous, and included all that there was in Joel's prophecy. It is my conviction that our problem with Acts 2:38 grew out of a false conclusion that if the gift of the Holy Spirit was miraculous, then the miraculous would have to continue beyond the period of revelation and confirmation. This does not follow, as I shall show later in the study.

JOEL'S PROPHECY

Joel's prophecy included spiritual gifts through the hands of the apostles. Some of the things in Joel's prophecy could only mean the gifts that Christians received through the laying on of the apostles' hands. "Your sons and your daughters shall prophesy" certainly means the gifts that were imparted by the apostles. The book of Acts shows that the apostles did impart gifts through the laying on of hands. The background of the apostles imparting spiritual gifts, such as Acts 8, is Joel's prophecy. Since Joel's prophecy included the gifts that believers would receive through the hands of the apostles, why should anyone be surprised that Peter promised what Joel's prophecy said? It seems to me that this is just what would be expected of the apostle Peter, as he had quoted Joel's prophecy, and what the apostles had received is not all that was included in Joel's prophecy. What the apostles had received

THE WORK OF THE HOLY SPIRIT

made it possible, through the laying on of their hands, to impart spiritual gifts, which also was included in the prophecy of Joel. Peter is dealing with the prophecy of Joel, having quoted it and showing that the outpouring of the Spirit on the apostles was the fulfillment of this prophecy. But it included more (that is, miraculous manifestations that would come through the laying on of the apostles' hands), and therefore the apostle Peter certainly would include this in the promise of the prophecy of Joel.

THE WORD "RECEIVE"

The word "gift" of Acts 2:38 is not the only key word in the passage. Let us study carefully another word. Peter said, "Ye shall RECEIVE the Holy Spirit." A study of the word "receive" will add additional proof as to what the gift of the Holy Spirit means. The word "receive" is found in the following passages according to Young's Concordance:

JOHN 7:39

1. "(But this spake he of the Spirit, which they that believe on him should receive: for the Holy Ghost was not yet given; because that Jesus was not yet glorified.)" (John 7:39.) John 7:39 is the first time the word "receive" is used in reference to the reception of the Spirit. I have already discussed this passage in the study of John. I have shown that the reception of the Spirit of John 7:39 is miraculous, and is parallel with Mark 16:17. The passage has Joel as its background and Pentecost and what developed from Pentecost in the foreground.

JOHN 20:21-23

2. The second mention of the word "receive" is in John 20:21-23: "Then said Jesus to them again, Peace be unto you: as my Father hath sent me, even so send I you. And when he had said this, he breathed on them, and saith unto them, Receive ye the Holy Ghost: Whose soever sins ye remit, they are remitted unto them; and whose soever sins ye retain, they are retained." This passage has also been studied and so there is no need to go into it again. The passage is John's account of the Great Commission and promises inspiration to the apostles. The promise that the apostles would receive the Holy Spirit is a promise of the miraculous.

ACTS 2:38

3. Acts 2:38 is the next time that the word "receive" is used, but I am passing over this passage for the present. I will come back to it later.

ACTS 8:15-17

4. We move now to the eighth chapter of Acts. The word "receive" is used twice in this chapter. "Who, when they were come down, prayed for them, that they might receive the Holy Ghost," (Acts 8:15). "Then laid they their hands on them, and they received the Holy Ghost," (Acts 8:17). Philip had gone to Samaria and had preached the gospel. The Samaritans had believed and had been baptized. The apostles which were at Jerusalem had heard that the Samaritans had received the Word of God and sent Peter and John down to Samaria. When Peter and John arrived, they prayed for them that they might receive the Holy Spirit (Acts 8:15). "Then laid they their hands on them and they received the Holy Spirit," (Acts 8:17). Luke tells us that the Samaritans received the Holy Spirit and makes it clear that their reception of the Spirit came through the hands of the apostles. So there is no question that when the Samaritans are reported to have received the Holy Spirit that it was miraculous.

Furthermore, this is the first time anyone is said to have received the Holy Spirit since Acts 2. I do not mean that others had not received miraculous endowments before this, because they certainly had. Philip could not have preached and performed miracles in Samaria without a miraculous endowment. What I am saying is that this is the first time the Bible specifically mentions someone receiving the Holy Spirit since Acts 2. The first recorded instance after Acts 2 of someone receiving the Holy Spirit was a miraculous reception. It is well also to keep in mind that this is an instance of Christians receiving the Holy Spirit during the period of the miraculous.

ACTS 10:47

5. "Can any man forbid water, that these should not be baptized, which have received the Holy Ghost as well as we?" (Acts 10:47). This is the next occurrence of someone receiving the Holy Spirit, that is, where the word "receive" is found. Peter asked, "Can any

THE WORK OF THE HOLY SPIRIT 141

man forbid water, that these should not be baptized, which have received the Holy Ghost as well as we?" It is not necessary to discuss this incident as all will agree that this was a miraculous reception of the Spirit.

ACTS 19:6

6. Passing to Acts 19, we find Paul at Ephesus. Paul asked the Ephesians if they had received the Holy Spirit since they had believed. What kind of reception was Paul asking about—miraculous or non-miraculous? The context surely shows that Paul was asking the Ephesians if they had received any miraculous endowment through the laying on of the hands of an apostle (Acts 19:6).

In the first place, it would have been foolish for Paul to have inquired if they had received a non-miraculous reception of the Spirit. Second, the fact that Paul laid his hands on them in verse 6, and they spake with tongues and prophesied, shows that Paul was asking about a miraculous reception. This is the second recorded instance of Christians receiving the Holy Spirit following their baptism. (Cornelius received the Spirit before he was baptized. This was special and was for the purpose of showing that the gospel was for Gentiles as well as Jews.) Is it not significant that in Acts 2:38 that Peter promised those that were baptized that they would receive the gift of the Holy Spirit? And in the book of Acts, we have two examples of people who were baptized receiving the Holy Spirit, and in both instances it was a miraculous reception through the hands of the apostles. Is it not also strange that there is not the first mention in Acts, after Acts 2, of anyone receiving the Holy Spirit in a non-miraculous way, unless it is Acts 2:38? Nor is there the slightest hint that anyone received a non-miraculous gift of the Spirit. Since the book of Acts mentions twice Christians receiving the Holy Spirit, and both times it was miraculous, if the gift of the Holy Spirit, in Acts 2:38 means a non-miraculous reception, is it not unusual that Luke records two instances of Christians receiving the Holy Spirit in a miraculous way, but he never one time gives an example of one being baptized and receiving the Holy Spirit non-miraculously? It seems to me that if such was the case, then in the miraculous period that surely this distinction would have been pointed out.

GALATIANS 3:2

7. The seventh passage that mentions someone receiving the Holy Spirit is Galatians 3:2: "This only would I learn of you, Received ye the Spirit by the works of the law, or by the hearing of faith?" This verse is often used to show that the Holy Spirit is received through the Word. Is this the meaning of Paul's question? It is important to keep in mind the general theme of the book. Why did Paul ask the Galatians if they received the Spirit by the works of the law or the hearing of faith? Judaizing teachers were troubling the churches of Galatia (Galatians 1:7). These false teachers were insisting that the Galatians needed to be circumcised and to keep the law (Galatians 5:1-4). They were trying to rob the Galatians of their liberty in Christ. The Galatian letter is an answer to these false teachers and to show that Gentiles had a right to the gospel on the same basis as the Jews, and it was not necessary for them to be circumcised. Paul insisted that if the Christians of Galatia accepted the claim of the Judaizing teachers, they would fall from grace (Galatians 5:4).

In order for the false teachers to have succeeded among the churches of Galatia, it would have been necessary for them to have proven that Paul was not an apostle of Christ. Thus, in the first verse of the letter, Paul affirms that he is an apostle of Christ: "Paul, an apostle, (not of men, neither by man, but by Jesus Christ, and God the Father, who raised him from the dead)," (Galatians 1:1). Then he develops this argument in Chapter 1 and the first fourteen verses of Chapter 2. In the last part of Chapter 2, Paul argues that righteousness was not through the law, but through Christ and the gospel. This is the background of Chapter 3.

When Paul asked, "Who hath bewitched you?" he had in mind the Judaizing teachers. If the Judaizing teachers could have successfully proven that Paul was not an apostle of Christ, then look at the consequences:
   a. If Paul was not an apostle of Christ, then the gospel he preached was not a genuine gospel.
   b. If the gospel Paul preached was not a genuine gospel, the Galatians were not Christians; they were counterfeits. This was what the Judaizing teachers were trying to get the Galatians to believe.
   c. The question in Galatians 3:2 is in this context.

The question is, Who is the false teacher—Paul or the Judaizers? Paul appealed to the Galatians' reception of the Spirit as an answer to the question as to which one was doing the false teaching—Paul or the Judaizers? Paul made this same argument in the Corinthian letter, except he stated it in a different way—I Corinthians 9:1-2. He first asked, "Am I not an apostle?" Then he says that though others may not consider him an apostle, that surely the Corinthians would not reject his apostleship, and then he stated the reason: "For the seal of my apostleship are ye in the Lord." The seal of Paul's apostleship, that established that the Corinthians were in the Lord, was the spiritual gifts that the Corinthians received through the hands of Paul. (See also II Corinthians 12:12.) In the Galatian letter, Paul had argued more extensively his apostleship than in the Corinthian letter. The problem had become more acute when Paul wrote the Galatian letter. But his question to the Galatians about their receiving the Spirit is, Who imparted the Spirit to the Galatians? Did the Judaizing teachers confirm themselves as apostles by imparting the Spirit through the laying on of their hands? How would a non-miraculous gift of the Spirit prove that Paul was an apostle? The Judaizers could as well have made the claim that the Galatians had received the Spirit non-miraculously as Paul could. In fact, if the non-miraculous reception of the Spirit could establish one as an apostle, anyone today could prove that he was an apostle.

But this is not all the evidence that the question of the reception of the Spirit in Galatians 3:2 means miraculous. Just three verses later, Paul uses the language of verse 1 where he speaks of works of the law and the hearing of faith: "He therefore that ministereth to you the Spirit, and worketh miracles among you, doeth he it by the works of the law, or by the hearing of faith?" (Galatians 3:5). The works of the law in Galatians 3:2 and 3:5 are just other ways of referring to the Judaizing teachers. The hearing of faith is a reference to the apostle Paul. What does Paul mean when he says, "He...that ministereth to you the Spirit"? The American Standard Version says, "supplieth." Is this not a direct statement that the Galatians received the Spirit by the laying on of Paul's hands? He is further asking them if they had received any miraculous gifts of the Spirit from these false teachers. Paul, in imparting gifts to the Galatians, provided proof of his apostleship, the genuineness of the gospel he preached, and the assurance to the Galatians that they were children of God by faith in Christ when baptized, and heirs of the promise of Abraham (Galatians

3:26-29). The fact that the Galatians had received no miraculous gift from the Judaizing teachers, was proof that they were false teachers. It ought to be clear that a non-miraculous reception of the Spirit would have served no purpose in relation to Paul's argument. When verse 5 reminded the Galatians that Paul had ministered to them the Spirit and worked miracles among them, it ought to be abundantly plain that the ministering of the Spirit was just as miraculous as the miracles. The question of receiving the Spirit in verse 2 is explained in unmistakable language in verse 5.

When Paul asked the Ephesians (Acts 19:2) if they had received the Spirit, was it not a question of receiving the Spirit miraculously through the apostles' hands? In a period of the miraculous operation of the Spirit, to ask the question about receiving the Spirit, would seem to me to naturally refer to a miraculous reception. I cannot conceive, in a period of miraculous operation of the Spirit, to ask one if he had received the Spirit, and make it mean anything other than a question of miraculous reception.

It is in this same context that Paul made the statement in Galatians 4:6. The question is still, Who are sons of God, those described in Galatians 3:26-29 or those that keep the law? In Galatians 4:6, Paul was simply answering the question that he had asked in Galatians 3:2 and defined in Galatians 3:5. Galatians 3:5 establishes that the Galatians had received the Spirit miraculously. So in Galatians 4:6 Paul made the point that they had received the Spirit, ministered by him (Galatians 3:5) because they were sons of God. God would not have given, through Paul, the Galatians any miraculous gifts if they had not been sons of God.

The contrast between the law and the gospel is made in Galatians 4:5. The contrast between the bondage of the law and the privilege of the gospel is summed up in Galatians 4:7 in the words "servant" and "son."

"...Received ye the Spirit by the works of the law, or by the hearing of faith?" (Galatians 3:2).
Question: From whom did you receive the Spirit—from Paul or the Judaizing teachers?
Answer: "He therefore that ministereth [supplieth, A.S.V.] to you the Spirit, and worketh miracles among you, doeth he it by the works of the law, or by the hearing of faith?"

Question:	Who confirmed his teaching by imparting miraculous gifts and working miracles—Paul or the Judaizing teachers?
Answer:	"And because ye are sons, God hath sent forth the Spirit of his Son into your hearts . . ."
Question:	Why did God give you miraculous gifts by me (Paul)?
Answer:	Because you are sons of God.

When one puts Galatians 3:2, 3:5, and 4:6 together, there is no difficulty. The statement in Galatians 4:6 is the answer to the questions that Paul had raised in Galatians 3:2. The statement in 4:6 is a further argument that develops from the previous chapter.

Let us trace the argument backward instead of forward:
1. The Galatians are sons.
2. The Judaizing teachers were denying that the Galatians were sons of God.
3. Proof that they are sons of God: The Galatians had received miraculous gifts.
4. From whom did the Galatians receive miraculous gifts? Answer: Paul (Galatians 3:5).
5. Since the Galatians had received the Spirit from Paul, Paul was an apostle of Christ as he claimed in Galatians 1:1.
6. Since Paul had proved his apostleship, the gospel he preached to the Galatians was a genuine gospel (Galatians 1:13).
7. The gospel of the Judaizing teachers was another gospel, which was not the gospel of Christ (Galatians 1:6).

This is the very heart of the Galatian letter. Who are the sons of God, Paul's converts by the gospel, who had received miraculous endowments through his hands as proof of his apostleship and the genuineness of the gospel he preached, or the converts of the Judaizers with their circumscision and the law? The statements about the Spirit in 3:2, 3:5, and 4:6 are in support of Paul's apostleship and the gospel he preached, thus showing that the Galatians were sons of God and heirs of the promise to Abraham (Galatians 3:26-29). The miraculous operation of the Spirit in an apostle, and the imparting of spiritual gifts, are the very foundation of establishing their apostleship. This is plain to any Bible student. Now as Paul was proving these very points in the book of Galatians, it should be evident that only a miraculous reference to the Spirit could establish this. As already mentioned, a non-miraculous indwelling could have been used as well by the false teachers as by Paul.

Suppose that someone should deny that I am preaching the gospel and that my converts are not sons of God. I answer, "They certainly are sons of God because they have the non-miraculous indwelling of the Holy Spirit." Would that prove that I was preaching the gospel? And would it prove that those converted by me were sons of God? In Galatians 3:2 Paul is presenting evidence to prove to the Galatians that they were sons of God. All three of these references are to establish this fact. Paul, who was an apostle, and could impart spiritual gifts, surely would not attempt to defend his apostleship, the gospel he preached, and the Galatian churches, by appealing to a non-miraculous indwelling of the Spirit as proof.

I JOHN 2:27

8. The last passage that speaks of receiving the Spirit is I John 2:27. "But the anointing which ye have received of him abideth in you, and ye need not that any man teach you: but as the same anointing teacheth you of all things, and is truth, and is no lie, and even as it hath taught you, ye shall abide in him." Was this what is called an ordinary, non-miraculous indwelling? I have seen the passage used to try to support this idea. But a casual reading of the verse will show that the anointing which they had received was miraculous. The statement, "...and ye need not that any man should teach you..." is a reference to the inspiration of those to whom John was writing, while the "any man" is directed toward uninspired false teachers. The anointing which they had received was miraculous gifts. To discern false teachers that claimed inspiration, they were told to try the spirits (4:1). This is a reference to the miraculous gifts of discerning spirits; that is, the gift to distinguish between one who is inspired by the Spirit and false teachers who claimed inspiration. How could a non-miraculous indwelling of the Spirit enable one to detect a false teacher? False teachers today are measured by the Bible, not the anointing of the Spirit. The gift of discerning spirits is mentioned in I Corinthians 12:10 and was necessary as a means of being able to distinguish between the ones that claimed to be inspired teachers, but were false teachers. The fact that the written Word is now the standard that teachers are tested by is positive proof that none now receive the anointing of the Spirit.

In debates that I have had with Pentecostals, they quoted this passage to try to support their claim, yet everyone of them used his Bible constantly in the debate. When I would attempt to get them to lay aside their Bibles and let the anointing, which they claimed to have received, teach them, not a one would accept the challenge. I offer this same challenge to brethren today that are quoting this passage to prove that they have received the anointing of the Spirit. Are they willing to enter into a discussion and rely on the anointing of the Spirit to teach them? If not, then their claim, based on this verse, is a false claim.

I have listed the eight references of receiving the Spirit and all of them are miraculous unless Acts 2:38 is the exception. Two instances, John 7:39 and John 20:22, were before Pentecost and pointed to the coming of the Spirit and the miraculous. The other five, excluding Acts 2:38, are all passages that referred to people that had miraculous gifts. Acts 2:38 was at the very beginning of this miraculous period. The two passages before Acts 2 prepare the way. The five that follow Acts 2 are examples of those who had miraculous gifts. When this is added up, it seems to me that one has a distinct Bible explanation of the gift of the Holy Spirit in Acts 2:38. Put together the six times the word "gift" is used with the eight times the Bible speaks of people "receiving the Spirit," and my conviction is that the "gift of the Spirit" means miraculous, as established by the Bible. If these arguments do not prove it, I must confess that I do not know how to prove anything by the Bible.

AN ANALYSIS OF ACTS 2

The day of Pentecost and the city of Jerusalem sets the stage for the events in Acts 2. The city of Jerusalem and the temple were the heart of Judaism. All that there was in Judaism was symbolized in the city and the temple. The church had its beginning in the city of Jerusalem because its roots were in the types, shadows, prophecies, and promises of the Old Testament. The Old Testament had been looking to this day and the things that would develop from it. The coming of the Holy Spirit upon the apostles was in fulfillment of the prophecy of Joel and the promise of Christ. Judaism had fulfilled its mission and given the Messiah to the world. The culmination of the work of Christ to make possible the redemption of man was now to be realized. The Christ that was rejected and crucified would be exonerated in the very city where He was rejected and crucified. The Holy Spirit, through the apostles, would set forth truth to reverse the verdict of the Jews and Pilate (John 16:7-11). A new covenant would be inaugurated, based on better promises, and offering full remission of sins through the blood of Christ. Here is the background of Acts 2.

The coming of the Spirit upon the apostles brought the question, "What meaneth this?" (Acts 2:12). Peter's sermon is in response to this question. Read the chapter carefully and notice that Peter used one of the words in their question throughout his sermon. Look how the word "this" threads its way through the chapter:
1. Now when "this" was noised abroad—(Acts 2:6)
2. What meaneth "this"—(Acts 2:12)
3. Be "this" known unto you—(Acts 2:14)
4. "This" is that—(Acts 2:16)
5. He hath shed forth "this"—(Acts 2:33)
6. Now when they heard "this"—(Acts 2:37)

The chapter can almost be outlined around the word "this." In response to their question, Peter quoted the prophecy of Joel. Joel's prophecy is the key to the outpouring of the Spirit on the apostles. But this prophecy includes more than the apostles. It includes the miraculous gifts that would be imparted by the apostles. This is clear from the mention of "sons and daughters, young and old, servants and handmaidens." The statement of Joel is a summary of the miraculous during the infancy of the church. It is not limited to the apostles and the household of Cornelius. The language used by Joel cannot be limited to these two events. This is a vital point in the prophecy of Joel that is usually overlooked and is essential to a proper understanding of the second chapter of Acts. I call attention to this because it has a bearing on the gift of the Holy Spirit in Acts 2:38. Keep in mind the question asked the apostles in verse 12. Peter was replying to their question. His reply begins with quoting Joel, but Joel's prophecy extends beyond what the apostles had received. It cannot be made to extend only to the household of Cornelius. This leaves only one other possible thing that it could include. The only other possible thing that can be included is the miraculous gifts that came through the laying on of the apostles' hands. The pouring out of the Holy Spirit on the apostles which qualified them for their work, the pouring out of the Spirit on Cornelius and his household to establish that the gospel was for the Gentile as well as the Jew, and the spiritual gifts that came through the laying on of the hands of the apostles are the sum of the miraculous work of the Spirit from Pentecost until revelation was completed and confirmed. All of this is summarized in the prophecy of Joel. Peter quoted the prophecy to show that what the apostle received was in fulfillment of Joel 2, but Joel's prophecy included the gifts that came through the laying on of the apostles' hands. This being true, why be surprised that Peter extended the prophecy of Joel to baptized believers?

THE WORK OF THE HOLY SPIRIT 149

Go back to the question in Acts 2:12. The inquiry was referring to the pouring out of the Spirit on the apostles. Peter replies that the answer to this question was found in Joel's prophecy. But the prophecy did not stop with the apostles being baptized in the Holy Spirit. The prophecy also included spiritual gifts that would come through the laying on of the apostles' hands. This is clear from the statement of Joel and from the development of the miraculous in the book of Acts. Since Peter was explaining Joel's prophecy, and the prophecy included spiritual gifts through the laying on of the apostles' hands, would it not be reasonable to conclude that Peter's promise of the gift of the Holy Spirit to believers would be what the prophecy promised? Joel's prophecy was the basis of Peter's discussion of the Holy Spirit. Joel's prophecy has nothing in it that is non-miraculous. Why would Peter quote a prophecy having to do only with the miraculous and then conclude by promising a non-miraculous gift without any explanation?

Again, let me remind the reader that the New Testament is written against the background of the Old Testament. The kingdom in the New Testament differs widely from the kingdom in the Old Testament. The first preaching of the gospel was to Jews who had an Old Testament background. One of the main problems of the New Testament was the Jew making the transition from the fleshly, limited, national kingdom of the Old Testament, to the spiritual, universal kingdom of the New Testament. Many of the characteristics that were peculiar to Judaism were the very opposite of the characteristics that are peculiar to Christianity. Judaism was tied to the fleshly descendents of Abraham, the land of Palestine, the city of Jerusalem, and the temple. Christianity is not based upon the blood of Abraham, but on the blood of Christ. Christianity does not have to do with the flesh of Abraham, but the faith of Abraham. Because of the fleshly nature of Judaism, there were distinctions that were based on the flesh. These were never meant to show respect of person, as God is no respecter of persons (Acts 10:34).

The arrangement of the temple had fleshly distinctions. Its purpose was twofold: a) It was to keep separate the lineage of Abraham to Christ. b) The limitation of fleshly blemishes was to symbolize spiritual truths of the gospel, but these symbols were not one of respect of person. The lamb without blemish was to foreshadow Christ, the perfect Lamb of God. But the Jews misread these and concluded that the Jew was better than others. This was the frame of mind of the Jews as the apostles proclaimed the gospel for the first time in Jerusalem. The pouring out of the Holy Spirit on the household of Cornelius shows the problem that was created in the New Testament from this arrangement. But this was because of the typical nature of Judaism. The prophecy of Joel anticipates this problem and is intended to show that these distinctions are not to be found in the church. Just as the pouring out of the Holy Spirit on Cornelius and his household was to prove that the Gentile stood on an equality before God, so the miraculous gifts to all men, without distinction, were to show that all were equal before God. While the gospel teaches that there are distinctions of function, it also teaches that there is equality before God for all. Under the gospel, a man is not any nearer to God than a woman. A Christian Jew is no nearer God than a Gentile. A free man is no nearer God than a slave. The miraculous gifts not only furnished revelation for the church during this period, but they also supplied evidence that all these distinctions in Judaism were gone. When a woman received a miraculous gift, it was evidence that spiritually she stood on the same equality with man. A woman receiving a miraculous gift did not prove that there were no distinctions of function and that a woman could do every thing that a man could do. I Corinthians 14:33 and 34, and I Timothy 2:10 to 12 show this. There were no women apostles, elders, or evangelists, and the reasons are given in the verses just cited. When a slave received a miraculous gift, it was proof that he was equal before God with a free man. All of this was to show that all men could be heirs of the promise to Abraham and that all men are one in Christ (Galatians 3:26-29).

Fleshly differences can even now affect the unity of the church. Consideration of the distribution of miraculous gifts to all ranks of men could have helped us see that God is not pleased with a pride of heart that will not allow all men to be brothers and one in Christ. Some today seem to think as the Jew did, that God respects the rich, not the poor; the educated, not the uneducated; the white race, not the black race. Such would profit from a careful study of the prophecy of Joel.

This is the meaning of Acts 2:39. It is a summary of the prophecy of Joel. The question asked the apostles was, "What meaneth this?" Peter's sermon was an explanation of what had occurred and appealed to the prophecy of Joel in his reply.

Compare Acts 2:39 and Acts 2:16 to 21:

Acts 2:39	Acts 2:17-18
To you and all that are afar off	Jew and Gentile—All flesh
Your children	Sons and daughters
As many as the Lord our God should call	Servants, handmaidens

THE WORK OF THE HOLY SPIRIT

A careful study of this passage, with this analysis, shows two things: 1) that the gospel was to be without distinction; 2) to establish that the gospel was to be without distinction, the gifts were given without distinction. A passage should always be studied in its context. Peter began his sermon with the prophecy of Joel and, as recorded by Luke, closed it with a summary of the prophecy. This is the thought through the chapter and with this in mind there will be no difficulty in seeing that verse 39 is a summary of Joel's prophecy. The question was about the miraculous (Acts 2:12 points back to Acts 2:1-4). Peter's reply was a prophecy that contained a promise of the miraculous. Peter referred to the promise of the Father in Acts 2:33 which can only be traced back to Joel's prophecy. (See Luke 24:49.) Since Peter had used the word "promise" in verse 33, which was based on Joel's prophecy, and Joel's prophecy included miraculous gifts without distinction to believers, why should the promise of Acts 2:39 refer to anything else? To insist that if the gift in Acts 2:38 is miraculous (then Acts 2:39 will prove the miraculous continues today), is to ignore the context of Acts 2:39. But someone is ready to say that if the gift in Acts 2:38 is miraculous, then either the miraculous must continue today, or else repentance and baptism for remission of sins cannot be preached today. But this does not follow. For example, Mark 16:16 teaches faith and baptism in order to be saved. But verses 17 and 18 speak of signs that followed believers. Does anyone have any problem with teaching Mark 16:16 today while leaving the signs of Mark 16:17 and 18 where they belong? Let me see if I can illustrate it for you.

MARK 16:16 and 17

| Believe | Baptize | Saved | These signs shall follow believers |

ACTS 2:38

| Repent | Be Baptized | Remission of sins | Gift of the Holy Spirit |

I make no claim to attempt to re-punctuate the Scriptures. The punctuation was not inspired, but was put in by translators. The verses were not put in by inspired writers. For the sake of illustration, let me rearrange Acts 2:38 and 39.

MARK 16:16	ACTS 2:38
He that believeth and is baptized shall be saved.	Repent and be baptized for the remission of sins.

MARK 16:17	ACTS 2:39
These signs shall follow them that believe.	Ye shall receive the gift of the Holy Spirit. For the promise is to you and to your children.

If the phrase, "the gift of the Holy Spirit," is put with verse 39 instead of 38, then Acts 2:38 is parallel with Mark 16:16 and Acts 2:39 is parallel with Mark 16:17. The promise of Acts 2:39 is the promise of Acts 2:33. The promise of Acts 2:33 is the promise of Joel, Acts 2:16 to 21. The promise of Joel was what the apostles had received (Acts 2:1-4; Acts 2:12). The promise of the prophecy of Joel also includes the gifts that would come through the hands of the apostles. It was necessary for the apostles to receive the Spirit in fulfillment of Joel's prophecy before the other part of Joel's prophecy could be fulfilled; that is, spiritual gifts through the hands of the apostles. This is the context of Acts 2:39. Since Peter had used the word "promise" in Acts 2:33, a reference to Joel's prophecy (Acts 2:16-21, Luke 24:49) and the promise of Joel's prophecy included spiritual gifts by the hands of the apostles to baptized believers (Mark 16:16-17), why would Peter not use the word "promise" in Acts 2:39 in reference to this? The phrase, "Even as many as the Lord our God shall call," is not a statement in relation to all men of all time receiving the promise mentioned. Acts 2:39 is a summary of Joel's prophecy, as already shown, and the phrase, "As many as the Lord our God shall call," is a promise that the Spirit would be given without distinction, just as Joel's prophecy had stated. The first part of Acts 2:39, "you" is equal to the Jew. "To all that are afar off" is a reference to the Gentiles, and both of these equal the "all flesh" of Joel's prophecy. Are not sons and daughters children? "Even as many as the Lord our God shall call" equals the servants and the handmaidens of Joel's prophecy, and all of these together show that miraculous endowments would be given without distinction; that is, they would be given to all ranks. Emphasis in Joel's prophecy and in Acts 2:39 is that spiritual gifts would be given without any distinction. Gifts being given without distinction were to show the oneness and the unity of those baptized into one body. The distribution of the gifts, as foretold in Joel's prophecy, is to underscore the truth that the gospel is for all without any distinction. It is a mistake to take Acts 2:39 out of the context of Acts 2.

REVIEW THE MIRACULOUS IN ACTS 2

1. Acts 2:1 to 4 is miraculous.

THE WORK OF THE HOLY SPIRIT

2. The question asked of the apostles in Acts 2:12 is a question about the miraculous.
3. The quotation of Peter from Joel is a reference only to the miraculous.
4. Acts 2:33 speaks only of the miraculous.

Does it not seem unusual that every reference to the Spirit from the first verse to verse 33 speaks of the miraculous, and then Peter, without any explanation, passes to the non-miraculous in verse 38. Place yourself in the audience on that Pentecost day. You have seen the miraculous manifestation of the Spirit. You ask for an explanation of the miraculous. The preacher quotes a passage that mentions only the miraculous and then you are promised the Spirit as a non-miraculous indwelling. What would be your reaction? In the days of miraculous manifestations, for an apostle to promise the Spirit and one receive no spiritual gift would have made that person question the credibility of the apostle. Surely, Peter would not, in his first sermon, make a promise that would have completely denied his credibility as an apostle.

Since the people had heard and seen the miraculous manifestations of the Spirit (Acts 2:33), just suppose that Peter baptized one for the remissions of sins, and following his baptism, the person inquired of Peter, "What about the promise of the gift of the Holy Spirit that you made?"

Peter replies, "You received the Spirit when you were baptized, but it is non-miraculous."

Can you not visualize the reaction? Since the apostles had the Spirit miraculously, would not the ones that were promised the Spirit expect to receive a miraculous manifestation? What would have happened in the period of the miraculous for one to have claimed to have the Spirit, but no manifestation?

This is even a valid challenge to those who claim the miraculous today. Do we not say to them, "Since you claim the miraculous, produce a manifestation (that is, restore sight to one blind from birth, or make one that is lame from birth walk)."

ACTS 5:32

"And we are his witnesses of these things; and so is also the Holy Ghost, whom God hath given to them that obey him," (Acts 5:32).

Acts 5:32 is sometimes used to support the argument that the gift of the Spirit in Acts 2:38 is non-miraculous. This passage does not add any scriptural support to the claim that the gift of Acts 2:38 is non-miraculous. The passage supports the very opposite and the position that I have taken concerning the gift of the Holy Spirit in Acts 2:38.

Look at the context of Acts 5:32. The Sadducees had accused the apostles of teaching false doctrine on the resurrection of Christ (Acts 4:2). Peter and John had healed the lame man (Acts 3:1-8). The healing of the lame man resulted in the people gathering in Solomon's Porch (Acts 3:11). Peter used the opportunity to preach, and among other things, preached the resurrection of Christ and stated that they were witnesses (Acts 3:15). The rest of Chapter 3 is a record of Peter's sermon. Chapter 4 begins with the reaction of the Sadducees to Peter's sermon and states that what disturbed the Sadducees was the apostles' preaching the resurrection of Christ (Acts 4:2). The Sadducees put Peter and John in jail and the next day questioned them as to the power and name by which they had healed the lame man. Acts 4:8 to 12 is Peter's reply, and his reply attributed the power to the healing of the lame man by Christ, who had been raised from the dead. They then threatened Peter and John and demanded that they cease preaching in the name of Christ (Acts 4:17). Peter and John returned to their own company and gave a report of what happened. Then they had prayer; the place was shaken; they were filled with the Holy Spirit and spake the Word with boldness (Acts 4:31). "And with great power gave the apostles witness of the resurrection of the Lord Jesus," (Acts 4:33). Passing over the selling of land and the death of Ananias and Sapphira, Acts 5:12 says that many signs and wonders were wrought by the apostles. The Sadducees put the apostles in prison, but an angel opened the door and told them to go speak all the words of this life. The High Priest, the captain, and the Chief Priest heard this and sent the captain to bring the apostles before the council, and they were questioned by the council and commanded not to teach any more in this name. Peter told the council that the apostles would obey God rather than men. He again states that Christ was raised from the dead (Acts 5:30). Acts 5:32 concludes Peter's defense of preaching the resurrection of Christ. The verse says, "And we [apostles] are his witnesses of these things..."

Question: What things?
Answer: The resurrection of Christ. "...And so also is the Holy Spirit, whom God hath given to them that obey him."
Question: What was the Holy Spirit a witness of?

THE WORK OF THE HOLY SPIRIT

Answer: The resurrection of Christ.
Question: How was the Holy Spirit a witness of the resurrection of Christ?
Answer: The miraculous manifestation of the Spirit through the apostles.

The question under consideration was the resurrection of Christ. The proof offered was: 1) The apostles were witnesses; that is, they had seen Christ after He was resurrected. 2) The Holy Spirit was also a witness of the resurrection of Christ. The miraculous manifestations of the Spirit through the apostles were proof that they were obedient to God, for God would not give a miraculous manifestation to a false teacher. Christians today cannot qualify on either count of Acts 5:32: 1) They are not witnesses of Christ's resurrection. 2) The Holy Spirit, in a Christian (non-miraculous), could not witness to the resurrection of Christ. Who would think of attempting to establish the resurrection of Christ today by saying the Holy Spirit dwelling in him proved that Christ arose from the dead?

Acts 5:32 offers a double testimony of the resurrection of Christ: the apostles who were witnesses, and the miraculous manifestations of the Spirit through the apostles. This is exactly what Jesus promised the apostles in John 15:26 and 27. Jesus promised that the Spirit would testify of Him (John 15:26). He also states that the apostles would be witnesses (John 15:27). Acts 5:32 is an example of the fulfillment of the promise in John 15:26 and 27. Acts 5:32, instead of supporting the idea of the gift of Acts 2:38 being non-miraculous, proves the very opposite.

Before I close this chapter, let me raise some questions. If the gift of the Holy Spirit is a non-miraculous gift that one receives when baptized, what does the Spirit do? Those that believe the Spirit leads and directs only through the Word are faced with explaining why one has received this gift of the Spirit, but the gift does not do anything for the Christian apart from the Word.

Then there are some that believe the gift of the Holy Spirit received at baptism does something for the Christian in addition to the Word. The ones that take this position are faced with the problem of identifying how the Spirit does this. Since miraculous manifestations have ceased, the only things left to identify the Spirit working are impressions and subjective feelings. This has been the claim of the denominational world through the years. They know the Spirit works in them, leads and directs, because they feel the Spirit. This position can only lead to subjective feelings being placed above revelation.

Second, does the interpretation that the gift of the Spirit is miraculous, lead to the conclusion that miracles continue today? The answer to this question is no. This has already been shown in the previous discussion. This is usually the main objection that I have had presented to the proposition that I have set forth in this chapter. As I close this chapter, let me say again that if the reader wants to still insist that the gift of the Holy Spirit is a non-miraculous gift received at baptism, and believes that the Spirit leads and directs the Christian only through the Word, I shall not make an issue out of it. This position has problems that I am unable to solve and this was one of the things that led me to restudy the Scriptures, and finally led to the conclusion that I have set forth in this chapter. If the reader wants to struggle with the problems that come from the position that one receives the gift of the Holy Spirit in a non-miraculous way when baptized, I grant him that privilege and assure him that I will have the highest respect for him. I only ask that I be granted the same privilege and respect. I simply ask that each one read and measure by the Word the things presented in this chapter, and draw his own conclusions as to whether or not I have proven by the Scriptures that the gift of the Holy Spirit was miraculous and ceased when revelation was completed and confirmed.

A WORD STUDY

In the previous chapter attention has been given to the meaning of the gift of the Holy Spirit. A further study of some words used in the New Testament will add clarification to this previous study.

I. MANIFESTATION

The word "manifestation" was used by Paul twice in his letters to the Corinthians. Paul used the word in his discussion of the gifts of the Spirit in I Corinthians 12. "But the manifestation of the Spirit is given to every man to profit withal," (I Corinthians 12:7). Since spiritual gifts were provided while revelation was being given and confirmed, it must be clear that there were some means of establishing this to avoid any deception by false teachers who also claimed inspiration. One of the means of avoiding any deception on the part of false teachers is found in the use of the word "manifestation" in connection with spiritual gifts. The word means "exhibition, disclosure, to make visible." This very argument is made by Peter in the second chapter of Acts. "Therefore being by the right hand of God exalted, and having received of the Father the promise of the Holy Spirit, he hath shed forth this, which ye now see and hear," (Acts 2:33). One of the proofs that the apostles had received the Holy Spirit was the manifestation that was visible. This is the very point that is intended by the word "manifestation" in I Corinthians 12:7. I Corinthians 12:7 prepares the way for the mention of the various gifts in the following verses. When anyone had a gift, there was always a manifestation; that is, an exhibition or visible evidence that he had a gift.

The second time Paul used the word "manifestation" is in II Corinthians 4:2: "But have renounced the hidden things of dishonesty, not walking in craftiness, nor handling the word of God deceitfully; but by manifestation of the truth commending ourselves to every man's conscience in the sight of God." The background of this chapter is II Corinthians 2:17: "For we are not as many, which corrupt the word of God: but as of sincerity, but as of God, in the sight of God speak we in Christ." Here Paul contrasted his preaching with that of false teachers. These false teachers were guilty of corrupting the Word of God. Chapter four and verse two is a further contrast between Paul and the false teachers. How could Paul have proved that his teaching was not false? It was by a manifestation of truth that commended the gospel to all that were honest enough to look at the evidence. The manifestation of the truth was such a visible, miraculous confirmation that any honest heart could see that Paul was indeed an apostle and his gospel was inspired. Here was a clear and unmistakable contrast. Paul's preaching was accompanied with manifestations that were visible for all to see.

In the period when there were direct and miraculous operations of the Holy Spirit, for one to claim to have received the Spirit and have no manifestation would have been foolish. No one would have believed the claim.

II. DEMONSTRATION

There is another word used by Paul that needs to be considered.

> And I, brethren, when I came to you, came not with excellency of speech or of wisdom, declaring unto you the testimony of God.
> For I determined not to know any thing among you, save Jesus Christ, and him crucified.
> And I was with you in weakness, and in fear, and in much trembling.
> And my speech and my preaching was not with enticing words of man's wisdom, but in demonstration of the Spirit and of power:
> That your faith should not stand in the wisdom of men, but in the power of God. (I Corinthians 2:1-5).

These verses set forth the contrast between Paul's preaching and that of the false teachers in Corinth. The preaching of the false teachers consisted only of "enticing words of man's wisdom." The Corinthians had nothing but the empty words of these false teachers to establish their claims. Paul did not depend on such means to establish the gospel he preached. He confirmed the gospel, testimony of God, in the demonstration of the Spirit and power. The word "power" denotes miraculous power to confirm the Word (Mark 16:20). But what was a demonstration in the Spirit? It was a visible manifestation of the Spirit that left no doubt as to whether the testimony proclaimed by Paul was inspired.

Paul's statement to the Thessalonians made plain the purpose of a demonstration in the Spirit. "For our gospel came not unto you in word only, but also in power, and in the Holy Spirit, and in much assurance; as ye know what manner of men we were among you for

THE WORK OF THE HOLY SPIRIT 159

your sake," (I Thessalonians 1:5). The Thessalonians did not have only Paul's word, but if they did not have only his word, what was there in addition to his word? The answer is found in the next phrase, "in power, and in the Holy Spirit." The gospel preached by Paul in Thessalonica was confirmed in the demonstration and manifestation of the Spirit. The purpose was that the Thessalonians might have full assurance that the gospel they had received was an inspired gospel. How would it have been possible for them to have had assurance without the miraculous confirmation? They did not have a New Testament to read and measure Paul's preaching by. We have a New Testament today and measure men's teaching by it. In what way could a non-miraculous indwelling of the Spirit provide assurance to anyone?

Again, it should be evident that in the period of direct revelation and miraculous confirmation, for one to have claimed to have the Spirit without either a demonstration or manifestation would have been useless. Who would have believed him? Any false teacher could have claimed he had the Spirit and would have had as much proof as an apostle if having had the Spirit was a reference to a non-miraculous indwelling. Try to visualize the situation if there had been two groups that had the Spirit during the time of direct revelation and confirmation. One group would have claimed to have received the Spirit and have a manifestation of the gift. A second group would have claimed to have the Spirit, but they would have had no manifestation. They could not have shown any visible sign that they had received the Spirit. Would anyone have accepted the claim of the second group?

We have a completed and confirmed revelation today. It is a mistake to read passages that were written to churches that had miraculous gifts and the references to their having received the Spirit, and equate that with our situation today when there are no miraculous gifts, nor do we need them. Confusion results when we fail to make this distinction.

It is my conviction that the misunderstanding of Acts 2:38 has led to reading into other passages that which was never there in the first place. The letters that were written to churches were to churches that had miraculous gifts. When references are made in the Epistles about their having received the Spirit, what would they have understood this to mean? When miraculous manifestations were visible in their assemblies, would they ever have thought of having the Spirit in a way that had no visible manifestation?

Consider the Corinthian letter. It is addressed to the church at Corinth (1:2). The very first thing mentioned after the salutation is the miraculous gifts of the Corinthians. References are made to miraculous endowments throughout the letter. Chapters 12 and 14 are given entirely to the discussion of miraculous gifts. Now read such passages as 3:16 and 6:19. "Know ye not that ye are the temple of God, and that the Spirit of God dwelleth in you?" (3:16). Are Chapters 1:5-8, and Chapters 12 and 14 written to the same people as Chapters 3 and 6? When Paul said that the manifestation of the Spirit is given to every man to profit withal (12:7), and there were miraculous manifestations in the assemblies as Chapters 12 and 14 show, what would the Corinthians understand the dwelling of the Spirit to mean in 3:16 and 6:19?

Look at the facts. Here was a church that assembled and there were miraculous manifestations of the Spirit in the assembly. A letter was written to the church correcting the abuses of these miraculous manifestations of the Spirit. The statement was made that the Spirit dwelled in them. Would it have ever occurred to these people that Paul was speaking of a non-miraculous indwelling? In a church that had miraculous manifestations of the Spirit, what would be the evidence that the Spirit was dwelling in them? Would it not have been the visible manifestations of the Spirit? In such a situation, would they have ever thought of having received the Spirit and it not having been a miraculous reception?

Someone might say today that the Corinthians knew they also had the Spirit in a non-miraculous indwelling as well as miraculous. But that is the very thing that Paul refuted in the letter. Read it for yourself: "But I will come to you shortly, if the Lord will, and will know, not the **speech** of them which are puffed up, but the **power**. For the kingdom of God is not in **word**, but in power," (4:19-20). Here were false teachers that claimed the Spirit, but who had no miraculous manifestations. All they had was speech; that is, words. Such were false apostles (II Corinthians 11:13-15). The statement that the kingdom is not "in word" means "word only." Compare I Thessalonians 1:5. The "power" means miraculous power to reveal and confirm—the manifestations of the Spirit. In a congregation that had miraculous gifts, for one to have claimed to have received the Spirit without a manifestation would have placed him in the same class with false teachers who had nothing but words without any manifestation.

THE WORK OF THE HOLY SPIRIT 161

Another objection that is raised is that the pronouns will not allow the indwelling of the Spirit in 3:16 and 6:19 to be miraculous. In 3:16 there are the pronouns "ye" and "you." In 6:19 the pronouns are "your" and "ye." But let us compare some other passages. In Chapter 1:5-8 Paul introduced the discussion of miraculous gifts in the church at Corinth. He even used the word "gift" in 1:7, and there is no doubt but that this means miraculous gifts. Now look at the pronouns: "That in everything YE...was confirmed in YOU...THAT YE...shall also confirm YOU...." These are statements that are about miraculous gifts. Yet Paul used the pronouns "ye" and "you" just as he did in 3:16 and 6:19. Thus, the attempt to avoid the fact that Chapters 3 and 6 were not written to the same people as Chapters 12 and 14 falls short by appealing to the pronouns.

Again, in Chapter 9:1-2, Paul used the pronouns "ye" and "you" in connection with the miraculous gifts that were in the church at Corinth. The seal of Paul's apostleship as proof that the Corinthians were in the Lord can only be a reference to the miraculous gifts they had received through the laying on of Paul's hands. The abundance of the gifts in the church at Corinth was evidence that Paul was "not a whit behind the very chiefest apostle," (II Corinthians 11:4-6).

But there is still a further problem in trying to make the pronouns of 3:16 and 6:19 allow for a distinction between the miraculous and the non-miraculous indwelling. If 3:16 and 6:19 mean a non-miraculous indwelling, they exclude the miraculous indwelling. Would it not have been rather strange for Paul to write to a church that had miraculous gifts, and say that the church knew the Spirit was in it, and exclude the miraculous manifestations as the evidence, without explaining anything about it? Were not the miraculous manifestations of the Spirit in the Corinthians proof that the Spirit was in them? If not, what was the evidence? It is beyond my ability to comprehend an apostle writing to a church that had miraculous endowments and tell them that they knew the Spirit was dwelling in them, and mean a non-miraculous indwelling.

Suppose the congregation which you attend had miraculous gifts just as the church at Corinth. Then a letter is written by an apostle that had laid hands on members of the congregation and imparted these miraculous gifts. The letter is written to correct the abuse of miraculous gifts. The letter mentions that the Spirit dwells in the members of the congregation that you are a part of. You have attended the assemblies regularly and have seen the manifestations of the Spirit. What would you understand the dwelling of the Spirit to mean? Would you think of the miraculous manifestations, or would you think the reference was to a non-miraculous indwelling? I am confident that no one would ever jump to the conclusion that the apostle who wrote the letter, and had imparted the miraculous gifts to the church, would be speaking of a non-miraculous indwelling.

Would this make it impossible to use I Corinthians 6:19 to show that the body is not to be abused? No, this would not follow. The principle stated in this verse is just as true today as it was when Paul wrote to the Corinthians. The miracles that Christ did to prove His Deity are now written, and prove through the written Word what they one time proved to those who saw His miracles (John 20:30-31). There is not a single truth that is lost as a result of the miracles being written instead of being performed for every generation. The same is true of I Corinthians 6:19. The miraculous manifestation of the Spirit in the church at Corinth is equal to the signs of John 20:30-31. The principle that is contained in I Corinthians 6:19 is established for us on the same basis.

The 12th and 14th chapters of I Corinthians deal with miraculous gifts. I do not think any would deny this. These gifts have ceased. But there are principles that are taught in both chapters that apply today. We are not exempt from the principles taught in these chapters just because the principles are found in a chapter dealing with miraculous gifts. For example, Paul used the physical body to show the unity of the church, or body of Christ. But this illustration was used by Paul as an illustration of the miraculous gifts that were in the church at Corinth. The various members of the body were used by Paul to illustrate the various miraculous gifts that the Corinthians had. Shall we conclude that the principle of the unity of the body cannot be applied today because it is found in a chapter dealing with miraculous gifts? I do not think anyone would draw such a conclusion. If the principle of unity which is taught in a chapter on miraculous gifts can still be used, even though the gifts have ceased, why is not the same true of I Corinthians 6:19, even though this is speaking of the miraculous gifts that were in the church at Corinth?

Again, the 14th chapter is given entirely to the discussion of the use of miraculous gifts in the assembly. Are the principles that are found in the chapter to be rejected because they are found in a chapter that deals with miraculous gifts? Surely no one would take this position. Notice some of the principles that are taught in the chapter:
1. The assemblies are to edify (I Corinthians 14:3).

THE WORK OF THE HOLY SPIRIT

2. A woman cannot teach over man in a mixed assembly (14:33-34).
3. All things are to be done decently and in order (14:40).

Here are three principles that we follow today. Yet they are found in a chapter that is discussing the proper use of miraculous gifts in the assembly. The miraculous gifts have ceased, but these principles and truths: 1) assemblies are to edify; 2) a woman cannot preach in an assembly where there are men; 3) things must be done decently, are just as applicable to us as they were to the Corinthians. If this is true, and it is, of Chapter 14, where the discussion is of the miraculous operation of the Spirit in the church at Corinth, why may not the same thing be true of the principle in I Corinthians 6:19, though the reference to the Spirit is of the miraculous manifestations of the Spirit that dwelt in the Corinthians.

Fornication was sinful for a Jew under the law. The Jew certainly did not have the non-miraculous indwelling of the Spirit as is claimed for Christians today. Sexual relations are reserved for marriage of proper subjects. Fornication was wrong before the Christian Age and is still wrong for the same reason. Fornication is wrong even for sinners. This very chapter shows this to be true (6:11). Paul made the appeal to the Corinthians because they had the Spirit in a miraculous way—spiritual gifts. He said, "... Know ye not that your body is the temple of the Holy Spirit which is in you, which ye have of God," (I Corinthians 6:19). Look at the word "know." What would be the first thing that would come to the mind of a church that had spiritual gifts when told that the Spirit was in them? Would such people not necessarily think of the Spirit in its miraculous manifestations? For example, if we had spiritual gifts today—miraculous manifestations—and the preacher said, "Know ye not that the Spirit dwells in you," what would you think he meant by the statement? Would you understand it to mean miraculous or non-miraculous? I am confident that no one would ever think of having the Spirit in any other way than miraculous. But this was the situation in which the statement was made to the Corinthians.

Pentecostals claim all the spiritual gifts today in the same manner that all the miraculous manifestations were claimed by the church at Corinth. Of course, they have none of these. But whoever heard a Pentecostal talk about having the Spirit and the audience understanding it to mean anything but miraculous? If this is true today with those who claim miraculous gifts, would it not have been doubly true in a church that actually had miraculous gifts?

The Corinthian letter was written to a church that had spiritual gifts. One of the main purposes of the letter was to correct the abuse of spiritual gifts. Chapters 3:16 and 6:19 were to the same people as Chapters 12 and 14. If not, then it becomes the responsibility of those who say these verses are not to the same people to present the proof. Where is the proof? Paul did not write anything in connection with these verses to indicate that he was speaking of the Spirit in a non-miraculous way.

If it had not been for the non-miraculous interpretation of the gifts in Acts 2:38, would not I Corinthians 3:16 and 6:19 have been considered in the context of the whole letter, which deals with spiritual gifts and not with a non-miraculous operation of the Spirit?

III. ANOINTED

Those that believe in the direct operation of the Holy Spirit today use the passages that speak of the anointing of the Spirit as a basis for their belief. Pentecostals try to use these passages to prove that spiritual gifts continue today. Some brethren that do not believe in spiritual gifts today use some of these passages to try to prove a non-miraculous indwelling of the Spirit, and an operation of the Spirit in the Christian apart from the Word. Denominational preachers who use these passages to prove a direct operation of the Spirit are wrong because there is no direct operation of the Spirit today on the sinner or the Christian. The Spirit works through the Word in converting the sinner and in edifying the Christian. Pentecostals are wrong because spiritual gifts ceased with the completion of revelation. Brethren that use these passages to support a non-miraculous indwelling and the operation of the Spirit in the Christian apart from the Word are wrong because the passages always refer to a miraculous operation of the Spirit.

1. Luke 4:18-19

The Bible is its best interpreter. Let the Bible explain the meaning of the anointing of the Spirit in Luke 4:18-19:

> The Spirit of the Lord is upon me, because he hath anointed me to preach the gospel to the poor; he hath sent me to heal the brokenhearted, to preach deliverance to the captives, and recovering of sight to the blind, to set at liberty them that are bruised,
> To preach the acceptable year of the Lord.

The phrase, "The Spirit of the Lord is upon me," explains the meaning of Christ being anointed to preach the gospel. Surely, no one would consider this anointing of Christ as being a non-miraculous anointing of the Spirit. John 3:34 is a commentary on Christ being anointed with the Spirit. The first mention of the anointing of the Spirit in the New Testament is a reference to Christ and means a miraculous anointing.

2. Acts 10:38

"How God anointed Jesus of Nazareth with the Holy Ghost and with power: who went about doing good, and healing all that were oppressed of the devil; for God was with him," (Acts 10:38). If there is any question as to the meaning of Christ being anointed with the Spirit, this verse settles it. Peter stated that "God anointed Jesus." But how did God anoint Jesus? The verse leaves no doubt. Jesus of Nazareth was anointed with the Holy Spirit and power. When Christ was anointed with the Holy Spirit and power, it was a miraculous anointing and miraculous power. Now we have an inspired interpretation of the anointing of the Spirit.

3. II Corinthians 1:21

"Now he which stablisheth us with you in Christ, and hath anointed us, is God," (II Corinthians 1:21). This statement was made by Paul, an apostle. In both of the Corinthian letters Paul was defending his apostleship against false teachers. Notice the following passages in II Corinthians: 2:17, 3:1, 4:1-7, 5:12, 5:19-20, 6:6-7, 10:8, 10:13, 11:1-6, 11:13-15, 11:23, 12:12-13, 13:3, 13:6 and 13:10. All of these passages struck at the false teachers that were disturbing the church at Corinth, and were denying that Paul was an apostle of Christ. It is in this context that Paul appealed to his being anointed of God.

The first part of the verse shows that Paul had in mind the miraculous gifts that he had as an apostle: "Now he which stablisheth us with you in Christ." Berry translates as follows: "Now he who confirms us with you unto Christ, and anointed us is God." Mark 16:20 shows that the Word was confirmed by signs and miracles. But the apostles were also confirmed as apostles by signs and miracles (II Corinthians 12:12-13). The Corinthians were confirmed as a God-approved church through the miraculous gifts they received through the hands of Paul (I Corinthians 1:6-7). The anointing that Paul received was the miraculous anointing that qualified him to be an apostle (Luke 24:49; Acts 1:8). Surely the anointing of an apostle cannot be proof of a non-miraculous anointing today. One might as well claim to be an ambassador of Christ today as to claim he has the anointing of the Spirit. One could as reasonably claim that he is the Pope and successor of an apostle. Paul was confirmed as an apostle by the signs and miracles that accompanied the gospel he preached. The Corinthians were stablished, or confirmed, with him in Christ by the miraculous gifts they received through his hands. Paul was confirmed as an apostle by the anointing of the Spirit. We have no living apostles today, and therefore no anointing of the Spirit. One might as well claim direct revelation which was promised to the apostles as to claim the anointing of the Spirit received by an apostle.

4. I John 2:18-27

Little children, it is the last time: and as ye have heard that antichrist shall come, even now are there many antichrists; whereby we know that it is the last time.

They went out from us, but they were not of us; for if they had been of us, they would no doubt have continued with us: but they went out, that they might be made manifest that they were not all of us.

But ye have an unction from the Holy One, and ye know all things.

I have not written unto you because ye know not the truth, but because ye know it, and that no lie is of the truth.

Who is a liar but he that denieth that Jesus is the Christ? He is antichrist, that denieth the Father and the Son.

Whosoever denieth the Son, the same hath not the Father: [but] he that acknowledgeth the Son hath the Father also.

Let that therefore abide in you, which ye have heard from the beginning.

If that which ye have heard from the beginning shall remain in you, ye also shall continue in the Son, and in the Father.

And this is the promise that he hath promised us, even eternal life.

These things have I written unto you concerning them that seduce you.

But the anointing which ye have received of him abideth in you, and ye need not that any man teach you: but as the same anointing teacheth you of all things, and is truth, and is no lie, and even as it hath taught you, ye shall abide in him. (I John 2:18-27).

THE WORK OF THE HOLY SPIRIT

THE CONTEXT

The anointing of verses 20 and 27 is sometimes used to try to prove that Christians today have a non-miraculous anointing of the Spirit. A study of the context of the verses, as well as the verses, shows that this is not a reference to a non-miraculous indwelling of the Spirit.

A. "The last hour . . ." This points to the end of the Jewish state. In a previous chapter, I have discussed the significance of the fall of Jerusalem and the end of the Jewish state. When John wrote this Epistle, he mentions the last hour because of the nearness of the overthrow of the temple and the Jewish state. The signs given by Christ enabled John to know that what Christ had foretold was now near at hand. Christ had said, ". . .When ye shall see all these things, KNOW THAT IT IS NEAR, EVEN AT THE DOORS," (Matthew 24:33). Paul used the phrase, ". . .as ye see the day approaching," (Hebrews 10:25). Since Christ had said, "Know that it is near, even at the door," John saw this and said it was the last hour. The attempt to project this still out in the future ignores the context. John said, ". . .Even NOW have there arisen many antichrists." The antichrists were working when John wrote the Epistle.

B. "They went out from us . . ." The antichrists refer to the ones that denied that Christ was the promised Messiah of the Old Testament and the Son of God. A study of the book of Acts will reveal who these were (Acts 21:20; Galatians 2:4). Because of Paul's opposition to these false teachers, the time came when they separated themselves completely from any claim to be in the church. "These be they who SEPARATE THEMSELVES, sensual, HAVING NOT THE SPIRIT," (Jude 19). The ones who separated themselves in Jude were the ones that John spoke of as "having gone out from us," (I John 2:19). The ones that Jude described as having not the Spirit are the ones that John pictured as being made manifest that they were not all of us (Jude 19; I John 2:19).

C. "But ye have an unction from the Holy One, and ye know all things," (I John 2:20). The anointing from the Holy One was the miraculous gifts that John's readers had received through the hands of an apostle. The last part of the verse is a direct statement showing inspired revelation. Miraculous gifts supplied knowledge by direct revelation. What man today gains any knowledge by a non-miraculous indwelling of the Spirit? Even those among us that insist that the Spirit works in Christians apart from the Word would not make the claim that the indwelling supplies any knowledge, or enables one to know the truth. One does not need the indwelling of the Spirit to interpret the written revelation given by the Spirit. It would be nonsense to say that one has to have the indwelling of the Spirit today to understand what the Spirit has said in the gospel. The gospel would be a sealed book to all men if it could not be understood without the Spirit being in one, explaining what the Spirit said in the book. The sensual man of Jude 19 was the false, uninspired teacher. The false teachers that John had in mind are of the same type, and are contrasted with inspired teachers that had miraculous gifts. The use of this verse to support the indwelling of the Spirit will end in the claim for miraculous gifts today.

D. "But the anointing which ye have received of him abideth in you, and ye need not that any man teach you: but as the same anointing teacheth you of all things, and is truth, and is no lie, and even as it hath taught you, ye shall abide in him," (I John 2:27). The false teachers were trying to seduce the ones to whom John was writing. The anointing was said "to teach you." What could a non-miraculous indwelling of the Spirit do either for John's readers or us today? Miraculous gifts furnished direct revelation which was "truth, and no lie." Included in the miraculous gifts was the gift of discerning of spirits. This gift supplied the miraculous ability to separate false teachers that claimed inspiration from those who actually were inspired. Instead of these false teachers having any manifestation of the Spirit, they are described by John as "being made manifest that they were not of us," by separating themselves from the church. The word "manifest" in verse 19 was used by John to show: 1) the lack of any miraculous manifestation on the part of these false teachers; 2) the only manifestation the false teachers had was showing they were false in leaving the church. A non-miraculous indwelling of the Spirit today would not: 1) supply any knowledge or truth; 2) would not enable anyone to be able to know who a false teacher was. All of this is now furnished through the written revelation. When John wrote this letter, there were miraculous gifts that furnished knowledge directly, and furnished the gift of discerning false spirits or teachers. This is the meaning of I John 4:1. False prophets were false teachers that claimed some kind of inspiration. The gifts of discerning spirits enabled the church and John's readers to expose these false prophets. No inspired teacher ever denied that Christ came in the flesh. False prophets were denying this.

Finally, 4:6 shows that anyone that denied what an apostle taught was a false teacher regardless of what his pretended claim might be. Paul made the same argument in I Corinthians 14:37: "If any man think himself to be a prophet, or spiritual, let him acknowledge that the things that I write unto you are the commandments of the Lord." I John 4:6 is the same thought simply stated in different words. The false teachers that John spoke of were those that denied that Christ was the Son of God. No man that had a miraculous gift ever was guilty of making any such denial. If one claimed some form of inspiration, as some surely did in that they were called false prophets. A further proof, in addition to the fact that one with a miraculous gift would not deny the Deity of Christ, was that such denial was a rejection of what the apostles taught about Christ. The apostles were His ambassadors, clothed with official power of inspiration, as Christ's representatives on earth (II Corinthians 5:20; Luke 24:49; Acts 1:8). This shows that not only the apostles who were guided by the Spirit never contradicted one another, but any one that had a spiritual gift never contradicted an apostle. The same Spirit that guided the apostles also guided one with a spiritual gift. There were diversities of gifts, but all gifts were manifestations of the same Spirit (I Corinthians 12:4). One might as well expect the Holy Spirit to contradict God or Christ as to think that anyone having a spiritual gift would contradict any other that had a gift. This is proof that those that claim to have spiritual gifts today are deceived and false teachers. They not only contradict one another in the doctrine that they teach, but they contradict the teaching of Christ and the apostles. Thus, John's argument of the anointing of the Spirit was to show that the ones to whom he wrote, could by these spiritual gifts, know that any man that denied that Christ had come in the flesh was a false teacher, for no one with a spiritual gift could ever teach any such doctrine. The anointing of the Spirit of I John 2:27 was a miraculous anointing. No one receives any such anointing today. Spiritual gifts ceased with the completion of revelation. One that had a spiritual gift was infallible in his teaching. A non-miraculous gift certainly does not assure a correct interpretation of the Scripture. If the anointing of I John 2:27 means a non-miraculous indwelling, then we have infallible men today. We now have an infallible Book, but no infallible men.

There are two other passages in I John that need to be discussed along with the anointing of 2:20-27. Before I discuss these passages, let me give the background of the book. False teachers were denying that Christ had come in the flesh (4:3). These false teachers pretended to be inspired. They were called false prophets by John (4:1). The fact that John called them false prophets shows their false claim to inspiration.

These false teachers denied the message of the apostles that Christ was God's Son in the flesh. The apostles preached that Jesus was the Christ, the Son of God. All that denied that Christ had come in the flesh denied the gospel preached by the apostles.

The false teachers' denial of Christ having come in the flesh opened the door to all kinds of corrupt living. These false teachers were saying that one could live as he wanted to. The letter was written to expose these false teachers. The letter was John's answer to these false doctrines.

The apostles were eyewitnesses. They had heard, seen, and handled Christ (1:1). Three of the five senses are mentioned in this verse to underscore the fact that the apostles were not deceived. Here was evidence that the apostles knew that Christ had come in the flesh. Since they were eye witnesses, they were qualified to testify to the reality of His humanity and His Deity.

The apostles had fellowship with both the Father and the Son (1:3). Others could have fellowship with God only through Christ, and this fellowship could only come through the message that the apostles proclaimed (1:3-5). The gospel proclaimed by the apostles concerning the Sonship of Christ, if accepted, imposed the responsibility of right living (3:5). False teachers were claiming to have fellowship with God while rejecting the humanity of Christ and, of course, this meant also rejecting His Deity. In order to succeed, it was necessary for these false teachers to discredit and repudiate the apostles. If the apostles could have been discredited, then the gospel they preached, declaring that Jesus was the Christ, the Son of God, would have been a counterfeit gospel.

The apostles were witnesses of Christ during His personal ministry and following His resurrection (Acts 1:8). But the apostles were not the only witnesses. The Holy Spirit, given to the apostles with miraculous manifestations, was also a witness (John 15:26-27; Acts 5:32). This is

THE WORK OF THE HOLY SPIRIT 171

the background of the book of I John. It is against this background that the statements are made in 3:24 and 4:13.

I JOHN 3:24

"And he that keepeth his commandments dwelleth in him, and he in him. And hereby we know that he abideth in us, by the Spirit which he hath given us," (I John 3:24). Also notice verse 23: "And this is his commandment, That we should believe on the name of his Son Jesus Christ, and love one another, as he gave us commandment." The name "Jesus" shows the humanity of Christ, and the word "Christ," His Deity. John used both words, "Jesus" and "Christ," to show that He was the Son of man and the Son of God.

The statement of John in 3:24 was John's defense against the false teachers who had repudiated the apostles, and who were seeking to get the people to whom John wrote to also repudiate the apostles. John insisted that the apostles knew that God abided in them because of the miraculous manifestation given them by the Spirit.

I JOHN 4:13

"Hereby know we that we dwell in him, and he in us, because he hath given us of his Spirit," (I John 4:13). John was making the same argument in this verse as in 3:24. This statement is in defense of the apostles and the message they preached. It is clear that this is the case as the next verse says, "And we have seen and do testify that the Father sent the Son to be the Saviour of the world," (I John 4:14). No one living today can make the claim of this verse. No one living today has seen Christ and there are no living eyewitnesses that can testify that God sent Christ to be the Saviour of the world. We are dependent upon those who were eyewitnesses and their testimony is found in the New Testament. I John 4:13 and 14 is the double testimony of the apostles and the Holy Spirit to the Sonship of Christ. The testimony of the Spirit was by direct revelation and miraculous manifestation as confirmation of the revelation that proclaimed Christ as the Son of God. This double testimony is the exact thing promised by Christ to the apostles in John 15:26-27, and as illustrated by Peter's statement in Acts 5:32. One might as well claim to have seen Christ in the flesh as to claim that the gift of the Spirit (I John 4:13-14) is a reflection of the premise of the book as stated in 1:1-5.

The miraculous manifestations of the Spirit in the apostles were proof that God dwelt in them and they dwelt in God. Suppose that someone today denied that you dwelt in God or Christ. Would you try to prove that you dwelt in Christ by appealing to having the Holy Spirit dwelling in you non-miraculously? This is the very claim that men make today that have not obeyed the gospel. They say that they have the Holy Spirit. If a non-miraculous indwelling of the Spirit proves that God dwells in a person, then any man can make this claim and no one can disprove it. We do not establish that we are in Christ by the indwelling of the Spirit, but by the gospel. While revelation was being given and confirmed, the miraculous manifestations of the Spirit were proof of the integrity of the apostles and of the churches that had miraculous gifts. What these miraculous gifts provided directly during this period is now furnished us by the Scriptures.

I JOHN 4:1-6

The apostles were of God (4:6). The proof that the apostles were of God was the miraculous manifestations of the Spirit (3:24, 4:13). False teachers rejected the apostles and denied the message the apostles taught, and such teachers were not of God as they claimed to be (4:6). The apostles were Christ's ambassadors, and as His representatives, they had been promised the Spirit to guide them into truth (John 16:13). Anyone that claimed inspiration and denied the teaching of an apostle was led by a false spirit (4:1). The same point is made by Paul in I Corinthians 14:37. Anyone that claimed a spiritual gift and refused to acknowledge anything taught by an apostle was ignorant; that is, he had no spiritual gift.

The Spirit of truth of I John 4:6 is the same as that promised to the apostles by Christ in John 14:16-17. Look at the contrast in John 14:17. In this verse you have "the Spirit of truth" in contrast with "whom the world cannot receive." "The Spirit of truth" is a promise of inspiration to the apostles. "Whom the world cannot receive" is the assurance that no false teacher would have inspiration. "Because it seeth him not" means that false teachers would have no manifestation to establish their claim of inspiration. "But ye know him" indicates the proof to the apostles that they really were inspired by the Spirit. The phrase, "For he dwelleth with you and shall be in you," refers to the miraculous powers of the Holy Spirit manifest in and through the apostles.

THE WORK OF THE HOLY SPIRIT

Now compare I John 4:1-6 with John 14:15-16. The "Spirit of truth" of I John 4:6 is the "Spirit of truth" (inspiration) of John 14:17. The spirit of error of I John 4:6 is equal to the teaching of false teachers who could not receive the Spirit of John 14:17. Since God is a God of truth, He could not, in keeping with His character, give any false teacher inspiration and miracles to confirm false teaching. John 14:16-17 is a divine commentary on I John 2:20, 3:24, 4:1-6, and 4:13.

There is nothing in any passage of I John to prove an ordinary non-miraculous indwelling of the Holy Spirit. It is as much a perversion of these passages to use them to prove a non-miraculous indwelling of the Spirit as it is to use John 14:16-17, 15:26-27, and 16:13 as a promise to Christians in general. All of these passages are speaking of miraculous gifts, not non-miraculous. These gifts have ceased. It is as reasonable and scriptural to claim the inspiration of the apostles today, or the gifts of I Corinthians 12, as to insist that I John 3:24 and 4:13 is proof of the indwelling of the Spirit today.

What the Spirit did directly then, He now does through the Word and only through the Word. A failure to realize this simple truth is to open the door for every kind of error and make the Spirit responsible.

IV. SEALED

"SPRAGIS," (seal) is found sixteen times in the New Testament. Thirteen of these are in the book of Revelation. The word always denotes a public mark or external sign, such as the seal on a letter. The instrument that makes the visible mark, or impression, is literally a "SEAL." A seal has an inscription on it. The inscription makes an impression. Each of these may be called a seal. Any one of these would be visible. Metaphorically, a seal may indicate secrecy and is so used in the book of Revelation. The word also denotes confirmation. Note the following:

1. "Seven seals," (Revelation 5:5)—Here the meaning is visible impressions indicating secrecy and security.
2. "...Till we have sealed the servants of our God," (Revelation 7:3)—Here is a reference to the instrument as a seal.
3. Abraham received the "sign of circumcision, a seal of the righteousness of the faith which he had yet being uncircumcised," (Romans 4:11). Circumcision in the person of Abraham was a seal, or confirmation, of his faith which he had in uncircumcision. The word is used here as a mark of confirmation.

4. "...For the seal of mine apostleship are ye in the Lord," (I Corinthians 9:2). The miraculous gifts that the Corinthians received through the hands of Paul confirmed him as an apostle and the Corinthians as being acceptable to God. (See II Corinthians 12:12.)

"SPHRAGIZO," (to seal) is used seventeen times with ten of them being in Revelation and used in the sense as already defined.

1. "So they went, and made the sepulchre sure, sealing the stone, and setting a watch," (Matthew 27:66)—Used to seal the tomb of Christ so that anyone removing the body would have to break the seal.
2. "Labour not for the meat which perisheth, but for that meat which endureth unto everlasting life, which the Son of man shall give unto you: for him hath God the Father sealed," (John 6:27). Christ was sealed as God's Son as He had the Spirit without measure (John 3:34). The visible signs, miraculous in their nature, were evidence that Christ was the Son of God. But all of these miracles were visible. God sealed His Son by the manifestation of the Holy Spirit.
3. "Who hath also sealed us," (II Corinthians 1:22)—This is a reference to the apostles. The apostles were sealed as the ambassadors of Christ by the manifestations of the Spirit. Manifestations of the Spirit were always visible. A non-miraculous indwelling of the Spirit would not seal or confirm the apostles as apostles. Paul was defending his apostleship in both of the Corinthian letters, but especially is this true of the second letter. The theme of the second letter could well be called "Paul's defense of his apostleship." But it was only by the miraculous manifestations of the Spirit that Paul's apostleship could have been established, and thus he was sealed by the Spirit.
4. "...Ye were sealed with that holy Spirit of promise," (Ephesians 1:13)—This passage is often used to contend for a non-miraculous indwelling. But consider a number of things which show that it is not a reference to a non-miraculous indwelling, but refers to the miraculous gifts which the Ephesians had received.

    Compare the following:
    a. "The Holy Spirit of promise" — "And, behold, I send the promise of my Father upon you: but tarry ye in the city of Jerusalem, until ye be endued with power from on high," (Luke 24:49). While this passage is specifically to the

THE WORK OF THE HOLY SPIRIT

apostles, it is a reference to Joel 2:28-32, which included spiritual gifts that were given through the hands of the apostles. See the discussion of John 7:38,39 and Mark 16:16,20. Joel's prophecy was the promise of the Father. Joel's prophecy was the promise of the Spirit. But Joel's prophecy was a promise of miraculous gifts, not non-miraculous. Ephesians 3:5 says, "...as it is now revealed unto his holy apostles and prophets by the Spirit." Ephesians 4:7-16 discusses miraculous gifts. Do not these passages indicate what is meant by the Spirit of promise in Ephesians 1:13?

b. "...In whom also after that ye believed..." (Ephesians 1:13)—Compare this with Acts 19:2: "...Have ye received the Holy Spirit since ye believed?" Is not the phrase in Ephesians 1:13 parallel with the question in Acts 19:2? In fact, does not the phrase in Ephesians 1:13 answer the question Paul asked in Acts 19:2?

c. "...Ye were sealed with that holy Spirit of promise," (Ephesians 1:13). Compare this phrase with the following: "And when Paul had laid his hands upon them, the Holy Spirit came on them; and they spake with tongues, and prophesied," (Acts 19:6). Acts 19:5 states that the Ephesians were baptized, but there is no mention of their receiving the Holy Spirit in consequence of their being baptized. But the next verse plainly states that they received the Holy Spirit when Paul laid his hands on them. In view of the record that is given in Acts 19 of the Ephesians receiving the Spirit through Paul's hands, speaking in tongues and prophesying, why should their being sealed with the Spirit mean a non-miraculous sealing they received when they were baptized?

d. The word "sealed"—The word means "something visible." A seal was to confirm or to certify something as genuine. Christ was sealed by the Spirit to confirm Him as God's Son and to certify Him as the promised Messiah of the Old Testament. The apostles were sealed by the Spirit to confirm and to certify them as the ambassadors of Christ. The seal on the Ephesians was the manifestations of the Spirit that confirmed them as God's people.

e. The seal of the Spirit was a public sign, mark, or certification that God had sent His Son and that He was all that He claimed to be. The seal of the Spirit on the apostles was a confirmation and certification that Christ had sent them as they claimed. The seal of the Spirit on the converts of the apostles was a confirmation and certification that God had received them. The seal of the Spirit on Christ was God's answer to all that denied that He was the Son of God. The seal of the Spirit on the apostles was God's answer to all that denied they were apostles. The seal on the Ephesians was God's answer to all that denied they were God's people.

Every "manifestation of the Spirit" was a confirmation of the apostles; a seal of their apostleship. The spiritual gifts bestowed upon converts by the hands of the apostles were a seal of the apostleship of the one who conferred the gifts, and it was a seal of certification that God had received them.

How could a non-miraculous indwelling of the Spirit be a seal in any of the above mentioned ways? It would be invisible. Suppose one buys a lot and takes the deed to the courthouse to have it recorded. If the deed is genuine, a seal of the county or state will be placed on it showing that it is a genuine deed. But suppose a question of ownership comes up, and it is taken to court. The judge calls for the deed. He looks for the seal of the county or state. He does not see a seal.

He asks, "Where is the seal?"

You reply, "The seal is on there because I had the deed recorded, but the seal is invisible."

What do you think the judge would reply?

Suppose someone denies that you are a Christian. You reply, "I have the evidence that I am a Christian. I have the 'seal of the Spirit.' "

Would a non-miraculous indwelling of the Spirit prove that one is a Christian today? One establishes that he is a Christian today by the Bible, not by the indwelling of the Spirit.

EPHESIANS 4:30

"And grieve not the holy Spirit of God, whereby ye are sealed unto the day of redemption," (Ephesians 4:30).

THE WORK OF THE HOLY SPIRIT 177

1. "Grieve not the Spirit"—A refusal to walk by the revelation given by the Spirit grieves the Spirit. While revelation was being given directly, one's refusal to live by the revelation of the Spirit and to follow a false teacher grieved the Spirit. This was not something that was new, except for the breadth of the miraculous gifts. "But they rebelled, and vexed his holy Spirit: therefore he was turned to be their enemy, and he fought against them," (Isaiah 63:10). Nehemiah 9:20, 30 shows that the Spirit, by inspiration, guided the prophets, and the nation rebelled against the teaching of the Spirit in the prophets. The church at Ephesus had miraculous gifts and these gifts furnished the revelation that should have directed them. When one rebelled against the teaching of the Spirit provided by the miraculous gifts in the church, he grieved the Spirit. The nation of Israel vexed, or grieved, the Spirit, but it was not because of non-miraculous indwelling in the Israelites, but their refusal to be taught and directed by the Spirit that was in the prophets. In the same manner, if the Ephesians refused to follow the teaching of the Spirit which was in the church by the gifts (Ephesians 4:7-8), it would grieve the Spirit. The church at Ephesus had the teaching of the Spirit by direct revelation; we have the teaching of the Spirit in a book. When they refused the teaching given directly by the Spirit, it would grieve the Spirit. When we refuse the teaching of the Spirit contained in the Book, not personally in us, the Spirit is grieved.

2. "Sealed by the Spirit"—This has already been discussed in my comments on Ephesians 1:13. I have already shown that it was the miraculous manifestations of the Spirit by which they were sealed. There is one additional thought in connection with Ephesians 4:30 to show that it is miraculous here just as in Ephesians 1:13. Look at the context in which the statement is found. Read Ephesians 4:7-16. Here are ten verses, and all of these verses are dealing with miraculous gifts. Beginning in verse 17, Paul gave some instruction on the proper kind of life for a Christian. This continues through verse 29. Then in verse 30, he said that the Ephesians were sealed by the Spirit. Suppose that verse 30 is read immediately following verse 16. Would anyone have any problem in seeing that the sealing was in connection with miraculous gifts? Ephesians 4:30 is in the same chapter and context that discusses miraculous gifts. To take the verse out of this context and make it mean a non-miraculous indwelling is to ignore a vital rule of Bible study; that is, that passages should be studied in their context. The subject of verse 30 is grieving and being sealed with the Holy

Spirit. The context in which this is found is one discussing miraculous gifts, not non-miraculous gifts. Ephesians 4:30 is a summary statement of the discussion of the miraculous gifts of verses 7-16.

3. "Unto the day of redemption"—Again, it is important to keep in mind the context of Ephesians 4:30. The background of this verse is the discussion of the miraculous gifts. The discussions of these miraculous gifts show their nature, purpose, and how long these gifts would continue. These gifts were to continue in the church until it reached a certain point. What was the time or point to be reached when miraculous gifts would cease? The time when revelation was completed.

I want to notice one particular phrase in 4:13. The phrase is "unto a perfect man." Berry translates the phrase as follows: "at a man full grown." The phrase is in contrast with the next verse that speaks of children. Thus, you have children, or infancy, in contrast with "man full grown" or maturity. These gifts were to last until the church arrived at maturity, as contrasted with the time when it was considered as a child. Is there anything that can aid in determining when a church reached its age of maturity? I believe so, and the Old Testament can contribute in determining this fact. Note the following:

a. The nation of Israel was a type of the church. The church is now the Israel of God (Galatians 6:16). It is spiritual Israel, not physical (I Peter 2:5,9).
b. The physical deliverance of the nation from bondage was a type of our spiritual deliverance from the bondage of sin (I Corinthians 10:2).
c. The infancy of the nation of Israel was a type of the infancy of the church. The wilderness wanderings of the nation of Israel were the period of its infancy. The nation reached its maturity when it entered Canaan. The promise to Abraham was that from him would come a nation (Genesis 12:2), and that his seed would possess the land of Canaan (Genesis 12:7). The land was essential for the nation to reach its maturity, or to become full-grown. This covered a period of approximately forty years. The wilderness wanderings were about thirty-eight years. There was about the same period of time from Pentecost until the end of the Jewish State in A.D. 70. The period from Pentecost to A.D. 70 covered the infancy of the church. The church reached its maturity when

revelation was completed. Spiritual gifts ceased and this occurred by the time the Jewish State ended in A.D. 70.

Consider the following points in connection with the phrase, "the day of redemption":
"The day"—The prophecy of Joel (2:28-32) gives the commencement, characteristics, and consummation of miraculous gifts. Notice how Joel pointed to the consummation of miraculous gifts: "The sun shall be turned into darkness, the moon into blood, before that great and terrible day of the Lord come." The language of Joel is not a reference to the end of time and Christ's personal return, but points to judgment on the Jewish State. Similar language is used in the Old Testament in describing the fall of Babylon. Read Isaiah 13 and note the similarity of the language in verses 10 and 13. The language here is descriptive of the fall or end of the Babylonian kingdom. This cannot be mistaken, as verse 17 mentions the Medes by name. The language of Joel is figurative as in Isaiah 13, and as Isaiah foresaw the judgment of God on Babylon, Joel foresaw judgment on the Jewish Nation.

Joel described the judgment on the Jewish Nation as "that great and terrible DAY OF THE LORD." The Hebrew letter was written to encourage the Hebrew Christians to endure the persecutions prior to and up to the fall of the Jewish Nation. In encouraging them to remain faithful, Paul exhorted them not to forsake the assembly and to increase their exhortations to help one another in the midst of the increasing persecutions. Then he used the phrase, "as ye see the day approaching." What day? That notable day that Joel foresaw (Acts 2:20). See also Matthew 24:33. The signs given by Christ would enable Christians to see the day approaching. Read also Hebrews 10:37.

But what about Ephesians 4:30, speaking of being sealed unto the day of redemption? Does redemption here mean redemption from sin? The answer is no. In Matthew's account of the prophecy of the fall of the nation, Matthew used the word "saved" of physical salvation, not salvation from sin. Matthew speaks of "the end," but it is not the end of life, but the end of the Jewish State (Matthew 24:13). See the previous word study of Matthew 24. But someone may say that, yes, Matthew uses the word "saved" as a reference to physical salvation, but not the word "redemption." That is correct, but Luke uses the word "redemption" instead of the word "saved." "And when these things begin to come to pass, then look up, and lift up your heads; for your redemption draweth nigh," (Luke 21:28).

Note the following in Luke's account:
Luke 21 is a prophecy of the fall of Jerusalem and the end of the Jewish State. Luke 21:20 leaves no doubt about this as reference is made to the Roman army encompassing the city.

Luke 21:25-26 is figurative language similar to that used by Isaiah and Joel, but Luke is speaking of the fall of the nation.

It is in this context that Christ said, "...Lift up your heads; for your redemption draweth nigh." This could not be a reference to redemption from sin, for redemption from sin began at Pentecost.

Luke 21:18 says, "But there shall not an hair of your head perish." This language makes it clear that Luke 21 points to the fall of the nation and the promise of a physical redemption to faithful Christians when that event occurred. The word "redemption" in Luke 21:28 is equal to the word "saved" of Matthew 24:22.

This accounts for the language in Ephesians 4:30. We have the day foretold by Joel. Joel saw not only the beginning of the miraculous operation of the Spirit for the giving and confirming of revelation, but he also saw the consummation of these miraculous gifts and this in view of a completed and confirmed revelation. The redemption of Ephesians 4:30 is the redemption foretold by Christ in Luke 21:28. The day of Joel and the redemption of Luke 21:28 belong together. Thus, in Joel, which is quoted by Peter, we have a summary of the miraculous operations of the Spirit which equals the seal of Ephesians 4:30. The day of Joel equals the day of Ephesians 4:30, but the day of Joel was the day of judgment on the Jewish Nation, and the end of the Jewish State consummated in the fall of the city. The redemption of Ephesians 4:30 is the redemption of Luke 21:28, which is not redemption from sin, nor the resurrection, but redemption from the persecution as already shown. Now Ephesians 4:30 ties in with the discussion of Ephesians 4:7-16. The gifts of Ephesians 4:7-11 are equal to the seal of Ephesians 4:30. The maturity of the church, which was to be reached when revelation was completed and confirmed, was equal to the day of redemption of Ephesians 4:30. The day of Joel is equal to the day of Ephesians 4:30 and the redemption of Luke

THE WORK OF THE HOLY SPIRIT

21:28 is equal to the redemption of Ephesians 4:30. Joel 2:28-32, Luke 21:14-28, Ephesians 4:7-16 with Ephesians 4:30, all add up to the fact that the miraculous gifts beginning with Pentecost for the revelation and the confirmation of the gospel had fulfilled this purpose by the time the Jewish State ended in A.D. 70, and by this time, all these miraculous gifts had ceased. We now have a completed revelation, and the church reached its maturity by the time of this event, leaving behind its infancy with these miraculous gifts.

Thus, instead of those who seek after these gifts today claiming that they enable themselves to attain a greater maturity and spirituality, the very opposite was true even while these gifts were available.

V. THE EARNEST OF THE SPIRIT

"Now he which stablisheth us with you in Christ, and hath anointed us, is God; Who hath also sealed us, and given the earnest of the Spirit in our hearts," (II Corinthians 1:21-22).

There are four words in these two verses that belong together: stablish (confirm), anointed, sealed, and earnest. The words "stablish (confirm), anoint, and sealed" have already been discussed. Each of these three words have to do with the miraculous work of the Spirit. What about the word "earnest"? It is being said that the earnest of the Spirit is the non-miraculous indwelling of the Spirit one receives when baptized, and is a down payment. Since the three other words all have to do with miraculous gifts, it would be strange that Paul would use a word in connection with these that was non-miraculous.

The word "sealed" and the word "earnest" are simply two different words expressing the same thought by two different figures of speech. The words "earnest" and "seal" both denote miraculous operations of the Spirit. Christ was anointed with the Holy Spirit and power. The words "Holy Spirit" and "power" are not two different things, but two words expressing the same thought. The same is true of "sealed" and "earnest" in I Corinthians 1:22. Both terms are used in connection with the miraculous operation of the Spirit. Regarding the word "earnest":

> The word is used three times in the New Testament, but always in a figurative sense. (II Corinthians 1:22) It is applied

to the gifts of the Holy Spirit which God bestowed upon the apostles, and by which he might be said to have hired them to be the servants of his Son; and which were the earnest, assurance, and the commencement of those far superior blessings which he would bestow on them in the life to come as the wages of their faithful service: in the two latter II Cor. 5:5; Ephesians 1:13, 14, it is applied to the gifts bestowed on CHRISTIANS GENERALLY upon whom, after baptism, THE APOSTLES LAID THEIR HANDS, and which were to them an earnest of obtaining a heavenly habitation and inheritance, upon the supposition of their fidelity—Cyclopedia of Biblical Theological, and Ecclesiastical Literature, McClintock and Strong, Vol., 3, p. 6.

Notice that McClintock and Strong say that the word "earnest" is a reference to the miraculous gifts which the apostles received and that Christians in general received through the hands of the apostles. The word "seal" is used in both II Corinthians 1:22 and Ephesians 1:13 and 14 with the word "earnest." The "seal" of the Holy Spirit was the miraculous manifestations of the Spirit that certified and guaranteed the integrity of the revelation given and obeyed. The "earnest" of the Spirit is a figurative term to indicate the inward enjoyment of the blessings of Christianity, because of the assurance given by miraculous manifestation. How could one enjoy the blessings of Christianity unless he was assured of the truthfulness of the gospel he had received? The "earnest," is the other side of the "seal." The "seal" to certify the integrity of the gospel given directly, and the "earnest," the assurance of the blessing promised therein.

VI. FILLED

Holiness people assume that every time the New Testament speaks of someone being filled with the Spirit, it means the baptism of the Spirit. The Scriptures show without doubt that this is not true. The Bible speaks of people being filled with the Spirit before the apostles received the baptism of the Spirit at Pentecost. Since there is no indication that anyone received what the Bible calls the baptism of the Holy Spirit before Pentecost, but certain ones were filled with the Spirit before Pentecost, it should be clear that to be filled with the Spirit does not mean to receive the baptism of the Holy Spirit.

For example, the phrase, "filled with the Spirit," is used three times in the first chapter of Luke. John was to be filled with the Spirit (Luke

THE WORK OF THE HOLY SPIRIT 183

1:15). Elisabeth was filled with the Holy Spirit (Luke 1:41). Zacharias was filled with the Holy Spirit (Luke 1:67). Here are three instances in one chapter where people were filled with the Spirit and not one of them had received the baptism of the Holy Spirit. It is a false assumption to insist that everyone that was spoken of as being filled with the Spirit had the baptism of the Spirit.

The phrase, "filled with the Spirit," denotes inspiration or miraculous power.

> In the Scriptures, to be filled with the Holy Spirit commonly signifies that degree of inspiration by which the ancient prophets spoke. Accordingly in this chapter it is applied to Elisabeth, to Mary, to Zacharias, and in each case a reference to inspiration, (Macknight).

Anyone that had a miraculous gift was filled with the Spirit, but everyone that had a miraculous gift was not baptized in the Holy Spirit. The different gifts of the Spirit were not a difference of the apostles being filled with the Spirit, the prophets being filled a little less, and ones with other gifts filled still less. The difference in gifts was a difference in power of manifestation in keeping with the distribution of the gifts. There were diversities of gifts, but the same Spirit operated in anyone that had a spiritual gift (I Corinthians 12:4).

> But unto every one of us is given grace according to the measure of the gift of Christ.
> Wherefore he saith, When he ascended up on high, he led captivity captive, and gave gifts unto men.
> (Now that he ascended, what is it but that he also descended first into the lower parts of the earth?
> He that descended is the same also that ascended up far above all heavens, that he might fill all things.)
> And he gave some, apostles; and some, prophets; and some, evangelists; and some, pastors and teachers; (Ephesians 4:7-11).

Ephesians 4:7 is a summary of all the spiritual gifts, or miraculous endowments. Ephesians 4:8 is a reminder of the promise that Christ made to the apostles in John 16:7-14. Ephesians 4:10 is a reference to the ascension of Christ and the promise that he made to the apostles that the Father, would send the Spirit in His name (John 14:26). The phrase, "that he might fill all things," of Ephesians 4:10 points to the miraculous gifts given to the apostles and believers through the hands of the apostles as the preceding verses and the following verses show. Now notice carefully the phrase, "that he might fill all things." Fill how? The context of this phrase shows that the filling of all things is a reference to the gifts mentioned in verses 7, 8, and 11. Thus, the following were said to be filled with the Spirit: 1) apostles, 2) prophets, 3) evangelists, 4) pastors, 5) teachers. Each of these mentioned were filled with the Spirit, but that is far from saying that all of these received the baptism of the Holy Spirit. The gift, or manifestation, of the Spirit of anyone having a gift was determined by the Spirit. "But all these worketh that one and the selfsame Spirit, dividing to every man severally as he will," (I Corinthians 12:11). "God also bearing them witness, both with signs and wonders, and with divers miracles, and gifts of the Holy Ghost, according to his own will," (Hebrews 2:4). Both of these verses teach that the gifts of the Spirit were determined by the Spirit of God. But anyone that had a gift was filled with the Spirit, though all did not have the same power. The supernatural operation of the Spirit in one that had a gift was determined by the Spirit in keeping with the office or function of the person that received the gift.

> For as we have many members in one body, and all members have not the same office [function—as apostle, prophet, evangelist, pastor, or teacher]:
> So we, being many, are one body in Christ, and every one members one of another.
> Having then gifts differing according to the grace that is given to us . . . (Romans 12:4-6).

The power of the Spirit was given according to the gift (Romans 12:6). Thus, anyone that had a gift was filled with the same Spirit, but all did not have the same miraculous power. The power was in keeping with the gift. While one that prophesied was filled with the Spirit (Luke 1:67), he did not have the same power given an apostle. For example, only the apostles had the power to impart spiritual gifts (Acts 8:14-17; II Corinthians 12:12-13; II Timothy 1:6).

When the problem of neglect arose concerning the Grecians' widows in Acts 6, the apostles told the brethren to seek out seven men "full of the Holy Spirit and wisdom," (Acts 6:3). Stephen was one of these and is described as one "full of faith, and of the Holy Spirit," (Acts 6:5). What was the significance of Stephen being filled with the Holy Spirit? The answer is found in Acts 6:8: "And Stephen, full of faith and power, did great wonders and miracles among the people." Full of the Holy Spirit in 6:5 becomes power in 6:8 and then power is defined by the words "wonders" and "miracles." Then 6:10 says, "And they were not able to resist the wisdom and the Spirit by which he spake." The King James has a little "s" for Spirit, but the A.S.V. has it capitalized, showing that it was the Holy Spirit and not the spirit of Stephen. These verses explain the qualification referred to in Acts 6:3. (Though there is no specific mention of the apostles imparting spiritual gifts before Acts 8, it is clear that they had imparted spiritual gifts as the brethren were told to select men that had gifts for seeing after the tables.) Stephen was full of the Holy Spirit and being full of the Spirit worked wonders, miracles, and spoke by inspiration.

There is additional proof that while everyone that had a spiritual gift was filled with the Spirit, all did not have the same power. Look at Acts 6 again. Stephen was not the only one of the seven that was "full of the Holy Spirit." The way verse 5 reads, might lead some to conclude that Stephen was the only one of the seven that was "full of the Holy Spirit," but this is not correct. The phrase, "full of faith and of the Holy Spirit," applies to all seven. This is shown from the statement made by the apostles in verse 3. The brethren were told to select seven men "...full of the Holy Spirit." Since the direction was to select seven men full of the Holy Spirit, this qualification applied to all seven. Thus, all that are named in verse 5 were men full of the Holy Spirit. Included in this number was Philip. Philip, like Stephen, was "full of the Holy Spirit." Philip, like Stephen, spoke by inspiration and confirmed what he taught by miracles (Acts 8:6-7). Philip was "full of the Holy Spirit," meaning the miraculous gifts of the Spirit. Even though Philip was "full of the Holy Spirit" and could speak by inspiration and work miracles, he did not have the same power as the apostles.

It is plain from the record in Acts 8 that Philip could speak by inspiration and work miracles, but he did not have all the powers that an apostle had. Philip could not impart spiritual gifts by laying his hands on those he had baptized. The apostles at Jerusalem heard that Samaria had received the Word of God and they sent Peter and John, apostles. Peter and John came to Samaria and laid their hands on the ones that had been baptized in Samaria, and they received the Holy Spirit. Simon saw that THROUGH THE LAYING ON OF THE APOSTLES' HANDS THE HOLY SPIRIT WAS GIVEN (Acts 8:18). Simon sought to buy this power—the power of an apostle to impart the Spirit by the laying on of hands (Acts 8:19). These verses show that the apostles had power that Philip did not have. The apostles had power to impart spiritual gifts; Philip did not. But now compare the following:
1. The apostles were filled with the Holy Spirit (Acts 2:4).
2. Philip was filled with the Holy Spirit (Acts 6:3-5; 8:6-7).

3. The apostles were filled with the Spirit when they were baptized in the Spirit.
4. Philip was filled with the Spirit, but was not baptized in the Spirit.
5. The apostles were filled with the Spirit when they were baptized in the Spirit, but they had power that Philip did not have.
6. Philip was filled with the Spirit, but not baptized in the Spirit, because he did not have the power that the apostles did.

This proves two things:
1. Anyone that had a gift of the Spirit was filled with the Spirit.
2. The phrase, "filled with the Spirit," is not always equal to being baptized in the Spirit.

The Spirit supplied the supernatural power needed in connection with the office of the one that received the Spirit. The very fact that the apostles were limited in number while spiritual gifts were abundant is proof that the apostles had a special office, or function, that was not common to everyone that had a spiritual gift. The special office of the apostles called for special powers. The baptism of the Holy Spirit supplied this power in keeping with the office, or function, of the apostles. The ones that had spiritual gifts, while said to be filled with the Spirit, did not have all the powers that the apostles did. It is not only unscriptural, it is not sensible that Christ would select a limited number of apostles with their special qualifications, and then give the same power to everyone equal to that of the apostles. The difference between the apostles and those that had spiritual gifts through the laying on of the hands of the apostles was not that the apostles were filled with the Spirit, while those having spiritual gifts were not filled with the Spirit, the difference was in the power possessed by the apostles in comparison with others who had spiritual gifts.

While there is no evidence that to be filled with the Spirit meant to be baptized in the Spirit, there is ample proof that being filled with the Spirit did not always mean baptized in the Spirit. The persons under consideration must be kept in mind along with the distinction between the apostles and those who received spiritual gifts through the hands of the apostles.

EPHESIANS 5:18

One other passage needs to be discussed in connection with the study on "filled with the Spirit." This is: "And be not drunk with wine, wherein is excess; but be filled with the Spirit; Speaking to yourselves in psalms and hymns and spiritual songs, singing and making melody in

THE WORK OF THE HOLY SPIRIT 187

your heart to the Lord," (Ephesians 5:18-19). Does this passage mean what it says? Is it a command to be filled with the Spirit? Does it mean that one is filled with the Spirit as he is filled with the Word, or gospel? While the last statement is true only in the sense in which one may be filled with the Spirit today, was this the sense of the statement made to the Ephesians? Consider some things that may help throw light on these questions.

First, consider some other passages:

> And they were all filled with the Holy Ghost, and began to speak with other tongues, as the Spirit gave them utterance (Acts 2:4).
>
> And when they had prayed, the place was shaken where they were assembled together; and they were all filled with the Holy Ghost, and they spake the word of God with boldness (Acts 4:31).
>
> Wherefore, brethren, look ye out among you seven men of honest report, full of the Holy Ghost and wisdom, whom we may appoint over this business (Acts 6:3).
>
> And the saying pleased the whole multitude: and they chose Stephen, a man full of faith and of the Holy Ghost, and Philip, and Prochorus, and Nicanor, and Timon, and Parmenas, and Nicolas a proselyte of Antioch (Acts 6:5).
>
> And Stephen, full of faith and power, did great wonders and miracles among the people (Acts 6:8).
>
> And they were not able to resist the wisdom and the spirit by which he spake (Acts 6:10).

Here are three examples of ones filled with the Spirit and the statement made that being filled with the Spirit, they spoke. This speaking by the Spirit was inspired speaking. These that were filled with the Spirit had miraculous gifts without exception. Unless Ephesians 5:18 is an exception, there is no mention of anyone being filled with the Spirit in the New Testament that did not have reference to a miraculous operation of the Spirit.

Second, is the objection that Ephesians 5:18 cannot refer to the miraculous operation of the Spirit a valid objection? The objection is based on the fact that it could not be a command (to be filled with the Spirit) and be a reference to the miraculous operation of the Spirit. Is it true that no one was ever commanded to be filled with the Spirit when a miraculous operation of the Spirit was involved? The answer is no.

II TIMOTHY 1:6

"Wherefore I put thee in remembrance that thou stir up the gift of God, which is in thee by the putting on of my hands," (II Timothy 1:6).

1. The gift referred to here was a miraculous gift. The word translated "gift" means "miraculous."
2. The gift came through the laying on of Paul's hands. There can be no question that the gift that Timothy had was a miraculous gift.
3. Timothy is commanded to "STIR UP THE GIFT OF GOD, WHICH IS IN THEE." Here is a command for Timothy to stir up the gift that he had. This shows that one that had a miraculous gift was expected to exercise the gift and it involved cooperation on the part of the one that had the gift. Since these gifts were for the edification of the church, it was necessary for the one having a gift to properly use it for his own edification, as well as the church's. The edification came through the revelation that was provided by means of the gift. I Corinthians 13 shows that the mind and proper motive of men were needed in the use of miraculous gifts. Christianity is voluntary. Since this is true, miraculous gifts did not make zombies out of those that possessed them. The revelation given by a miraculous gift was infallible, but the Spirit did not take over and operate against one's will. II Timothy 1:7 shows the reason for the command for Timothy to "stir up the gift." "For God has not given us the Spirit of fear; but of power, and of love and of a sound mind." The enemies of Christianity were not to cause Timothy to cease to use his gift. The Spirit would not lay hold of Timothy and by supernatural power take his tongue and preach the gospel, or teach the church, without his own willingness and consent. It is a mistake to think that spiritual gifts did not demand the use of proper motives and consent of the one that had a gift. If one that had a gift pleased God in the use of that gift, it was necessary that all the motives and other proper actions, that characterize us today in proper service to God, also accompanied that teaching, preaching, singing, praying, and worship. Spiritual gifts did not give those that had them any advantage over us today who have no spiritual gifts, but instead a spiritual Book. We do not have miraculous gifts today, but instead we have natural gifts. God does not force us to use our gifts against our will. Such service would be contrary to all the principles of Christianity. Miraculous gifts did not set aside these principles of Christianity for those who had the gifts.

Since this was true in connection with spiritual gifts, there is nothing strange about those having them being commanded to be filled with the Spirit, or to stir up the gift. In II Timothy 1:6 we have the positive command to Timothy in the use of a spiritual gift. The negative is given in I Timothy 4:14: "Neglect not the gift that is in thee, which was given thee by prophecy, with the laying on of the hands of the presbytery." This passage does not teach, as some claim, that others than apostles could impart spiritual gifts. Timothy was selected by prophecy; that is, a prophet or by the gift of prophecy in Paul. The elders laid hands on Timothy to set him aside, or separate him for the work of an evangelist, not to impart a spiritual gift. II Timothy 1:6 says plainly that the miraculous gift that Timothy had came through Paul's hands.

But notice that Timothy was commanded not to neglect the gift that he had. Thus, in two instances a command is given in connection with the use of miraculous gifts. One command is positive—"Stir up the gift." The second is negative—"Neglect not the gift." The objection to Ephesians 5:18 being a command because no command was given to use miraculous gifts is not true. If "be filled with the Spirit" is not a reference to the miraculous gifts, it cannot be on the basis that it is a command. If Timothy was told not to neglect a miraculous gift, but stir up the gift, should one be surprised to find a command to a church that had miraculous gifts to be commanded to not neglect or stir up the gifts it had? Be filled with the Spirit of Ephesians 5:18 is just another way of stating the same thing that Paul told Timothy. The Ephesians had miraculous gifts (Acts 19:1-6; Ephesians 1:13; 4:7-16; 4:30). The power of the Spirit did not operate constantly in one that had a miraculous gift; that is, every minute—but as the occasion called for it. These gifts were for the edification of the church (I Corinthians 12:7; 14:3), and were used in the assemblies. But as already mentioned, the use of these gifts involved the cooperation of the one that had the gift; that is, it was to be used voluntarily and with the understanding and consent of the one that had the gift. "And the spirits of the prophets are subject to the prophets," (I Corinthians 14:32).

I THESSALONIANS 5:19

There is still one other passage that shows the same principle in the use of miraculous gifts. "Quench not the Spirit," (I Thessalonians 5:19). Again, here is a command issued to a church. It is a command relative to miraculous gifts. It is clear that this is a command in connection with the use of miraculous gifts as the next verse says, "Despise not prophesyings," (5:20). The context indicates that the command to prove all things was directed toward those that had the gift of discerning of spirits. The command to the Thessalonians to "Quench not the Spirit" is the negative of Ephesians 5:18. Macknight gives the following rendering of the passage:

> Quench not the gifts of the Spirit, by hindering others to exercise them, or by neglecting to exercise them yourselves, or by exercising them with strife and tumult. Highly esteem the gift of prophesying; for it is the most useful of all spiritual gifts, being that by which the church is edified, exhorted and comforted. Do not believe every teacher pretending to inspiration; but examine all things offered to you, comparing them with the doctrine of Christ, and of his apostles, and with former revelations: and hold fast that which, upon examination, is found good.
>
> Here the Spirit denotes the miraculous gifts which were bestowed on the first Christians, called Hebrews 2:4 "Distributions of the Holy Spirit." From this precept, as well as from that to Timothy "Stir up the gift of God which is in thee," II Timothy 1:6, it appears that even the miraculous gifts might be improved; and that the continuance of them with individuals, depended in a great measure upon the right temper of their minds, and upon the proper use which the spiritual men made of their gifts.

If the Thessalonians were commanded not to "quench the Spirit," a reference to miraculous gifts, why would it be a strange thing for Paul to command the Ephesians to "be filled with the Spirit?" The command to the Ephesians points to the assembly as the next verse shows. Spiritual gifts were to be used in the assemblies as I Corinthians 14 and I Thessalonians 5:19-20 both teach. When the Ephesians assembled and exercised these miraculous gifts, would they not be filled with the Spirit? I have already shown that when one spoke by inspiration, he was filled with the Spirit. Ephesians 5:18 is the positive, while I Thessalonians 5:19 gives the negative. This is the only difference between the two passages.

Does someone ask how this may be reconciled with Colossians 3:16? There is no difficulty here. In the period of miraculous gifts, did not the Word dwell in them through the means of these gifts? How else did the Word dwell in either an individual or church that had miraculous gifts unless it was through these gifts? The same thought is expressed in I Corinthians in different words. "That in every thing ye are enriched [richly in Colossians] by him, in all utterance, and in all knowledge," (1:5). The statement to the Corinthians is one discussing miraculous gifts. Notice also the word "wisdom," (Colossians 3:16). The seven selected for service from the church in Jerusalem were to be men "full of the Holy Spirit and wisdom," (Acts 6:3). Stephen's enemies could not resist (that is, refute) the wisdom and the Spirit by which he spake (Acts 6:10).

The objection may be raised that these verses speak of singing and therefore they could not include miraculous gifts. Is this a valid objection? It is certain that there was inspired singing, and I do not mean the "Shakespeare kind" of inspiration. Look at the clear statement that says there was inspired singing: "How is it then, brethren? when ye come together, every one of you hath a PSALM, hath a doctrine, hath a tongue, hath a revelation, hath an interpretation. Let all things be done unto edifying," (I Corinthians 14:26). The psalm here can only mean an inspired psalm, as everything referred to in the verse was miraculous. Indeed, how could pagans who had no Old Testament, and the New Testament was not yet written, have been able to sing a psalm unless it was inspired? This passage teaches there were those who sang psalms by inspiration, otherwise, it would not make sense to include psalms in a chapter and verse that was dealing with miraculous gifts. If there were inspired psalms, and there were, what was a spiritual song? A spiritual song was an inspired song. While there were miraculous gifts, the services of the assemblies were under the complete direction of the Spirit through the use of these gifts. These miraculous gifts furnished the knowledge and revelation for edification. I Corinthians 14 teaches that entire assemblies were carried out by means of miraculous gifts. The assemblies were characterized by inspired preaching, prophecy, praying, and singing. Would it not have been appropriate to have said to a church whose services were characterized by all these, "be filled with the Spirit"?

After completing these comments on Ephesians 5:18, I happened to be reading Volume II of the <u>Millenial Harbinger</u> and ran across the following by Alexander Campbell. Lest some think that what I have said is far-fetched, consider carefully Campbell's comments along the same line. The following is taken from an article "Dialogue on the Holy Spirit":

T. To this passage you might add many others, such as Rom. xv. 19. I will not speak of any of those things which Christ has not wrought by me, to make the Gentiles obedient by word and deed, through mighty signs and wonders **by the power of the Spirit of God**; so that from Jerusalem and round about unto Illyricum, I have fully preached the Gospel of Christ"—"Yea," says Peter of his fellow Apostles, I Ep. i. 12. "they have preached the gospel to you with the Holy Spirit sent down from heaven"—"For," says Paul to the Thessalonians, I Ep. i. . "our gospel came not to you in word only, but also in power and in the Holy Spirit, and in much assurance." This power of the Holy Spirit is also called **"the hand of the Lord,"** Acts xi. 21. "And the hand of the Lord was with them, and a great number believed and turned to the Lord." And thus the Lord had opened the heart of Lydia, that she attended to Paul, Acts xvi. 14. But all these passages, and many others to the same effect, only prove that the arguments of the Holy Spirit are of two sorts, words and actions; and the actions are only to confirm the word, to enable persons to do as the Thessalonians did, receive the word with much assurance. Hence the Lord not only promised to confirm or prove the testimony of the Apostles, but did actually go forth with them, **confirming the word** with all power, and signs and wonders, and thus opened the hearts of the hearers to receive the gospel. Had the gospel not been confirmed by demonstrations of the power of God inimitable, no one's heart or ears would have been opened to attend to it. But when it came not in word only, but in demonstration of the Spirit and of power, they could not but attend to it. But all this was implied in my remarks to you the other evening, when it was said that the power of every argument is in its **meaning**. And unless it be made certain it has no meaning at all. All that is necessary to overcome the world, is to be assured that the gospel is true. Its arguments can have no weight, unless they are regarded as indubitably certain. That Jesus Christ will give eternal life to all who obey him, is an argument to obedience; but it is not only necessary that the words be intelligible, but that his ability and faithfulness to bestow eternal life be indubitably proved: and this requires the demonstrations of the Spirit and of power.

A. I anticipated that this would be your method of getting out of the difficulty.

T. I do not get out of the difficulty, for there is none. Every person must know that any proposition must be proved before there is any argument in it; and the proof must be of the same nature with the proposition. If the proposition be merely human, good human testimony or evidence will sustain it; but if it be divine and supernatural, no less than divine and supernatural proof can sustain it. Paul's argument in the passage quoted is, in brief, "I sought not to persuade you Corinthians by human eloquence or the powers of rhetoric, by curious logical or rhetorical orations, but I came declaring only the testimony of God concerning Jesus of Nazareth, and by the demonstrations of the presence of God's Spirit and power I proved it; and so your assurance or faith rests not on my reasonings, but on the power of God which accompanied that testimony.

A. I am satisfied with this resolution of the difficulty. You understand all the gifts of the Holy Spirit mentioned in the New Testament necessary to confirm the testimony.

T. No, sir; this is not all. The gifts of the Holy Spirit had more to do than this. They were necessary to develop the religion, as well as to prove it. Hence all the diversities of gifts mentioned I Cor. xii. xiii. xiv. chapters, are classified under two heads; first, those which revealed the religion, and those which proved it. The spiritual gifts necessary to teach the religion were "the word of wisdom," "the word of knowledge," "the gift of prophesy," "the interpretation of tongues," and to these might, in one sense, be added "the discerning of spirits." To confirm the religion there were "faith," or a firm persuasion that they were able to perform miracles; "the gift of healing diseases;" "powers," or an ability to perform such works as Peter did on Ananias and Sapphira, and Paul on Bar Jesus; "the gift of foreign tongues:" this was necessary to teach all nations, but as necessary to confirm the word; and the gift of "inworking," or imparting spiritual gifts to others by the imposition of hands. But on these gifts I would advise you to read the 2nd volume of the Christian Baptist, as they are expatiated on in that volume at considerable length. This I advise to prevent mistakes concerning our sentiments on this very important subject.

A. Well, now I am reminded of one of my difficulties, and that I may have it fully examined, I will propose one of my questions—Why is it that the Apostles exhorted their converts "to pray in the Holy Spirit," "to quench not the Spirit," "to be filled with the Spirit"?

T. I am glad that you have made this a question; for much depends upon understanding not merely these and similar expressions, but the state of things in the primitive church which gave rise to these precepts of the Apostles. I therefore beseech you to hear me patiently.

The churches gathered by the first proclamation of the gospel were either Jews or ignorant Pagans; and most churches were composed of both. "Know," says Paul to the Corinthians, when he began to write on spiritual gifts, "Know that you were Gentiles, carried away unto these **dumb idols**, even as you were led." This church "came behind in no gift," because it much needed them. Its members had every thing to learn. Destitute of any written revelation—**the Old Testament they had not, and the New was not then written**—they required all the gifts bestowed in that age. This was true of all the churches, save those in Judea; and **these had no letters written to them by the Apostles.**

These churches out of Judea had every thing to learn, and could not have a single spiritual thought but as they were taught either by inspired men, or by the Holy Spirit. But the inspired Apostles must travel every where, and could not long continue in any one place; and, therefore, it was necessary that these candlesticks, newly lighted up, should be constantly supplied with fresh oil. Hence all those spiritual gifts were bestowed on the first converts for perfecting them. They could neither speak in the church, pray, nor sing, without supernatural aid.

Writings of all sorts were scarce; and many had not the ability to read, had they had the writings of the Apostles all completed in their hands. In these congregations, then, every thing was done by the suggestion of the Holy Spirit. Moreover, it was more compatible with the genius of the religion, and with its prosperity in the world, that it should be set up by such means. The same wisdom which made Apostles out of rude fishermen, and hid the gospel treasure in these humble vessels, chose to fill rude barbarians and ignorant pagans with supernatural gifts, that the excellency of the power might appear divine and not human. Other reasons may be assigned; but these appear sufficient to commend the Divine economy in introducing the Christian institution.

By the Spirit of God they spake, prophesied, sang, prayed, and exhorted. Even women, as well as men, prayed and prophesied in the church. Because, according to Joel, in those days, the last of the Jewish age, God promised to pour out of his Spirit on **all flesh**, Jew and Gentile, and on both sexes; "your sons and your daughters shall prophesy." One Evangelist had four daughters, all prophetesses; that is, they all spoke by inspiration: for this is the meaning of prophesying. It matters not whether the inspiration respect past, present, or future relations or things, he or she who speaks by inspiration **prophesies**. Corinthian women were exhorted by Paul concerning their praying and prophesying in the church.

The gift of **discerning spirits** was then necessary to prevent imposition. Some possessed this gift; and therefore the prophets were commanded to speak but two or three sentences at a time, that those possessed of this gift might judge whether they spake according to the Spirit of God.

They are novices in the christian scriptures and religion who cannot discriminate between the order of edification in the primitive church, while under the guidance of **spiritual** men, from that which was to be the result of that order, when that which is perfect is come. That which was "**in part**," has now ceased; for "prophecies have failed." "That which is perfect," the complete revelation, is come.

We must, then, discriminate between the church in her infancy, during her minority, because the Apostles have taught us to discriminate. "When I was a child I thought as a child," says Paul to this people, to whom he expounds the nature and design of spiritual gifts; and to the church as a child the same Apostle says, It pleased Jesus when he ascended to bestow gifts—Apostles, Prophets, Evangelists, Pastors and Teachers, for the **fitting of the saints** for the service of the Lord, that they might not continue children, but grow up by these gifts to the full measure of the christian stature, to full grown men under Christ the Lord.

The literal body of Christ was literally formed by the Holy Spirit, and afterwards that body was filled with the Holy Spirit: so his metaphorical body, the church, was formed by the Holy Spirit in these gifts, and when formed it became the temple of that Spirit, and was filled with it. There is one body, and but one body of Christ composed of Jewish and Gentile disciples, and they have been builded together for an habitation of God through the Spirit. Hence **the Spirit is promised only to them who believe.** Every body has its own spirit, and the body of Christ has the spirit of Christ.

These are but hints, but they respect matters of the greatest importance to correct and comprehensive views of christianity. Ignorance of these matters is one principal cause of the present opposition to the ancient gospel and the ancient order of things. We professed the christian religion for years without hearing a hint on these subjects; and even now we seldom or ever hear them named by those declaimers about the Holy Spirit. They neither appear to understand what they say themselves, nor the things of which they so strongly affirm.

Let it be noted here, and I pray you to keep this proposition in mind, viz: **That every part of the christian worship, and all the means of edification in the primitive church, during its infancy, or while it was under the guidance of spiritual men, was performed by the immediate suggestion of the Holy Spirit.** Hence such expressions as these: "Quench not the Spirit;" that is, as explained by what follows, "despise not prophesyings"—"Pray in the Spirit"—"Be filled with the Spirit," singing psalms, hymns, and songs suggested by the Spirit—"I will sing in the Spirit," "I will pray in the Spirit;" but I will sing and pray in a known tongue, that by my singing and praying I may edify others, as well as worship the Lord.

Sometimes a whole congregation expressed all the same words at the same instant of time, the Holy Spirit suggesting to each individual all the same ideas and expressions at one and the same impulse. Thus the whole church kneeled down in Jerusalem, and with one accord, all uttered the same words at the same instant.

Pagans could neither know how, or for what to pray, unless they had been thus taught. Even the disciples of John and of Jesus, during the personal ministry of these two prophets, were taught by them how, and for what to pray. To pray in accordance with the economy under which we are placed, is a matter of some moment to all who have correct conceptions of God.

A. I cannot express the ideas which throng upon each other in my mind: but I must break silence and tell you, that really these are matters of which I have scarcely ever had a thought before; I never heard so much to explain to my satisfaction numerous passages in the Epistles, as I have now heard. I can now see why many things are connected together, which I never before understood. For example, "Quench not the Spirit" is succeeded by "despise not prophesyings," and that is succeeded by "prove all things and hold fast that which is good." I now see the association of ideas in the Apostle's mind. He exhorted the Thessalonians to stir up the gifts of the Spirit; to exercise the gift of prophesying; and, though some pretended to it who did not possess it, they were neither to contemn the gift, nor to cease from exercising it, but **prove** whether he that spake, spake by the Spirit; and so soon as this was proved, they were to hold fast that which was good. In this way my thoughts are running upon these passages as you proceed. I now understand another expression which I never before understood—"Be filled with the Spirit." I could not see, on the Calvinian or Arminian hypothesis, how any person could be **commanded** to be filled with the Spirit, any more than with any Divine attribute, inasmuch as that Spirit is not subject to the will of man; but as they cherished in their minds the word of Christ, and spake to one another in psalms, hymns, and spiritual songs, they were filled with the Holy Spirit—and it was not incompatible with those gifts to **command** the christians to exercise them.

T. And if you would read the exhortations delivered to the Ephesians and Colossians, both of which letters were written about the same time, while Paul was a prisoner, and while the same associations of ideas were in his mind, you will see that Paul explains himself. The parallel passages in the two Epistles read thus: Ep. v. 18, 19. "Be not drunk with wine, wherein is excess," or by which comes dissoluteness, "but be filled with the Spirit. Speak to one another in psalms, hymns, and spiritual songs, singing and making melody in your hearts to the Lord." In the Colossians, ch. iii. 16. it reads—"Let the word of Christ dwell in you richly; and with all wisdom teach and admonish one another, in psalms, hymns, and spiritual songs, singing with gratitude in your heart to the Lord." In both epistles these words are preceded and succeeded by exhortations precisely similar, only in a few instances verbally different. Compare them accurately, and no doubt can exist that the same connexion of things was before the mind of the Apostles in each. Hence it follows, that **to be filled with the Spirit, and to have the word of Christ dwelling richly in one,** are of the same import in Paul's mind; and as a means to this end, christians were to abound in singing psalms, hymns, and spiritual songs.

But this only by the way. You will find a hundred passages to yield to this great principle of interpretation, or rather to this view of the primitive worship and means of edification.

A. Methinks another passage opens to my view: "Stir up the gift which is in you, which was given you according to prophecy by the laying on of the hands of the eldership." Paul's hands were among these, as appears from another passage—"The gift which was given you by the imposing of my hands." Timothy was designated by one of those prophets which had the gift of discerning spirits as a suitable person to act as an Evangelist, and as an agent for Paul in Ephesus. As such he is commanded to **stir up** the gift, not to **quench the Spirit**, but to exercise his gift to edification and comfort.

T. Yes—but this will lead us into another matter; and perhaps it may be a profitable one at some other time; for indeed much of what pertains to the common order which ought to exist in a church, and to the officers which are necessary to its perfection, may be learned incidentally from the gifts of the Holy Spirit of which we are now speaking. But recollect that we are straying off from the subject on which we began.

A. Pardon me. I have been so much engrossed in this view of the ancient worship, that I have forgotten all my questions, and all my thoughts too on the original topic of inquiry.

T. Let us then dismiss the subject for the present, and meet again. You will find it advantageous to read the whole New Testament once through from the 1st chapter of the Acts to the last epistle, with this **single** idea in your eye; and observe, as you proceed, in what new and clear light it presents many passages to your mind. Recollect the proposition is this: **That the whole worship and edification of the primitive church, in its** infancy, was directed by inspired men; and that the Spirit suggested the songs, prayers, exhortations, and, indeed, all the discourses which were useful to the congregation: and that every thing incompatible with these suggestions was reprobated by the Apostles and those judges who had the gift of discerning spirits. But let me add, excesses and indiscretions occurred then, even among those who possessed the spiritual gifts; and this is no more than might have been expected in that age, by those who best understood the nature of those gifts, for even now, when a perfect and well proved revelation is possessed by us, how often do we err, even in the most common matters, requiring only prudence and discretion!

SPIRITUAL

Today, we think of the word "spiritual" as meaning one whose mind is directed by the gospel and is motivated by the principles of the gospel. A spiritual man today would be one whose life is controlled by the gospel. This is true because we now have a completed and confirmed written revelation. A spiritual man is one whose mind is filled with the law of the Spirit (Romans 8:2), the gospel.

In the study of the New Testament, it is important to remember that at first there was no written revelation. Revelation was given directly by the Spirit. The gospel that we now have in a book was at first in men that had the Spirit directly. In the time when there were miraculous gifts for the revelation of the Word, "spiritual" had a different significance than today where we have the Word, not in the man, but in the BOOK. It is important to keep this in mind in the study of the Holy Spirit and His work.

The second chapter of I Corinthians introduces and defines the meaning of the word "spiritual." It is important that one understands Paul's use of the word in this chapter. In I Corinthians 2:13, Paul uses the word "spiritual" in contrast with "natural" in 2:14.

Through the years denominational preachers have made the natural man the sinner and then pushed the idea that the sinner could not understand the written Word unless aided by the direct operation of the Spirit. This interpretation of I Corinthians 2:13, 14 is based on the Calvinistic doctrine of total depravity. The doctrine of total depravity is that the sinner is dead and can do nothing without a direct operation of the Spirit to enable him to believe, and repent, in order to become a Christian. (I use the order of denominational teaching as to what makes one a Christian. J.F.C.) Since the sinner is dead and can do nothing, the Word of God is a dead letter. He may read the Bible, but he cannot understand it without the Spirit to enlighten him as to its meaning. Recently, I have read one or two articles written by gospel preachers that have taught this same thing on I Corinthians 2. A bulletin sometime back said that the sinner could not understand the written Word unless the Spirit interpreted it for him. When one makes the natural man the sinner and the spiritual man one that has the direct operation of the Spirit to interpret the written Word, he makes the mistake of not seeing the difference between the time when the Word was revealed directly by the Spirit and the present when there is no direct revelation as we now have a completed, written revelation.

First, the Corinthian letter was written to a church, not sinners (I Corinthians 1:2). Secondly, the church at Corinth had miraculous gifts, and no church has these gifts today. Thirdly, the church at Corinth did not have a complete, written New Testament. Fourthly, we now have a complete, written New Testament. The miraculous gifts stood in relation to the church at Corinth as the written Word stands in relation to a church today.

The church at Corinth had the Word through Paul, who had the Word by direct revelation and through the miraculous gifts in the church. Paul was inspired by the Spirit. The church at Corinth was inspired through the miraculous gift in it. There is no preacher that is inspired today by the Spirit. There is no church that is inspired by miraculous gifts today. There is as much difference in the church at Corinth and one today as there is a difference between an apostle who had the Spirit directly and a preacher today who does not have the Spirit miraculously.

THE SPIRITUAL MAN VS. THE NATURAL MAN

Who are the spiritual man and the natural man of I Corinthians 2? The book will explain the difference if one will allow it to do so. When Paul wrote the letter, it was not divided into chapters and verses. Paul introduced the spiritual man and the natural man in Chapter 1. He used other words in discussing the same thing in the first chapter.

Consider the following:
1. "Paul, an apostle of Jesus Christ through the will of God," (1:1)—Paul calls himself an apostle because there were false teachers in Corinth that denied his apostleship (I Corinthians 9:1).

2. Paul introduced the letter by discussing miraculous gifts in the Corinthian church (1:4-8).

3. The Corinthians had been called into the fellowship of Christ through the inspired preaching of Paul. Paul's preaching did not deny the "faithfulness" of God as promised in the Old Testament. Paul's gospel was the culmination of the promises of the Old Testament, especially the promise of Abraham (Genesis 22:18). Judaizing teachers were denying that the Corinthians were in fellowship with God through Christ. The Judaizing teachers were attempting to use the pride, fleshly appeal, love of human learning of the Gentile Christians at Corinth. They were doing this to promote their Judaistic teachings. The Jews had a special pride in their fleshly descent from Abraham, but the Jews were not the only ones that could be appealed to through fleshly pride. The Gentiles were subject to fleshly pride, just as we may be today. This made it possible for the false teacher to appeal to the Corinthians. It was through the fleshly pride of the Corinthians that the false teachers were deceiving the Corinthians and denying Paul's apostleship. Who were the ones that were examining Paul if it was not these false teachers and their followers in the church (I Corinthians 9:3)? Who were the ones questioning Paul's apostleship, if not these false teachers? Why were they questioning Paul's apostleship if it was not because they did not like Paul's gospel that placed both Jew and Gentile on equality in one body?

I Corinthians 1:9 is directed toward those who had been influenced by Judaistic teaching that denied the gospel Paul preached was in harmony with the Old Testament promises. The preceding verse concerning the gifts in the church at Corinth was to prove the genuineness of the gospel Paul preached and the fact that the Corinthians were genuine Christians. The miraculous gifts in the church confirmed this.

The command that they all speak the same thing certainly included a reminder not to listen to false teachers who were not guided by the Spirit. Indeed, how could the church at Corinth speak different doctrines as long as it was directed by the

THE WORK OF THE HOLY SPIRIT

revelation given through miraculous gifts? Can one conceive of the Holy Spirit teaching different doctrines in the church at Corinth? Surely not. But someone was teaching a different doctrine. Who was it, if not these false teachers? Someone was deceiving the Corinthians. It certainly was not the Holy Spirit through the miraculous gifts which provided revelation for the church. (See I Corinthians 15:33.) Of course, there were false teachers who followed the pagan philosophy of Corinth, but the Corinthian letter was written in answer to both kinds of false teaching, Jewish and Corinthian. It is also well to keep in mind that the revelation of the gospel given through the gifts in the church at Corinth had to be followed willingly. The gifts did not force the practical conduct that should have resulted from the revelation.

4. I Corinthians 1:17: "For Christ sent me not to baptize, but to preach the gospel: not with wisdom of words, lest the cross of Christ should be made of none effect."

This statement shows Paul's commission and what it included. Paul's statement that he was not sent to baptize had no connection with his preaching baptism. He was sent (commissioned as an apostle) to preach. "Preach" here means receiving the revelation of the gospel. He had to be sent to be an apostle. The revelation of the gospel was an apostolic function. Baptizing was not an apostolic function. An apostle could baptize, but that was not what he was primarily commissioned for. An apostle was commissioned to receive and reveal the gospel (Ephesians 3:3-6). One did not have to be commissioned to baptize, but he did have to be sent to be an apostle. The word "sent" of I Corinthians 1:17 tells what Paul means. The very commission Paul was under required preaching baptism (Mark 16:16). The question Paul asked in Romans 10:15, "And how shall they preach, except they be sent?" was not, How shall one preach unless a church sends and supports him? He is speaking of chosen, selected ones, commissioned by God and inspired to preach or proclaim the Word of God. This kind of preaching had to do with receiving the revelation of God's Word. Suppose Christ had not selected the twelve apostles and endued them with the power of the Holy Spirit to preach the gospel? Who would have ever been able to call on the name of the Lord? Who would have been able to believe on Christ? How would anyone have heard of Christ? This is the meaning of I Corinthians 1:17. Preaching, which involved receiving the revelation of the gospel, belonged to the apostolic office. Baptizing did not depend on one being an apostle.

5. "Not with wisdom of words," (I Corinthians 1:17)–this phrase is contrasted with Paul being sent to preach the gospel by inspiration. Thus, you have one commissioned and inspired to preach the gospel in contrast with false teachers who were neither commissioned by Christ, nor inspired. Paul's preaching was in word and power, that is, miraculous, while the false teachers had nothing but speeches and words (I Corinthians 4:19). The inspired preaching of Paul set forth the cross as the means of salvation. The false teachers used only the art of human wisdom and words to set forth their doctrine.

"The wisdom of the wise, and understanding of the prudent," strikes at the human wisdom and human understanding based purely on human reasoning (1:19). "The wisdom of God" (inspired preaching) is contrasted with the wisdom of the world (1:21). The wisdom of God means inspired revelation which is called preaching in the last part of the verse. God made possible man's redemption through Christ and selected simple men through which to reveal the gospel so that "no flesh should glory in his presence," (1:29).

When Paul came to Corinth, he did not use the deceit and art of human methods in setting forth the gospel (2:1). His speech and "preaching was not with [the] ENTICING WORDS OF MAN'S WISDOM, but in the demonstration of the Spirit and of power," (2:4). The phrase, "enticing words," is descriptive of the deceptive means of artful, persuasive words to mislead people. Paul did not have to resort to any such methods. His preaching was confirmed by demonstration of the Spirit and power. The wisdom of the world, of Chapter 1, becomes speeches and "enticing words of man's wisdom" in 2:4. The "words of man's wisdom" equals what man is able to know by his own faculties apart from any inspired revelation. The faith of the Corinthians did not rest on the wisdom of men—just speeches and enticing words, their faith rested on a revelation that was confirmed by miracles (2:5).

"Howbeit we speak wisdom . . ." (2:6)– Paul also spoke wisdom, but what kind? Inspired and confirmed wisdom. The false teachers in Corinth spoke wisdom, but what kind? It was uninspired and unconfirmed by any miracle. Here is the inspired gospel Paul preached in contrast with the uninspired and unconfirmed teaching of false teachers who were disturbing the Corinthians.

"But we speak the wisdom of God in a mystery, even the hidden wisdom, which God ordained before the world [ages] unto our glory," (2:7). The wisdom of God in a mystery was the purpose of God to save both Jew and Gentile through Christ in one body, the church, which He had promised to Abraham before the Jewish Age, (Genesis 12:1-7; 22:18; Ephesians 3:1-6, 10, 11, 21; Galatians 3; I Corinthians 12:13). Verse 7 must surely be directed toward Judaizing teachers, for why else would Paul appeal to the Old Testament in writing to a Gentile church? Neither the Jewish ecclesiasticism nor the Roman Government (Pilate) understood God's purpose as announced in the Old Testament. Their lack of understanding led to their crucifying Christ (2:8).

I Corinthians 2:9: "But as it is written, Eye hath not seen, nor ear heard, neither have entered into the heart of man, the things which God hath prepared for them that love him."

The things that God had prepared for the ones that love Him were the things of the gospel of redemption: purposed, planned, promised, and announced in type, shadows, and prophecies in the Old Testament. Not one of the things purposed, planned, promised, and announced in the Old Testament originated in the heart of man. They had their origin in the mind of God and were revealed by the Holy Spirit to man. Man did not discover the first one of the basic principles of redemption as promised in the Old Testament and fulfilled in the New. The promises, prophecies, types, and shadows of the Old Testament were of divine origin and the meaning of these and their fulfillment in the New Testament was through inspired interpretation and explanation. Their meaning in the New Testament came by revelation to the apostles by the Spirit (2:10).

I Corinthians 2:11: "For what man knoweth the things of a man, save the spirit of man which is in him? even so the things of God knoweth no man, but the Spirit of God." No man could know the mind of God unless God revealed it. This was the work of the Holy Spirit. Man could not know the mind of God by his own mind. "...The things of God [the gospel of redemption] knoweth no man...." This statement does not mean that one cannot understand what God has revealed in His Word, but that man could never have known what God's will was if God had not revealed it.

I Corinthians 2:12: "Now we have received, not the spirit of the world, but the spirit which is of God; that we might know the things that are freely given to us of God." "Now we have received, not the spirit of the world"—the spirit of the world is equal to the wisdom of the world, what man could know by his own mind and reason. The spirit of the world was all that the false teachers had, the wisdom of the world. The apostles and the Corinthians through the hands of Paul had received the Spirit miraculously for revelation. The miraculous gifts the apostles had received are equal to the phrase, "wisdom of God." The apostle John declared, "They are of the world [false teachers] therefore speak they of the world [uninspired speaking, the wisdom of the world] and the world heareth them," (I John 4:5). Paul said, "For the time will come when they will not endure sound doctrine; but after their own lusts shall they heap to themselves teachers, having itching ears; And they shall turn away their ears from the truth, and shall be turned unto fables (II Timothy 4:3, 4). This is the reason that John said the world heareth them. They would not listen to the truth and would hear only what they wanted to hear. This teaching had grown when John wrote I John, but it had already started when Paul wrote the Corinthian letter. ". . .He that knoweth God [through miraculous gifts which provided revelation—'the things of God knoweth no man'—see I Corinthians 2:11] heareth us [apostles]; he that is not of God [false teachers not commissioned by God and having not received the Holy Spirit to guide them] heareth not us [apostles]. Hereby know [by the gifts of the Holy Spirit] we [apostles] the Spirit of truth [truth revealed to the apostles by the Spirit, the wisdom of God of I Corinthians 2], and the spirit of error," (I John 4:6). The spirit of error is the wisdom of the world, uninspired teaching that is false. The Spirit that the apostles received was the Spirit of truth (John 14:17; 16:13), for guiding them into the revelation of the truth of the gospel. The spirit of the world was the spirit of error, the wisdom of the world which was human in its origin, coming only from the mind and wisdom of man.

I Corinthians 2:13: "Which things also we speak, not in the words which man's wisdom teacheth, but which the Holy Ghost teacheth; comparing spiritual things with spiritual." "Which things also we [i.e., we, apostles] speak [inspired speaking], not in the words which man's wisdom teacheth," (i.e., teaching devised in the heart of man, human in origin, the spirit of the world, the wisdom of man).

I Corinthians 2:14: "But the natural man receiveth not the things of the Spirit of God: for they are foolishness unto him: neither can he

THE WORK OF THE HOLY SPIRIT

know them, because they are spiritually discerned." "...The natural man...."—the man guided by his own wisdom, the wisdom of the world, uninspired teaching, the false teachers in Corinth, the man teaching without any revelation.

"...Receiveth not the things of the Spirit..."—Christ had promised the Spirit to the apostles. When He promised the Spirit to the apostles, He said plainly, "...Whom the world cannot receive because it seeth him not, neither knoweth him," (John 14:17). The Holy Spirit was never promised to any false teacher, but it is clear from the Epistles that some false teachers claimed inspiration. Indeed, it would be impossible for one to be directly guided by the Spirit and teach error. The Holy Spirit is the Spirit of truth. The world of John 14:17 is equal to the natural man of I Corinthians 2:14. The Spirit of truth which was promised to the apostles and which they received at Pentecost, to guide them into the revelation of truth, is contrasted with the world which could not receive the Spirit, but had only the Spirit of the world (I Corinthians 2:12), the spirit of error (I John 4:6).

"...Neither can he know them..."—the truth had to be revealed by inspiration. The apostles were inspired by the Holy Spirit which they had received (I Corinthians 2:10). No man could know the truth unless it had been revealed by the Holy Spirit. The Holy Spirit was not promised to the world, especially Jewish leaders who belonged to the world of Judaism. The Jews had been God's people in the Old Testament. All of this was changed at Pentecost. The Jewish leaders would not accept this change. They still claimed to be God's people, though the Jewish kingdom of the Old Testament had now become the synagogue of Satan (Revelation 3:9). Pentecost showed the apostles in the forefront while the Jewish leaders were on the defensive. It was the apostles that received the Holy Spirit, not the Jewish leaders. How could the Jewish leaders have received the Spirit as He was never promised to them. The Jewish leaders could make all the claims they wanted to, the one thing they could not do was confirm their claims with any miracle. This was one of the things that distinguished the apostles from every Jewish leader and false teacher.

"...Neither can he know them..."—the truth was made known by the Holy Spirit. The false teachers had not received the Holy Spirit; therefore, they could not know or teach what was true.

"...They are spiritually discerned,"—the truth was given by the Holy Spirit as promised to the apostles. One that was not inspired by the Holy Spirit could not receive or reveal any truth.

I Corinthians 2:15: "...He that is spiritual [the apostles—the inspired man, the one with miraculous gifts] judgeth all things..."—the revised has "discerned" for "judgeth." Thus, the apostles discerned all things by inspiration of the Holy Spirit. There was even the gift of discerning of spirits, discerning false teachers claiming the Spirit.

"...Yet he himself [apostles] is discerned of no man,"—the very nature of the office of an apostle carried with it credentials that established it so that no one needed to discern or judge if he were an apostle (II Corinthians 12:12).

I Corinthians 2:16: "For who hath known the mind of the Lord, that he may instruct him? But we have the mind of Christ." No one knows the mind of the Lord except the Spirit (I Corinthians 2:11). Man did not know one thing about what was needed for his redemption. Man could never have conceived the scheme of redemption, and if it had been possible to conceive it, he could not have brought to pass the provisions that were required for making redemption possible. Man was spiritually bankrupt. Only God could provide a sacrifice that would atone for sin. Thus, God planned, provided, and then revealed unto man the entire scheme of redemption.

"But we [apostles] have the mind of Christ." How did the apostles have the mind of Christ? Certainly, it was not by self-discovery, by the spirit of the world, by worldly wisdom, by human faculties. The apostles had the mind of Christ by the Holy Spirit (I Corinthians 2:10-13).

The spiritual man of I Corinthians 2 is the inspired man, and particularly the apostles. The natural man was the one that sought to teach (before the New Testament was written) without being inspired by the Holy Spirit. His teaching had its origin within his own heart, came from his own uninspired mind or faculties, and is aptly described as natural.

There is not the first suggestion of the following in I Corinthians, Chapter 2:
1. That the natural man is the sinner—he is, like all men, a sinner, but not "the sinner."
2. There is not the slightest hint that the natural man is a sinner that cannot understand the Bible when he reads it. Sinners may misunderstand the Bible, but it will be for reasons that keep

anyone from understanding; i.e., prejudice, making up his own mind what he wants the Bible to teach before he ever studies it, or the attempt to avoid what it teaches; or a lack of desire and willingness to obey the truth. Any one of these will keep a person from understanding the truth and this includes Christians as well as sinners. But not one of these have anything to do with one being a sinner, totally depraved as claimed by Calvinists, which results in his being unable to understand the Bible when he reads it.

3. There is not the first indication in this chapter that one must have the indwelling Spirit today to understand the Scriptures.

The entire discussion beginning in I Corinthians 1:18 through all of the second chapter is a discussion of divine wisdom given by inspiration of the Holy Spirit to selected and chosen men (1:27), commissioned and sent (1:17), for the purpose of revealing His will as they were directly guided by the Holy Spirit. This is put in contrast with those who were teaching false doctrine and had nothing but speeches and words (4:19), and is called worldly wisdom because its origin is from the world, not heaven; teaching that is the product of the human mind and heart. I Corinthians 2 was written by Paul in defense of his apostleship. Chapter 2, like Chapter 9, was Paul's answer to those who denied that he was an apostle: "Mine answer to them that do examine me is this..." (9:3). "Since ye seek a proof of Christ speaking in me..." (II Corinthians 13:3). The spiritual man of I Corinthians 2 is the inspired man, and in particular, Paul an apostle. The natural man is the uninspired man, and specifically, the false teacher in Corinth who had nothing but the spirit of the world, not the Holy Spirit.

There could be no greater perversion of the truth than to take a passage that is contrasting inspired revelation through chosen men, with uninspired false teachers (natural men) whose teaching was of human origin, and make the passage refer to a sinner that has a completed open Bible before him and insist that he cannot understand what he reads unless the Holy Spirit dwelling in him interprets it for him. This claim would make it impossible for a sinner to ever know what the truth is. It is certain that a sinner does not have the Spirit dwelling in him. But, if the indwelling of the Spirit is essential to the Spirit interpreting the Scriptures, how will a sinner ever come to a knowledge of the truth? If one answers that he will have to let someone else who has the Spirit interpret it for him, then he will have to take someone else's word for what the truth is. He could not do as the Bereans did, search the Scriptures to see if the teaching was true (Acts 17:11). The Bereans were sinners at the time they were searching the Scriptures and they were doing this checking on a man that was inspired by the Spirit, Paul an apostle. This is surely a strange development if the natural man of I Corinthians 2 is the sinner and cannot understand the Scriptures without the indwelling of the Spirit to interpret it for him.

The consequences of making the natural man the sinner and the indwelling of the Holy Spirit the interpreter of the Scriptures today would be infallibility. Does anyone think that the Holy Spirit in one, and interpreting the Scriptures, would ever be guilty of misinterpreting His own revelation? This would make a pope (infallible) out of everybody. Are we ready to accept the infallibility of the "Pope"? This interpretation would end in making popes of all. This is the result of applying passages that contrast chosen men (apostles) who were promised the Spirit to guide them in receiving revelation, with men that were false teachers. False teachers today are those who pervert the written revelation, not men that are not guided by a direct operation of the Spirit. The preacher today that teaches the wisdom of God, teaches that which is found in written revelation, not what he receives by a direct operation of the Spirit.

I Corinthians 14:37: "If any man think himself to be a prophet, or spiritual, let him acknowledge that the things that I write unto you are the commandments of the Lord." I Corinthians 14:37 is a commentary on the spiritual man. A spiritual man, according to this verse, was one that was guided directly by the Spirit, one having a miraculous gift. Miraculous gifts have ceased and there are no spiritual men in this sense today. The only spiritual person today is the one described in the introduction of the discussion of the subject.

There are two other passages that show the meaning of spiritual and natural as already defined. James 3:15: "This wisdom descendeth not from above, but is earthly, sensual, devilish." Notice the context of this verse: "Who is a wise man and endued with knowledge among you?" (3:13). The wisdom of 3:15 is described in 3:14. It lies "against the truth." This is simply another way of referring to false teaching. It was false teaching in opposition to the truth. The wisdom of 3:15 is identified as to origin.

1. Negative—"...descendeth not from above." It was not wisdom of

THE WORK OF THE HOLY SPIRIT

divine revelation, and in this instance was not wisdom given through miraculous gifts.
2. Positive—this wisdom is "earthly." Its origin is from earth, not heaven.
3. This wisdom is "sensual," ("natural" of I Corinthians 2:14). Its origin was from within man, the worldly wisdom of I Corinthians.
4. It was "devilish"—the lie or false doctrine of James 3:14. This wisdom was of human origin and served the aims and purposes of the devil. The devil has his apostles (II Corinthians 11:11-13). The devil is a liar and the father of lies (John 8:44).

"For where envying and strife is, there is confusion and every evil work," (James 3:16). Here are the consequences of this type wisdom. The doctrine is false and produces evil results, envy and strife, confusion and evil work.

"But the wisdom that is from above is first pure, then peaceable, gentle, and easy to be intreated, full of mercy and good fruits, without partiality, and without hypocrisy," (James 3:17). "...The wisdom that is from above..."—this is the wisdom of God given through the spiritual man of I Corinthians 2:11-13, especially the apostles, but it also included ones who received spiritual gifts through the hands of the apostles. This wisdom is the wisdom of divine revelation, first given directly by the Holy Spirit through the gifts of the Spirit, and now contained in the written Word.

The wisdom given by direct revelation was pure, not mixed with human wisdom. It was unadulterated by human defilement. It was the wisdom in the words of the Spirit and not in the words of man's wisdom. Again, the contrast between the spiritual and the sensual (natural) is one between those miraculously endowed and those whose wisdom had its origin from earth, within the mind and heart of men. The contrast in James is the same as that in I Corinthians.

There is one other passage that drives the nail down in the definition already given. "These be they who separate themselves, sensual [natural, as in I Corinthians 2:14; James 3:15], having not the Spirit," (Jude 19). The sensual man of this verse is the natural man of I Corinthians 2:14. He is the one guided by worldly wisdom following the inclinations of his own heart and flesh. "...Having not the Spirit," is the negative of I Corinthians 2:11-13, where the positive is given of those who had the Spirit miraculously, which provided inspired revelation. "...Having not the Spirit" equals receiving no revelation of their teaching. While the same word is not used, the sense of the meaning of sensual is given in Jude 10: "But these speak evil of those things which they **know not** [things given by direct revelation which they did not have]: but what they know naturally [by their own human wisdom, the wisdom of the world], as brute beasts, in those things they corrupt themselves." Their wisdom was the product of the human mind and heart, not the wisdom that came by revelation. Their so-called knowledge was human and not divine. These are the same as the ones described as sensual in verse 19, who had not the Spirit; that is, had no miraculous gift of the Spirit.

All of these passages are related to the time when revelation was in the process of being given directly and are to show the distinction between those who taught by inspiration, and the ones who claimed to be teachers but were not inspired by the Spirit. There was a world of difference between both the natural man, and one having the Spirit then, and the present day where we have a completed written revelation. It is a monumental mistake to say the natural man is the sinner who has a copy of the New Testament to read and cannot understand what he reads without the aid of the direct operation of the Spirit. This is the doctrine of Calvin, not the doctrine of the apostles.

The following from the pen of Alexander Campbell is to the point on I Corinthians 2:14:

> Let it, then, be distinctly noticed, from all these premises, that these gifts had for their object, first, the revelation of the whole christian doctrine; and secondly, the confirmation of it; and without them, no man could either have known the truth or believed it. To this effect does the apostle reason, I Cor. ii. 9-16. He shews that none of the princes, the legislators, or wise men of Judea, Greece or Rome, ever could, by all their faculties, have discovered the hidden wisdom, "which God had determined before the Mosaic dispensation began, should be spoken to the honor of those apostles, gifted by the Holy Spirit." For so it was written, "Eye has not seen, and ear has not heard, and into the heart of man (before us apostles) those things have not entered, which God has prepared for them who love him. But God has revealed them (those unseen, unheard, and unknown things) to us (the apostles) by his Spirit"—"Which things (before unknown, unheard, and unseen,) also we (apostles)

speak (to you Gentiles and Jews, that you may know them) not in words taught by human wisdom, (in Judea, Greece or Rome,) but in words taught by the Holy Spirit, explaining spiritual things in spiritual words." "Now, an animal man, (whether a prince, a philosopher, a legislator, or a rhetorician, in Judea, Greece, or Rome, by the means of all arts and sciences) receives not the things of the Spirit of God, for they are foolishness to him; neither can he know them, (by all his faculties and attainments,) because they are spiritually examined" (by the light which revelation and not reason affords.) "But the spiritual man (the man possessed of a supernatural gift) examines, indeed, all things; yet he cannot be examined by any animal man (because such cannot judge of the principles suggested to him by the Spirit;) for what man (who is merely animal) has known the mind of the Lord, (his deep designs respecting Jews and Gentiles, now made known to us apostles,) who will (or can) instruct him (the spiritual man.) But we (apostles) have the mind of Christ," and are able to instruct your spiritual men, with all their gifts. O! you Corinthians! How has this beautiful passage been perverted by system into a meaning the most remote from the mind of the Spirit! The translation above given is most consistent with the original, and, indeed, is the translation of Dr. McKnight, who seems to have rendered all those passages that speak of spiritual gifts, in all the epistles, much more accurately and intelligibly than any other translator we have seen. The animal man, or what our translators call a natural man, spoken of by the apostle, is quite another sort of a man than the Calvinistic or Arminian natural man. The apostle's natural man, or his animal man, was a man who judged of things by his animal senses or reason, without any revelation of the spirit; but the natural man of modern systems, is a man who possesses the revelation of the Spirit, and is in the "state of nature" as it is called. The apostle's natural man's eye had never seen, his ear had never heard, his heart never conceived any of those things written in the New Testament—our natural man's ear has heard, and it has entered into his mind to conceive, in some way or other, the things which were revealed by the Holy Spirit to the apostles. To argue from what is said of the one by the apostle, to the other, is a gross sophism, though a very common one; and by many such sophisms is the word of God wrested to the destruction of thousands.

ROMANS 8

Romans 8 is a difficult chapter. I do not propose to settle all the difficulties in the chapter. I do want to study it, as no study of the Holy Spirit would be complete without including Romans 8.

THE BOOK OF ROMANS

It will be necessary to look at the book of Romans before discussing the eighth chapter. It is my conviction that understanding the overall teaching of Romans is the key to the eighth chapter. The eighth chapter must be considered in the light of the purpose of the book.

Theme

1. The theme of the Roman letter is the gospel as God's power to save (1:16). While this is the theme of the book, it is not the purpose of the book. The theme establishes the purpose, but there is a definite point established in the book. The purpose of the letter is found in Chapter 15. This is the reason that it is important to see the book as a whole. A failure to read the entire book to get its thought, leads to missing the purpose of the book. Since the purpose is found in Chapter 15, if one does not read the whole book before beginning a detailed study, he will be through with the book and never grasp its purpose.

Purpose

2. The purpose of the book is to show the unity of Jew and Gentile in the church. This is vital to an understanding of the Roman letter. A glance at Chapter 15 establishes the following: a) Paul was on his way to Jerusalem with a collection from Gentile churches for Jewish Christians (15:30-32). b) He was concerned over the problem which the Judaizing teachers had created by insisting that Gentiles be circumcised and keep the law. The question of circumcision had brought about a strained relationship and Paul was seeking to avoid a divided church—one Jewish and one Gentile. c) He was hoping and praying that this collection from Gentile churches for Judean churches would help to relieve the strained relationship and heal the wounds. It was not his

THE WORK OF THE HOLY SPIRIT

purpose to sacrifice the truth; i. e., that the Gentiles should not be circumcised and keep the law. It was his prayer that the collection would help Jewish Christians to become more receptive to the Gentiles, belonging to the same body with equal spiritual blessings.

Problems and Answers

3. The Roman letter explores the problems that were causing the trouble and sets forth the answer. The conclusion of the Roman letter is that both Jew and Gentile are one through Christ in the church.

Future Plans

4. Paul had completed his work in regions where he had been preaching. "But now having no more place in these parts, and having a great desire these many years to come unto you; Whensoever I take my journey into Spain, I will come to you: for I trust to see you in my journey, and to be brought on my way thitherward by you, if first I be somewhat filled with your company," (15:23-24). As Paul considers his future plans, he proposes to broaden his efforts to carry the gospel to Spain. Paul was not one who operated as a "loner." Geographically, Antioch was no longer a logical base from which to work. Paul wanted to establish a working relationship with Rome, and from there evangelize Spain. This would enable him to continue his apostolic ministry to the Gentile world. As Paul thought of the church in Rome, a congregation that he had never visited, the question arose: Is the church the body of Christ and do Christians all around the world, both Jew and Gentile, belong to this one body? This is the significance of Romans 16:16. "Salute one another with an holy kiss. The churches of Christ salute you"—this statement is made to underscore the unity of the church, made up of both Jews and Gentiles. "Salute one another with an holy kiss" is a reminder of the tender ties that bind Christians together. The phrase, "churches of Christ," was not written by Paul to provide a scriptural term to describe the church, though it does such. Churches (plural) show that all congregations go to make up the one body. It made no difference whether they were Jewish churches in Judea, Gentile churches in Asia, or the church in Rome, they all belonged to the one body. Chapter 16:17-18 is a warning of the problem that had arisen that could have affected the unity of Jew and Gentile. False teachers were seeking to

undermine the unity with their false doctrine that was contrary to the doctrine of Christ. "Now I beseech you, brethren, mark them which cause divisions and offences contrary to the doctrine which ye have learned; and avoid them. For they that are such serve not our Lord Jesus Christ, but their own belly; and by good words and fair speeches deceive the hearts of the simple," (16:17-18). These false teachers are in the background of the book of Romans. The contents of the book, and the arguments in the book, show that these false teachers were the Judaizers who were seeking to bind circumcision on the Gentiles. The book also is an answer to Jews that rejected the gospel.

AN ANALYSIS OF THE BOOK
Introduction 1:1-17

There are four main divisions in the Roman letter. The first seventeen verses compose the introduction to the book. The introduction sets the stage for the discussion found in the three major divisions which follow. The first verse of the book suggests the contents: "Paul . . . an apostle,"—he was not just an apostle; he was an apostle of Christ. Saul, the Jew, was a servant of Jesus Christ, and an apostle of Christ rejected by the Jews. Paul was an apostle of Christ, the Saviour that the Judaizers were rejecting and making void the grace of God through Christ by their insistence on circumcision of the Gentiles.

> But if, while we seek to be justified by Christ, we ourselves also are found sinners, is therefore Christ the minister of sin? God forbid.
> For if I build again the things which I destroyed, I make myself a transgressor.
> For I through the law am dead to the law, that I might live unto God.
> I am crucified with Christ: nevertheless I live; yet not I, but Christ liveth in me: and the life which I now live in the flesh I live by the faith of the Son of God, who loved me, and gave himself for me.
> I do not frustrate the grace of God: for if righteousness come by the law, then Christ is dead in vain. (Galatians 2:17-21).

It was necessary for Paul to defend his apostleship and his being an apostle of Christ to the Gentile world. It was this that aggravated the Judaizing teachers (Galatians 2:8; Acts 22:21-22). "Paul, an apostle of

Christ to the Gentiles, separated unto the gospel of God." The gospel that Paul preached as an apostle of Christ, offering salvation to Jew and Gentile in the one body, was the gospel of God. Paul's gospel of redemption to Jew and Gentile alike was the gospel of God, because God promised it by the prophets in the Old Testament.

Paul's gospel was not a denial of the Old Testament, but the realization of what the Old Testament promised in Christ. "(Which he had promised afore by his prophets in the holy scriptures,)" (Romans 1:2). Thus, the Roman letter is a defense of Paul's apostleship as the servant of Christ, promised in the Old Testament.

"Concerning his Son Jesus Christ our Lord, which was made of the seed of David according to the flesh; And declared to be the Son of God with power, according to the spirit of holiness, by the resurrection from the dead," (Romans 1:3-4). The resurrected and living Christ was the source of grace by which Paul became an apostle for the obedience of faith among all nations: "By whom we have received grace and apostleship, for obedience to the faith among all nations, for his name," (1:5). The obedience to the faith sets the tone of the letter and suggests the contrast of the obedience of the gospel with that of Judaism. Furthermore, the obedience to the faith is not limited to Jews, as was Judaism, but is open to all nations, Gentiles as well as Jews. The Roman letter begins and ends with the emphasis that the gospel is the fulfillment of the Old Testament and is open to all men alike, Jew and Gentile. Romans 1:5 introduces the letter, showing that the obedience of faith is open to Jew and Gentile alike. But the sixteenth chapter closes upon this same note: "But now is made manifest, and by the scriptures of the prophets, according to the commandment of the everlasting God, made known to all nations for the obedience of faith," (Romans 16:26).

Since the gospel was for all nations, the Christians in Rome are among the called: "Among whom are ye also the called of Jesus Christ," (Romans 1:6). The "called" of the gospel was not limited to the Jews, but to all that were in Rome, whether Greek or barbarian, wise or unwise (Romans 1:14). The love of God was not limited to the Jew, but was universal in its longing to redeem the lost. The saints at Rome, in responding to the call of the gospel, were numbered among the beloved of God: "To all that be in Rome, beloved of God, called to be saints: Grace to you and peace from God our Father, and the Lord Jesus Christ," (Romans 1:7).

"For God is my witness, whom I serve with my spirit in the gospel of his Son, that without ceasing I make mention of you always in my prayers," (Romans 1:9). God witnessed the gospel preached by Paul through the miraculous endowments given to Paul by the Spirit.

> That I should be the minister of Jesus Christ to the Gentiles, ministering the gospel of God, that the offering up of the Gentiles might be acceptable, being sancitified by the Holy Spirit.
> I have therefore whereof I may glory through Jesus Christ in those things which pertain to God.
> For I will not dare to speak of any of those things which Christ hath not wrought by me, to make the Gentiles obedient, by word and deed,
> Through mighty signs and wonders, by the power of the Spirit of God; so that from Jerusalem, and round about unto Illyricum, I have fully preached the gospel of Christ.
> Yea, so have I strived to preach the gospel, not where Christ was named, lest I should build upon another man's foundation: (Romans 15:16-20).

God was also a witness to Paul's apostleship by the laying on of Paul's hands to impart spiritual gifts (Romans 1:11). ". . . Whom I serve with my spirit . . ." (Romans 1:9). Again, we have a contrast between the gospel and the law. The law purified the flesh, not the spirit. "For if the blood of bulls and of goats, and the ashes of an heifer sprinkling the unclean, sanctifieth to the purifying of the flesh," (Hebrews 9:13). The gospel sanctified Paul's own spirit through the blood of Christ and purged his conscience from dead works to serve the living God. "How much more shall the blood of Christ, who through the eternal Spirit offered himself without spot to God, purge your conscience from dead works to serve the living God?" (Hebrews 9:14).

This is another key verse for the correct interpretation of the Roman letter. The law was fleshly; the gospel is spiritual. This is the meaning of John 4:24: "God is a Spirit: and they that worship him must worship him in spirit and in truth." All acceptable worship must come from man's spirit and be directed by the truth of the gospel. Paul affirmed that God testified to his being an apostle of Christ by the miraculous gifts given him, and that his gospel was the gospel of God, and that he served God with his spirit in this gospel, which was also the gospel of His Son.

THE WORK OF THE HOLY SPIRIT

Then Paul drew his conclusion concerning the gospel. In spite of the opposition of Jews and Judaizing teachers, he was not ashamed of the gospel of Christ: "For I am not ashamed of the gospel of Christ: for it is the power of God unto salvation to every one that believeth; to the Jew first, and also to the Greek. For therein is the righteousness of God revealed from faith to faith: as it is written, The just shall live by faith," (Romans 1:16-17). Paul would not allow the opposition of the Jews and Judaizing teachers to make him ashamed of the gospel, because it was God's power to save. The claim of the Jews and the Judaizing teachers that salvation was through the law and the attempt to bind the law on the Gentiles, by requiring circumcision, was a false doctrine and did not save. The gospel of God which Paul preached offered salvation to everyone.

The word "everyone" strikes the universal note of the gospel that Paul preached. But it was this universal offer that Paul's enemies despised. While the gospel was universal in its offer, the Jew had the privilege of hearing it first, but this was never intended to suggest that he was superior to the Gentile, or the Gentile was to be a second-class citizen in the church. The Gentile was entitled to all of the spiritual blessings of the gospel by the obedience of faith. The flesh of Abraham, that one time excluded the Gentiles, no longer had anything to do with who could enjoy the blessings of God. God's plan and provision for righteousness is now found in the gospel and is appropriated by the obedience of faith. The gospel is a system of faith, not flesh. One becomes a Christian by faith and lives the Christian life by faith. It is not faith alone, but the obedience of faith (Romans 1:5; 16:26). Therefore, it is from faith to faith. Salvation by faith, offered in the gospel to both Jew and Gentile, was anticipated in the Old Testament. The Jew and the Judaizers were perverting the Old Testament in their attempt to hold onto it and refusing to accept the Gentile on an equal basis in the church. This is why Paul quoted Habakkuk 2:4: "... the just shall live by his faith." The very Bible of the Jew, the Old Testament, foresaw the gospel of salvation by the obedience of faith. This was to be offered to Jew and Gentile without distinction. One of the chief characteristics of the Roman letter is the universal principles discussed in it.

UNIVERSAL PRINCIPLES IN THE ROMAN LETTER

1. There is a universal need: "For all have sinned, and come short of the glory of God," (Romans 3:23).
2. There is a universal Saviour: "Therefore as by the offence of one

judgment came upon all men to condemnation; even so by the righteousness of one the free gift came upon all men unto justification of life. For as by one man's disobedience many were made sinners, so by the obedience of one shall many be made righteous," (Romans 5:18-19).
3. There is a universal gospel: "For I am not ashamed of the gospel of Christ: for it is the power of God unto salvation to every one that believeth; to the Jew first, and also to the Greek," (Romans 1:16). "By whom we have received grace and apostleship, for obedience to the faith among all nations, for his name," (Romans 1:5). "But now is made manifest, and by the scriptures of the prophets, according to the commandment of the everlasting God, made known to all nations for the obedience of faith," (Romans 16:26).
4. There is a universal way of redemption: "For therein is the righteousness of God revealed from faith to faith: as it is written, The just shall live by faith," (Romans 1:17). The universal way of redemption is by faith, not flesh. It is not by faith alone, but the obedience of faith (Romans 1:5; 1:17; 16:26).
5. There is universal treatment: "For there is no respect of persons with God," (Romans 2:11).
6. There is a universal standard of judgment: "But we are sure that the judgment of God is according to truth against them which commit such things," (Romans 2:2). "In the day when God shall judge the secrets of men by Jesus Christ according to my gospel," (Romans 2:16).
7. There is a universal judgment: "Or despisest thou the riches of his goodness and forbearance and longsuffering; not knowing that the goodness of God leadeth thee to repentance? But after thy hardness and impenitent heart treasurest up unto thyself wrath against the day of wrath and revelation of the righteous judgment of God; Who will render to every man according to his deeds," (Romans 2:4-6).

These universal principles run throughout the entire Roman letter. But why argue these universal principles? Why did Paul set forth these universal principles in the Roman letter? What called for Paul to establish these universal truths? Paul's life as an apostle of Christ was spent in preaching the gospel to Jew and Gentile; especially Gentiles, as he was an apostle to the Gentiles, and defending the integrity of the universal gospel which he preached. This is the reason that Paul speaks of "my gospel." The truth of the gospel Paul preached was not any different from the gospel preached by the other apostles, but since he was sent to the Gentile world and was called on to defend his preaching to the Gentile world, it is this particular characteristic that made it "his gospel." The Roman letter sets the universal gospel in contrast with the temporary, national, limited exclusiveness of Judaism. The law of Moses was temporary, fleshly, and national. The gospel of Paul was universal, individual, and spiritual. This is the reason for the discussion of the law in the book of Romans. The gospel with its ample provisions, universal principles, is contrasted with the limitations of the law. These truths are vital in understanding the Roman letter. The main body of the book looks at these principles and shows that the gospel of grace is the only hope of both Jews and Gentiles. Keeping these things in mind, consider this brief outline of the book.

THREE MAJOR DIVISIONS OF THE ROMAN LETTER

I. The problem of sin and its solution (Chapter 1:18 to 8:39): Sin and its consequences are set forth in the Old Testament and its solution in the gospel.
II. The problem of the Jews (Chapters 8, 9, and 10): The Jews' misunderstanding of the law led to their rejection of Christ and the gospel.
III. The problem of application to conduct of the righteousness, which is by the obedience of faith (Chapters 12 to 16):
   A. Will the righteousness, which is by the obedience of faith, work in the everyday problems of life? Will the righteousness, which is by the obedience of faith, bring unity among men, both Jew and Gentile, in the one body, which is the church?
   B. These last chapters set forth the importance of understanding and applying the principles of the gospel in daily conduct so that all men can live together in harmony and peace.

FIRST MAIN DIVISION – CHAPTER 1:18-8:39

It is necessary to get a bird's-eye view of the book in order to appreciate and understand the eighth chapter. Chapter 8 is the conclusion of the first section that deals with the problem of sin and its solution. From Chapter 1:18 through Chapter 7, Paul traces the origin and development of sin down through the Old Testament. He shows that no solution to sin was found in paganism or Judaism. He accepts the fact that Judaism was a God-ordained religion, but its design was temporary and preparatory because it offered no real solution to the problem of sin. Since the law could not solve the problem of sin, there had to be something beyond the law, and that which was beyond the law was Christ and the gospel. In order to prove this truth, it was necessary for Paul to discuss the nature of the law, its weaknesses and its purpose. The various aspects of the law with its weaknesses in dealing with the problem of sin is developed and contrasted with the gospel in the first seven chapters. But if the law could not solve the problem of sin, how and where could its solution be found? The concluding chapter, Chapter 8 of the first section, answers this question. Paul's approach to the problem of sin was to trace God's promise to Abraham from its beginning through Judaism to its culmination in Christ and the gospel. The promise of God to Abraham did not end with the law, but came through the channel of the Jewish Nation, and culminated in Christ and the gospel. The substance of Paul's argument in this connection was that the church, made up of both Jew and Gentile, was the end product of the promise, and was God's solution to the problem of sin.

Why did Paul approach the question from this standpoint? The Jews had rejected Christ and, following Pentecost, many of them still refused to accept Christ and the gospel. Since the Jews were God's people before Christ came into the world, they were insisting that they were still the elect, even though Christ had come. In contending they were God's chosen people, they were denying the integrity of the gospel that Paul preached. This is the reason for Paul's discussion of the Jew in Chapters 9, 10, and 11. If, after the coming of Christ, the Jews remained God's chosen people, it follows that the gospel that Paul preached, in offering redemption by the obedience of faith to Jew and Gentile alike, was false. The Roman letter is really Paul's defense of his gospel of grace, appropriated by the obedience of faith, placing Jew and Gentile in one body in the church, and standing on equality before God.

If it was necessary for Paul to defend the gospel he preached, why was it necessary? His gospel must have been under attack from some source. What was the source? In addition to the Jews who refused to accept Christ and the gospel, there were those who accepted it under false pretenses, or without understanding its full implication. (See Acts 15 and the entire book of Galatians.) Judaistic teachers followed Paul's trail wherever he went preaching the gospel, and sought to subvert the churches he established. They denied that he was an apostle of Christ, repudiated the gospel of Christ he preached, and attempted to lead his converts to accepting circumcision and the law (Galatians 5:1-4). Paul's refusal to bow to these false teachers finally landed him in a Roman

THE WORK OF THE HOLY SPIRIT

prison. The Roman letter is Paul's in depth answer to the Jews who despised the gospel he preached, and to the Judaizing teachers who were perverting his certified gospel (Galatians 1:7-13; Romans 16:17-18). This raised the question as to how Paul could establish the truth of the gospel in his defense against all of his opposers. Two appeals are made in the letter: 1) The discussion and the development of the Old Testament show the weaknesses of the law and appeal to the prophets who announced beforehand the coming of Christ and the gospel. 2) The second appeal is to the miraculous gifts he had as an apostle and the apostolic gift of imparting spiritual gifts:

> Now the God of hope fill you with all joy and peace in believing, that ye may abound in hope, through the power of the Holy Ghost.
> And I myself also am persuaded of you, my brethren, that ye also are full of goodness, filled with all knowledge, able also to admonish one another.
> Nevertheless, brethren, I have written the more boldly unto you in some sort, as putting you in mind, because of the grace that is given to me of God,
> That I should be the minister of Jesus Christ to the Gentiles, ministering the gospel of God, that the offering up of the Gentiles might be acceptable, being sanctified by the Holy Ghost.
> I have therefore whereof I may glory through Jesus Christ in those things which pertain to God.
> For I will not dare to speak of any of those things which Christ hath not wrought by me, to make the Gentiles obedient, by word and deed,
> Through mighty signs and wonders, by the power of the Spirit of God; so that from Jerusalem, and round about unto Illyricum, I have fully preached the gospel of Christ.
> Yea, so have I strived to preach the gospel, not where Christ was named, lest I should build upon another man's foundation:
> But as it is written, To whom he was not spoken of, they shall see: and they that have not heard shall understand.
> For which cause also I have been much hindered from coming to you.
> But now having no more place in these parts, and having a great desire these many years to come unto you;
> Whensoever I take my journey into Spain, I will come to you: for I trust to see you in my journey, and to be brought on my way thitherward by you, if first I be somewhat filled with your company.

But now I go unto Jerusalem to minister unto the saints. (Romans 15:13-25).

For I long to see you, that I may impart unto you some spiritual gift, to the end ye may be established; (Romans 1:11).

In the Roman letter, Paul deals with all the basic issues of sin and redemption in answering both the Jew and the Judaizing teachers. This accounts for his discussion of the law. Since the law could not save the Jew, what hope could the Judaizing teacher offer to the Gentiles by binding on him circumcision and submission to the law?

> Now we know that what things soever the law saith, it saith to them who are under the law: that every mouth may be stopped, and all the world may become guilty before God.
> Therefore by the deeds of the law there shall no flesh be justified in his sight: for by the law is the knowledge of sin.
> But now the righteousness of God without the law is manifested, being witnessed by the law and the prophets:
> Even the righteousness of God which is by faith of Jesus Christ unto all and upon all them that believe: for there is no difference:
> For all have sinned, and come short of the glory of God;
> Being justified freely by his grace through the redemption that is in Christ Jesus:
> Whom God hath set forth to be a propitiation through faith in his blood, to declare his righteousness for the remission of sins that are past, through the forbearance of God;
> To declare, I say, at this time his righteousness: that he might be just, and the justifier of him which believeth in Jesus.
> Where is boasting then? It is excluded. By what law? of works? Nay: by the law of faith.
> Therefore we conclude that a man is justified by faith without the deeds of the law.
> Is he the God of the Jews only? is he not also of the Gentiles? Yes, of the Gentiles also:
> Seeing it is one God, which shall justify the circumcision by faith, and uncircumcision through faith.
> Do we then make void the law through faith? God forbid: yea, we establish the law. (Romans 3:19-31).

Notice the phrase, "But now," in Romans 3:21. This phrase puts the law, which made none righteous, in contrast with the righteousness

THE WORK OF THE HOLY SPIRIT 225

of the gospel. The righteousness of the gospel was witnessed by the law and the prophets. The law witnessed the righteousness of the gospel in its types and shadows. The prophets witnessed of the righteousness of the gospel in the promises and prophecies of the prophets. Isaiah is filled with prophecies concerning Christ, the gospel, and the church (Isaiah 2:1-4, 7-14, 9:6, 11:1-10, 35:8, 42:1-4, the entire fifty-third chapter, 56:5, 62:1-2). These prophecies from Isaiah are but a few of the prophecies in the Old Testament which witnessed to the righteousness which would be through Christ found in the gospel, located in the church, and offered to both Jew and Gentile alike upon the same basis, by the obedience of faith. Why did Paul make the contrast and why did he appeal to the prophets if there were not those who refused to accept the fact that Christ was the fulfillment of these prophecies? Why did Paul go into detail in showing that the law could not save unless there were Jews and Judaizing teachers who were teaching that it did save? If these false teachers were right, Paul was wrong. If Paul was right, they were wrong. It is vital to keep these things in mind in the study of Romans 8 or one is sure to misunderstand Paul's conclusions in this chapter.

The eighth chapter cannot be isolated from 1:18 through Chapter 7. How can one understand Paul's conclusion in this chapter if he does not see:

1. What Paul was working to establish.
2. How he established his conclusion. (It is my conviction that a failure to see the relationship of this chapter to the entire first division of the book is the basic reason for the difficulties that have arisen with the chapter.)
3. The "now" of Romans 8:1 sets the tone of Paul's conclusions of the first division of the book. The "now" of this verse is the culmination of Paul's development of the promise to Abraham and the purpose and the weaknesses of the law.

Chapter 8 is an expanded commentary of 3:19 to 31. The first four verses of Chapter 8 form the foundation for the discussion in the chapter.

> There is therefore now no condemnation to them which are in Christ Jesus, who walk not after the flesh, but after the Spirit.
> For the law of the Spirit of life in Christ Jesus hath made me free from the law of sin and death.

> For what the law could not do, in that it was weak through the flesh, God sending his own Son in the likeness of sinful flesh, and for sin, condemned sin in the flesh:
> That the righteousness of the law might be fulfilled in us, who walk not after the flesh, but after the Spirit. (Romans 8:1-4).

Notice the phrase, "There is therefore now," in 8:1. "Therefore" puts the chapter in contrast with something. What is the contrast? Evidently, the contrast is with what precedes Chapter 8. The chief contrast that Paul has made from 2:17 through Chapter 7 is the contrast between the law and the gospel. The word "now" of verse 1 further establishes the contrast.

> Therefore by the deeds of the law there shall no flesh be justified in his sight: for by the law is the knowledge of sin.
> But now the righteousness of God without the law is manifested, being witnessed by the law and the prophets, (Romans 3:20-21).
> For when we were in the flesh, the motions of sins, which were by the law, did work in our members to bring forth fruit unto death.
> But now we are delivered from the law, that being dead wherein we were held; that we should serve in newness of spirit, and not in the oldness of the letter (Romans 7:5-6).

Notice the contrast made between the law and the gospel, by the use of the phrase, "But now." It is this same contrast in Chapter 8. What is the situation "now"? There is no condemnation. Where is there no condemnation? In Christ. Where was condemnation until "now"? Under the law. "Therefore by the deeds of the law there shall no flesh be justified in his sight, for by the law is the knowledge of sin." Why was freedom from condemnation found in Christ?

> Whom God hath set forth to be a propitiation through faith in his blood, to declare his righteousness for the remission of sins that are past, through the forbearance of God;
> To declare, I say, at this time his righteousness: that he might be just, and the justifier of him which believeth in Jesus. (Romans 3:25-26).

Even those who lived under the law before the coming of Christ could not be saved apart from Christ and the atoning power of His blood. If the ones that lived under the law before the coming of Christ

THE WORK OF THE HOLY SPIRIT

could not be saved except through faith in His blood, how much less could the law do after Christ came? Yet, there were those Jews who continued to reject Christ, and the Judaizing teachers, who claimed to accept Him, but still insisted upon holding on to the law. The Roman letter is Paul's answer to the false claims of the Jews who still rejected Christ and the Judaizing teachers who pretended to accept Him, while holding to the law. The "now" of Romans 8:1 is the "now" of Christ and the gospel contrasted with the past and the law.

Before beginning a study of Chapter 8, let us take a brief survey through the first seven chapters. Notice carefully the following which Paul has developed in the first seven chapters:

1. Paul traced the downward plunge of man in sin (Chapter 1:18 forward).
2. He proved that both Jew and Gentile were under sin (3:9).
3. He answered the charge of some that he was encouraging evil (3:8; 6:1).
4. Paul proved that the law could not save (3:20).
5. Paul proved that salvation was for Jew and Gentile alike (1:16).
6. Paul showed that salvation was through Christ and the gospel by the obedience of faith, not by the works of the law (1:5; 3:20).
7. Paul showed that the promise to Abraham was of faith that it might be by grace. The promise was not limited to the seed, which was of the law (Jew), but to those who were of the faith of Abraham (4:16).

Both the Jew, who had rejected Christ, and the Judaizing teachers were denying these principles that Paul had established. Chapter 8 summarizes all of these principles and answers the arguments of those who opposed Paul's gospel, which was spiritual, not fleshly, and for Jew and Gentile alike.

WHO WALK NOT AFTER THE FLESH

The word "flesh" is used in two ways: 1. A reference to Judaism, which was a fleshly, carnal religion.

> Which was a figure for the time then present, in which were offered both gifts and sacrifices, that could not make him that did the service perfect, as pertaining to the conscience;
> Which stood only in meats and drinks, and divers washings, and carnal ordinances, imposed on them until the time of reformation....

> For if the blood of bulls and of goats, and the ashes of an heifer sprinkling the unclean, sanctifieth to the purifying of the flesh: (Hebrews 9:9, 10, 13).

But not only was Judaism fleshly and carnal, but its corruption by the Jews and Judaizing teachers overlooked sin and encouraged sin. Their perversion of it added to their breaking of it and dishonoring God (Romans 2:23). This in turn led to God's name being blasphemed among the Gentiles (Romans 2:24). Thus, they not only could not keep the law as given, but in an attempt to be saved by it, sought to make the law condone sin.

The word "flesh" is sometimes used as a synonym for the word "Judaism." The old covenant left its subjects in the flesh where it found them. The old covenant was addressed to them as men in the flesh. Neither righteousness, nor eternal life, was enjoyed in it. Even those that lived under it could only be saved by the provisions of a better covenant (Romans 3:25-38). The Judaizing teachers sought to bind the law on Gentile Christians and, in so doing, only left them in the flesh. If the old covenant was a covenant in the flesh, and apart from the new covenant left the Jew still in the flesh, what could it do for the Gentile but leave him where it found him, in the flesh? Paul insisted in the Roman letter, and in other Epistles, that it was not the flesh that made one a child of God. " . . . They which are the children of the flesh, these are not the children of God . . . " (Romans 9:8). Who are the children of God? Answer: The children of promise. The children of promise culminated in Christ and the gospel, and are those who are children of God by faith in Christ when baptized (Galatians 3:26-27). In answer to the Judaizers who were disturbing the Christians at Corinth, Paul stated: "Wherefore henceforth know we no man after the flesh: yea, though we have known Christ after the flesh, yet now henceforth know we him no more," (II Corinthians 5:16). Macknight gives the following paraphrase of this verse:

> Wherefore since Christ died for all, we, the apostles of Christ, from this time forth in the exercise of our ministry show respect to no man more than another on account of his being a Jew according to the flesh, and even if we have formally esteemed Christ on account of His being a Jew, yet now we esteem Him no more on that account.

In writing to the Philippians, Paul makes the same argument:

> Though I might also have confidence in the flesh. If any other man thinketh that he hath whereof he might trust in the flesh, I more:
> Circumcised the eighth day, of the stock of Israel, of the tribe of Benjamin, an Hebrew of the Hebrews; as touching the law, a Pharisee. (Philippians 3:4-5).

In all of these passages, the word "flesh" is used to equal Judaism.

Romans 7:5 makes it clear that the meaning of "in the flesh" sometimes is a reference to Judaism: "For when we were in the flesh, the motions of sins, which were by the law, did work in our members to bring forth fruit unto death," (Romans 7:5). "In the flesh" of this verse is equal to being under the law, which was a fleshly system. It is important to keep this in mind as this is included in its use in Romans 8. Finally, Galatians 3:3 establishes the fact that "in the flesh" is used in reference to Judaism: "Are ye so foolish? having begun in the Spirit, are ye now made perfect by the flesh?"

The gospel, received through miraculous gifts of the Spirit to Paul, an apostle, and the gifts of the Spirit which the Galatians had received, is that which is indicated by the phrase, "begun in the Spirit." The word "Spirit" here is really equal to the gospel, which was received by the revelation of the Spirit. "Are ye now made perfect by the flesh"—the law, which was carnal, or fleshly, is that which is signified by the phrase, "by the flesh." Judaizing teachers were seeking to persuade Gentile Christians who had accepted the gospel to also be circumcised and to keep the law. These false teachers were insisting that the gospel was not sufficient. They were teaching Gentiles that in order to be saved, they must accept circumcision and the law. The phrase, "made perfect by the flesh," is a synonym for the law, or the Judaistic system. This was an argument that Paul answered not only in the Galatian letter, but also in the Roman letter.

2. The word "flesh" is also used to denote the body. "But put ye on the Lord Jesus Christ, and make not provision for the flesh, to fulfil the lusts thereof," (Romans 13:14).

> Now the works of the flesh are manifest, which are these; Adultery, fornication, uncleanness, lasciviousness,
> Idolatry, witchcraft, hatred, variance, emulations, wrath, strife, seditions, heresies,

Envyings, murders, drunkenness, revellings, and such like: of the which I tell you before, as I have also told you in time past, that they which do such things shall not inherit the kingdom of God. (Galatians 5:19-21).

The avenue of sin is through its appeal to the flesh. The word "flesh" is used also in this sense. In answering some who had charged Paul's gospel of grace of encouraging sin, Paul shows that such is not true. Paul made it plain that the gospel of grace, which frees one from the bondage of sin, through the blood of Christ, is no license to sin. Rather than the gospel of grace giving one a license to sin, his body is to be used in the service of righteousness.

Likewise reckon ye also yourselves to be dead indeed unto sin, but alive unto God through Jesus Christ our Lord.
Let not sin therefore reign in your mortal body, that ye should obey it in the lusts thereof.
Neither yield ye your members as instruments of unrighteousness unto sin: but yield yourselves unto God, as those that are alive from the dead, and your members as instruments of righteousness unto God.
For sin shall not have dominion over you: for ye are not under the law, but under grace. (Romans 6:11-14).

It is for this reason that Paul states his conclusion in Romans 8 that one is not a debtor to the flesh and to allow the flesh to control ends in death. "Therefore, brethren, we are debtors, not to the flesh, to live after the flesh. For if ye live after the flesh, ye shall die: but if ye through the Spirit do mortify the deeds of the body, ye shall live," (Romans 8:12-13).

THE WORD "SPIRIT"

The word "Spirit" is also used in two ways in the New Testament:

1. The word is used sometimes as a synonym of the gospel. The gospel is spiritual. It has to do with man's spirit. The word "Spirit" is sometimes used where it simply means the gospel. The old covenant was a covenant of the letter and not a covenant of spirit. Judaism, with all of its privileges, was only the shadow of better things to come. The condition of the Jew under the law was as different from the Christian under the gospel as flesh is different from spirit. Their standing under the law was as much

unlike the Christian under the gospel as the difference in the position of a servant and a son. This is the reason that Paul represents the Jew as being under the flesh, while being under the law or covenant of the letter. While Christians are represented as being in the Spirit, or being under the covenant of the Spirit. The service of the Jew is spoken of as a service in the "oldness" of the letter. A Christian's service is in the newness of spirit. Paul speaks of the Jew while under the covenant of the letter as in bondage, or slavery, and possessed of the spirit of slaves, but when in the covenant of the Spirit, as being sons of God and possessing the spirit of adoption. Paul then concludes that believing Jews are no longer servants, but have been raised to the rank of sons (Galatians 4:7). The state of the Jew, is represented under the covenant of the letter, but believing Christian Jews are under the covenant of the Spirit. The bondage of the Jew under the first covenant forms a contrast to the liberty and freedom under the new covenant. The same contrast between the law and the gospel is made in II Corinthians 3. Note in particular verse 6: "Who also hath made us [apostles] able ministers of the new testament; not of the letter [the law], but of the spirit [the gospel]: for the letter killeth [the law], but the spirit giveth life [the gospel]." The new covenant is called spirit, while the old is called letter. In the old, a letter was presented to the eye, but in the new it is written on the heart (spirit). The tables of the old covenant were stone; the table of the new covenant is the spirit or the mind of man. The letter when engraved on stone was cold and dead as the stone itself. It could not give life. The gospel, when believed, received into man's spirit or mind, motivates man's spirit in loving obedience. Christians are not "in the flesh," the letter, the law, or Judaism; but "in the spirit," the gospel, and the new covenant. All the institutions under the old terminated in the flesh. They sanctified and purified the flesh (Hebrews 9:13). The new covenant is fitly called a covenant of Spirit, because it has to do, not with the flesh, but the mind of the spirit of man. It is true that there are written words in the New Testament, as there were written words in the Old Testament. But there is a moral fitness in the words of the New Testament to be the medium of the inspiration of the Holy Spirit. As the spirit of all goodness, righteousness, and truth, there was a moral fitness in the engraven words on stone to be the medium of inspiration of bondage and fear. The covenant of the letter could not inspire men with the spirit of sons. It demanded what it did not impart strength to give. It presented a perfect rule, but left man unable to conform to its demands. The more a Jew understood it, the less comfort he received from it. When rightly understood, it filled his heart with the spirit of bondage, and ended in condemnation and death. The new covenant is morally adapted to inspire the spirit of adoption and sonship. This is the reason that the spirit is sometimes contrasted with flesh—spirit being used for the gospel, flesh being used for the law.

2. A second use of the phrase, "in the spirit," is to indicate the miraculous and the direct operation of the Spirit by which the gospel was given and confirmed. It is used in this way to emphasize the gospel, in contrast with false teachers who were uninspired and who could not confirm their teaching. "But I will come to you shortly, if the Lord will, and will know, not the SPEECH of them which are puffed up, but the POWER. For the kingdom of God is not in WORD, but in POWER," (I Corinthians 4:19-20). "For our gospel came not unto you in WORD ONLY, but also in POWER, and IN THE HOLY SPIRIT, and in much assurance; as ye know what manner of men we were among you for your sake," (I Thessalonians 1:5).

Notice the phrases in this verse which prove the integrity of the gospel Paul preached to the Thessalonians: a) "... our gospel came not in WORD ONLY...." Was the gospel that Paul preached to the Thessalonians really a genuine gospel? If so, where was the proof? Could the Thessalonians be sure that the gospel which they had received was not a counterfeit? Did the Thessalonians have anything more than Paul's word that the gospel he preached was the true gospel? The answer is yes. The gospel received by the Thessalonians was one that came IN POWER and in the HOLY SPIRIT. The word "power" indicates the supernatural, or miraculous power; power that demonstrated, the manifestation of power that was visible to the eye (Acts 2:33).

If the gospel came in power, where did this power come from? The source of the power was the Holy Spirit. The phrase, "in the Spirit," simply means the source of the gospel preached, and the miraculous manifestations to confirm it as a divine revelation. Because the gospel had been preached in the Spirit, the Thessalonians received this with full assurance that it was the genuine gospel given by God, and that Paul was an apostle of Christ.

The phrase, "in the Spirit," also includes the miraculous gifts given by the laying on of hands by the apostles. Macknight comments as follows on this phrase in I Thessalonians 1:5: "The Holy Spirit here denotes those spiritual gifts of prophecy, healing diseases, speaking foreign languages, and the interpretation of languages which the apostles communicated to believers for the purpose of edifying one another and for confirming the truth of the gospel." The direct operation of the Spirit not only provided revelation, but carried with it the miraculous manifestations, which were the credentials of the credibility of the gospel. The credibility of the gospel is now found in the Book. The credibility of the ones that proclaim the gospel is measured by the Book. The preacher today proves his message by the Bible, not by miracles. This accounts for the language used to contrast the gospel and its messengers with false teachers who opposed it in the apostolic age. The heart of the Roman letter is Paul's defense of the gospel in opposition to Judaizing teachers. It is an answer to all the false claims of these teachers. This accounts for the lengthy discussion in the book of the law and its inability to save. This is the reason that three whole chapters are given to the discussion of the Jew (Chapters 8, 9, and 10). The eighth chapter is Paul's conclusion and arguments concerning the law and the gospel in the first division of the letter.

ROMANS 8:9

"But ye are not in the flesh, but in the Spirit, if so be that the Spirit of God dwell in you. Now if any man have not the Spirit of Christ, he is none of his," (Romans 8:9). It is important to study this verse in the context of the whole Roman letter as well as the eighth chapter. This verse is appealed to as proof that the Spirit personally dwells in the Christian. But it must be remembered that the statement was made in the context of the things Paul has already discussed.

"But ye are not in the flesh . . . "—this is a direct statement made to the Romans that they are not in Judaism. Does one ask, Why would Paul say to the Gentiles, "You are not in Judaism"? Let it be remembered that this is exactly what the Judaizing teachers were working to accomplish. They were willing to accept a Gentile Christian, provided he would be circumcised and keep the law. Everywhere Paul preached, Judaizing teachers followed and tried to convince Christians of the need of being circumcised and keeping the law. This is the basic argument discussed in the entire Galatian letter, and while it is discussed more in detail in the Galatian letter, it is also in the background in the Roman letter. The false teachers were contending that the gospel was all right as far as it went, but it did not perfect the Christian (Galatians 3:3). If a Gentile accepted circumcision and the law to be complete, would he not then be in the flesh; that is, under the law, in Judaism, as opposed to being in Christ? (Galatians 5:4). Furthermore, Judaizing teachers, in appealing to Christians to accept circumcision, encouraged licentious living. These teachers lived that kind of life and certainly would not forbid it to their converts. "For they that are such serve not our Lord Jesus Christ, but their own belly . . . " (Romans 16:18). "(For many walk, of whom I have told you often, and now tell you even weeping, that they are the enemies of the cross of Christ: Whose end is destruction, whose God is their belly, and whose glory is in their shame, who mind earthly things.)" (Philippians 3:18-19). These were walking "in the flesh,"; that is, perverted Judaism and the evil life encouraged through such teachings.

IN THE SPIRIT

"In the Spirit" is put in contrast with "not in the flesh." Christians were not in Judaism as false teachers were insisting, but if they were not in Judaism as these false teachers claimed, where was the proof? The proof was "in the Spirit." Paul's argument here, in answer to the false teachers, is the same as in I Thessalonians 1:5. How would "in the Spirit" answer false teachers? The miraculous manifestation was proof of the gospel received by the Romans. There were spiritual gifts in the church at Rome (Romans 12:3-8). Paul had said in the introduction of the letter that he wanted to come to Rome to impart spiritual gifts (Romans 1:11). But why would Paul want to impart spiritual gifts to a church that already had gifts? The impartation of spiritual gifts through the hands of Paul would further confirm Paul as an apostle of Christ and the genuineness of the gospel he preached. It is clear that Paul knew that the gospel he preached, setting aside the law and placing Jew and Gentile in one body of the church, was opposed at Rome, as well as everywhere else. If Paul could visit Rome and impart spiritual gifts to some in the church, this would settle any fears that the Judaizing teachers might have created about Paul and "his gospel." Paul wanted to go to Rome to impart spiritual gifts, not because the church in Rome did not have any, but to establish his apostleship to the Roman brethren, as well as impart spiritual gifts to any in Rome who had had no access to an apostle to receive a gift.

Lest some think that "in the Spirit" does not mean "to be inspired by," let me give what Thayer says. Here is his comment on the phrase, "in the Spirit": "To be in the power of, to be actuated by, to be inspired by the Holy Spirit, (see Romans 8:9)." The same phrase is found in Revelation 1:10 and 4:2. While some may question whether

THE WORK OF THE HOLY SPIRIT 235

1:10 means the inspiration of John, though I think it clearly refers to his being inspired to receive the revelation of the vision in the book, as the rest of the verse indicates, there can be no doubt of the meaning "being inspired by the Spirit" in 4:2.

> After this I looked, and, behold, a door was opened in heaven: and the first voice which I heard was as it were of a trumpet talking with me; which said, Come up hither, and I will shew thee things which must be hereafter.
> And immediately I was in the spirit; and, behold, a throne was set in heaven, and one sat on the throne. (Revelation 4:1-2).

There cannot be any question but what "in the Spirit" of Revelation 4:2 refers to the inspiration of John in receiving the revelations, or visions, which are presented in the book of Revelation. Here is proof from Thayer, a recognized scholar, that "in the Spirit" means "to be inspired by the Spirit." This is miraculous power. But not only do we have proof from Thayer that "in the Spirit" means "to be inspired by," we have a divine commentary on the meaning of the phrase, "in the Spirit," in Revelation 4:2. "In the Spirit" in Revelation 4:2 means "to be inspired by." Thayer further adds that "the phrase in the Spirit is used in opposition to the phrase, in the flesh." "In the flesh" and "in the Spirit" are used in opposition one to another. "In the flesh" was equal to Judaism, or the law, and particularly a reference to the false teachers, who were "natural men," uninspired (I Corinthians 2:14); "sensual, having not the Spirit," (Jude 19).

"In the Spirit" of Romans 8:9 is equal to being inspired by the Spirit. " . . . If so be that the Spirit of God dwell in you,"—since "in the Spirit," according to Thayer, means "inspired by," the dwelling in the Spirit in this phrase would mean "miraculous indwelling." This is a reference to the miraculous gifts in the church at Rome (Chapter 12:3-6).

There are other passages that teach that the dwelling of the Spirit was a reference to miraculous gifts. "Know ye not that ye are the temple of God, and that the Spirit of God dwelleth in you?" (I Corinthians 3:16; see also I Corinthians 6:19). These statements were made to a church that had miraculous gifts. The letter was written to the church (I Corinthians 1:2). The church at Corinth had miraculous gifts (Chapters 12, 14). One of the main things that is discussed in the Corinthian letter is spiritual gifts. Would it not seem that a letter which was written to a church (with one of the main things discussed being spiritual gifts), when the Spirit was said to dwell in the church, be a reference to the miraculous gifts that were in the church. If not, why not?

There is still another passage that speaks of the indwelling of the Spirit that confirms the fact that the indwelling was a reference to a miraculous indwelling: "That good thing which was committed unto thee keep by the Holy Ghost which DWELLETH IN US," (II Timothy 1:14). That which was committed to Timothy was the gospel. He was to keep that which had been committed to him by the Holy Spirit. Surely, Timothy would not be admonished to keep the gospel which had been committed to him by a non-miraculous indwelling of the Holy Spirit. "Which dwelleth in us"—"us" equals Paul, as well as Timothy. In what way did the Spirit dwell in Paul? Was not the dwelling of the Spirit in Paul miraculous? Surely, Paul, who was an apostle, would not speak of the Spirit dwelling in him and mean non-miraculous indwelling. The gospel was committed to Paul by inspiration and this was by the miraculous power of the Holy Spirit.

But how did the Spirit dwell in Timothy? Here is the answer: "Wherefore I put thee in remembrance that thou stir up the gift of God, which is in thee by the putting on of my hands," (II Timothy 1:6). "Neglect not the gift that is in thee, which was given thee by prophecy, with the laying on of the hands of the presbytery," (I Timothy 4:14). The gift that Timothy was to stir up was one that he had received from Paul. This certainly was miraculous. The spiritual gift which Timothy received from Paul is mentioned in the same chapter where the Spirit is said to dwell in Timothy. The indwelling of the Spirit in Timothy in this verse is likewise a reference to the miraculous indwelling. Now we have another verse that speaks of the Spirit dwelling in one, but it was a miraculous indwelling. The gift of II Timothy 1:6 belongs to the apostolic period when there were spiritual gifts. The indwelling of the Spirit in verse 14 belongs to the apostolic age when they had the Spirit with miraculous manifestations.

I Corinthians 3:16 and 6:19 speak of the indwelling of the Spirit. The letter was addressed to the church (I Corinthians 1:2); the church had spiritual gifts (Chapters 12 to 14). One of the main sections of the book deals with spiritual gifts (Chapters 12 to 14). Would it not follow that when the writer speaks of the Spirit dwelling in the church, that he had reference to the Spirit dwelling in the church because it had spiritual gifts? The Bible speaks of the indwelling of the Spirit in Paul and Timothy. Paul was an apostle and the Spirit dwelt in him

THE WORK OF THE HOLY SPIRIT 237

miraculously. Timothy had a spiritual gift received through the laying on of Paul's hands, and thus the indwelling of the Spirit in Timothy was miraculous.

There is only one other passage that uses the word "dwell" in connection with the Spirit: "Hereby know we that we dwell in him, and he in us, because he hath given us of his Spirit," (I John 4:13). John said that he knew that God dwelt in him because "He hath given us [apostles] of His Spirit." This statement is made in answer to false teachers who repudiated the apostles. The next verse proves that such is the case: "And we [apostles] have seen [I John 1:1] and do testify [bear witness—I John 1:2] that the Father sent the Son to be the Saviour of the world." Verse 14 is a direct reference to I John 1:1, 2, which shows that John is speaking of the apostles. The Bible speaks of the Spirit dwelling in the apostles, but how did the Holy Spirit dwell in the apostle? Was it a miraculous indwelling or a non-miraculous indwelling? How was the Holy Spirit promised to the apostles? Was it promised to them miraculously or non-miraculously? Here is the answer:

> And I will pray the Father, and he shall give you another Comforter, that he may abide with you for ever;
> Even the Spirit of truth; whom the world cannot receive, because it seeth him not, neither knoweth him: but ye know him; for he dwelleth with you, and shall be in you. (John 14:16-17).

The promise of the Spirit to the apostles was miraculous. In this same context, read John 14:26, 15:26-27, and 16:13. The first mention of the indwelling of the Spirit is the promise of the miraculous indwelling of the Spirit. The indwelling of the Spirit is mentioned five times: Romans 8:9, I Corinthians 3:16, 6:19, II Timothy 1:6, and I John 4:13. In each of these instances the statement is made to a church that had spiritual gifts, or an individual who had a spiritual gift. The church at Rome, as well as the church at Corinth, had spiritual gifts (Romans 12:3-6). Indeed, without a New Testament, since it had not been written, and without an apostle in Rome, how could the church in Rome have functioned without spiritual gifts?

"And I myself also am persuaded of you my brethren that you are also full of goodness, filled with all knowledge and able also to admonish one another," (Romans 15:14). How could the church in Rome be filled with knowledge and able to admonish one another unless it was by the means of spiritual gifts? At the time Paul wrote this statement to the church at Rome, they did not have a New Testament. It seems to me that the only way that they could have had the knowledge of which Paul spoke, and be able to admonish one another, was by the spiritual gifts that were in the church at Rome, but since the church at Rome had spiritual gifts (Romans 12:3-6 shows), and were filled with all knowledge (which would involve inspiration), when Paul said to the church at Rome that the Spirit dwelt in them, did this not add further evidence to what had already been said to show that the indwelling of the Spirit in Romans 8:9 is a reference to the miraculous indwelling—not a non-miraculous indwelling? "In the Spirit" of Romans 8:9 is equal to being inspired by the Spirit. This is evidence that the dwelling of the Spirit in the next part of the verse is a reference to the miraculous indwelling that was contrasted with those in the flesh, who were uninspired teachers. The teacher that was "uninspired," not "in the Spirit" but "in the flesh," did not belong to Christ. " . . . If any man have not the Spirit of Christ, he is none of his," (Romans 8:9), was the proof that he was a false teacher. He was uninspired; guided only by fleshly, human wisdom. He was a teacher who had only words; no miraculous power to confirm the Word (I Corinthians 4:19-20). The statement, "If any man have not the Spirit of Christ, he is none of his," is directed toward those who were false teachers, and were disturbing the church in Rome; in fact, were disturbing all the churches which Paul had established, as well as churches elsewhere. This is Paul's statement to the church at Rome as a means of distinguishing between those who were guided by the Spirit, having a spiritual gift, preaching the same gospel he preached; and distinguishing them from false teachers who were uninspired, having not the Spirit, and therefore not belonging to Christ.

Were there such people in view in the Roman letter? Let us see if we can find some who had only speeches or words. Is there a reference to some in the Roman letter who were uninspired teachers? The answer is yes.

> Now I beseech you, brethren, mark them which cause divisions and offences contrary to the doctrine which ye have learned; and avoid them.
> For they that are such serve not our Lord Jesus Christ, but their own belly; and by GOOD WORDS AND FAIR SPEECHES, deceive the hearts of the simple. (Romans 16:17-18).

Here were some that had only speeches, just as Paul described in I Corinthians 4:19-20. What did these men lack? Having not the Spirit of

Romans 8:9, or miraculous power to confirm their teaching. What did Paul command the Romans to do with these teachers? "Mark them." These are the same ones that are said not to have the Spirit and did not belong to Christ in Chapter 8:9.

There is further proof in the New Testament that this is a contrast between an inspired teacher and false teachers who were uninspired and who could not confirm their teaching. "But the anointing which ye have received of him abideth in you, and ye need not that any man teach you: but as the same anointing teacheth you of all things, and is truth, and is no lie, and even as it hath taught you, ye shall abide in him," (I John 2:27). Notice John's statement, "... Ye need not that ANY MAN teach you." Who is the "any man" of this verse? He is the uninspired man. Those who were false teachers who were seeking to seduce the one that John was writing to. The word "seduce" characterized the method of these false teachers. The people that John wrote to had the anointing of the Spirit—spiritual gifts—which provided revelation so they were not dependent on uninspired teachers. The "any man," uninspired teacher of I John 2:27, is the same as the false spirits they were commanded to try or prove in I John 4:1. The "any man" of Romans 8:9, having not the Spirit, did not belong to Christ. They were false teachers. They were teaching things contrary to the doctrine of Christ and causing division (Romans 16:17). The false teachers were not servants of Christ, but served their own bellies. They were uninspired teachers who could not confirm their teaching, having only speeches. Their speech was with enticing words of man's wisdom and not in the demonstration and the power of the Spirit (I Corinthians 2:4). If the Romans had accepted the speeches of these false teachers, their faith would have stood in the wisdom of man and not in the power of God, just as Paul said of the Corinthians (I Corinthians 2:5). Since Paul had said that he had hoped to come to Rome to impart spiritual gifts as confirmation of his apostleship, (and of course this would confirm his gospel of the equality of both Jews and Gentiles in one body), why would he want to do this unless there were those who opposed him as an apostle and the gospel he preached? Who were these, if not Judaizing teachers? How could the Romans detect these teachers? Such teachers were "in the flesh, not in the Spirit"; that is, uninspired in their teaching. They were unable to confirm their teaching. Why? Because they did not have the Spirit of Christ. Since they did not have the Spirit of Christ, they were false teachers and did not belong to Christ.

ROMANS 8:11

"But if the Spirit of him that raised up Jesus from the dead dwell in you, he that raised up Christ from the dead shall also quicken your mortal bodies by his Spirit that dwelleth in you." The Spirit that raised up Christ from the dead was a miraculous operation of the Spirit. Would it not be rather strange reasoning for Paul to appeal to a miraculous operation of the Spirit to prove a non-miraculous operation? As already pointed out in verse 9, "in the Spirit" meant "to be inspired by, under the power of the Spirit," (Thayer); this was a reference to spiritual gifts. Then Paul followed this by a reference to the Spirit that raised Christ from the dead, which surely was miraculous. "... He that raised up Christ from the dead shall also quicken your mortal bodies by the Spirit that dwelleth in you." This is sometimes interpreted to mean the resurrection of the body. If this is correct, this would still mean a miraculous operation of the Spirit, for a non-miraculous operation would not raise the body from the grave. But there are difficulties with this interpretation. If it is the indwelling of the Spirit that assures the resurrection of the body from the grave, what about the resurrection of sinners who could not have the indwelling of the Spirit? The preceding verse says the body is dead. The death spoken of here is not physical death, but the fact that the body is dead to the power and control of sin. Paul's argument here was, in substance, the same as that which he had already made in Chapter 6. Notice his arguments in Chapter 6: 1) Grace does not mean that one may continue to live a life of sin (6:1). 2) Christians have died to sin and therefore can no longer live a life of sin (6:2). 3) Christians die to sin in being baptized into Christ (Romans 6:3-5). 4) In being baptized into Christ, the old man is crucified and the body of sin is destroyed (6:6). In dying to sin, the Christian is freed from the guilt and the power of sin (6:7). 6) Christians, in being dead to sin, are alive to God through Christ (6:11). 7) Through the atonement of Christ, sins can be forgiven and Christians are not to let sin reign in their mortal bodies. They are not to be controlled by the lusts of the body (6:12). 8) Christians are not to yield the members of their body as instruments of sin, but to use the instruments of the body in the service of righteousness (Romans 6:13). The reason that the body is freed from sin, and sin no longer has dominion over the body, is because the law has been abolished. Under the law, sin had dominion. The law, as a system, did not provide any escape from the dominion of sin. The blood of animals did not take away sin (Hebrews 10:1-4). But under grace, the blood of Christ atones for sin. A Christian is no longer in bondage to the flesh. Sin does not have dominion over him. Even when the Christian sins, provisions are

THE WORK OF THE HOLY SPIRIT 241

made in the gospel for his forgiveness, and sin does not have dominion over him. But the provision under grace does not include a life of sin. The Christian, being freed from the dominion of sin, is to use his body in righteous living, not the sinful indulgence of the flesh. The miraculous gifts that dwelt in the church until revelation was completed provided the instructions that they were to follow in righteous living. Since Christians are freed from sin, and sin does not have dominion over them, they are not debtors to the flesh (Romans 8:12). Paul appeals to the Romans not to submit to the Judaizing teachers with their fleshly religion, nor to allow the false teachers to influence them to live according to the lust of the flesh.

ROMANS 8:14

"For as many as are led by the Spirit of God, they are the sons of God." It is true that one is led by the Spirit through the written Word today, but it should be remembered that when Paul wrote the Roman letter, the written revelation had not been completed and churches were led by the Spirit, by the spiritual gifts which they received through the hands of an apostle. The phrase, "as many," strikes at the Judiazing teachers who did not have the Spirit and who did not belong to Christ (Romans 8:9). This statement is made to show that both Jew and Gentile were sons of God and the proof of their being sons of God was spiritual gifts that provided the revelation which led them, and of course this would include the revelation of the gospel by the apostles and the miraculous manifestations of the apostles to confirm this revelation. Spiritual gifts were given to Christians without distinction, whether Jew or Gentile, male or female, bond or free, to establish the spiritual equality of all. False teachers were opposed to all being sons of God by faith (Galatians 3:26-29). God answered their false teaching, not only by the gospel preached by Paul, but also in bestowing spiritual gifts on the Gentiles, as well as the Jews. Joel had foretold that spiritual gifts would be given without distinction, and one of the purposes of spiritual gifts being given without distinction was to show that the gospel was for all, Jew and Gentile alike. Spiritual gifts, given to the Gentiles, presented an argument that no Judaizing teacher could answer. These gifts furnished the revelation, which was to lead or guide, until revelation was completed. The church in Rome had spiritual gifts (Romans 12:3-6). This was proof that those who were in the church at Rome were sons of God. The context of this verse seems to me to demand this interpretation: 1) The Spirit dwelt in them (Romans 8:9). 2) False teachers did not have the Spirit to guide them (Romans 8:9). 3) It was the miraculous operation of the Spirit that raised Christ from the dead (Romans 8:11). 4) The leading of the Spirit in 8:14 was by the indwelling of the Spirit mentioned in the preceding verses. If one makes the indwelling in the preceding verses non-miraculous, then he must switch from being led by the indwelling of the Spirit to being led by the Spirit in the written Word. While the latter is true now, this was not the case when Paul wrote the Roman letter. The miraculous indwelling then did lead through the revelation given directly. The miraculous indwelling, spiritual gifts, also was evidence that the Gentiles were sons of God. Spiritual gifts in the church at Rome were proof that the Christians in Rome were sons of God, and these spiritual gifts in the church at Rome were an answer to the Judaizing teachers who denied that Gentiles were sons of God as well as Jews.

ROMANS 8:15

"For ye have not received the spirit of bondage again to fear; but ye have received the Spirit of adoption, whereby we cry, Abba, Father." This verse adds evidence that the interpretation given to verse 14 is correct. Gentile Christians did not have to fear the spirit of bondage again. This is descriptive of the disposition that characterized those under the law. The law engendered a spirit of bondage and fear (Galatians 4:23). How could it do otherwise? It was a law that demanded perfection, but there are no perfect people. It was a law that no man could keep and therefore did not justify (Romans 3:20). The law left man under the curse since he could not do all the things that were "written in the book of the law," (Galatians 3:10). Apart from Christ, there was no redemption from that curse (Galatians 3:13). Sin held dominion over men under the law (Romans 6:14). The law could not free the conscience from sin (Hebrews 10:1-4). All of this ended in condemnation and death. The spirit, begotten by the law, was the spirit, or disposition, of bondage and fear. "And deliver them who through fear of death were all their lifetime subject to bondage," (Hebrews 2:15). The spirit of the law, or the disposition that went with it, is described in Hebrews 12:18-21:

> For ye are not come unto the mount that might be touched, and that burned with fire, nor unto blackness, and darkness, and tempest,
> And the sound of a trumpet, and the voice of words; which voice they that heard intreated that the word should not be spoken to them any more:
> (For they could not endure that which was commanded, And if so much as a beast touch the mountain, it shall be stoned, or thrust through with a dart:

And so terrible was the sight, that Moses said, I exceedingly fear and quake:)

The concluding statement of these verses which says that "Moses said, I exceedingly fear and quake," is symbolic of the bondage and fear that characterized the law. These verses which describe the scene at the giving of the law denote the disposition produced under the law. It was enough to make men shake in their boots. This was all that the Judaizing teachers had to offer with their "Judaistic gospel," which could not be called a gospel, for it was not good news. "But ye have received the spirit of adoption, whereby we cry, Abba, Father." Here is the disposition produced by the gospel. It does not beget a spirit of fear and bondage. The grace of the gospel offers freedom from the guilt, condemnation, and death produced by sin. The gospel made it possible for Gentile Christians to draw near in the full assurance of faith, with a conscience cleansed from sin when they were baptized into Christ (Hebrews 10:22; I Peter 3:21). The gospel does not result in a disposition of bondage and fear. Hebrews 12:22-24 presents the contrast of the gospel and the law:

> But ye are come unto mount Sion, and unto the city of the living God, the heavenly Jerusalem, and to an innumerable company of angels,
> To the general assembly and church of the firstborn, which are written in heaven, and to God the Judge of all, and to the spirits of just men made perfect,
> And to Jesus, the mediator of the new covenant, and to the blood of sprinkling, that speaketh better things than that of Abel.

The gospel promotes a disposition of loving obedience. The Christian has been freed from the dominion of sin through the blood of Christ and serves God in the spirit of sonship, and not slavery. Here is Paul's appeal to Gentile Christians to not forsake the gospel and allow the Judaizing teachers to bring them into the bondage of the law. Who, in his right mind, would want to forsake the gospel with its privileges and blessings, for the bondage and fear of the law? But this was what the false teachers, with good words and fair speeches, were attempting to do. May I add that I have grave fear that many who claim to be Christians today, attempt to serve God with a disposition that characterized those under the law, rather than serving Him with a disposition of sonship which belongs to the gospel. The gospel should make us fear sin, but not be afraid of God.

ROMANS 8:16

"The Spirit itself beareth witness with our spirit, that we are the children of God." It should be kept in mind that Paul is appealing to evidence to establish: 1) His apostleship, in answer to Judaizing teachers who denied that he was an apostle of Christ. 2) Paul was seeking to prove the genuineness of the gospel being for both Jew and Gentile alike. 3) Paul was answering false teachers who denied that he was an apostle, that his gospel was genuine, and that the gospel was for both Jew and Gentile. 4) How could Paul defend his apostleship, the integrity of the gospel he preached, and show that the gospel included both Jew and Gentile? The answer was the miraculous confirmation of the gospel which he preached (Mark 16:20; Hebrews 2:3-4). What was the credential of an apostle if not the miraculous operation of the Spirit (II Corinthians 12:12)? Why was it necessary for Paul to prove his apostleship? He was an apostle especially to the Gentiles; he contended that the gospel was for the Gentile as well as for the Jew. He opposed all that sought to bind the law on the Gentile. This was the reason Paul and his apostleship were so bitterly denounced by Judaizing teachers. It was these false teachers that Paul was answering in Romans 8. Paul makes the same appeal in Chapter 15:16-20:

> That I should be the minister of Jesus Christ to the Gentiles, ministering the gospel of God, that the offering up of the Gentiles might be acceptable, being sanctified by the Holy Ghost.
> I have therefore whereof I may glory through Jesus Christ in those things which pertain to God.
> For I will not dare to speak of any of those things which Christ hath not wrought by me, to make the Gentiles obedient, by word and deed,
> Through mighty signs and wonders, by the power of the Spirit of God; so that from Jerusalem, and round about unto Illyricum, I have fully preached the gospel of Christ.
> Yea, so have I strived to preach the gospel, not where Christ was named, lest I should build upon another man's foundation:

Notice the following in these verses: 1) Paul states that he is an apostle of Christ to the Gentiles (16). 2) While he was an apostle of Christ, the gospel he preached was the gospel of God. He called it the gospel of God to connect the gospel he preached with the promises of the Old Testament, especially God's promise to Abraham, which was that "in thy seed" should all the nations of the earth be blessed. This promise was not limited to the Jews. 3) He next calls attention to the

THE WORK OF THE HOLY SPIRIT

fact that the Gentiles who accepted the gospel were acceptable to God. 4) The proof of the Gentiles being acceptable to God was the spiritual gifts bestowed upon Gentiles, the outpouring of the Spirit on Cornelius, and the spiritual gifts that Gentile Christians received. The spiritual gifts were evidence that Gentiles were sanctified; that is, set apart from the world and acceptable to God. God would not have bestowed spiritual gifts on Gentiles through the hands of an apostle if they had not been acceptable to God on the same basis as the Jew. 5) Paul appealed to the things that Christ had wrought by him to convince the Jews that the gospel was for the Gentiles as well as for the Jews. The Gentiles were convinced by word and deed. The "word" of this verse is the gospel Paul preached. "Deed" is equal to the miracles that confirmed the Word, or the gospel that Paul preached, and spiritual gifts bestowed on Gentiles through the hands of Paul. This is shown in the next verse: "Through mighty signs and wonders, by the power of the Spirit of God," (15:19). Macknight gives the following paraphrase of verse 19: "By the power of miracles performed by me on the sick and maimed, and what is still greater, by the power of the gift of the Spirit of God communicated by me to the Gentiles." The arguments made in these verses show that there were those that denied the apostleship of Paul, the integrity of the gospel he preached, and denied that the Gentiles converted by Paul were children of God. In the same manner, Paul was answering the Judaizing teachers in Romans 8. Paul's testimony (the gospel he preached) was not limited to his word. The Holy Spirit witnessed (testified—confirmed by miracles) "with our Spirit." This verse indicates the double testimony of the apostles and the testimony, or witness, of the Holy Spirit through the apostles. Christ had told the apostles that the Holy Spirit would testify (bear witness of him) and that the apostles would also bear witness of him (John 15:26-27). As an eyewitness, the apostles were able to testify concerning Christ as the Son of God, and of course this resulted in the gospel. But the Holy Spirit, by miraculous manifestations, would accompany the testimony of the apostles. The witness of the Holy Spirit in the apostolic age was the miraculous manifestation of the Spirit that confirmed the Word. The miraculous manifestation of the Spirit bore witness to the truth of the gospel preached by the apostles and answered all false teachers who opposed the apostles and the gospel they preached. While it is true that the Holy Spirit bears witness through the written Word today, it must be remembered that before the New Testament was completed, the witness of the Holy Spirit was direct in revealing the Word and confirming it. The question under consideration by Paul in Romans is the question of the truthfulness and integrity of the gospel he preached, that placed both Jew and Gentile in one body. How could Paul prove this? What could he appeal to, to establish the credibility of the gospel for both Jew and Gentile? Answer: The witness, testimony of the Spirit, in miraculous power manifest in signs and miracles. It is a mistake to take these statements out of the "time period" (direct revelation and confirmation) and move them past that period to one of a completed and confirmed, written revelation. When Paul wrote the Roman letter, the Spirit worked directly. The Spirit guided Paul directly in the writing of this Epistle. There were still miraculous gifts. The church in Rome had miraculous gifts (Romans 12:3-6). Paul said that he wanted to go to Rome to impart spiritual gifts, which would, of course, confirm his apostleship before the very eyes of the Roman brethren, and would be a final answer to Judaizing teachers that denied his apostleship and the gospel that he preached. There is another statement in the next chapter that adds strength to the interpretation that I have given Romans 8:16: "I say the truth in Christ" is Paul's affirmation of the gospel he preached extending the offer of salvation to both Jew and Gentile in one body. "I lie not"—it must be evident that someone had accused Paul of lying. Paul's denial of lying is an answer to the Judaizing teachers who charged that he was teaching a lie. "My conscience bearing witness"—this is parallel with "our spirit" of 8:16. "In the Holy Spirit"—how could Paul's conscience (spirit) and the Holy Spirit bear witness? The Holy Spirit's witness to Paul, and through him, was certainly by miraculous manifestations. It was not the witness of the written Word that bore witness with Paul's conscience. The Spirit was writing the Word through Paul. The Spirit likewise was confirming the Word by miracle through Paul. The witness of the Spirit, in and through an apostle, was direct and miraculous. Surely, the direct and miraculous witness of the Spirit by an apostle is not the same as the witness through the Word today. Of course, the Spirit's witness is by the Word today, but this witness, or testimony, was first given directly and miraculously to the apostles. What we now have in the written Word was given then directly and supernaturally. It was the supernatural manifestation that confirmed the testimony received by the apostle. It was this miraculous confirmation of the Word that Paul appealed to in answer to the Judaizing teachers. All of this is NOW in the written Word. It was not THEN as the Word was in the process of being revealed. Judaizing teachers were denying the revelation which Paul received. Paul's reply was that the witness of the Spirit, miraculous manifestation, answered these false teachers and established that the gospel he preached in Christ was no lie. It is this same thought that is in 8:16. Judaizing teachers denied that Paul and his converts were children of God. Paul's reply was that the Spirit witnessed, furnished miraculous confirmation that both Paul and his converts were children of God.

THE WORK OF THE HOLY SPIRIT

Let me give a New Testament example of what a reference to the Holy Spirit witnessing meant during the period of direct revelation and confirmation. "Save that the Holy Spirit witnesseth in every city, saying that bonds and afflictions abide me," (Acts 20:23). Notice: 1) The Holy Spirit witnessed. 2) The Holy Spirit witnessed "saying...." 3) Question: Was this witness of the Holy Spirit saying through the written Word then, or was the witness by direct revelation? Answer: Move over one chapter and the answer is found. "And as we tarried there many days, there came down from Judaea a certain PROPHET, named Agabus. And when he was come unto us, he took Paul's girdle, and bound his own hands and feet, and said, Thus saith the Holy Ghost, So shall the Jews at Jerusalem bind the man that owneth this girdle, and shall deliver him into the hands of the Gentiles," (Acts 21:10-11). Here we have an inspired interpretation of Paul's reference to the witness of the Holy Spirit in Acts 20:23. Acts 20:22 refers to Jerusalem. Verse 23 refers to "bonds and afflictions." Acts 21:11 refers to "Jerusalem" and "bonds and afflictions." But now notice, the witness of the Holy Spirit in Acts 20:23 comes through a prophet in Acts 21:10 and 11. Was the Holy Spirit witnessing through Agabus "saying"? Was this not a direct revelation of the Spirit to the prophet? Was this not a miraculous revelation by which the Spirit witnessed to Paul by a prophet? We now have the witness of Agabus to Paul in the written Word, but it was not in the written Word when Agabus received it and when the Holy Spirit witnessed by the prophet to Paul. It would be a mistake to take Acts 20:23 and insist that the passage meant the Spirit witnessed at that time through the written Word. It is correct to say that what the Spirit then witnessed directly is now written in the Word, and the witness, which was at first by direct revelation, is now done only through the written Word. It is in this same context that Paul speaks of the witness of the Spirit in Romans 8:16. It is my conviction that in the apostolic age, the meaning of "witness of the Spirit" was a reference to inspiration and miraculous confirmation. This was how the Spirit witnessed in the apostolic age (Acts 1:8). Witnessing in the New Testament sense meant always inspired testimony and the miraculous that accompanied the testimony. It is never used of one simply telling some experience. If Paul related an experience, it was inspired testimony, giving that experience to defend the gospel. One can no more witness today than he can speak by direct inspiration. We now have the testimony of inspired witnesses in the New Testament and we proclaim their testimony, not our uninspired experiences. Macknight comments as follows on Romans 8:16:

> By this argument the apostle proved the great honor of being the sons of God was not restricted to the Jews. All who

believe are the sons of God, as is evident from their possessing the spirit of God's children. Besides, in the first age, the sonship of the Gentiles was demonstrated by the spiritual gifts bestowed on them. The former of these attestations the apostles had described unto the name of the spirit of adoption: the latter he speaks of in this verse and calls it the Spirit because of the spiritual gifts comes from the Spirit. And as these testimonies concurred in establishing the same fact, the apostles justly affirmed that the Spirit of God in the first age bear witness of believers that they were the children of God. Hence God is said to have sealed the believing Gentiles as His sons, by giving them the Spirit.

ROMANS 8:26-27

Likewise the Spirit also helpeth our infirmities: for we know not what we should pray for as we ought: but the Spirit itself maketh intercession for us with groanings which cannot be uttured.

And he that searcheth the hearts knoweth what is the mind of the Spirit, because he maketh intercession for the saints according to the will of God.

The most common interpretation of these verses is as follows: When a Christian cannot find words to express his petition, the Holy Spirit takes his groanings and intercedes for him to God. I am fully conscious of some of the difficulties of these verses. In dealing with difficult passages, it is always wise not to be dogmatic in rejecting an interpretation that does not violate any other scriptural principle, and not be dogmatic in offering an explanation. It is in this spirit that I offer what I think is the meaning of these verses. Before looking at the verses, it is important to see the basis of Paul's discussion:

1. Chapter 8 is the conclusion of the first division of the Roman letter.
2. Chapter 8 is a summary of Paul's conclusions reached as the result of his discussion in the previous chapters.
3. Chapter 8 also contains the arguments and evidences to establish that the gospel was for both Jew and Gentile. This was to answer Judaizing teachers.
4. Paul's method in the Roman letter was to approach it from the past and develop his theme down to Pentecost and the outgrowth of Pentecost. In this he appealed to the coming of the Spirit in His

miraculous manifestations, given to both Jew and Gentile, to establish that the gospel was for both.
5. Especially prominent in Paul's approach was the promise to Abraham and its culmination in Christ, with all the spiritual blessings being offered to Jew and Gentile alike in Christ.
6. Paul positioned himself back in the Old Testament and looked through the telescope of the Old Testament and saw the development of redemption down through the pages of the Old Testament until it reached its climax in Christ and the gospel.

Read the Roman letter and look at the little word "now," and watch how this word throws the Old and the New Testament into contrast, with special emphasis on the law and the gospel. Here is just one example: "Therefore by the deeds of the law there shall no flesh be justified in his sight: for by the law is the knowledge of sin. But now the righteousness of God without the law is manifested, being witnessed by the law and the prophets," (3:20-21). The righteousness of which Paul speaks was foreshadowed in the law and the prophets, but could only be realized in Christ and the gospel (3:20-26). These same truths are still under consideration in Chapter 8. Paul's method of approach in the previous part of the book is still his approach in Chapter 8. It is my conviction that this is one of the keys to understanding this chapter.

Is there another possible explanation of Romans 8:26 and 27, other than the previous one mentioned? I believe there is another interpretation that harmonizes with the general teaching of the Bible and also the context of Romans 8. My study of the Scriptures establishes the fact that it was the work of the Holy Spirit to reveal the mind of God to man, through selected men, and confirm the revelation as a genuine revelation from God. Numerous passages make this point clear. Following man's sin and separation from God, it was necessary for God to reveal His Word to man, or man would never have known God's will. But the revelation of God's will calls for a supernatural revelation. A supernatural revelation made it necessary for those who received the revelation to have proper credentials, to avoid counterfeit and deception. This accounts for the direct operation of the Spirit in revelation and confirmation. Because the gospel was to be preached to the whole world, miraculous gifts were given not only to the apostles to receive the revelation and confirmation of the gospel, but also to churches who had spiritual gifts. An additional purpose of a church receiving spiritual gifts, especially Gentile churches, was to establish the fact that Gentiles were acceptable to God just as the Jews. If Romans 8:26 and 27 mean that the Spirit takes the groanings of the

Christian and makes them known to God, this is a direct reversal of the general work of the Spirit in revealing the mind of God to man. I can understand why it was necessary for the Spirit to reveal the mind of God to man, but it is a little difficult for me to understand why God needs the Spirit to interpret man's needs to Him. Of course, the fact that I cannot understand something does not mean that it is not so. While on the other hand, if an interpretation can be offered that harmonizes with the general teaching of the Bible and the context in which it is found, it seems to me to be more reasonable to at least consider the interpretation.

There is still another problem with the explanation that these verses teach that the Spirit takes the groanings of the Christian and interprets them to God today. If this is true, then this work of the Spirit is confined to the Christian Age. There is not the slightest indication that the Spirit did this either in the Patriarchal or the Jewish Age. But there were people who had burdens before the Christian Age. There were those who groaned under their burdens before the Christian Age. There were those who prayed under such burdens before the Christian Age. For example, Thayer, on page 587, on the word "groaning," gives Romans 8:26 and Acts 7:34 together. Acts 7:34 is a reference to Israel in Egyptian bondage. They groaned; God heard their groanings. The Holy Spirit did not take their groanings and interpret them to God. If God could hear the groanings of the Israelites while they were in Egyptian bondage, without the Holy Spirit interpreting their prayer to Him, why may not God likewise hear the groanings of Christians today?

Is there an explanation that harmonizes with the general teaching of the Scriptures, that it was the work of the Holy Spirit to reveal and confirm the Word of God? In the apostolic age, there was inspired prayer. Just as the Holy Spirit revealed the mind of God for instruction, the Holy Spirit also revealed prayer. Look at I Corinthians 14:14: "For if I pray in an unknown tongue, my spirit prayeth, but my understanding is unfruitful." The tongue was a gift (I Corinthians 12:10). If one spoke in a tongue, it was by direct revelation. If one prayed in a tongue, it was by a direct revelation. A prayer in a tongue was an inspired prayer, but inspired prayer was not limited to the one that had the gift of tongues. Paul only mentions this type of inspired prayer in I Corinthians 14 because he was discussing the abuse of tongues. A commentary on this type prayer is found in Jude 19 and 20. Verse 19 speaks of uninspired teachers; sensual (animal, fleshly); having not the Spirit; that is, uninspired teachers. Then verse 20 says,

THE WORK OF THE HOLY SPIRIT 251

"...praying in the Holy Spirit." "Praying in the Holy Spirit" was praying by the inspiration of the Spirit. Just as the one of I Corinthians 14 that prayed in a tongue, prayed by inspiration, so the one of Jude 20 that prayed in the Holy Spirit, prayed an inspired prayer. I think there is also additional evidence to support this fact. In John 14:15 and 16, Christ promised the apostles the Holy Spirit as a Comforter. I have already discussed this in a previous chapter, but the word that is translated "Comforter" is broader than our word "comforter." Vine gives the following: "Then generally one who pleads another's cause, an intercessor, advocate," <u>W. E. Vine Expository Dictionary of New Testament Words.</u> Now consider the following:

1. The promise of the Comforter to the apostles was the miraculous gift of the Spirit to equip them for their work as apostles.
2. Included in the meaning of the word according to Vine was that of an intercessor.
3. This promise of the Holy Spirit to the apostles as an intercessor would be in connection with their work of receiving and confirming revelation. This involved the miraculous work of the Spirit.
4. The Holy Spirit inspired prayer (I Corinthians 14:14; Jude 19).
    a. This was revelation.
    b. This was the revelation of the prayer.
    c. The revelation of the prayer was the Spirit's intercession.
5. This harmonizes with the work of the Holy Spirit in giving and confirming revelation.
6. If an inspired sermon was a revelation given by the Spirit, why would not an inspired prayer be a revelation of the Spirit?
7. An inspired prayer harmonizes with the general teaching of the Bible, that the work of the Holy Spirit was revelation and confirmation.

Vinson has the following comment on the word "intercession":

The verb signifies to fall in with a person; to draw near so as to converse familiarly; hence it is not properly intercession in the accepted sense of that term, but rather approach to God in free and familiar prayer. Intercession in the passages cited is not to make intercession but to intervene, interfere; thus, in Romans 8:26, it is not the Spirit that pleads in our behalf, but that He throws Himself into our case, takes part in it.

This is exactly what the Spirit did in an inspired prayer. In revealing the prayer, He threw Himself into it, took part in it. This interpretation at least harmonizes with the work of the Holy Spirit in revealing God's will. I think, furthermore, that it also harmonizes with the general teaching of the Roman letter, which included a discussion of spiritual gifts. Since this interpretation at least harmonizes with the general work of the Spirit in revealing God's will, it seems to me that at least it deserves some consideration. The quotation by Campbell in a previous chapter pointed out that the entire assemblies were under the direction of the Spirit by the spiritual gifts in the church. All of the Epistles to the churches were to Gentile churches. This accounts for the numerous statements concerning spiritual gifts to these churches and the instruction given for the use of spiritual gifts.

While Macknight does not give this as his interpretation of Romans 8:26, he admits that it is a possible interpretation: "Perhaps the apostle meant that the Spirit helped their infirmities by inspiring them with a proper prayer." And then he cites I Corinthians 14:15 as an explanation. I Corinthians 14:15 is a reference to an inspired prayer, that was not in a tongue. I Corinthians 14:15 was an inspired prayer. This interpretation harmonizes with the work of the Spirit in revelation and confirmation. In inspiring the prayer, the Holy Spirit was making known the mind of God to man. This passage, like the other verses, should be studied in the context of apostolic age when the Spirit worked directly and miraculously.

RECEIVING THE SPIRIT TODAY

The passages that speak of receiving the Spirit have been discussed. Each statement that refers to receiving the Spirit was either before Pentecost and the coming of the Spirit in miraculous power, or during the time following Pentecost when there were miraculous endowments. There is not the first reference made to one receiving the Spirit as a non-miraculous indwelling. Consider the following:
1. The promise of the Holy Spirit was miraculous (Joel 2:28-32).
2. The passages in Matthew, Mark, Luke, and John which speak of the coming of the Spirit have Joel as their background, with Pentecost in view.
3. The specific instances of people receiving the Spirit in the book of Acts are all miraculous reception of the Spirit.
    a. The apostles (Acts 2:1-4)
    b. The Samaritans through the hands of the apostles, Peter and John (Acts 8:14-17)
    c. The household of Cornelius (Acts 10:44-47)
    d. The Ephesians by the laying on of Paul's hands (Acts 19:2-6)

THE WORK OF THE HOLY SPIRIT 253

The promise of the Holy Spirit was miraculous. The fulfillment was in keeping with the promise and each specific mention of those who were said to have received the Spirit was miraculous.
1. Where is the promise that the Holy Spirit would be received non-miraculously?
2. Where is the specific mention of someone receiving the Spirit non-miraculously?
3. Why was the Holy Spirit promised? The Holy Spirit was promised to the apostles to provide inspiration for the revelation and the confirmation of the gospel. The Holy Spirit was promised to believers (Mark 16:17-20) to provide the means of evangelizing, and for instruction for edification until the New Testament was completed. The apostles received the Holy Spirit so they would have the Word which was then being revealed. The apostles imparted spiritual gifts to provide the Word in churches while the Word was being revealed and as confirmation of their apostleship (II Corinthians 12:12). Believers received the Holy Spirit; that is, spiritual gifts, as proof that all distinctions between Jew and Gentile were abolished in the church. Churches, especially Gentile churches, received the Spirit; that is, spiritual gifts, as proof of their sonship; that is, their being acceptable to God on the same basis as the Jew.

These things set forth the basis of the promise of the Holy Spirit. The fulfillment was in harmony with the promise. There is not one of these needs today. We do not need living apostles, as they now function through the Word. Since there are no living apostles to impart spiritual gifts to believers, it is certain that no one receives the Spirit to provide a spiritual gift. Gentiles do not receive the Spirit as Cornelius did, as the outpouring on Cornelius was a one-time occurrence. The promise of the Spirit was miraculous and the reception was miraculous, and the miraculous has ceased. Why do we need to receive the Spirit today?
1. We do not need to receive the Spirit to furnish revelation, for revelation is completed.
2. We do not need to receive the Spirit to supply confirmation, as revelation and confirmation went together. When one ceased, the other ceased.

Since revelation and confirmation have ceased, the faith has been once for all delivered to the saints. What would reception of the Spirit provide today? What the reception of the Spirit one time furnished miraculously and directly is now furnished through the written Word. If the written Word does not furnish everything that was one time given miraculously and directly, will someone identify what it is that the reception of the Spirit now supplies non-miraculously? Do we receive the Spirit today? Let me ask another question: Are there miracles today? The answer to this last question is no, but the reception of the Spirit in the apostolic age and the miraculous were tied together. If one received the Spirit then, it was miraculous. The attempt to find a miraculous reception of the Spirit and a non-miraculous reception of the Spirit, in my judgment, is the very thing that has caused the confusion today. We have no problems generally in leaving miracles in the apostolic age. Since the reception of the Spirit and the miraculous belong together, why not leave the reception of the Spirit in the apostolic age with miracles? Someone may ask, But what do we receive today? We receive the gospel, the teaching of the Spirit. Is the gospel complete? If so, what could the Spirit supply today apart from the gospel? If the Spirit supplies something apart from the gospel, then it must be evident that the gospel is not complete. If the gospel is complete, and the Spirit does not furnish anything apart from the gospel, would not the reception of the Spirit be a useless reception? It seems to me that our problem has come from the attempt to make a distinction where there is none in the New Testament. We can leave the miracles in the apostolic age where they belong, but then we attempt to make a distinction between the miraculous and the non-miraculous reception of the Spirit. This is a distinction that the New Testament does not make. This is the source of the confusion. The following by brother Guy N. Woods is to the point on this question. Read it and ponder it. It strikes at the very root of the problem on the Holy Spirit and His work.

THE HOLY SPIRIT AND THE SAMARITANS
Guy N. Woods

"Now when the apostles that were at Jerusalem heard that Samaria had received the word of God, they sent unto them Peter and John: who, when they were come down, prayed for them, that they might receive the Holy Spirit: for as yet it was fallen upon none of them: only they had been baptized into the name of the Lord Jesus. Then laid they their hands on them, and they received the Holy Spirit." (Acts 8:14-17.) Immediately after the death of Stephen, the first martyr to the Christian religion following the establishment of the church, a massive wave of persecution engulfed the disciples in the city of its birth; and all the saints, with the exception of the apostles, were scattered abroad, and they "went every where preaching the word."

THE WORK OF THE HOLY SPIRIT 255

(Acts 8:4) Among those expelled was Philip, one of the seven (Acts 6:1-6), who went down to the city of Samaria and "preached Christ" to them. Details of his preaching are more particularly indicated in Acts 8:12, where it is said that he preached "good tidings concerning the kingdom of God and the name of Jesus Christ," in consequence of which "both men and women" are said to have "believed" and to have been "baptized."

When word of this came to the ears of the apostles in Jerusalem two of their number—Peter and John—were delegated by the entire group to go to Samaria. On arrival in that city, Peter and John prayed that all those who had received the word (obeyed the gospel), might also **receive** the Holy Spirit, then they laid hands on them, and the historian informs us that "they **received** the Holy Spirit." (Acts 8:17.)

(1) It is significant that notwithstanding the fact that these people in Samaria had "**received** the word" and thus were saved, they had not in consequence thereof "**received**" the Holy Spirit. This is plainly, clearly and unequivocally affirmed by the sacred writer: "For as yet it was fallen upon none of them: only they had been baptized into the name of the Lord Jesus." This says, in effect: "They had not **received** the Holy Spirit; they had only been baptized in water." It must follow therefore that any theory regarding the reception of the Holy Spirit which alleges that it is automatically **received** in consequence of being baptized in water is in conflict with the facts emerging in this event in Samaria. How is it possible for one seriously to contend that the Samaritans **received** the Holy Spirit **simply** and **solely** because they had been baptized, when the text asserts positively and specifically that they had not?

If, to this, it is replied that they had **received** a non-miraculous measure, but not that measure which came through the laying on of apostles' hands, then they had **received** the Holy Spirit! If, at this point, they **had received** the Holy Spirit it could not be truthfully asserted that they had **not received** the Holy Spirit; but, such, by implication, is clearly declared. Therefore, prior to the coming of the apostles, and subsequent to their obedience to the gospel, they had **not received** the Holy Spirit. Any theory, therefore, which alleges that the Samaritans **had received** the Holy Spirit prior to the coming of the apostles, Peter and John, is untenable, and in conflict with the facts. The truth is, as the context indisputably shows, the Samaritans received the Holy Spirit through the imposition of the apostles' hands, and not because they had been baptized in water. The phrase, "the gift of the Holy Spirit," in

Acts 2:38, must be construed in the light of these facts. If the demurrer is offered that here, "the gift of the Holy Spirit" is promised to all who repent and are baptized, we answer that in Mark 16:16-18, our Lord, having said, "He that **believeth** and is baptized shall be saved," added, "And these signs shall accompany them that believe: in my name shall they cast out demons; they shall speak with new tongues; they shall take up serpents, and if they drink any deadly thing, it shall in no wise hurt them; they shall lay hands on the sick, and they shall recover." Though these signs accompanied believers, they were in consequence of the bestowal of miraculous powers, and not the result of having obeyed the gospel. This fact is made to appear again and again, in the sacred writings.

A clear instance of this may be seen in Acts 19:1-6: "Paul...came to Ephesus, and found certain disciples: and he said unto them, Did ye **receive** the Holy Spirit when ye believed?" **Believed** here is a synecdoche for **saved**. The meaning is, "Did you receive the Holy Spirit when ye were saved?" But, such a question, by Paul, is wholly unaccountable on the assumption that the reception of the Holy Spirit necessarily follows the conditions of salvation. Were such the case, Paul would simply have asked, "Have you obeyed the gospel?" or, "Are you saved?" knowing that an affirmative answer to this query would necessitate the conclusion that they had received the Holy Spirit. It is clear that no such assumption characterized the apostle. His question clearly establishes the fact that it is possible for one to be saved, **yet not have received** the Holy Spirit! The conclusion is irresistable that the reception of the Holy Spirit did not automatically and necessarily follow salvation. Its reception was dependent, not on baptism, but on the imposition of apostles' hands, except in the case of Holy Spirit baptism, administered only by the Lord. But, neither was the baptism of the Holy Spirit concurrent with baptism in water; the apostles, on Pentecost, were baptized in the Holy Spirit, long **after** they were baptized in water; and the household of Cornelius received the baptism of the Holy Spirit **before** they were baptized in water. (Acts 10:1ff.)

(2) Philip, himself miraculously endowed, through the laying on of the apostles' hands (Acts 6:6), was not an apostle, and the power to transmit the Holy Spirit in this manner was not his. This accounts for the fact that it was necessary for Peter and John (who were apostles) to come to Samaria in order to impart to the people, who had obeyed the gospel, the Holy Spirit. Be it remembered **that they were Christians** (Acts 8:12), yet, they had not received the Holy Spirit: "For as yet he was fallen upon none of them..." (verse 16): "Then laid they their

THE WORK OF THE HOLY SPIRIT

hands upon them, **and they received the Holy Spirit**" (verse 17). To the point prior to the arrival of Peter and John, "none" had received the Holy Spirit; they received the Spirit when Peter and John laid hands on them, and through their response to the preaching of Philip.

Inasmuch as only the apostles had the power to transmit the Holy Spirit through the imposition of hands, it follows that with the passing of the apostles this power terminated. We stand in relation to the situation in Samaria at the point where those people were prior to the arrival of the apostles, and following their obedience to the gospel. **They** believed; they were baptized; they were saved. (Acts 8:12; Mark 15:15, 16.) We have believed; we have been baptized; we are saved. But, there are no apostles living today to lay hands on us. It was through laying on of apostles' hands that they **received** the Holy Spirit. It is, therefore, futile to claim to have **received** the Holy Spirit in a situation where inspiration asserts that such has not been done.

It is truly distressing that there has been an erosion of the true doctrine of **the measures** of the Spirit among us in recent years. Many, unknowingly, or without proper perception, have espoused the denominational doctrine of direct and/or immediate spiritual influence. Others, contemptuous of the views characteristic of the Restoration movement, boldy advocate such. Measures of the Spirit are not varying amounts of the Spirit himself, but greater or less **portions of power** which the Holy Spirit exercised through people. Miraculous powers, such as those which were to follow the "believers" of Mark 16:16-18, and "the gift of the Holy Spirit," identified in Acts 10:45, as enabling one to speak in tongues were measures peculiar to the apostolic age, and thus no longer available. Today the Holy Spirit leads (Rom. 8:14), enables us to identify God as our Father (Gal. 4:6), and produces fruit in our lives (Gal. 5:16-24), by **means** of the Word of Truth which the Holy Spirit provided through the pens of inspired men (I Cor. 2:13). He does so in no other way. The all-sufficiency of the Word, **in every good work** (are there others???) is by the Holy Spirit himself affirmed. (2 Tim. 3:16,17.)

SOME FINAL THOUGHTS

THE GOSPEL A SYSTEM OF FAITH

Redemption is offered to a lost world through a system of faith. One becomes a Christian through the obedience of faith (Romans 1:5): "By whom we have received grace and apostleship, for obedience to the faith among all nations, for his name." One lives the Christian life by faith (Hebrews 10:38): "Now the just shall live by faith." Man becomes righteous by the obedience of faith and remains righteous by obedience of faith: "For therein is the righteousness of God revealed from faith to faith: as it is written, The just shall live by faith," (Romans 1:17). The gospel offers righteousness to the sinner through the atonement of Christ. The Christian continues in righteousness through the atonement of Christ. The obedience of faith enables one to become righteous because of the blood of Christ. The obedience of faith makes it possible for one to remain righteous because of the blood of Christ.

> But if we walk in the light, as he is in the light, we have fellowship one with another, and the blood of Jesus Christ his Son cleanseth us from all sin.
> If we say that we have no sin, we deceive ourselves, and the truth is not in us.
> If we confess our sins, he is faithful and just to forgive us our sins, and to cleanse us from all unrighteousness.
> If we say that we have not sinned, we make him a liar, and his word is not in us. (I John 1:7-10).

The difference in the law and the gospel is a distinction that is based on the difference in the atonement. The only atonement under the law, as a system, was the blood of animals. But the blood of animals could not take away sin: "For ye had compassion of me in my bonds, and took joyfully the spoiling of your goods, knowing in yourselves that ye have in heaven a better and an enduring substance," (Hebrews 10:3-4). The blood of Christ does remit sins (Matthew 26:28; Acts 2:38; Hebrews 9:14). "For this is my blood of the new testament, which is shed for many for the remission of sins," (Matthew 26:28). This is the very heart of the contrast between the law and the gospel. The law and the gospel are two different systems. The law could not justify because no man could keep it perfectly, and when one came short under the law, there was no atonement that could forgive sins. One cannot live perfect under the gospel, but the atonement of Christ

THE WORK OF THE HOLY SPIRIT

makes provisions for forgiveness under the gospel. Christ is the very heart of the gospel. It is Christ that makes the difference between the law and the gospel. There is as much difference between the law and the gospel as there is between Moses and Christ. Moses could lead the children of Israel out of physical bondage, but he could not deliver them from the bondage of sin. Christ makes free from the bondage of sin: "And ye shall know the truth, and the truth shall make you free," (John 8:32). Christ is the fundamental difference between the law and the gospel. The apostles and the evangelists of the New Testament preached Christ, not the Holy Spirit.

> Then Philip opened his mouth, and began at the same scripture, and preached unto him Jesus. (Acts 8:35).

> And I, brethren, when I came to you, came not with excellency of speech or of wisdom, declaring unto you the testimony of God.
> For I determined not to know any thing among you, save Jesus Christ, and him crucified.
> And I was with you in weakness, and in fear, and in much trembling.
> And my speech and my preaching was not with enticing words of man's wisdom, but in demonstration of the Spirit and of power:
> That your faith should not stand in the wisdom of men, but in the power of God. (I Corinthians 2:1-5).

> For we preach not ourselves, but Christ Jesus the Lord; and ourselves your servants for Jesus' sake. (II Corinthians 4:5).

It has been no problem for most in the church to see that it is Christ and not the Holy Spirit that makes possible the salvation of the sinner. It is not necessary today for the Holy Spirit to do anything directly in order for the sinner to be saved. What the Holy Spirit does for the sinner today, He does through the Word and it is the blood of Christ that saves, not the Holy Spirit. But does someone say, Yes, but the New Testament promised the Holy Spirit to Christians, not sinners? Did not Cornelius receive the Holy Spirit before he became a Christian? The answer, of course, is yes, but that does not prove the sinner must receive the Holy Spirit before he can be converted today. Cornelius received the Holy Spirit, not for his benefit, but for the benefit of others. Cornelius would have gladly accepted the gospel if someone would have preached it to him and the church accepted him as equal to

Jewish Christians. Those who attempt to use Cornelius as proof of a direct operation of the Spirit on the sinner today take it out of the time period to which it belongs. The question still remains why the promise of the Holy Spirit to Christians? The answer is simple. Judaism was not evangelistic. The church is to carry the gospel into all the world. How did the church in the apostolic age do this? It could not do it by providing a written New Testament. Since there was no written New Testament, how could the church evangelize unless it had the Word to preach? How did the church have the Word before it was written? The church had the Word through spiritual gifts that came through the hands of the apostles. This was one of the main reasons for the gift of tongues. The gift of tongues enabled the church to preach the gospel to other nations and every creature just as the Great Commission authorized. The gift of tongues also confirmed the revelation preached (Mark 16:16-20). Here is the reason for the promise of signs, including tongues to believers, in the Commission as given by Mark (Mark 16:16-20; I Corinthians 14:22). We have no need for the gift of tongues today because we have a written revelation which can be translated into other languages, and the one preaching can learn the foreign language. The Spirit was promised to Christians so that through spiritual gifts the church could edify itself. The theme of I Corinthians 14 is edification. "But he that prophesieth speaketh unto men to edification, and exhortation, and comfort," (I Corinthians 14:3). Everything that was done in the assembly was to edify. Anything that did not edify was not to be used. It was because the assemblies were to edify that Paul discussed spiritual gifts in I Corinthians 14. The abuse of the gift of tongues by the Corinthians was not resulting in edification. But we do not need spiritual gifts for the church to edify itself today. The Word furnishes all that we need for edification. The church in the apostolic age had no written New Testament for edification. The Holy Spirit through spiritual gifts provided edification for the church in the apostolic age—exactly what the written Word provides for the church today.

Finally, the Holy Spirit was promised to Christians, and especially Gentile Christians, to prove that they were acceptable by God. Spiritual gifts in a church established two things: 1) the credibility of the apostles that imparted the spiritual gift, and 2) the genuineness of the church as being one approved by God. This appeal to spiritual gifts in the church is made by Paul in answer to Judaizing teachers that denied that he was an apostle of Christ and that the churches he established were churches approved by God. We do not need to receive the Holy Spirit today to establish the credibility of the apostles or the church being acceptable by God. We use the written Word to establish the credibility of the apostles and to prove that a church today is a New Testament church.

A non-miraculous indwelling of the Holy Spirit would not supply a single one of the three needs that spiritual gifts provided Christians and churches before the New Testament was written. Everything the Holy Spirit provided for Christians and churches directly THEN is NOW furnished in the New Testament. Here are the reasons that the New Testament promised the Holy Spirit to Christians. But the promise of the Holy Spirit to Christians was miraculous, temporary, and ceased when the New Testament was completed (Mark 16:16-20). It was the revelation of the gospel by spiritual gifts that was the means of evangelizing and edifying even when a church had these gifts. It was the visible manifestation in these gifts that assured churches that they were acceptable to God and thereby gave them the strength to live the Christian life in the face of all opposition.

The Holy Spirit never directly, apart from the revelation and the assurance with the genuineness of the revelation, gave strength to live the Christian life. If the Holy Spirit gives strength directly and apart from revelation to live the Christian life today, then it seems to me that one of two things must follow: the doctrine of the impossibility of apostasy is correct, for if the Holy Spirit takes over, apart from the truth, and empowers the Christian to overcome sin, how can the Christian fall? Secondly, if the Holy Spirit directly and apart from the Word empowers the Christian to overcome sin, and the Christian is overcome by sin, then the Holy Spirit has failed the Christian. Becoming a Christian is a voluntary action motivated by the truth of the gospel. Living the Christian life is also voluntary and still motivated by the truth of the gospel. The misunderstanding of the denominational world of this fact has contributed to its false teaching on the necessity of the Holy Spirit working directly on the sinner to empower him to obey the truth. Once the Holy Spirit has empowered him to obey the truth in becoming a Christian, then the Spirit continues this work, and it makes it impossible for a Christian to apostatize. We have rejected the first, but some have accepted the second premise, while refusing to also accept the doctrine of the impossibility of apostasy.

What does the Indwelling of the Holy Spirit Do Today?

1. It cannot give faith for faith comes by the Word of God (Romans 10:17).

2. It cannot give love to God for the gospel is the motive for love to God (I John 4:8).
3. It cannot make us love one another for gratitude in response to the love of God and the gospel is the basis of love among brethren (John 13:34-35). Even the miraculous indwelling did not produce love in the church at Corinth (I Corinthians 13).
4. It cannot produce the spirit of sonship, as the contents of the gospel produces the spirit of sonship, rather than the spirit of bondage that characterized the law (Romans 8:15).
5. It cannot give knowledge for knowledge comes from the Word itself.
6. It cannot give strength for it is faith based on the Word of God that gives strength for living. (Read the entire eleventh chapter of Hebrews.)
7. It cannot empower to overcome sin for we overcome through the blood and the Word (Revelation 12:11).
8. It cannot produce spirituality for the gospel makes one spiritual. Even the miraculous indwelling in the Corinthians did not make them spiritual (I Corinthians 3:1-3).
9. It cannot give growth for we grow by the Word of God (I Peter 2:2).
10. It would not make one unselfish. The church at Corinth had miraculous gifts, but these gifts did not make the Corinthians liberal. (II Corinthians, Chapters 8 and 9.)
11. It would not keep one from sinning. Even the baptism of the Holy Spirit did not keep Peter from sin (Galatians 2:11). Surely, non-miraculous indwelling would not accomplish more than the baptism of the Holy Spirit.
12. The Holy Spirit does not work miracles today, as the miracles are now written (John 20:30-31).
13. The Holy Spirit does not give revelation today as revelation is completed (Jude verse 3).
14. The Holy Spirit does not work miracles of confirmation, as confirmation ended when revelation ended (Mark 16:16-20).

What does the Holy Spirit do today that He does not do by the Word?

SOME BASIC ERRORS OF PENTECOSTALISM

1. One of the most fundamental errors of Pentecostalism is that it exalts the Holy Spirit above Christ. I know Pentecostals render lip service to Christ by shouting, "Praise His Name," but in reality

they deny the power of the blood of Christ. They talk about "the fullness of the Spirit," but reject the "fullness of the power of the blood." Their doctrine is that the blood of Christ saves, but the blood of Christ does not sanctify. Pentecostalism separates salvation and sanctification, making sanctification a second blessing received when one receives the baptism of the Holy Spirit. Their theory is that one can be saved without complete surrender or giving one's self up to God. While they would not state this, as I have, this is what their teachings result in. How do they claim one receives the baptism of the Holy Spirit? They say it is by yielding one's self completely over to God, and then the Holy Spirit will take over. While yielding one's self completely over to God and praying, he can then receive the baptism of the Holy Spirit. If this does not mean that one can be saved without complete surrender, what does it mean? If this theory does not mean that the blood of Christ will save but not sanctify, what does it mean? If this does not mean that one reaches the highest heights in Christianity by the Holy Spirit and not by Christ, what does it mean? It has always been a mystery to me why it was Christ who became incarnate, suffered the mockery of men, died the ignoble death on the cross, and then the Holy Spirit should end up getting the glory and the honor. The Bible teaches that the Holy Spirit glorifies Christ, not himself. "Howbeit when he, the Spirit of truth, is come, he will guide you into all truth: for he shall not speak of himself; but whatsoever he shall hear, that shall he speak: and he will shew you things to come. He shall glorify me: for he shall receive of mine, and shall shew it unto you," (John 16:13-14).

About the only glory that Pentecostals give Christ is for "sending the Holy Spirit to baptize and to sanctify." False teachers, by their philosophy, vain deceit, and traditions of men, were refusing to give Christ pre-eminence and Paul condemned them. "And he is the head of the body, the church: who is the beginning, the firstborn from the dead; that in all things he might have the pre-eminence," (Colossians 1:18). "For in him dwelleth all the fulness of the Godhead bodily," (Colossians 2:9). Pentecostals, with their doctrine of the second blessing of sanctification and baptism of the Holy Spirit, just as surely deny the pre-eminence of Christ.

The Body Over the Soul

2. Still another false doctrine of Pentecostals is in giving more emphasis to the body than the soul. I receive <u>Abundant Life</u>

published by Oral Roberts Evangelistic Association, Inc. I have a copy before me and have checked to see what the main theme of this issue is. Like all others, the entire issue talks about miracles today. The chief miracles that he wants to pray with people about are healing and financial success. In reading this issue, one would think that bodily healing and financial gain are the whole burden of the gospel. The New Testament teaches that Christ came to save from sin, not just to heal the sick or to sign a note for financial security.

"For the Son of man is come to seek and to save that which was lost," (Luke 19:10). While it is true that emotional ills affect the body and that true Christianity will cure these ills, these cures are not miracles. Man is a unit—body, soul, and spirit. A divided heart and divided loyalties produce emotional conflicts and these in turn may affect one physically. James says that a double-minded man is unstable in all of his ways (James 1:8). A literal reading of James 1:8 would be a man with two souls. This indicates divided loyalties of the person described by James. Sin not only separates from God, and separates man from man, but it can also "split" one's personality. Divided loyalties make for instability. The faith once for all delivered to the saints, when accepted, unites one with God and also brings unity and peace into one's life. The gospel does this. It does not take a miracle to bring this about. But there may be bodily ills that do not come from divided loyalties and emotional problems. The blind do not receive their sight miraculously today. Those crippled from birth do not walk by a miracle of healing (Acts 3). The miracles of Christ were to confirm the Word. The Word has been completed. The main emphasis of the gospel is redemption, not bodily healing. The body will decay, but the Spirit lives forever.

> For which cause we faint not; but though our outward man perish, yet the inward man is renewed day by day.
> For our light affliction, which is but for a moment, worketh for us a far more exceeding and eternal weight of glory;
> While we look not at the things which are seen, but at the things which are not seen: for the things which are seen are temporal; but the things which are not seen are eternal. (II Corinthians 4:16-18).

Even the ones that Roberts attempts to interest in their souls are appealed to on the basis of this so-called bodily healing. Tied to the emphasis of bodily healing, Pentecostals insist that miracles include financial success. The very issue previously mentioned gives the so-called testimony of a "money miracle." The primary blessings of the gospel are spiritual. "Blessed be the God and Father of our Lord Jesus Christ, who hath blessed us with all spiritual blessings in heavenly places in Christ," (Ephesians 1:3). Temporal blessings are secondary. "But seek ye first the kingdom of God, and his righteousness; and all these things shall be added unto you," (Matthew 6:33).

The emphasis that Pentecostals and the premillennial doctrine give to temporal blessings confuses the temporal, earthly blessings of Judaism with the spiritual blessings of the new covenant. God promises to take care of His people in the New Testament, but the gospel nowhere promises a chicken in every pot to every Christian. The only "money miracle" recorded in the New Testament is the one where Christ sent Peter fishing, and Peter caught a fish and found the money to pay taxes. I have often wondered why men like Oral Roberts who talk about "money miracles" do not go fishing instead of asking people to send in the "seed money" for a miracle. Why do they not try a little fishing to get their money instead of appealing to people to send them money? It would be interesting to see a Pentecostal explain why Christ and Paul had so little of this earth's goods if the Bible promises "money miracles." Christ told a potential follower, "foxes have holes, and the birds of the air have nests; but the Son of man hath not where to lay his head," (Luke 9:58). Paul described his hardships in II Corinthians 11:23-28:

> Are they ministers of Christ? (I speak as a fool) I am more; in labours more abundant, in stripes above measure, in prisons more frequent, in deaths oft.
> Of the Jews five times received I forty stripes save one.
> Thrice was I beaten with rods, once was I stoned, thrice I suffered shipwreck, a night and a day I have been in the deep;
> In journeyings often, in perils of waters, in perils of robbers, in perils by mine own countrymen, in perils by the heathen, in perils in the city, in perils in the wilderness, in perils in the sea, in perils among false brethren;
> In weariness and painfulness, in watchings often, in hunger and thirst, in fastings often, in cold and nakedness.
> Beside those things that are without, that which cometh upon me daily, the care of all the churches.

Included in this list of hardships were hunger and thirst, cold and nakedness. Did Paul lack Roberts' "seed faith" and fail to give God "seed money" to produce a "money miracle"? The gospel places the real values of life in the spiritual realm, not the material. It is a perversion of the whole nature of the gospel to try to make it a money-making gospel. The emphasis that Pentecostals give to bodily healing and financial success gives more attention to the body than the soul. The gospel of redemption gives spiritual values and the soul pre-eminence.

THE TONGUE QUESTION

First Corinthians 14 has become the basis of the so-called tongue speaking today. Pentecostals claim to speak in a tongue that is not a language. A tongue that is not a language is a contradiction of terms. The word "tongue" in the Bible is used: a) of the tongue as a member of the body (James 3:5-6): "Even so the tongue is a little member, and boasteth great things. Behold, how great a matter a little fire kindleth! And the tongue is a fire, a world of iniquity: so is the tongue among our members, that it defileth the whole body, and setteth on fire the course of nature; and it is set on fire of hell."

b) It is used as a language (Acts 2:4, 6, 8):

And they were all filled with the Holy Ghost, and began to speak with other tongues, as the Spirit gave them utterance . . . .

Now when this was noised abroad, the multitude came together, and were confounded, because that every man heard them speak in his own language . . . .

And how hear we every man in our own tongue, wherein we were born?

The Bible knows nothing of a tongue that is not a language. The theme of I Corinthians 14 is edification. Edification is based on knowledge and understanding. The very fact that Paul commanded the one that spoke in a tongue to keep silent, unless there was an interpreter so the church could be edified, is proof that edification demands understanding. First Corinthians 14:3 says, "But he that prophesieth speaketh unto men to edification, and exhortation, and comfort."

1. Prophecy edified the church:
"He that speaketh in an unknown tongue edifieth himself; but he that prophesieth edifieth the church, " (I Corinthians 14:4).

THE WORK OF THE HOLY SPIRIT

2. Prophecy was greater than tongues unless tongues were interpreted so that the church could be edified:
"I would that ye all spake with tongues, but rather that ye prophesied: for greater is he that prophesieth than he that speaketh with tongues, except he interpret, that the church may receive edifying," (I Corinthians 14:5).
3. A tongue not understood was of no profit to the assembly because it did not edify:
"Now, brethren, if I come unto you speaking with tongues, what shall I profit you, except I shall speak to you either by revelation, or by knowledge, or by prophesying, or by doctrine?" (I Corinthians 14:6).
4. Even a trumpet that was sounded without a specific meaning was useless. Unless a soldier understood the specific meaning of a sound of the trumpet, it would have no effect on him. That is, he would not make preparation for battle. Again, the illustration of the trumpet shows the necessity of understanding or it was without any value:
"And even things without life giving sound, whether pipe or harp, except they give a distinction in the sounds, how shall it be known what is piped or harped? For if the trumpet give an uncertain sound, who shall prepare himself to the battle?" (I Corinthians 14:7-8).
5. The tongue was to speak words easy to understand so that what was spoken might be known; that is, understood. Otherwise, it was just speaking into the air:
"So likewise ye, except ye utter by the tongue words easy to be understood, how shall it be known what is spoken? for ye shall speak into the air," (I Corinthians 14:9).
   a) The tongue was to speak words. Words indicate language.
   b) The words were to be words that could be understood. The words "word" and "understood" show that the speaking whenever done was to be in words that could be understood so they would edify.
6. There are many kinds of voices in the world and none without signification:
"There are, it may be, so many kinds of voices in the world, and none of them is with signification," (I Corinthians 14:10).
There is no such thing as a voice that is not a language. All voices have signification. Why? Because every voice is a language and has a signification for the one that understands the language. This verse makes it clear that the tongues of this chapter are languages.

Consider the following:
>No voice is without signification.
>For a voice to have signification, it must be understood and to be understood, it must be a language.
>Therefore, every voice is a language and there is no such thing as a voice that is not a language.
>The so-called tongues of today are without signification.
>But there is no tongue that is without signification (I Corinthians 14:10).
>Therefore the so-called tongue of today is not a tongue as it has no signification.

7. If the one that heard the voice (tongue) did not understand what was said, he would be as a barbarian:
"Therefore if I know not the meaning of the voice, I shall be unto him that speaketh a barbarian, and he that speaketh shall be a barbarian unto me," (I Corinthians 14:11).
And the speaker would be as a barbarian. Here is a contrast of the speaker and the hearer. The word "barbarian" is used to describe both the speaker and the hearer. The word "barbarian," in reference to the hearer, is a language—the native tongue of the hearer. Since the word "barbarian" is used in reference to the language of the hearer, the word would also be used as a language of the speaker. It must follow that the voice (tongue) of the speaker was a language, but not the language of the hearer. It could not make sense to use the word "barbarian" meaning language of the hearer, and then use the same word for the speaker and it not mean a language. The so-called tongue of today is not a language. Verse 11 is another denial that the word "tongue" in this chapter is used as reference to something that is not a language.

8. Seek that ye may excel to the edifying of the church:
"Even so ye, forasmuch as ye are zealous of spiritual gifts, seek that ye may excel to the edifying of the church," (I Corinthians 14:12).
The purpose of assemblies were to edify. Spiritual gifts were not for the benefit of the one possessing the gift, but were to be used for the edification of the assemblies. The so-called tongues of today do not edify the assemblies, but are exercised purely for the one that is supposed to be speaking in a tongue. This verse would eliminate the so-called tongues of today. Since spiritual gifts were for the assemblies and not for the individuals, the tongue could not be for private use. Since a tongue that was not understood by

THE WORK OF THE HOLY SPIRIT

those in the assembly was forbidden except when there was someone to interpret, this likewise would eliminate their use today.

9. "I thank my God, I speak with tongues more than ye all," (I Corinthians 14:18).
   Paul was an apostle. Tongues were for evangelism. Tongues enabled the one that possessed the gift to teach in the language of the audience. Acts 2 is an example of the apostles exercising this gift. The contrast here is that of Paul who could speak in many languages while the ones in Corinth that possessed the gift of tongues spoke in only one language.
10. This statement by Paul, an apostle, shows that the word "tongue" in this chapter means "language" just as Acts 2, and all attempts to make tongues an unknown language is futile:
    "Yet in the church I had rather speak five words with my understanding, that by my voice I might teach others also, than ten thousand words in an unknown tongue," (I Corinthians 14:19).
    Five words spoken in a language understood by the audience are worth more than ten thousand words that the audience cannot understand. Pentecostals follow the very opposite of what Paul did. They would rather speak five words understood by no one than ten thousand words that can be understood.
11. "In the law it is written, With men of other tongues and other lips will I speak unto this people; and yet for all that will they not hear me, saith the Lord," (I Corinthians 14:21).
    This verse is a quotation from Isaiah 28. The tongue here was the Assyrian language which the Jews did not understand. The fact that Paul quoted from Isaiah, where the reference is to the language of the Assyrians, again establishes the fact that the tongues of I Corinthians 14 means language.
12. "Wherefore tongues are for a sign, not to them that believe, but to them that believe not: but prophesying serveth not for them that believe not, but for them which believe," (I Corinthians 14:22).
    Tongues are for a sign to unbelievers. This shows the following:
    a) Tongues were for evangelism enabling the apostles and those who received this gift through the hands of an apostle to teach others the gospel.
    b) The tongue confirmed the gospel (Mark 16:17-20). If the hearer did not understand the language, it could not be a sign and instead of confirming the Word, produced the opposite results. The unbeliever thought the tongue speaker was mad.

13. "If any man speak in an unknown tongue, let it be by two, or at the most by three, and that by course; and let one interpret," (I Corinthians 14:27).

    The one that spoke in a tongue was to speak two or three sentences and let one interpret. If there was no interpreter, he was to remain silent. The fact that what was spoken in a tongue could be interpreted by one who had the gift of interpretation, is further evidence that the tongue was a language. The interpretation into a language that the assemblies could understand made it possible for the revelation to edify. Again, this makes it clear that all that was done in the assemblies was to be done for edification. Anything that did not edify the assemblies was forbidden.

WHAT ABOUT PRAYING FOR THE GIFT OF INTERPRETATION?

The 14th chapter of I Corinthians is not only perverted in trying to find in it a tongue that is not a language, but it is also perverted in the attempt to try to use it to prove that one could receive a spiritual gift in answer to prayer. One rule of Bible study is that difficult passages must be interpreted in the light of other plain passages: "Wherefore let him that speaketh in an unknown tongue pray that he may interpret," (I Corinthians 14:13).

Does verse 13 prove that the gift of interpretation could be received in answer to prayer? This brings up the question as to what the New Testament teaches about spiritual gifts. The New Testament teaches beyond question that spiritual gifts came only through the hands of the apostles. Imparting spiritual gifts was the chief sign of an apostle:

> Am I not an apostle? am I not free? have I not seen Jesus Christ our Lord? are not ye my work in the Lord?
> If I be not an apostle unto others, yet doubtless I am to you: for the seal of mine apostleship are ye in the Lord. (I Corinthians 9:1-2).
>
> Truly the signs of an apostle were wrought among you in all patience, in signs, and wonders, and mighty deeds. (II Corinthians 12:12).

Paul defended his apostleship on the basis of his imparting spiritual gifts to the Corinthians. If spiritual gifts came in answer to

THE WORK OF THE HOLY SPIRIT 271

prayer, then Paul's defense of his apostleship on the basis of imparting spiritual gifts to the Corinthians was nonsense. They could have replied that they received their gifts by prayer, not through the laying on of his hands. The Judaizing teachers could have had prayer meetings to encourage the Corinthians to pray for gifts as well as Paul could. Philip could have conducted a prayer meeting in Samaria as well as the apostles, Peter and John, if spiritual gifts came simply by one praying for the gift.

> Now when the apostles which were at Jerusalem heard that Samaria had received the word of God, they sent unto them Peter and John:
> Who, when they were come down, prayed for them, that they might receive the Holy Ghost:
> (For as yet he was fallen upon none of them: only they were baptized in the name of the Lord Jesus.)
> Then laid they their hands on them, and they received the Holy Ghost.
> And when Simon saw that through laying on of the apostles' hands the Holy Ghost was given, offered them money,
> Saying, Give me also this power, that on whomsoever I lay hands, he may receive the Holy Ghost. (Acts 8:14-19).

Consider the following in connection with the account of the Samaritans receiving spiritual gifts:

1. Philip could perform miracles, but he could not impart spiritual gifts to the Samaritans. If spiritual gifts came in answer to prayer, why could Philip not pray as well as the apostles? Verse 17 says, "Then laid they their hands on them, and they received the Holy Spirit." Here is the plain, simple statement that it was by the laying on of the apostles' hands that the Samaritans received the Holy Spirit and thus received spiritual gifts.
2. Simon saw that through the laying on of the apostles' hands, the Holy Spirit was given, verse 18. Again, the record is careful to state that Simon saw that through the laying on of the apostles' hands the Holy Spirit was given. What these verses do not state is:
   a) That the Samaritans received the Holy Spirit in answer to prayer.
   b) That when Simon saw the apostles praying that the Holy Spirit was given, he asked them for the power of prayer so that he could impart spiritual gifts.

If spiritual gifts came through anyone praying, then Simon was foolish to offer money for the power that Peter and John had. Simon did not ask Peter and John to teach him how to pray so that he could impart spiritual gifts to others. Verse 19 states that Simon said he wanted "this power that on whomsoever I lay hands, he may receive the Holy Spirit." Simon did not ask for the power of prayer that for whomsoever he prayed, they might receive the Holy Spirit. Look again at what these verses state. Acts 8:17 states that the apostles laid hands on them and they received the Holy Spirit. Verse 18 says that Simon saw it was by the laying on of the apostles' hands that the Holy Spirit was given. In Acts 8:19 Simon said, " . . . Give me also this power, that on whomsoever I lay hands, he may receive the Holy Spirit." The statement is made three times in these verses that the Holy Spirit was given by the laying on of hands. Not a single verse states that the Holy Spirit was received in answer to prayer.

> He said unto them, Have ye received the Holy Ghost since ye believed? And they said unto him, We have not so much as heard whether there be any Holy Ghost.
> And he said unto them, Unto what then were ye baptized? And they said, Unto John's baptism.
> Then said Paul, John verily baptized with the baptism of repentence, saying unto the people, that they should believe on him which should come after him, that is, on Christ Jesus.
> When they heard this, they were baptized in the name of the Lord Jesus.
> And when Paul had laid his hands upon them, the Holy Ghost came on them; and they spake with tongues, and prophesied. (Acts 19:2-6).

In Ephesus, Paul laid hands on the Ephesians and the Holy Spirit came upon them. Again, spiritual gifts came through the hands of an apostle:

"Wherefore I put thee in remembrance that thou stir up the gift of God, which is in thee by the putting on of my hands," (II Timothy 1:6). Timothy received a gift by the putting on of Paul's hands. I Timothy 4:14 cannot change the direct statement made by Paul to Timothy in II Timothy 1:6. The presbyters did not impart any spiritual gift to Timothy. Paul says the gift Timothy had, came through his hands. This statement is too positive for any mistaking what Paul meant as to how Timothy received the spiritual gift.

Paul, in writing to the Romans, said, "For I long to see you, that I may impart unto you some spiritual gift, to the end ye may be established," (Romans 1:11). If spiritual gifts came in answer to prayer of the one seeking the gift, then there was no need for Paul to want to go to Rome to impart spiritual gifts. The church in Rome was not dependent on Paul's presence for a prayer meeting. These passages establish the fact that spiritual gifts came only through the hands of an apostle. Spiritual gifts were not received simply by one praying for a gift. Any interpretation of I Corinthians 14:13 that contradicts the truth, that spiritual gifts were given through the hands of an apostle, cannot be correct.

There is still additional proof that the one who had the gift of tongues is not directed to pray for the gift of interpretation. "If any man speak in an unknown tongue, let it be by two, or at the most by three, and that by course; and let one interpret," (I Corinthians 14:27). This verse states that if any man speaks in a tongue, "let it be by two, or at the most by three, and that by course; and let **one** interpret." This is a command for the one that spoke in a tongue, which would include praying in a tongue, to let one interpret; that is, let another interpret. If the one that spoke in a tongue could receive the gift of interpretation in answer to prayer, why did Paul not say let him remain silent until he received the gift of interpretation in answer to prayer.

One of the things that characterized spiritual gifts was that they were of such a nature so as to avoid someone counterfeiting them. If the one that prayed or spoke in a tongue had been allowed to interpret his own speaking, no one would have known whether he had really spoken in a tongue or not. But when another had the gift of interpretation, and gave the interpretation of the tongue, it assured the assembly of the genuineness of the inspiration of the tongue. Thus, verses 27 and 28 forbid the tongue speaker to do his own interpreting. Verse 13 must harmonize with verses 27 and 28. Can verse 13 be explained so that it harmonizes?

1. Does it harmonize with the truth that spiritual gifts came only through the hands of an apostle?
2. Does it harmonize that when one spoke in a tongue, another with the gift of interpretation was to interpret the tongue?

The answers are yes. The sense of verse 13 is, "Wherefore let him that speaketh in an unknown tongue pray that he [one] may interpret." This harmonizes with the truth that spiritual gifts were imparted by the apostles and with verses 27 and 28 where the one that spoke in a tongue was to let another one interpret. Verse 13 is not a direction for the one that spoke in a tongue to pray for the gift of interpretation, but rather to pray so that the prayer could be interpreted by one that had the gift of interpretation. The next verse shows that it is the prayer that is to be interpreted: "For if I pray in an unknown tongue, my spirit prayeth, but my understanding is unfruitful," (I Corinthians 14:14). If the prayer of verse 14 is not interpreted, it is unfruitful to the assembly. The phrase of verse 13, "that he may interpret," is a reference to the one that has the gift of interpretation, not a prayer to receive the gift of interpretation. There is no authority in this verse for one praying for the gift of interpretation. If one could receive the gift of interpretation in answer to prayer, why could he not receive the gift of prophecy, the gift of tongues, the gift of healing, or any other of the spiritual gifts in the same manner? But if one could receive spiritual gifts in answer to prayer, then the credentials of the apostles are completely destroyed. The chief credential of an apostle was that of the impartation of spiritual gifts. Surely, Paul who was an apostle and defended his apostleship by appealing to his imparting spiritual gifts to the church at Corinth, would not have been so inconsistent as to have told the Corinthians that spoke in tongues to pray for the gift of interpretation. If this verse is understood so that the one who spoke; that is, prayed in a tongue, was to speak or pray in such a manner so that the one who had the gift of interpretation could interpret the prayer, and thereby the audience could be edified, it harmonizes with the truth that spiritual gifts were imparted through the hands of an apostle, and with verses 27 and 28 where Paul tells the one that spoke in a tongue to remain silent unless there be one to interpret. The phrase of verse 27, "and let one interpret," is the key to the proper understanding of I Corinthians 14:13, plus the fact, that verse 14 shows that Paul is speaking of interpreting the prayer and not praying for the gift of interpretation. The so-called tongues of today are not the tongues of I Corinthians 14. Praying for the baptism of the Holy Spirit and spiritual gifts is without any Bible basis. Spiritual gifts were given for the edification of the church and as a means of evangelizing while the Word was in the process of being revealed. When revelation was completed, all of these spiritual gifts ceased. There is not the slightest hint in I Corinthians 14 that spiritual gifts can be received today.

PENTECOSTALISM AND TONGUES

Pentecostalism has grown tremendously in the last few years. Its proponents are seen constantly on TV and heard on radio. It has found among its famous adherents some of the personalities of TV. It has also made inroads into the successful business world. The method of neo-pentecostalism is to use some TV personalities or persons who have become rich. These people give their "testimony" as to how the baptism of the Holy Spirit and speaking in tongues has changed their lives. They attribute all their success to the experience of the baptism of the Holy Spirit and speaking in tongues. The method of using popular stars of our day has an appeal to multitudes of people.

Pentecostals also claim that the experience of speaking in tongues is the ultimate of spirituality. In view of the growth and the claims of these people, there is a need for measuring their claims by the Bible. All testimonies of every TV star and successful businessman cannot establish their claims. They must prove them by the Bible. The Bible test is what I shall apply to their claims. If Pentecostalism cannot pass this test, it must be rejected. "Prove all things; hold fast that which is good." (Thess. 5:21)

PROPHECY

The foundation of all miraculous operations of the Holy Spirit is prophecy. The background of this is found in the calling, the commission, and the credentials of Moses. (Exodus 3 & 4) Abraham is called a prophet one time. This was because Abraham was the channel of blessing for all the families of the earth. (Gen. 2:7; 12:3) In the broader view of the prophet, Moses is considered as the first one.

"Whom the heaven must receive until the times of restitution of all things, which God hath spoken by the mouth of all his holy prophets since the world began. For Moses truly said unto the fathers, A prophet shall the Lord your God raise up unto you of your brethren, like unto me; him shall ye hear in all things whatsoever he shall say unto you. And it shall come to pass, that every soul, which will not hear that prophet, shall be destroyed from among the people. Yea, and all the prophets from Samuel and those that follow after, as many as have spoken, have likewise foretold of these days. Ye are the children of the prophets, and of the covenant which God made with our fathers, saying unto Abraham, And in thy seed shall all the kindreds of the earth be blessed." (Acts 3:21-25)

Thus, the account of Moses gives the background and principles in relation to prophecy, its importance, and the miraculous that accompanies it. The principles of revelation and inspiration are set forth in the calling, commission, and the credentials of Moses. It required (1) a specific call, (2) a specific commission, and (3) specific credentials to confirm the **call, commission,** and **revelation** that came through Moses as a prophet.

"And the Lord said, I have surely seen the affliction of my people which are in Egypt, and have heard their cry by reason of their taskmasters; for I know their sorrows; and I am come down to deliver them out of the hand of the Egyptians, and to bring them up out of that land unto a good land and a large, unto a land flowing with milk and honey; unto the place of the Canaanites, and the Hittites, and the Amorites, and the Perizzites, and the Hivites, and the Jebusites. Now therefore, behold, the cry of the children of Israel is come unto me: and I have also seen the oppression wherewith the Egyptians oppress them. Come now therefore, and I will send thee unto Pharaoh, that thou mayest bring forth my people the children of Israel out of Egypt.

"And Moses said unto God, Who am I, that I should go unto Pharaoh, and that I should bring forth the children of Israel out of Egypt? And he said, Certainly I will be with thee; and this shall be a token unto thee, that I have sent thee: When thou hast brought forth the people out of Egypt, ye shall serve God upon this mountain. And Moses said unto God, Behold, when I come unto the children of Israel, and shall say unto them, The God of your fathers hath sent me unto you; and they shall say to me, What is his name? what shall I say unto them? And God said unto Moses, I AM THAT I AM: and he said, Thus shalt thou say unto the children of Israel, I AM hath sent me unto you. And God said moreover unto Moses, Thus shalt thou say unto the Children of Israel, The Lord God of your fathers, the God of Abraham, the God of Isaac, and the God of Jacob, hath sent me unto you: this is my name for ever, and this is my memorial unto all generations." (Exodus 3:7-15)

"And it shall come to pass, if they will not believe thee, neither harken to the voice of the first sign, that they will believe the voice of the latter sign. And it shall come to pass, if they will not believe also these two signs, neither hearken unto thy voice, that thou shalt take of the water of the river, and pour it upon the dry land: and the water which thou takest out of the river shall become blood upon the dry land." (Exodus 4:8-9)

A prophet was an inspired spokesman for God. This called for confirmation to establish that the revelation was divine in origin. It required

THE WORK OF THE HOLY SPIRIT 277

supernatural evidence that the revelation through him was supernatural in origin.

It is also interesting to note that written revelation began with Moses: "Do not think that I will accuse you to the Father: there is one that accuseth you, even Moses, in whom ye trust. For had ye believed Moses, ye would have believed me: for he wrote of me. But if ye believe not his writings, how shall ye believe my words?" (John 5:45-57)

The call, commission, and credentials of Moses become the type for the call, commission, and credentials for the apostles in the New Testament. The nature of prophecy demanded the miraculous. Revelation could only be given through miraculous means.

"And he said, Certainly I will be with thee, and this shall be a token unto thee, that I have sent thee: When thou hast brought forth the people out of Egypt, ye shall serve God upon this mountain. And Moses said unto God, Behold, when I come unto the children of Israel, and shall say unto them, The God of your fathers hath sent me unto you; and they shall say to me, What is his name? what shall I say unto them: And God said unto Moses, I AM THAT I AM: and he said, Thus shalt thou say unto the children of Israel, I AM hath sent me unto you. And God said moreover unto Moses, Thus shalt thou say unto the children of Israel, The Lord God of your fathers, the God of Abraham, the God of Isaac, and the God of Jacob, hath sent me unto you: this is my name for ever, and this is my memorial unto all generations." (Exodus 3:12-15)

Forthtelling and foretelling required the miraculous. In Moses we have the first primary prophet, and in connection with him the fundamental nature of prophecy. Here is the background and the foundation of the miraculous. If one is to understand the miraculous in giving and confirming revelation, it is necessary that he grasp the principles set forth in this account of Moses. It is evident that prophecy forms the basis of the miraculous and that all other miraculous operations were related to this one. Here's the reason for Paul's direction to the church at Corinth.

Let a man so account of us, as of the ministers of Christ, and stewards of the mysteries of God. Moreover it is required in stewards, that a man be found faithful. But with me it is a very small thing that I should be judged of you, or of man's judgment: yea, I judge not mine own self. For I know nothing by myself; yet am I not hereby justified: but he that judgeth me is the Lord. Therefore judge nothing before the time, until the Lord come, who both will bring to light the hidden things of darkness, and will make manifest the counsels of the hearts: and then shall every man have praise of God." (I Cor. 4:1-5)

While it is true that prophecy edified, Paul places it above tongues because prophecy was primary and tongues were secondary.

THE PURPOSE OF THE MIRACULOUS

Supernatural knowledge requires supernatural evidence for confirmation. The two main gifts that Pentecostals claim are tongues and healing. A tongue was like prophecy in that it was an inspired utterance. Prophecy was an utterance in words given by God.

> "I will raise them up a Prophet from among their brethren, like unto thee, and will put my words in his mouth; and he shall speak unto them all that I shall command him." (Deut. 18:18)

Verse 17 says "the Lord said unto me ... " The verse quoted states that the words a prophet spoke were God's words. Thus prophecy or revelation was an utterance of God. A tongue was also an utterance in words given by God.

> "And when the day of Pentecost was fully come, they were all with one accord in one place. And suddenly there came a sound from heaven as of a rushing mighty wind, and it filled all the house where they were sitting. And there appeared unto them cloven tongues like as of fire, and it sat upon each of them. And they were all filled with the Holy Ghost, and began to speak with other tongues, as the Spirit gave them utterance. And there were dwelling at Jerusalem Jews, devout men, out of every nation under heaven. Now when this was noised abroad, the multitude came together, and were confounded, because that every man heard them speak in his own language." (Acts 2:1-6)

A **tongue** was an inspired utterance in a language by the speaker. If the speaker did not know the language, it is evident that the words were given by the Spirit. (This is an argument for verbal inspiration.) Thus, a tongue, like prophecy, was an inspired utterance, an inspired word of God. Words given by God demand complete acceptance and obedience.

> "I will raise them up a Prophet from among their brethren, like unto thee, and will put my words in his mouth; and he shall speak unto them all that I shall command him. And it shall come to pass, that whosoever will not hearken unto my words which he shall speak in my name, I will require it of him." (Deut. 18:18-19)

THE WORK OF THE HOLY SPIRIT

Peter quotes this from Moses and applies it to his hearers in Jerusalem:

"For Moses said unto the fathers, A prophet shall the Lord your God raise up unto you of your brethren, like unto me; him shall ye hear in all things whatsoever he shall say unto you. And it shall come to pass, that every soul, which will not hear that prophet, shall be destroyed from among the people." (Acts 3:22-23)

Paul says the same thing to the Thessalonians:

"Therefore, brethren, stand fast, and hold the traditions which ye have been taught, whether by word, or our epistle." (II Thess. 2:15)

"And if any man obey not our word by this epistle, note that man, and have no company with him, that he may be ashamed." (II Thess. 3:14)

An inspired utterance was to be accepted and obeyed. False prophets claimed their utterances were from God. Any utterance that claimed to be from God but was not from him was to be rejected.

"But the prophet, which shall presume to speak a word in my name, which I have not commanded him to speak, or that shall speak in the name of other gods, even that prophet shall die." (Deut. 18:20)

Jeremiah gives a clear warning against false prophets that claimed to be uttering God's word.

"Mine heart within me is broken because of the prophets; all my bones shake; I am like a drunken man, and like a man whom wine hath overcome, because of the Lord, and because of the words of his holiness. For the land is full of adulterers; for because of swearing the land mourneth; the pleasant places of the wilderness are dried up, and their course is evil, and their force is not right. For both prophet and priest are profane; yea, in my house have I found their wickedness, saith the Lord. Wherefore their way shall be unto them as slippery ways in the darkness: they shall be driven on, and fall therein: for I will bring evil upon them, even the year of their visitation, saith the Lord. And I have seen folly in the prophets of Samaria; they prophesied in Baal, and caused my people Israel to err. I have seen also in the prophets of Jerusalem an horrible thing: they commit adultery, and walk in lies: they strengthen also the hands of evildoers, that none doth return from his wickedness: they are all of them unto me as Sodom, and the inhabitants thereof as Gomorrah. Therefore thus saith the Lord of hosts concerning the prophets; Behold, I will feed them with wormwood, and make them drink the water of gall: for from the prophets of Jerusalem is profaneness gone forth into all the land. Thus saith the Lord of hosts, Harken not unto the words of the prophets that prophesy unto you: they make you vain: they speak a vision of their own heart, and not out of the mouth of the Lord. They say still unto them that despise me, The Lord hath said, Ye shall have peace; and they say unto every one that walketh after the imagination of his own heart, No evil shall come upon you. For who hath stood in the counsel of the Lord, and hath perceived and heard his word? who hath marked his word, and heard it? Behold, a whirlwind of the Lord is gone forth in fury, even a grievous whirlwind: it shall fall grievously upon the head of the wicked. The anger of the Lord shall not return, until he have executed, and till he have performed the thoughts of his heart: in the latter days ye shall consider it perfectly. I have not sent these prophets, yet they ran: I have not spoken to them, yet they prophesied. But if they had stood in my counsel, and had caused my people to hear my words, then they should have turned them from their evil way, and from the evil of their doings. Am I a God at hand, saith the Lord, and not a God afar off? Can any hide himself in secret places that I shall not see him? saith the Lord. Do not I fill heaven and earth? saith the Lord. I have heard what the prophets said, that prophesy lies in my name, saying, I have dreamed, I have dreamed. How long shall this be in the heart of the prophets that prophesy lies? yea, they are prophets of the deceit of their own heart; Which think to cause my people to forget my name by their dreams which they tell every man to his neighbor, as their fathers have forgotten my name for Baal. The prophet that hath a dream; and he that hath my word, let him speak my word faithfully. What is the chaff to the wheat? saith the Lord. Is not my word like as a fire? saith the Lord; and like a hammer that breaketh the rock in pieces? Therefore, behold, I am against the prophets, saith the Lord, that steal my words every one from his neighbour. Behold, I am against the prophets, saith the Lord, that use their tongues, and say, He saith. Behold, I am against them that prophesy false dreams, saith the Lord, and do tell them, and cause my people to err by their lies, and by their lightness; yet I sent them not, nor commanded them: therefore they shall not profit this people at all, saith the Lord." (Jeremiah 23:9-32)

"Now we beseech you, brethren, by the coming of our Lord Jesus Christ, and by our gathering together unto him, That ye be not soon shaken in mind, or be troubled, neither by spirit, nor by word, nor by letter as from us, as that the day of Christ is at hand." (II Thess. 2:1-2)

It was vital to test all utterances that claimed to be God's word. The utterance that passed the test was to be accepted, and the utterance that did not pass the test was to be rejected.

"Beloved, believe not every spirit, but try the spirits whether they are of God: because many false prophets are gone out into the world." (I John 4:1)

When one spoke in tongues and the language was understood, it was evidence of a miracle, and that was confirmation of the utterance being the word of God. But when one spoke in a tongue not understood, it lacked supernatural evidence to prove that it was an inspired utterance from God. Since the tongue not understood lacked the necessary supernatural evidence to establish it as an utterance from God, how could one that heard it determine whether it was true or false? He could not unless there was a interpreter. This is the reason for the regulations governing tongues in First Corinthians 14 which required an interpreter. If there was no interpreter the one who could speak in a tongue was to remain silent. The reason is plain. Speaking in a tongue was an inspired utterance. It was like prophecy in this point. An inspired utterance was God's word and was to be accepted and obeyed. Since there were false prophets claiming to utter God's word, it was necessary that every claim be tested to determine whether it was from God or from a man's own heart.

"Thus saith the Lord of hosts, Hearken not unto the words of the prophets that prophesy unto you: they make you vain: they speak a vision of their own heart, and not out of the mouth of the Lord." (Jeremiah 23:16) "For who hath stood in the counsel of the Lord, and hath perceived and heard his word? who hath marked his word, and heard it? (v. 18)

"I have not sent these prophets, yet they ran: I have not spoken to them, yet they prophesied." (v. 21)

"I have heard what the prophets said, that prophesy lies in my name, saying, I have dreamed, I have dreamed. How long shall this be in the heart of the prophets that prophesy lies? yea, they are prophets of the deceit of their own heart;" (v. 25, 26)

"The prophet that hath a dream, let him tell a dream; and he that hath my word, let him speak my word faithfully. What is the chaff to the wheat saith the Lord." (v. 28)

"Therefore, behold, I am against the prophets, saith the Lord, that steal my words every one from his neighbour. Behold, I am against the prophets, saith the Lord, that use their tongues, and say, He saith." (v. 30, 31)

How could one determine whether a tongue was an inspired utterance from God when in a language not understood? There was no way unless there was an interpreter and the interpreter provided the supernatural evidence showing the utterance was God's word. The call, commission, and credentials of Moses lay the foundation for the work of the apostles in the New Testament. The apostles were called and commissioned by Christ and were given credentials to establish their call and commission. They were infallible teachers.

> "But when they deliver you up, take no thought how or what ye shall speak: for it shall be given you in that same hour what ye shall speak. For it is not ye that speak, but the Spirit of your Father which speaketh in you." (Matt. 10:19-20)

> "But when they shall lead you, and deliver you up, take no thought beforehand what ye shall speak, neither do ye premeditate: but whatsoever shall be given you in that hour, that speak ye: for it is not ye that speak, but the Holy Ghost." (Mark 13:11)

> "Settle it therefore in your hearts, not to meditate before what ye shall answer: For I will give you a mouth and wisdom, which all your adversaries shall not be able to gainsay nor resist." (Luke 21:14-15)

> "But the Comforter, which is the Holy Ghost, whom the Father will send in my name, he shall teach you all things, and bring all things to your remembrance, whatsoever I have said unto you." (John 14:26)

> "Howbeit when he, the Spirit of truth, is come, he will guide you into all truth: for he shall not speak of himself; but whatsoever he shall hear, that shall he speak: and he will shew you things to come." (John 16:13)

It is interesting to note that Christ, in speaking of the inspiration of the apostles in Matthew 10:19-20, also calls them prophets.

> "He that receiveth a prophet in the name of a prophet shall receive a prophet's reward; and he that receiveth a righteous man in the name of a righteous man shall receive a righteous man's reward." (Matt. 10:41)

The prophet of verse 41 is a reference to the apostles in the first part of the chapter. The prophet in the New Testament had the power to discern the false.

> "And, lo, a spirit taketh him, and he suddenly crieth out; and it teareth him that he foameth again, and bruising him hardly departeth from him." (Luke 7:39)

> "The woman answered and said, I have no husband. Jesus said unto her, Thou hast well said, I have no husband: For thou hast had five husbands; and he whom thou now hast is not thy husband: in that saidst thou truly. The woman saith unto him, Sir, I perceive that thou art a prophet." (John 4:17-19)

> "And thus are the secrets of his heart made manifest; and so falling down on his face, he will worship God, and report that God is in you of a truth." (I Cor. 14:25)

THE WORK OF THE HOLY SPIRIT

The apostles had this power as a part of their function:

"But a certain man named Ananias, with Sapphira his wife, sold a possession, And kept back part of the price, his wife also being privy to it, and brought a certain part, and laid it at the apostles' feet. But Peter said, Ananias, why hath Satan filled thine heart to lie to the Holy Ghost, and to keep back part of the price of the land? Whiles it remained, was it not in thine own power? why hast thou conceived this thing in thine heart? thou hast not lied unto men, but unto God. And Ananias hearing these words fell down, and gave up the ghost: and great fear came on all them that heard these things. And the young men arose, wound him up, and carried him out, and buried him. And it was about the space of three hours after, when his wife, not knowing what was done, came in. And Peter answered unto her, Tell me whether ye sold the land for so much? And she said, Yea, for so much. Then Peter said unto her, How is it that ye have agreed together to tempt the Spirit of the Lord? behold, the feet of them which have buried thy husband are at the door, and shall carry thee out. Then fell she down straightway at his feet, and yielded up the ghost: and the young men came in, and found her dead, and, carrying her forth, buried her by her husband. And great fear came upon all the church, and upon as many as heard these things." (Acts 5:1-11)

"And when they had gone through the isle unto Paphos, they found a certain sorcerer, a false prophet, a Jew, whose name was Bar-jesus: Which was with the deputy of the country, Sergius Paulus, a prudent man; who called for Barnabas and Saul, and desired to hear the word of God. But Elymas the sorcerer (for so is his name by interpretation) withstood them, seeking to turn away the deputy from the faith. Then Saul, (who also is called Paul,) filled with the Holy Ghost, set his eyes on him, And said, O full of all subtilty and all mischief, thou child of the devil, thou enemy of all righteousness, wilt thou not cease to pervert the right ways of the Lord? And now, behold, the hand of the Lord is upon thee, and thou shalt be blind, not seeing the sun for a season. And immediately there fell on him a mist and a darkness; and he went about seeking some to lead him by the hand. Then the deputy, when he saw what was done, believed, being astonished at the doctrine of the Lord." (Acts 13:6-12)

"And there sat a certain man at Lystra, impotent in his feet, being a cripple from his mother's womb, who never had walked: The same heard Paul speak: who stedfastly beholding him, and perceiving that he had faith to be healed, Said with a loud voice, Stand upright on thy feet. And he leaped and walked." (Acts 14:8-10)

The apostles could determine false prophets. Paul, an apostle, regulated the use of prophetic gifts. In First Corinthians 14, he used the apostolic right to accept or refuse to recognize one that claimed inspiration. "But if any man be ignorant, let him be ignorant." (I Cor. 14:38) The books of the New Testament were written by an apostle or by one that passed under apostolic sanction.

"Aristarchus my fellowprisoner saluteth you, and Marcus, sister's son to Barnabas, (touching whom ye received commandments: if he come unto you, receive him;)" (Col. 4:10)

"Only Luke is with me. Take Mark, and bring him with thee: for he is profitable to me for the ministry." (II Tim. 4:11)

"Luke, the beloved physician, and Demas, greet you." (Col. 4:14)

Thus the New Testament comes to us through either apostolic writing or apostolic sanction of the writer. Any utterance that claims to be from God must pass this test. If the prophecy or utterance (tongue) contradicts scripture, the claim must be rejected. There is no way that a so-called tongue today can have apostolic sanction since all the apostles are dead. This is but another argument showing that the miraculous was never intended beyond the age of a completed revelation and its confirmation through the apostles.

If an utterance denied Christ, it was to be rejected.

"And every spirit that confesseth not that Jesus Christ is come in the flesh is not of God: and this is that spirit of antichrist, whereof ye have heard that it should come; and even now already is it in the world." (I John 4:3)

But it did not follow that because an utterance spoke well of Christ that it was divine and was to be accepted. (I Kings 13:11-32, Matt. 8:29, Mark 1:24, Acts 16:17, Matt. 7:21-23) Some claim to work miracles in his name, but one is not to accept it just because he claims to be a Christian.

"Beware of false prophets, which come to you in sheep's clothing, but inwardly they are ravening wolves. Ye shall know them by their fruits. Do men gather grapes of thorns, or figs of thistles? Even so every good tree bringeth forth good fruit; but a corrupt tree bringeth forth evil fruit. A good tree cannot bring forth evil fruit, neither can a corrupt tree bring forth good fruit. Every tree that bringeth not forth good fruit is hewn down, and cast into the fire. Wherefore by their fruits ye shall know them." (Matt. 7:15-20)

The fruit of a prophet is not his good deeds but his doctrine. The word "prophet" signifies inspired teaching. The fact that Jesus warns of false prophets shows that he has reference to teaching — not deeds.

The claim to the gift of prophecy or tongues without confirmatory evidence is false doctrine. (Deut. 18:20-22) A good life is not the basis of Matthew 7:15-20. It is true that right doctrine believed and obeyed will produce a good life, but this is not what Christ was dealing with. The general rule would be that a right life and inspiration belong together. But this certainly was not the case with Balaam. (Num. 22-24, II Pet. 2:15, Jude 11) The church at Corinth could not lay claim to any superior spiritual state. The church at Corinth could not claim that a good life was the basis of their having spiritual gifts. One should not accept the Pentecostal claims since they cannot pass the test of apostolic sanction. It is foolish to accept the claim of Pentecostals today.

DISTRIBUTION OF GIFTS

The means of the distribution of gifts was like the means of determining real gifts from counterfeit. Since it took apostolic sanction for a gift to be determined an actual gift, it must follow that the distribution of gifts could only be through an apostle's hand.

"Now when the apostles which were at Jerusalem heard that Samaria had received the word of God, they sent unto them Peter and John: Who, when they were come down, prayed for them, that they might receive the Holy Ghost: (For as yet he was fallen upon none of them: only they were baptized in the name of the Lord Jesus.) Then laid they their hands on them, and they received the Holy Ghost. And when Simon saw that through laying on of the apostles' hands the Holy Ghost was given, he offered them money, Saying, give me also this power, that on whomsoever I lay hands, he may receive the Holy Ghost. But Peter said unto him, Thy money perish with thee, because thou hast thought that the gift of God may be purchased with money. Thou hast neither part nor lot in this matter: for thy heart is not right in the sight of God. Repent therefore of this thy wickedness, and pray God, if perhaps the thought of thine heart may be forgiven thee. For I perceive that thou art in the gall of bitterness, and in the bond of iniquity." (Acts 8:14-23)

"And it came to pass, that, while Apollos was at Corinth, Paul having passed through the upper coasts came to Ephesus: and finding certain disciples, He said unto them, Have ye received the Holy Ghost since ye believed? And they said unto him, We have not so much as heard whether there be any Holy Ghost. And he said unto them, Unto what then were ye baptized? And they said, Unto John's baptism. Then said Paul, John verily baptized with the baptism of repentance, saying unto the people, that they should believe on him which should come after him, that is, on Christ Jesus. When they heard this, they were baptized in the name of the Lord Jesus. And when Paul had laid his hands upon them, the Holy Ghost came on them; and they spake with tongues, and prophesied." (Acts 19:1-6)

It's significant that the ones in Acts 19 spoke in tongues and prophesied.

Acts 18 gives the account of the beginning of the church at Corinth. Nothing is said in Acts 18 of Paul's imparting spiritual gifts, but the silence of Acts 18 does not prove that he did not impart gifts to the church at Corinth. Evidently the events of Acts 8 and 19 were intended to establish the rule for receiving spiritual gifts. It was to be understood when not stated. Does someone say, "But how can you prove this?" I can prove it by Paul. First Corinthians 12-14 proves that the church had gifts. I Cor. 1:5-8, I Cor. 13:1-3, II Cor. 12:12 provide the evidence that the **gifts came through the hands of the apostle Paul.**

Furthermore, there is no indication that anyone received any miraculous gift while Paul was away from Corinth. If the church received gifts apart from Paul's hands, then his argument in his defense of his apostleship in that he imparted spiritual gifts to the church at Corinth is destroyed. The chief argument of Paul in defense of his apostleship was that the church at Corinth had received spiritual gifts from him. If one member could have received a gift in Paul's absence (no other apostle visited Corinth), a false teacher could have repudiated his apostolic claim based on their gift through his hand.

There is no record in Acts of Timothy's receiving a miraculous gift by the hands of Paul; but is this proof that he did not? The answer is No. Acts 8 and 19 give the rule. It was understood when not stated. We are not left to guess about this. "Wherefore I put thee in remembrance that thou stir up the gift of God, which is in thee by the putting on of my hands." (II Tim. 1:6) The passage states that Paul laid his hands on Timothy and imparted spiritual gifts to him.

The book of acts is not a detailed account of every instance of the distribution of gifts through the hands of the apostles. The book of Acts shows the process and the purpose. Acts 8 and 19 set forth the rule. It was to be understood in all other cases where people had spiritual gifts that those gifts came through apostolic hands.

This is similar to obedience to the gospel. The obedience of faith includes repentance, confession, and baptism. When one or more of these is mentioned and the others are not, the ones not mentioned are to be understood as being included. The same principle is true about spiritual gifts. When a person had a spiritual gift, if it is not stated that the gift was received through the hands of an apostle, it is to be understood that this was so, based on Acts 8 and 19.

THE WORK OF THE HOLY SPIRIT

The Galatians received spiritual gifts through the hands of Paul. "He therefore that ministereth to you the Spirit, and worketh miracles among you, doeth he it by the works of the law, or by the hearing of faith?" (Gal. 3:5) Paul was defending his apostleship against the charge of Judaising teachers.

"Paul, an apostle, (not of men, neither by man, but by Jesus Christ, and God the Father, who raised him from the dead;)" (Gal. 1:1) "I marvel that ye are so soon removed from him that called you into the grace of Christ unto another gospel: Which is not another; but there be some that trouble you, and would pervert the gospel of Christ." (v. 6-7) "For I neither received it of man, neither was I taught it, but by the revelation of Jesus Christ." (v. 12)

The rule of Acts 8 and 19 that the distribution of a gift through the hands of an apostle is true in the case of the Galatians.

The church at Rome had miraculous gifts. It's likely that the church at Rome was started by some that were in Jerusalem on Pentecost or by some that were scattered in Acts 8. There may have been some in Rome who received gifts through Paul's hands. The list of names in Romans 16 would certainly include those who had been converted by Paul and had received gifts through the laying on of his hands. All indications are that no apostle had visited Rome. Any converts in Rome that had no access to an apostle had not received any gift. Therefore, Paul's desire to go to Rome to impart spiritual gifts to those who had none. "For I long to see you, that I may impart unto you some spiritual gift, to the end ye may be established;" (Romans 1:11) Why did Paul not simply tell them to pray that they might receive a gift? Paul knew that the distribution of the gifts came through apostolic hands. Romans 1:11 follows the rule for the distribution of the gifts through the hands of an apostle as set forth in Acts 8 and 19.

SUMMARY

"How shall we escape, if we neglect so great salvation; which at the first began to be spoken by the Lord, and was confirmed unto us by them that heard him; God also bearing them witness, both with signs and wonders, and with divers miracles, and gifts of the Holy Ghost, according to his own will?" (Heb. 2:3-4)

This passage gives a summary of the personal ministry of Christ; the great commission given by Christ to the apostles; the revelation of the gospel to the apostles, with miraculous confirmation of it; and the distribution of the gifts through the hands of the apostles. McKnight paraphrases verse 4 as follows: "God himself bearing joint witness to the salvation preached by the Lord and his apostles both by signs and wonders and miracles of divers kinds which enabled these preachers to perform, and by distribution of the gifts of the Holy Ghost which they bestowed, not according to their will, but according to his own pleasure." Hebrews 2:3-4 summarizes and confirms the procedure of Acts 8 and 19. Spiritual gifts came only through the hands of the apostles. The limitation of the distribution of spiritual gifts by the hands of an apostle can mean only one thing: spiritual gifts were limited to the day of living apostles. There are no living apostles today; therefore the claims of Pentecostalism are false. They can neither heal nor speak in tongues.

THE PURPOSE OF GIFTS

The purpose of gifts proves that they are not received today. The distribution of gifts through the hands of the apostles had the same purpose as the other powers of an apostle. The distribution of a gift through the hands of an apostle was his credential. But the credentials of an apostle were proof of his inspiration and the confirmation of his message.

"And they went forth, and preached every where, the Lord working with them, and confirming the word with signs following." (Mark 16:20)

"How shall we escape, if we neglect so great salvation; which at the first began to be spoken by the Lord, and was confirmed unto us by them that heard him; God also bearing them witness, both with signs and wonders, and with divers miracles, and gifts of the Holy Ghost, according to his own will?" (Heb. 2:3-4)

In fact, the distribution of spiritual gifts was the chief sign of an apostle:

"Truly the signs of an apostle were wrought among you in all patience, in signs, and wonders, and mighty deeds." (II Cor. 12:12)

"Then Simon himself believed also: and when he was baptized, he continued with Philip, and wondered, beholding the miracles and signs which were done. Now when the apostles which were at Jerusalem heard that Samaria had received the word of God, they sent unto them Peter and John: Who, when they were come down, prayed for them, that they might receive the Holy Ghost: (For as yet he was fallen upon none of them: only they were baptized in the name of the Lord Jesus.) Then laid they their hands on them, and they received the Holy Ghost. And when Simon saw that through laying on of the apostles' hands the Holy Ghost was given, he offered them money, Saying, Give me also this power, that on whomsoever I lay hands, he may receive the Holy Ghost." (Acts 8:13-19)

THE WORK OF THE HOLY SPIRIT

The distribution of gifts through the hands of an apostle was like the other powers of the apostles; it was intended for the confirmation of the gospel given through him. When the revelation of the gospel was completed and confirmed, this gift, like the other powers of an apostle, ceased. Note the following:

1. Spiritual gifts came only through the hands of an apostle.
2. The distribution of gifts through the hands of an apostle was like the other powers of an apostle.
3. The distribution of gifts through the hands of an apostle confirmed his apostleship and the gospel he preached.
4. The gospel revealed through the apostles has been completed and confirmed.

It must follow that the claim of any miraculous power — particularly healing and tongue — is a false claim and must be rejected.

It is true that gifts had specific purposes within themselves, but these were also fulfilled within the age of living apostles. The purpose of Old Testament prophecy and of New Testament apostles and prophets was to bear witness to the Messiah. (Heb. 2:1-4) The prophets of the Old Testament pointed to his coming. John the Baptist was the last of the Old Testament prophets.

"For all the prophets and the law prophesied until John." (Matt. 11:13)

"The law and the prophets were until John: since that time the kingdom of God is preached, and every man presseth into it." (Luke 16:16)

The coming of Christ, his sinless life, death, burial, resurrection, and ascension fulfilled Old Testament prophecy. "The Lord thy God will raise up unto thee a Prophet from the midst of thee, of thy brethren, like unto me; unto him shall ye harken;" (Deut. 18:15) Peter's second sermon in Acts 3 shows that Christ fulfilled Deuteronomy 18:15.

The apostles provide infallible proof that he was the fulfillment of the Old Testament.

"For Moses truly said unto the fathers, A prophet shall the Lord your God raise up unto you of your brethren, like unto me; him shall ye hear in all things whatsoever he shall say unto you. And it shall come to pass, that every soul, which will not hear that prophet, shall be destroyed from among the people." (Acts 3:22-23)

The apostles, in providing infallible proof that Christ was the fulfillment of the Old Testament, at the same time provided the gospel of redemption from sin — the faith once for all delivered to the saints. (Jude 3) When this was accomplished, there was no further need for miraculous endowment. The entire book of Hebrews is a treatise showing that the preaching of Christ by the apostles was the final stage of revelation:

> "God, who at sundry times and in divers manners spake in time past unto the fathers by the prophets, Hath in these last days spoken unto us by his Son, whom he hath appointed heir of all things, by whom also he made the worlds; Who being brightness of his glory, and the express image of his person, and upholding all things by the word of his power, when he had by himself purged our sins, sat down on the right hand of the Majesty on high;" (Heb. 1:1-3)

THE IMPORTANCE OF PROPHECY

I've already shown the importance of the calling, commission, and credentials of Moses. He is considered the first of the prophets. (Acts 3) I also called attention to the fact that prophecy was the foundation of the miraculous in relation to revelation and confirmation. It is not by accident that the Bible makes prophecy the base of the operation of the miraculous. Prophecy demands inspiration.

The prophetic in relation to revelation and inspiration shows its cessation.

> "For I testify unto every man that heareth the words of the prophecy of this book, If any man shall add unto these things, God shall add unto him the plagues that are written in this book:" (Rev. 22:18)

Since God made prophecy and the prophets the foundation of all the miraculous, is it not significant that the last book of the New Testament is one of prophecy? It was given through John, an apostle, thus showing the prophetic nature of the apostles. Written revelation had its beginning with Moses, a prophet. (Deut. 18:18-22) The New Testament closes with a book of prophecy given through an apostle to whom revelation and confirmation had been given. The book of Revelation was written to establish the completeness and finality of the redemption provided through Christ and proclaimed through the apostles. The warning given in Revelation 22:18 is not just a warning against adding to the book of Revelation. It is a signal of the end of prophecy, and with the end of prophecy the end of the miraculous. Since prophecy was the foundation of the miraculous, the cessation of prophecy signaled the completion of Revelation, the end of inspiration, and the cessation of all miraculous operations of the Holy Spirit. Revelation 22:18 is a warning that all claims to miraculous powers are false.

Prophecy stands for all miraculous powers:

"Charity never faileth: but whether there be prophecies, they shall fail; whether there be tongues, they shall cease; whether there be knowledge, it shall vanish away." (I Cor. 13:8)

Look at the passage. Prophecy is first. This is not by accident. It was the basis of all miraculous operation, therefore listed first. We have prophecy, tongues, and knowledge. These three equal divine revelation. That is, they stand for the whole of miraculous powers and a full, completed revelation. In like manner, "the words of the prophecy of this book" stands for the whole miraculous power, and indicate their ceasing. The book of Revelation is the crown, or pinnacle, of revelation. Prophetic in its nature, it was a symbol of the end of prophecy and, with it, all other miraculous gifts; the reason being that, revelation being completed, there was no need for miraculous powers to continue.

TONGUES

Tongues were a part of the package of gifts. In addition, a tongue was a part of the revelation that God gave to Israel. One of the reasons many misunderstand the Bible is their failure to see its unity and unfolding message. The Old Testament is the background of the tongues of the New Testament. The book of Deuteronomy contains Moses' farewell addresses to the nation of Israel. This book is a commentary on the failure of the generation that died in the wilderness, and contains a message of warning to those who were entering into Canaan.

The 28th chapter of Deuteronomy contains promises and blessings for the nation if they would obey; and curses if they were disobedient. Beginning in verse 15, through the rest of the chapter, Moses gives a long list of warnings and the consequences of rebellion against God. In the midst of these warnings to the nation there is one that is of particular interest in connection with the study of tongues:

"And they shall be upon thee for a sign and for a wonder, and upon thy seed for ever." (Deut. 28:46)

Is it not strange that Moses used the word "sign" in this connection? Strong defines the word "sign" of this verse as follows: "A signal, as a flag, beacon, monument, omen, prodigy, or evidence." Wilson, in his word studies, gives the following: "A sign, mark, or token, which brings to mind, shows, or confirms anything either past, present, or to come; which excites attention or consideration; which distinguishes one thing from another; or is an inducement to believe what is affirmed, professed, or promised. The prophets were accustomed to afford tokens of some more distant event foretold; or as a proof and test of some great and important event to add to the prophecy some other prediction having a nearer issue, the fulfillment which would be a token or sign of the accomplishment of the more distant." The unbelief and disobedience of the nation would bring about judgment and the judgment was to be a sign. But what was this judgment?

"Because thou servedst not the Lord thy God with joyfulness, and with gladness of heart, for the abundance of all things; Therefore shalt thou serve thine enemies which the Lord shall send against thee, in hunger, and in thirst, and in nakedness, and in want of all things: and he shall put a yoke of iron upon thy neck, until he have destroyed thee. The Lord shall bring a nation against thee from far, from the end of the earth, as swift as the eagle flieth; a nation whose tongue thou shalt not understand;" (Deut. 28:47-49)

The judgment was to be through a nation whose language they did not understand. Now we have the Bible meaning of "tongues" as a sign. (1) It was to be a sign to Israel of her disobedience. (2) It was a language of another nation, and thus a language and not some kind of unintelligible jabber. Any interpretation of tongues must harmonize with this background in the Old Testament.

THE APPLICATION

Let us see if the Old Testament makes any application of Deuteronomy 28:46-49. If so, then we will have an inspired interpretation and application.

"But they also have erred through wine, and through strong drink are out of the way; the priest and the prophet have erred through strong drink, they are swallowed up of wine, they are out of the way through strong drink; they err in vision, they stumble in judgment. For all tables are full of vomit and filthiness, so that there is no place clean.

"Whom shall he teach knowledge? and whom shall he make to understand doctrine? them that are weaned from the milk, and drawn from the breasts. For precept must be upon precept, precept upon precept; line upon line, line upon line; here a little, and there a little: For with stammering lips and another tongue will he speak to this people." (Isaiah 28:7-11)

The picture here is of an unbelieving and rebellious people. The drunk mock and accuse Isaiah of treating them like babies in his continued call for righteous living. But, because the people refuse to hear the prophet, God will speak to them through Assyria, a nation whose language they did not understand. This was to be a sign, when they were conquered by another nation, an alien nation, whose language they did not understand. But of what was it a sign? Deuteronomy 28:46-49 supplies the answer. God's judgment, brought upon them through an alien nation, was a sign of their alienation from God. Rest was offered through the prophet, but they refused to hear: "To whom he said, This is the rest wherewith ye may cause the weary to rest; and this is the refreshing: yet they would not hear." (Isa. 28:12) Moses' warning of the consequence of rebellion is now prophesied of by Isaiah. It came to pass, and it was intended as a sign of their alienation from God as a result of their unbelief and disobedience.

These points should be remembered: (1) Moses specifically connects this conquering nation "whose tongue thou shalt not understand" with the nation of Israel. (2) It was an alien tongue, or foreign language. (3) It was to be a sign to the nation. (4) It was the sign of the nation's alienation from God. Here is an inspired application. No one is left to subjective proof concerning the question.

"Thou shalt not see a fierce people, a people of a deeper speech than thou canst perceive; of a stammering tongue, that thou canst not understand." (Isa. 33:19)

While the Assyrians would overrun the northern kingdom, penitence and confession of sin would spare Jerusalem. The tongue of the Assyrians would not be among those in Judah. But what was the reason Jerusalem was not captured?

"Then said Eliakim and Shebna and Joah unto Rabshakeh, Speak, I pray thee, unto thy servants in the Syrian language; for we understand it: and speak not to us in the Jews' language, in the ears of the people that are on the wall." (Isa. 36:11)

Sennacherib and his army were defeated (Isaiah 37). But why was Jerusalem not also overrun as the northern kingdom was? The answer is found in Isaiah 33:14-17. The remnant of Judah, the believing, obedient part of the nation, supplies the answer:

"And the remnant that is escaped of the house of Judah shall again take root downward, and bear fruit upward: For out of Jerusalem shall go forth a remnant, and they that escape out of mount Zion: the zeal of the Lord of hosts shall do this." (Isa. 37:31-32)

The capture of the ten tribes by Assyria was a sign of its alienation from God. The safety of Jerusalem was because of the faith of Hezekiah in listening to Isaiah, the prophet, and in turning to God. Here is the reason Judah did not fall and there was no alien tongue among them.

JEREMIAH

We have seen the application Isaiah made on Deuteronomy 28:46-49. Now let us look at Jeremiah's application,

> "How shall I pardon thee for this? thy children have forsaken me, and sworn by them that are no gods: when I had fed them to the full, they then committed adultery, and assembled themselves by troops in the harlots' houses. They were as fed horses in the morning: every one neighed after his neighbour's wife. Shall I not visit for these things? saith the Lord: and shall not my soul be avenged on such a nation as this?

> "Go ye up upon her walls, and destroy; but make not a full end: take away her battlements; for they are not the Lord's. For the house of Judah have dealt very treacherously against me, saith the Lord. They have belied the Lord, and said, It is not he; neither shall evil come upon us; neither shall we see sword nor famine: And the prophets shall become wind, and the word is not in them: thus shall it be done unto them. Wherefore thus saith the Lord God of hosts, Because ye speak this word, behold, I will make my words in thy mouth fire, and this people wood, and it shall devour them. Lo, I will bring a nation upon you from far, O house of Israel, saith the Lord: it is a mighty nation, it is an ancient nation, a nation whose language thou knowest not, neither understandest what they say." (Jer. 5:7-15)

Remember the curses of Deuteronomy 28. Keep in mind in particular the warning about enemy nations when Israel turned aside in unbelief. Jeremiah gives a picture of a nation that has forsaken God (v. 7). The sinfulness of the nation calls for God's visitation in judgment (v. 9). The judgment was to be brought through an alien nation — a nation whose language they did not understand. Did Israel's being conquered by a nation whose language they did not understand have any meaning for them? If they read Deuteronomy 28:46-49 they could have known that being ruled by an alien nation, a people whose language they did not speak, was a sign of their alienation from God.

The Old Testament gives the background essential for understanding what the New Testament teaches about tongues. Remember these principles: (1) A tongue was a language. (2) The introduction of the subject by Moses to Israel shows that it had a special meaning to the nation of Israel. (3) When conquered by a foreign nation it was a sign of Israel's alienation from God. (4) This laid the foundation for tongues in the New Testament.

THE WORK OF THE HOLY SPIRIT 295

The books of Matthew, Mark, Luke, and John give the account of Christ coming to his own nation and the bulk of the nation rejecting him.

"He came unto his own, and his own received him not. But as many as received him, to them gave he power to become the sons of God, even to them that believe on his name:" (John 1:11-12)

The believer of verse twelve is a reference to the remnant of the nation that accepted Christ. The bulk of the nation refused Christ. The nation refused to accept Christ as king.

"But they cried out, Away with him, away with him, crucify him. Pilate saith unto them, Shall I crucify your King? The chief priests answered, We have no king but Caesar. Then delivered he him therefor unto them to be crucified. And they took Jesus, and led him away." (John 19:15-16)

Christ was God's last call to the nation:
"God, who at sundry times and in divers manners spake in time past unto the fathers by the prophets, Hath in these last days spoken unto us by his Son, whom he hath appointed heir of all things, by whom also he made the worlds; Who being the brightness of his glory, and the express image of his person, and upholding all things by the word of his power, when he had by himself purged our sins, sat down on the right hand of the Majesty on high;" (Heb. 1:1-3)

"O Jerusalem, Jerusalem, thou that killest the prophets, and stonest them which are sent unto thee, how often would I have gathered thy children together, even as a hen gathereth her chickens under her wings, and ye would not!" (Matt. 23:37)

Their rejection of Christ and his crucifixion showed their alienation from God. Read all of Matthew 23. In the rejection of Christ and their crucifying him, their house was left to them desolate. "Behold, your house is left unto you desolate." (Matt. 23:38) God no longer would accept their worship in the temple.

On the first Pentecost following Christ's rejection by Israel, the Holy Spirit came upon the apostles and they spoke in tongues.

"And when the day of Pentecost was fully come, they were all with one accord in one place. And suddenly there came a sound from heaven as of a rushing mighty wind, and it filled all the house where they were sitting. And there appeared unto them cloven tongues like as of fire, and it sat upon each of them. And they were all filled with the Holy Ghost, and began to speak with other tongues, as the Spirit gave them utterance." (Acts 2:1-4)

There were men out of every nation that heard the apostles speaking in their own languages.

"And there were dwelling at Jerusalem Jews, devout men, out of every nation under heaven. Now when this was noised abroad, the multitude came together, and were confounded, because that every man heard them speak in his own language." (Acts 2:5-6)

The tongues of the New Testament were for a double purpose: (1) They provided a means of preaching the gospel to the world when there was no written revelation. (2) They were a sign to Israel of its alienation from God. Acts 10 presents the same picture. Cornelius, a Gentile speaking in tongues, was a sign to the Jewish nation of its alienation from God. For one in the nation of Israel to have God's blessing he would have to leave behind him Judaism and accept the gospel of Christ. Jew and Gentile stood on the same level in Christ. Cornelius, an alien speaking in tongues, was evidence that men of every nation were acepted of God and at the same time a sign to the Jewish nation of its alienation from God. Read Acts 10 against the background of Deuteronomy 28, Isaiah 28, Isaiah 33, and Jeremiah 5. There can be no mistake about the significance of Cornelius' speaking in tongues. It confirmed the acceptance of the Gentiles and the alienation of the Jewish nation from God. Acts 19:1-6 is additional proof of the same thing. Consider Ephesus and its distance from Jerusalem. Here are people speaking in tongues and prophesying. This signals two things: (1) A worldwide gospel and (2) an end to the Jewish system. Notice also that tongues and prophecy are together in this instance.

THE TONGUES OF CORINTH

What about the tongues of Corinth? Do they fit into the same pattern?

"In the law it is written, With men of other tongues and other lips will I speak unto this people; and yet for all that will they not hear me, saith the Lord. Wherefore tongues are for a sign, not to them that believe, but to them that believe not: but prophesying serveth not for them that believe not, but for them which believe." (I Cor. 14:21-22)

It is important to consider carefully Paul's argument in these verses. When one understands Paul's purpose in these verses he'll have a key to understanding some of the controversy about tongues. Paul quotes Isaiah 28:11-12. Remember Isaiah's application here of Deuteronomy 28:46-41. Why would Paul quote this passage if he did not have in mind the principle applied by Isaiah? It is evident that Paul is making the same application that Isaiah did, for he also quotes the last part of Isaiah

THE WORK OF THE HOLY SPIRIT

28:12, "and yet for all that will they not hear me, saith the Lord." The principle set forth in Isaiah is used by Paul in his application at Corinth.

Furthermore, Paul's quotation of Isaiah 28:11 settles the question as to the meaning of the tongues in I Corinthians 14. The tongue of Isaiah 28 was a language, the language of the Assyrians. There can be no quibble about the language of Isaiah 28. Paul's use of the Isaiah passage shows that the tongue he's discussing is also a language. If the tongues of I Corinthians 14 were not languages, then Paul's use of Isaiah 28 is entirely out of place; that is, his quoting this passage would not make any sense at all. Therefore, the only correct exegesis of I Corinthians 14 there can be is that the tongues were languages.

The word "wherefore" of verse 22 shows Paul's logical conclusion. The word "for" denotes purpose. Tongues had a purpose. What was the purpose? Tongues were for a sign. A sign of what? To whom were tongues a sign? Answer: "not to them that believe, but to them that believe not." Is that not the very argument made by Moses' introduction of the signs and tongues in Deuteronomy 28, and the exact application made by both Isaiah and Jeremiah? The warning of Moses and the applications by Isaiah and Jeremiah were to the unbelief of the nation of Israel. Where was the problem in Corinth coming from? Was it not from the Judaising teachers?

> "But what I do, that I will do, that I may cut off occasion from them which desire occasion; that wherein they glory, they may be found even as we. For such are false apostles, deceitful workers, transforming themselves into the apostles of Christ. And no marvel; for Satan himself is transformed into an angel of light. Therefore it is no great thing if his ministers also be transformed as the ministers of righteousness; whose end shall be according to their works." (II Cor. 11:12-15)

> "Are they Hebrews? so am I. Are they Israelites? so am I. Are they the seed of Abraham? so am I. Are they ministers of Christ? (I speak as a fool) I am more; in labours more abundant, in stripes above measure, in prisons more frequent, in deaths oft." (II Cor. 11:22-23)

Could it be by accident that Paul quoted Isaiah 28:11? Consider the phrase "this people." To what people does "this people" refer in Isaiah? Surely it is to the unbelieving nation of Israel. But was this not also the condition of the nation when Paul wrote to the Corinthians? "Well; because of unbelief they were broken off, and thou standest by faith. Be not highminded, but fear." (Rom. 11:20) Here is Paul's description of the nation, except for the remnant that obeyed the gospel. Paul insists that tongues were for a sign to the unbelievers. His quotation from Isaiah shows that he had in mind in particular the unbelief of the Jewish nation. An ecstatic tongue would not have made any sense as a sign to the unbelieving nation that it was alienated from God. A foreign language would have, if they had read the Old Testament and accepted the statement of Moses and its applications by Jeremiah and Isaiah. It would also have warned them of the impending judgment coming from the Roman nation, as foretold by Christ in Matthew 24, Mark 13, and Luke 21.

The utterance in Gentile tongues in Acts 2 was a sign of the end of God's special relationship to the nation. It signaled the unbelief of the nation that rejected Christ, and was a call to accept the gospel in order to have God's blessings.

The prophecy from Joel shows that all stood on the same level before God. Whatever distinctions there may have been in the past were all gone. The nation, as such, had turned aside in unbelief. Therefore, Peter's exhortation to "Save yourselves from this crooked generation." (Acts 2:40 ASV) The fall of the nation in A.D. 70 was the climax of the Jewish rejection of the covenant of the promise with Abraham. This left nothing but the gospel as man's only hope, for the Jew or the Gentile. Christ had warned the nation of this:

> "Hear another parable: There was a certain householder, which planted a vineyard, and hedged it around about, and digged a winepress in it, and built a tower, and let it out to husbandmen, and went into a far county: And when the time of the fruit drew near, he sent his servants to the husbandman, that they might receive the fruits of it. And the husbandmen took his servants, and beat one, and killed another, and stoned another. Again, he sent other servants more than the first: and they did unto them likewise. But last of all he sent unto them his son, saying, They will reverence my son. But when the husbandmen saw the son, they said among themselves, This is the heir; come, let us kill him, and let us seize on his inheritance. And they caught him, and cast him out of the vineyard, and slew him. When the Lord thereof of the vineyard cometh, what will he do unto those husbandmen? They say unto him, He will miserably destroy those wicked men, and will let out his vineyard unto other husbandmen, which shall render him the fruits in their seasons. Jesus saith unto them, Did ye never read in the scriptures, The stone which the builders rejected, the same is become the head of the corner: this is the Lord's doing, and it is marvellous in our eyes? Therefore say I unto you, The kingdom of God shall be taken from you, and given to a nation bringing forth the fruits thereof." (Matt. 21:33-43)

> "And when ye shall see Jerusalem compassed with armies, then know that the desolation thereof is nigh. Then let them which are in Judaea

flee to the mountains; and let them which are in the midst of it depart out; and let not them that are in the countries enter thereinto. For these be the days of vengeance, that all things which are written may be fulfilled. But woe unto them that are with child, and to them that give suck, in those days! for there shall be great distress in the land, and wrath upon this people. And they shall fall by the edge of the sword, and shall be led away captive into all nations: and Jerusalem shall be trodden down of the Gentiles, until the times of the Gentiles be fulfilled." (Luke 21:20-24)

Speaking in tongues in the New Testament served as a means of preaching the gospel to the world. But it was also a sign of something else. While it confirmed the gospel, it was a sign to the nation of Israel, specifically, of the nation's alienation from God.

Once the thing for which the tongue was a sign became evident to the whole world, there was no further need for the sign. When Rome destroyed Jerusalem and the temple, that destruction told the entire world that the nation was alienated from God and that they were no longer his people. When this was done, what further need was there for tongues?

The completion of the New Testament as a written revelation made tongues no longer necessary. Thus the two purposes that tongues served: (1) The preaching of the gospel to the world when there was no written revelation, and (2) A sign to the nation of Israel of its alienation from God. When the nation fell, it left no further place for tongues. God's judgment on the nation left not one single need for a tongue.

If the religious world had placed the proper interpretation on tongues, there would be no such doctrine as premillennialism. Tongues signified the unbelief of the nation. When God used Rome to bring judgment on the nation, it signaled their rejection of the Abrahamic covenant and God's rejection of the nation.

"For ye are all the children of God by faith in Christ Jesus. For as many of you as have been baptized into Christ have put on Christ. There is neither Jew nor Greek, there is neither bond nor free, there is neither male nor female: for ye are all one in Christ Jesus. And if ye be Christ's, then are ye Abraham's seed, and heirs according to the promise." (Gal. 3:26-29)

When this was accomplished, it left no place for tongues. It's no wonder that most Pentecostals are also premillennialists. The two usually go together. One would expect the cessation of tongues with the ashes of the temple and the completion of a written revelation.

I CORINTHIANS 13

Does I Corinthians 13 harmonize with the things that I have presented? "For we know in part, and we prophesy in part. But when that which is perfect is come, then that which is in part shall be done away." (v. 9-10) Note carefully the passage. There is the part, then there is the perfect; the fragment, then the complete. If the complete thing has arrived, then any claim to tongues (one of the "parts") is false. What is the complete thing? It is not Christ, and it is not heaven. There is no mention of Christ in the chapter. It would be strange to have such a vague reference to Christ, as this surely would be, since he is not mentioned anywhere else in the chapter. It is not heaven. Heaven is foreign to the context. There is not a single reference to heaven in the entire section that deals with the miraculous gifts (Chapters 12-14). Furthermore, heaven would destroy the contrast between the part and the complete thing. The contrast is not between the life now and the one to come, but between a part and a whole. What is the complete thing? The whole is composed of the parts: prophecy, tongues, and knowledge. These three equal divine revelation. The whole, or complete thing, is the written revelation — the New Testament. The complete revelation of God was given through miraculous gifts. When the revelation was completed, the gifts ceased.

THE APOSTOLIC "WE"

Read carefully I Corinthians 13:9. "For we know in part, and we prophesy in part." Why did Paul use the personal pronoun "we"? He does **not** say, "now Ye know in part and ye prophesy in part." Compare this verse with I Corinthians 1:5, where he introduces the discussion of the miraculous gifts: "That in every thing ye are enriched by him, in all utterance, and in all knowledge." Notice how he uses the word "ye" in that passage. Why the personal pronoun "we" in I Corinthians 13:9? Paul's apostleship was under attack from false teachers. He uses the pronoun "we" as a reference to the apostles. He does the same thing in I Corinthians 2. The "we" in I Corinthians 2:6, 7, 12, 13, 16, and the "us" in verse 10, are all used in reference to the apostolic office. False teachers denied that Paul was equal to the rest of the apostles since he was not with Christ in his personal ministry. For this reason, Paul uses the pronoun "we" to show his equality with the other apostles. "Therefore whether it were I or they, so we preach, and so ye believed." (I Cor. 15:11) I Corinthians 2 has to do with the revelation given to the apostles. The "we" in 13:9 is an inspired "we" — a specific reference to the apostles and, therefore, the revelation and inspiration of the apostles.

THE WORK OF THE HOLY SPIRIT

Is it not true that the apostles received the revelation in part and then wrote it in completeness? Is that not what we have today? It's plain that the pronoun "we" was intended to signify the apostles, and the revelation of the gospel through them. When that was completed, the "part" ceased. The part and the whole are tied to the apostles. When they finished their work and had given the faith "once for all delivered unto the saints" (Jude 3, ASV), the part stopped. The apostles have completed their work. We have the complete thing — the New Testament. When one admits that apostolic revelation is complete, he admits that the gifts have ceased. The "we" in I Corinthians 13:9 settles the matter as to the ones that are under consideration. Paul used that pronoun to designate specifically the apostles. There's not the slightest question about the completeness of revelation today. Therefore, there is no question left about the miraculous gifts. The work of the apostles has ceased. Their work was the revelation of the gospel of Christ. The revelation of the gospel of Christ has been completed, and therefore the gifts that the apostles had, and provided to others by the laying on of hands, has ceased. The claims of Pentecostals to be able to heal and speak in tongues is a false claim.

I CORINTHIANS 13:12

"For now we see through a glass, darkly; but then face to face: now I know in part; but then shall I know even as also I am known."(I Cor. 13:12)

This passage, and those just discussed, is a reference to the partial knowledge while revelation was being given through miraculous gifts, as contrasted with full knowledge when revelation was completed. When revelation was completed, the Jewish state ended. It left nothing but Christ and the church. (Rev. 10:7) When revelation was completed, one could fully know the will of God. When one looks in a mirror he does not see another, he sees himself. The American Standard version (ASV) translates it "but then shall I know fully." Question: Can one know fully the will of God today? Do we have the full will of God in the New Testament? Is there still some revelation to be added to the New Testament? The answers to these questions are clear. We do have the full revelation of God. There is to be no further revelation. Look at verse 2: "And if I have the gift of prophecy, and know all mysteries ..." (ASV) What does the "know" of verse 2 mean? It is a reference to knowledge based on divine revelation. In like manner, the "know" of verse 12 is the knowing that rests on divine revelation. We now have that in the New Testament. The "know" of Paul was knowledge in part, because revelation was in the process of being given.

When completed, there would be no further need for the miraculous that supplied the part. Is there anything in chapter 13 to identify the "know" of verse 12? There certainly is a key to the specific knowledge under consideration.

"And if I have the gift of prophecy, and know all mysteries and all knowledge; and if I have all faith, so as to remove mountains, but have not love, I am nothing." (I Cor. 13:2, ASV)

Here are both the word "know" ("understand" in KJ) and the word "knowledge." Can one determine the how of "know" and the what of "knowledge" in verse 2? Two other words identify the how of "know" and the what of "knowledge." The "gift of prophecy" tells the how, and "mysteries" tells the what.

"For this cause I Paul, the prisoner of Jesus Christ for you Gentiles, If ye have heard of the dispensation of the grace of God which is given me to youward: How that by revelation he made known unto me the mystery; (as I wrote afore in few words, Whereby, when ye read, ye may understand my knowledge in the mystery of Christ) Which in other ages was not made known unto the sons of men, as it is now revealed unto his holy apostles and prophets by the Spirit; That the Gentiles should be fellowheirs, and of the same body, and partakers of his promise in Christ by the gospel:" (Eph. 3:1-6)

Here is a further divine commentary on the "know" and the "knowledge" of I Corinthians 13:2. Notice that the words in I Corinthians 13:2 are used by Paul in these verses in Ephesians. In the place of "prophecy" in I Corinthians 13:2, Paul used the words "apostles" and "prophets." Substituting the words "apostles" and "prophets" for the word "prophecy" in the Corinthian passage, we have the exact idea given. Look at the words: **Apostles** and **prophets** made **known mystery** and **knowledge**. Here is the how of "know" in I Corinthians 13:2. It was through miraculous gifts. Here is the what that is known: **the mystery.** This is specific written revelation.

Finally, Paul specifies the medium of completed revelation — apostles and prophets. Does anyone have any problem with the meaning of the Ephesian passage? I think no one would contend that the revelation (miraculous) of this passage continues today or will continue in heaven. But the **know, mystery, knowledge, apostles,** and **prophets,** by the **Spirit,** are parallel with the same words in I Corinthians 13:2.

Since there can be no question about the "know" and the "knowledge" of verse 2, can it be established that this is the same "know" and "knowledge" of verse 12? Keep in mind the **prophecy, know,**

THE WORK OF THE HOLY SPIRIT 303

and **knowledge** of verse 2. Let us follow the thought through the chapter. "Charity never faileth: but whether there be **prophecies,** they shall fail; whether there be **tongues,** they shall cease; whether there be **knowledge,** it shall vanish away." (I Cor. 13:8) Notice the things in the verse. In verses 1 and 2 we have tongues, prophecies, and knowledge. In verse 8 we have prophecy, tongues, and knowledge. I have already shown the meaning of "know" and "knowledge" in verse 2. Can anyone doubt that verse 8 is a reference to the same "know" and "knowledge"? There can be no mistake about this.

Let us continue to trace our "know." "For we know in part, and we prophecy in part." (I Cor. 13:9) Here are two of our words: "know" and "prophesy." But what kind of "know"? Answer: the **know of prophecy.** Since the "prophesy" was in part, the "know" was in part. The "prophesy" of verse 9 is the same prophecy that we have traced through the chapter. It is prophecy that had to do with revelation.

"But when that which is perfect is come, then that which is in part shall be done away." (I Cor. 13:10) Now, watch verse 10: The word "but" is a contrasting word. What is being contrasted? It will not do to jump the track and ignore Paul's previous thoughts. There is no question but that, up to this point, Paul is discussing miraculous gifts in connection with the revelation of the gospel. The **perfect** (complete) is introduced by a contrasting word and does not refer to anything but the revelation of the gospel. Paul has already identified the "part" with "prophesy" in verse 9. Prophesy ties the "part" to revelation. Thus the contrast is between partial revelation, while the gospel was being revealed through the apostles and prophets, and completed revelation when the parts (miraculous gifts) would be done away.

Now we are ready for verse 12. "I know in part" has been used by Paul in relation to prophecy or miraculous gifts (verse 9). But this is a reference to the revelation of the gospel. The "know" has been proven to be the knowing by revelation and inspiration. The "but then shall I know fully" (ASV) of verse 12 is parellel to "But when that which is perfect is come" of verse 10. The "know in part" and the "know fully" is the same contrast as that of verses 9 and 10. A contrast between partial knowledge while revelation was being given by miraculous gifts and a completed written revelation with the cessation of gifts since they are no longer needed. Paul puts "knowing in part" with prophecies and tongues. Paul uses tongue and prophecies to equal divine revelation. Paul stated definitely that prophecies and tongues, which equal divine knowledge given by miraculous gifts, would cease (v. 8). Paul set the time of cessation of prophecies and tongues to be when revelation was completed. (v. 10). Paul illustrates the "part" as equal to childhood and the "whole" as equal to maturity or manhood. Evidently Paul did not think that spiritual gifts were the ultimate of spirituality. Paul closes his discussion by insisting that when revelation was completed one would have all that he needed. Therefore, there is no place left for miraculous gifts today. Paul completely refutes the Pentecostal claim for spiritual gifts today. Shall we believe Paul or the claims of Pentecostals?

THE GROWING ARGUMENT

"And now abideth faith, hope, charity, these three; but the greatest of these is charity." (I Cor. 13:13)

Pentecostals claim that one has not reached the ultimate in living unless one has experienced the baptism of the Holy Spirit and speaking in tongues. If this proposition is correct, then there is an intrinsic value in the gift of tongues. This must be true if one cannot reach the peak in spirituality without the gift. There has to be something in the gift of tongues itself. But Paul completely repudiates this claim. He says that tongues without love are like sounding brass or a tinkling cymbal (V.1). Paul uses figures which suggest noise, and perhaps even a ritual; but he says that of themselves, tongues are nothing. Speaking in a tongue apart from love is valueless. But, according to Pentecostals, speaking in a tongue is the highest spiritual experience. Paul denies that this is true.

In the second place, Pentecostals claim that one of the chief fruits of the baptism of the Holy Spirit and speaking in tongues is love. Again, Paul denies that this is true. The Corinthian church was lacking in love. It was not lacking in spiritual gifts (spiritual gifts — not the baptism of the Holy Spirit). If the position of Pentecostals is true (that spiritual gifts produce the fruit of love), the church in Corinth should have been the most loving church in the New Testament; but it was not. The lack of love in the church was the reason for I Corinthians 13, the "Love chapter." The church had the gifts, but not the love. So, down goes another claim of Pentecostals, that spiritual gifts are a short cut to love.

In the third place, Pentecostals contend that the Holy Spirit, through spiritual gifts, brings about unity. They teach that this is the road to unity, and that people of all denominations are receiving spiritual gifts — thus producing unity. This was surely not the case in Corinth. The church had an abundance of spiritual gifts and yet was the most divided church mentioned in the New Testament. "Now I beseech you,

THE WORK OF THE HOLY SPIRIT

brethren, by the name of our Lord Jesus Christ, that ye all speak the same thing, and that there be no divisions among you; but that ye be perfectly joined together in the same mind and in the same judgment." (I Cor. 1:10) If the Holy Spirit, through spiritual gifts, did not bring unity in a single congregation, by what stretch of the imagination can Pentecostals sustain their claim today? Indeed, they cannot. Nowhere does the Bible teach that unity rests upon some kind of "experience." The New Testament teaches clearly that Christ, and the word of the gospel through the apostles, is the basis of unity.

"And when he had so said, he shewed unto them his hands and his side. Then were the disciples glad, when they saw the Lord. Then said Jesus to them again, Peace be unto you: as my Father hath sent me, even so send I you." (John 20:20-21)

Now one can see the place and the importance of Paul's admonition concerning the more excellent way (I Cor. 12:31). The more excellent way is not the way of gifts, but the way of salvation. The word "way" is never used in reference to spiritual gifts. It is always used to mean the way of life through Christ.

"Jesus saith unto him, I am the way, the truth, and the life: no man cometh unto the Father, but by me." (John 14:6)

"And desired of him letters to Damascus to the synagogues, that if he found any of this way, whether they were men or women, he might bring them bound unto Jerusalem." (Acts 9:2)

"But when divers were hardened, and believed not, but spake evil of that way before the multitude, he departed from them, and separated the disciples, disputing daily in the school of one Tyrannus." (Acts 19:9)

None of these passages mentions one thing about the "way of the Spirit." Even in the Corinthian letter, Paul spoke of his ways "in Christ" (I Cor. 4:17). In view of I Corinthians 2:1-5, how could anyone ever conclude that the "more excellent way" of I Corinthians 12:31 was the way of spiritual gifts? The way of salvation through Christ is the way of love. Love has an intrinsic value; it gives meaning to spiritual gifts (I Cor. 13:1-3). Love has qualities that spiritual gifts do not possess (I Cor. 13:4-7). Since love possesses values and qualities which spiritual gifts do not have, love abides (I Cor. 13:13).

The foundation of a spiritual life is based on faith, hope, and love. Spiritual gifts are not essential for a single one of these today. Faith is based on the testimony of the scriptures: "So then faith cometh by hearing, and hearing by the word of God." (Rom. 10:17) Hope is based on the scriptures: "For whatsoever things were written aforetime were written for our learning, that we through patience and comfort of the scriptures might have hope." (Rom. 15:4) Love is based on the scriptures: "We love him, because he first loved us." (I John 4:19)

The knowledge of the love of God comes to us through the scriptures. The three essentials of spirituality are based on scriptures — not spiritual gifts. One might have a spiritual gift and be lacking in love, a fundamental of Christianity and spirituality; but one cannot have love apart from the word of God. The word of God abides; and therefore faith, hope, and love abide. No one has a spiritual gift today because there is no place for it.

THE CESSATION OF PROPHECY FORETOLD

I have shown that prophecy was the basis of the miraculous, beginning with Moses. The nature of prophecy demanded the miraculous, in both forthtelling and foretelling. Foretelling was beyond the power of man. The future was known only to God. Therefore, when future events were foretold hundreds of years before they occurred, it had to be through miraculous revelation.

"Who hath wrought and done it, calling the generations from the beginning? I the Lord, the first, and with the last; I am he." (Isa. 41:4)

"That they may see, and know, and consider, and understand together, that the hand of the Lord hath done this, and the Holy One of Israel hath created it. Produce your cause, saith the Lord; bring forth your strong reasons, saith the King of Jacob. Let them bring them forth, and shew us what shall happen: let them shew the former things, what they be, that we may consider them, and know the latter end of them; or declare us things for to come. Shew the things that are to come hereafter, that we may know that ye are gods: yea, do good, or do evil, that we may be dismayed, and behold it together. Behold, ye are of nothing, and your work of nought: an abomination is he that chooseth you. I have raised up one from the north, and he shall come: from the rising of the sun shall he call upon my name: and he shall come upon princes as upon morter, and as the potter treadeth clay. Who hath declared from the beginning, that we may know? and beforetime, that we may say, He is righteous? yea, there is none that sheweth, yea, there is none that declareth, yea, there is none that heareth your words." (Isa. 41:20-26)

"Behold, the former things are come to pass, and new things do I declare: before they spring forth I tell you of them." (Isa. 42:9)

"Thus saith the Lord, thy redeemer, and he that formed thee from the womb, I am the Lord that maketh all things; that stretcheth forth the heavens alone; that spreadeth abroad the earth by myself; That

THE WORK OF THE HOLY SPIRIT

frustrateh the tokens of the liars, and maketh diviners mad; that turneth wise men backward, and maketh their knowledge foolish; That confirmeth the word of his servant, and performeth the counsel of his messengers; that saith to Jerusalem, Thou shalt be inhabited; and to the cities of Judah, Ye shall be built, and I will raise up the decayed places thereof:" (Isa. 44:24-26)

"I will go before thee, and make the crooked places straight: I will break in pieces the gates of brass, and cut in sunder the bars of iron:" (Isa. 45:2)

"Declaring the end from the beginning, and from ancient times the things that are not yet done, saying, My counsel shall stand, and I will do all my pleasure:" (Isa. 46:10)

"I have even from the beginning declared it to thee; before it came to pass I shewed it thee: lest thou shouldest say, Mine idol hath done them, and my graven image, and my molten image, hath commanded them. Thou hast heard, see all this; and will not ye declare it? I have shewed thee new things from this time, even hidden things, and thou didst not know them. They are created now, and not from the beginning; even before the day when thou heardest them not; lest thou shouldest say, Behold, I knew them." (Isa. 48:5-7)

All of these passages set forth the fact that God alone can see the future. His seeing the future is contrasted with man's inability to foretell the future. God's ability to foresee the future is not only contrasted with man's inability; God challenges man to match him in foretelling the future.

Fulfilled prophecy confirms the word of the prophet (Isa. 44:26). Fulfilled prophecy not only confirms the prophet, it shows up the counterfeit claims of liars, diviners, and wise men (Isa. 44:25). These passages establish the vital nature of prophecy in the revelation of the will of God and mark it with credibility, because prophecy is a "word miracle." Unlike miracles of healing, fulfilled prophecy stands as an argument of inspiration for every generation. It has no need for being repeated. The fulfilled events stand as witness to the inspiration of the prophet and mark the Bible as God's book. One should not be surprised that prophecy became the base of all miraculous operations of the Spirit. The fulfilled event had within it the seeds of its own confirmation apart from any other miracle.

Now that I have established prophecy as the base of all the miraculous, if I can establish the cessation of prophecy, I will with one stroke destroy the claim of any miraculous gifts today. This is the proposition that I shall seek to establish. I have shown that one element of prophecy was foretelling the future. I shall now seek to show that prophecy foretold the cessation of prophecy itself. The same Spirit that inspired Paul to announce the cessation of prophecy was in the prophets of the Old Testament. One should not be surprised that the Holy Spirit in the prophet would announce the end of prophecy.

"And whiles I was speaking, and praying, and confessing my sin and the sin of my people Israel, and presenting my supplication before the Lord my God for the holy mountain of my God; Yea, whiles I was speaking in prayer, even the man Gabriel, whom I had seen in the vision at the beginning, being caused to fly swiftly, touched me about the time of the evening oblation. And he informed me, and talked with me, and said, O Daniel, I am now come forth to give thee skill and understanding. At the beginning of thy supplications the commandment came forth, and I am come to shew thee; for thou art greatly beloved: therefore understand the matter, and consider the vision. Seventy weeks are determined upon thy people and upon thy holy city, to finish the transgression, and to make an end of sins, and to make reconciliation for iniquity, and to bring in everlasting righteousness, and to seal up the vision and prophecy, and to anoint the most Holy. Know therefore and understand, that from the going forth of the commandment to restore and to build Jerusalem unto the Messiah the Prince shall be seven weeks, and threescore and two weeks: the street shall be built again, and the wall, even in troublous times. And after threescore and two weeks shall Messiah be cut off, but not for himself: and the people of the prince that shall come shall destroy the city and the sanctuary; and the end thereof shall be with a flood, and unto the end of the war desolations are determined. And he shall confirm the covenant with many for one week: and in the midst of the week he shall cause the sacrifice and the oblation to cease, and for the overspreading of abominations he shall make it desolate, even until the consummation, and that determined shall be poured upon the desolate." (Dan. 9:20-27)

All Bible students admit that this passage is a difficult one. But in spite of the difficulties, there are some things that are evident: (1) It is a prophecy of the Messiah that was to come. (2) The Messiah was to come to Jerusalem. (3) The Messiah would be cut off; i.e., die. (4) His death would be to atone for sins (make an end of sin and make reconciliation for iniquity). (5) He would bring in an everlasting righteousness (the forgiveness of sin). (6) There would be a desolation of the city and the temple.

Here are six things that are clear, both in the prophecy and in their fulfillment in the New Testament. (1) Christ of the New Testament is the promised Messiah (Matt. 1). (2) He came to Jerusalem. (The books

THE WORK OF THE HOLY SPIRIT

of Matthew, Mark, Luke, and John establish this.) (3) He was cut off, or crucified (Acts 2:23). (4) His death atoned for sins (Rom. 5:9-11). (5) His atonement for sin, his resurrection, and his ascension back to the right hand of God brought in everlasting righteousness (Rom. 3:24-26). (6) The rejection of the Messiah by the Jewish nation, his crucifixion, and the nation's rejection of the gospel brought about the desolation of the city (Luke 21:20-24; Christ, in Matthew 24:15, specifically identified Daniel as the prophet who foretold the events that were soon to come to pass. Luke 21:22 also identified Daniel by the phrase "that all things that are written may be fulfilled." This fulfillment came when Rome destroyed the city and the temple in A.D. 70.)

"SEAL UP THE VISION AND PROPHECY"

This phrase is of interest. I think it is significant in the context of the previous things mentioned. It is important to note that it is not just "seal up the vision." This would have been sufficient if the prophecy of Daniel alone was all that was under consideration. Furthermore, the American Standard version translates "and seal up vision" — not "**the** vision," as in the King James.

Again, the passage says "seal up the vision and prophecy" — not "**the** prophecy." "Vision" equals divine revelation, or prophetic knowledge (I Cor. 13:2). (See the discussion of I Corinthians 13 in an earlier part of this treatise.) "Phophecy" equals miraculous revelation. Thus, Daniel is to seal up vision (prophetic knowledge) and prophecy (miraculous revelation). The margin of both the King James and the American Standard version has the word "prophet" instead of "prophecy."

The coming of Christ, his death, resurrection, and ascension, made possible full atonement for sin, beginning at Pentecost. The everlasting righteousness foretold by Daniel (possible only because of the atoning power of the blood of Christ) began at the Pentecost of Acts 2. The thrust of the whole Roman letter is an argument for the righteousness that is by faith — and not by the merits of the law (Rom. 1:16-17; 3:27-28). Paul was rejected by the Jewish nation, not because he was contending for what would be, but because he was contending for what was already a fact of redemption. Both Jews and Gentiles had been saved, through the obedience of faith, from sin through the blood of Christ that reconciled (Eph. 2:12-22).

The church was now the nation of God. God no longer considered nations, as such (I Pet. 2:9). God had created the nation of Israel to be a light to the pagan world of darkness (Isa. 43:10, 44:8). The Jews misunderstood this fact and, instead of being a light, became darkness by being like other nations. When Pentecost came, there was no further place for one nation to be used as a light to other nations. The gospel of redemption, made possible through the blood of Christ, could be preached to **every** creature in **every** nation. The gospel reaches out to individuals — not nations. The disciples of Christ — Christians — are the light of the world. This left no place for the Jewish nation. The Jews, except for the "remnant" (Rom. 9:27), blinded by their misconceptions of God and of their mission as an example (light) to the pagan world, refused to accept this fact. The nation wanted to hold on to their claim that they were God's people. God settled the question as to who were the people of God, the church as the nation of Israel, when he used Rome to destroy the temple.

Prophecy started with Moses (Acts 3:22; Ex. 4:15-16; Ex. 7:1-2). Written revelation began with Moses (John 5:47; Gen. 3:15, 12:3, 18:18, 22:18, 49:10; Deut. 18:15-18). The nation was to be the channel through which the promised seed was to come. When he came, the nation rejected him. His death, resurrection, and ascension made redemption a reality, beginning at Pentecost (Acts 2). But when the nation refused the gospel, there was left nothing but a political nation. The Jewish nation was no different from pagan Rome except in ritualism and pretension. The journey from wanting to be like the nations around her (I Sam. 8:5) had reached its culmination when Pilate said, "Shall I crucify your King?" and the chief priests answered, "We have no king but Caesar." (John 19:15) They had requested a king to be like the nations around them, and now the high priests acknowledge that they have a king of another nation.

Following the crucifixion of Christ, his resurrection, ascension, and Pentecost, the bulk of the nation closed their eyes and ears to the gospel. Their table, "perverted Judaism," became a trap and brought recompense, God's judgment, upon the unbelief of the nation. (Psa. 69:23; Rom. 11:8-11) From Pentecost until the destruction of the temple by the Romans, what was there in the temple? It was left desolate (Matt. 28:38). God's presence was not in the temple. Christ became priest at Pentecost. His sacrifice for sin and his priesthood set aside the sacrifice of the priesthood of the law (Heb. 7). Sinful man approached God through Christ and his sacrifice beginning at Acts 2. That left no place for animal sacrifices or Jewish priests.

When the tabernacle was completed, God's presence entered it (Ex. 40). The holiness of God made it impossible for sinful man to have fellowship with God except on the basis of sacrifice and priesthood (Lev. 1-10; read also Lev. 16). But beginning at Pentecost, man's approach to God was through Christ and his sacrifice. Thus, from Pentecost until the temple was destroyed, there was nothing holy about

THE WORK OF THE HOLY SPIRIT 311

the temple. It was God's presence in it that had made it holy, but God no longer dwelt in the temple. God dwelt in the church (Eph. 2:11-22; II Cor. 6:14-18). In view of the fact that God no longer dwelt in the temple, what would have been wrong with either a Jew or a Gentile going not only into the temple, but even into what had been the most holy place? The answer is, nothing. If Paul had carried a Gentile into the temple, why would it have been wrong? God's presence, which formerly had made the temple holy, was not there. Since it was the presence of God that had made it holy in the first place, how could there have been anything holy about it when God no longer dwelt in it? It was nothing but the misconception of the Jews who continued to attribute holiness to it. Who had ever dreamed of there being anything holy in the temple following Pentecost? The most holy place was moved from Jerusalem to heaven, with Christ as high priest (Heb. 9:24). This did not await the fall of the Jewish state. This began at Pentecost. James and the elders at Jerusalem were simply mistaken when they encouraged Paul to go into the temple as though there were any service that could be rendered unto God through the sacrifices of the Old Testament. It was a God-forsaken, empty house. The attitude of the Jews toward the temple showed their total misunderstanding of what had happened beginning at Pentecost. When the book of Acts closed, their eyes were still blinded, and nothing was left but judgment (Acts 28:26-27).

Daniel foretold the coming of Christ, the preaching of the gospel of redemption, and, with the revelation of the gospel, the cessation of the prophet, and the end of the Jewish state. Ellicott makes the following comment on the phrase "to seal up": " . . . the impression of the translators being that all visions and prophesies were to receive their complete fulfullment in the course of these seventy weeks. It appears, however, to be more agreeable to the context to suppose that the prophet is speaking of the absolute cessation of all prophecies (I Cor. 13:8)." Daniel, in foretelling the culmination of redemption in Christ and the church, also announced the cessation of the prophet and, with the prophet, the end of the miraculous operation of the Spirit. Thus, with prophecy as the foundation of Revelation, and the miraculous confirmation that accompanied it, the announcement of the end of prophecy would of necessity include the end of the miraculous gifts that were associated with prophecy. A completed revelation left no place for a prophet and, therefore, no place for miraculous gifts. All claims for the miraculous gifts — the speaking in tongues or any other direct operation of the Spirit today — is contrary to all that the scriptures teach.

ZECHARIAH 13:1-6

"In that day there shall be a fountain opened to the house of David and to the inhabitants of Jerusalem for sin and for uncleanness.

"And it shall come to pass in that day, saith the Lord of hosts, that I will cut off the names of the idols out of the land, and they shall no more be remembered: and also I will cause the prophets and the unclean spirit to pass out of the land. And it shall come to pass, that when any shall yet prophesy, then his father and his mother that begat him shall say unto him, Thou shalt not live; for thou speakest lies in the name of the Lord: and his father and his mother that begat him shall thrust him through when he prophesieth. And it shall come to pass in that day, that the prophets shall be ashamed every one of his vision, when he hath prophesied; neither shall they wear a rough garment to deceive: But he shall say, I am no prophet, I am an husbandman; for man taught me to keep cattle from my youth. And one shall say unto him, What are these wounds in thine hand? Then he shall answer, Those with which I was wounded in the house of my friends." (Zech. 13:1-6)

The subject of demon possession is a difficult one. I do not pretend to know a great deal about it. I do know that the Bible teaches that there were people possessed of demons and that Christ and the apostles cast out demons. Any attempt to weaken this by saying that the recorded accounts were the result of Christ's accepting a superstition which existed during the first century must be totally rejected by those who accept his diety.

Zechariah 13 points to Christ as a fountain, an atonement for sin. Verse 2 is a prophecy of the end of demon possession. Since it took a miraculous operation of the Spirit to cast out demons, the cessation of the miraculous would have left no means for dealing with demons if they continued beyond the period of miracles. The atonement of Christ limited the work of Satan (Matt. 12:22-30). The casting out of demons demonstrated the power of Christ over Satan. The apostles' casting out of demons demonstrated their apostolic power, proved the gospel they preached, and confirmed the claim of Christ. When the gospel was revealed, the faith "once delivered unto the saints" (Jude 3), there was no further need of the miraculous. In the passing away of the miraculous, there also would be the cessation of demon possession.

Notice that Zechariah not only foresaw the passing of demon possession, but also the passing of the prophets. Since prophecy stands for the entire miraculous operation of the Spirit, one should not be surprised that Zechariah combines the passing of both, the prophecy and

THE WORK OF THE HOLY SPIRIT 313

demon possession.

Verses 3 through 6 picture a time when there would be no genuine prophets. Thus, any claim to be a prophet would be an evident lie. Since the prophet would cease, any attempt to prophesy would produce shame. The garment worn by prophets would no longer be used as a means of deceit by false prophets. The garment identified the prophet. None wearing the garment of a prophet signified a time when there would be no genuine prophet to counterfeit. Verses 5 and 6 show the refusal to make any claim to prophesy. When questioned as to the wounds in his hands, he would lie about it by saying he had been wounded in the house of his friends. There was a practice among heathen priests of cutting themselves while attempting to prophesy, as seen in I Kings 18:28: "And they cried aloud, and cut themselves after their manner with knives and lancets, till the blood gushed out upon them."

This entire section of the book of Zechariah is intended to foretell the cessation of the prophet. The picture of no one being willing to admit to being a prophet establishes this fact. The truth of the matter is, if men believe the Bible, the claim on the part of any to be a prophet or to have any miraculous gift would be marked as a lie.

Any claim to speak in the name of the Lord today by direct operation of the Holy Spirit is a lie (Zech. 13:3). The claim to speak in a tongue by a direct operation of the Holy Spirit is a lie. Zechariah foresaw the end of phophecy, and with it the end of the miraculous operation of the Holy Spirit. Whom shall I believe: one to whom the word of the Lord came, who is called a prophet and whose prophecy is dated (Zech. 1:1), or Pentecostals who falsely claim to have miraculous gifts? It is not difficult for me to accept both Daniel and Zechariah who, by inspiration, foresaw the cessation of the prophets, and with them the passing of miraculous gifts. Daniel 9 and Zechariah 13 confirm Paul in I Corinthians 1:5-8 and I Corinthians 13:1-13. Thus do both the Old and the New Testaments deny the claim today of Pentecostal speaking in tongues.

SCRIPTURE INDEX
(**Bold type** indicates extensive discussion)

GENESIS	Page
6	37,38,41,61
6:3	37
6:22	43
12	43,56
12:1-7	205
12:2	57,178
12:3	49,57
12:7	57,178
18	20
22:18	49,202,205
49:10	49

EXODUS	
3:12-15	277
4:1	11
4:8,9	12,276
40	310

LEVITICUS	
1-10	310
16	310

NUMBERS	
22-24	285
22:38	35
24:13	35

DEUTERONOMY	
18:18	278
18:15-18	278
18:17-20	279
18:18-20	48,285
28	291
28:46-49	291,292

II SAMUEL	
7:10-13	49

I KINGS	
18:28	313

NEHEMIAH	
9:13-30	38,177

PSALMS	
19	10
19:7	24

ISAIAH	
2:1-4	54,225
7:14	48,225
9:6	48,225
11:1-10	225
13	179
28	269
28:7-11	292
33:19	293
35:8	225
36:11	293
37:31-32	293
41:4	306
41:20-26	306
42:1-4	225
42:9	306
43:10	309
44:8	309
44:24-26	307
45:2	307
46:10	307
48:5-7	307
53	225
55:8,9	10
56:5	225
62:1,2	225
63:10	177

JEREMIAH	
5:7-15	294
23:9-32	280,281

DANIEL	
2,7	47,54
9	47,54
9:20-27	46,308

JOEL
2 .... **43-46,61**,113,116,119,125, 127,138,139,148,149,152,195
2:28-32 .. 68,69,78,80,81,82,84,86, 108,111,175,179,181,252

HABAKKUK
2:4 219

ZECHARIAH
1:1 313
4:6 30
13:1-6 312
14 46

MALACHI
3,4 43,46
3:8-12 47
4:1 54

MATTHEW
1:1 49
3 80
3:1-12 .... **77-80**
3:2 84,108
3:7 63
3:10-12 68
3:11 81,82,84,96,109
5:17 44
6:33 265
7:7,8 90
7:15-20 284
10 .... **80-82**
10:16-20 128
10:16-42 .... **68,69**
10:19,20 282
10:32,33 18
10:41 282
11:13 289
12:22-30 312
16:19 119,120
21:33-43 298
22:42 48
23 50
23:33 63,79
23:36 47,58,61,62,63,71
23:37,38 63,295
24 .... 46,48,**61-67**,69, 74,75,179
24:3 70
24:5 49
24:8 74
24:13 51,179
24:15 46
24:21 47
24:22 51,71,180
24:24 49
24:29 61,68
24:30 50
24:33 167,179
24:34 47,58,71
24:35 47,48
25 48
25:31-46 81
26:28 258
27:66 174
28:7 101
28:16 88
28:16-20 102
28:17 88
28:18-20 .... **69,70**,81,**82,83**,87, 101,102,103
28:20 94,95,96,100

MARK
1:4 109
1:15 59,109
9:1 .... **83,84**,109
13 .... 48,**61-65**,67
13:9-13 48,129
13:11 282
13:24,25 61,68
16:9-13 87
16:14-20 .... **85-106**, 117,118,119,253,260,261,262,269

16:15,16	257
16:16	112,118,175,203
16:16-18	**151,152**,256,257
16:17	139
16:20	16,33,73,74,158,165, 175,244,288

LUKE

1:15	29,**106,107**,183
1:41	107,183
1:67	107,183,184
1:76	107
4:18,19	**164,165**
9:39	282
9:58	265
11:2	109
11:13	**107-111**
16:16	289
19:10	264
21	48,**61-65**,68,180
21:11	68
21:13-15	48,129,282
21:14-28	181
21:18	51,180
21:20	46,180
21:20-24	299
21:22	67
21:28	180,181
22:29	121
24:33-36	88
24:36-48	87,89
24:41,42	88
24:44-49	102,103,**111-113**
24:49	84,134,151,152, 166,169,174

JOHN

1:11,12	295
3:34	165,174
4:17-19	282
4:24	44,218
5:45-47	277

6:27	174
7:38,39	**114-119**,139,147,175
8:32	259
8:44	211
10:41	106
13:34,35	262
14	24,**119-127**
14:6	305
14:15-17	172,173,206,207, 237,251
14:26	97,183,237,282
15	24,**119-127**,251
15:6	91
15:26,27	155,170,171,173, 237,245
16	24,**119-127**,251
16:7,8	109,136
16:7-11	147
16:7-16	115,116,183
16:13	172,206,237,282
16:13,14	263
19:15,16	295,310
20:19-23	87,88
20:20,25,28	88
20:20,21	305
20:21-23	139
20:22	147
20:30,31	16,162,262

ACTS

1:3	102
1:4-9	103
1:6-9	99,102
1:8	84,97,109,121,166, 169,170,247
2	33,36,46,70,71,78, 80,81,111,112,126,133, 140,141,**147-153**,269
2:1-4	4,84,97,121,252,295
2:5-6	296
2:1-6	278
2:1-37	50

Reference	Pages
2:4	71,185,187,266
2:6,8	266
2:12	78
2:16	46
2:20	179
2:30,31	70
2:33	32,157,232
2:36	112
2:38	18,112,116,**130-134**,137,139,140,141,147,154,155,159,164,256,258
2:40	71
2:41	23
2:43	5
3	4,264
3:11-15	154
3:21-25	275
3:22,23	279,289
4:2,17,33	154
4:31	154,187
5:12,30	154
5:32	7,**153-155**,170,171
6:1-6	255
6:3-10	184,185,187,191
6:6	256
7:34	250
8	57,85,86,111,117,133,138,185
8:4	57,117,255
8:6,7	185
8:12	255,256,257
8:12-18	105
8:13-19	288
8:14-19	110,111,184,252,254,271,272
8:14-23	285
8:15-17	140
8:16	256
8:17-18	85,185,255
8:19	185
8:20	134,137
8:26,29	21
8:35	259
9	4,57
9:2	305
9:6	103
10	36,57,135,256
10:32,33	18
10:34	36,149
10:38	**165**
10:44-47	252
10:45	132,**135**,137,257
10:46	4
10:47	**140,141**
10:48	18
11	36,57
11:15	84
11:17	**135**,137
11:21	192
13:6-12	283
14:8-10	283
15	222
16:14	192
16:31	18
17:11	210
19	30,86,117,133,175
19:1-7	106,118,189,252,256,272
19:2	8,144,175
19:6	4,8,141,175
19:1-6	286
19:9	305
19:19,20	8
20:22,23	247
20:32	24
21:10,11	247
21:20	167
22:10	103
22:21,22	216
25:4,6	59
26:31,32	53
28:22	54
28:26,27	311

ROMANS
Outline	221
1:1	120
1:1-17	**216-219**
1:5	18,43,117,220,227,258
1:9	44
1:11	106,224,234,273
1:16	6,32,214,227
1:16,17	44,220,258,287
1:18	227
2:2,4-6,11,16	220
2:23,24	228
3:8,9	227
3:19-31	224,225
3:20,21	226,227,242
3:20-26	249
3:23	219
3:25,26	226
3:25-31	228
3:27	309
4:11	173
4:12	7,43
4:13	43
4:16	227
5:18,19	220
6:1	227
6:1-13	240
6:11-14	230,242
7:5,6	226,229
8	221,222,225,227,229,244,245,248,249
8:1	225,227
8:1-4	226
8:2	200
8:9	29,**233-239**,240,241
8:11	**240,241**,242
8:12	230,241
8:14	257
8:14-16	**241-248**
8:15	262
8:26,27	19,**248-252**
9	222
9:8	228
10	222
10:15	203
10:17	7,19,261,305
11	222
11:20	297
12:3-6	184,234,235,237,238,241,246
13:11,12	65,66
13:14	229
15	214
15:8	73,74
15:13-25	223,224
15:4	305
15:14	237
15:16-20	218,244
15:19	192,245
15:23,24	215
15:30-32	214
16	60
16:16	215
16:17,18	215,216,223,234,238,239
16:20	50,56,59,66
16:25	56
16:26	217,219,220

I CORINTHIANS
1:2	201,235,236
1:4-8	**71-76**,160,161,202
1:5	191
1:6,7	165
1:9	202
1:10-17	18
1:17	203,204
1:18,27	209
1:19,21,29	204
2	200,201,**204-213**
2:1-5	157,239,259,305

2:7-16	12	14:14	250,251,274
2:13	11,200,257	14:15	252
2:14	200,235	14:25	282
3:1-4	18,262	14:21,22	296
3:16	**160-164**,235,236,237	14:22	260
4:1-5	278	14:26	191
4:17	305	14:27,28	273,274
4:19,20	160,204,207,232,238	14:32	189
6:11	163	14:33,34	150,163
6:19	**160-164**,235,236,237	14:37	120,172,210
7:26,29	66	14:37,38	11,169,284
9:1,2	71,72,73,143,161, 174,202,270	14:40	163
9:3	202,209	15:1-4	73
10:2	178	15:33	203

II CORINTHIANS

11	18
12	18,72,157,160,162, 164,173,193,235,236
12:4	169,183
12:7	34,157,189
12:8	72
12:10	146,250
12:11	184
12:13	205
12:28	120
12:31	305
13	18,71,72,188,193, 236,262,301,303
13:2	301,302
13:8	15,291
13:8-10	92,300
13:10	76
13:13	304
14	18,34,72,160,162, 163,164,190,191,193, 235,236,251,260,266,274
14:1	18
14:3	189,260,273,274
14:3-27	**266-270**
14:13	273,274

1:21	**165,166**,181
1:22	174,181
2:17	157,165
3	75,231
3:1	165
3:6	231
4:1-7	165
4:2	157
4:5	259
4:16-18	264
5:5	182
5:7	31
5:12,19	165
5:16	228
5:20	120,165,169
6:6,7	165
6:14-18	311
8	262
9	262
10:8	113,165
10:13	165
11:3	6
11:4-6	161-165
11:5	73

11:11-13 211
11:12-15 297
11:13-15 6,160,165
11:22,23 297
11:23 165
11:23-28 265
12:10 146
12:12 33,73,122,143,165,
    174,184,208,244,253,270,288
13:3 165,209
13:6 165
13:8 33
13:10 113,165

GALATIANS

1 142
1:1 142,145
1:1-12 287
1:6 145
1:7 142
1:7-9 6,10
1:7-13 223
1:11,12 10,121
1:13 145
2 31,142
2:4 167
2:8 216
2:11-14 16,36,262
2:17-21 216
3 55,205
3:2 .... **142-146**
3:3 229,233
3:5 143,144,145,287
3:8 55
3:10,13 242
3:19,22-29 55
3:26,27 228
3:26-29 144,145,150,241,299
4 55
4:5 144

4:6 144,145,257
4:7 144,231
4:23 242
5 55
5:1-4 23,142,222,234
5:6 7
5:16-24 257
5:19-21 230
6:16 57,178

EPHESIANS

1:3 265
1:13 174,175,177,189
1:13,14 182
2:12-22 309
3:1-6,10,11,21 205
3:1-8 39,302,311
3:3 121,136
3:3-6 33,56,60,203
3:5 175
3:7 .... **136**,137
4:7,8 177
4:7-11 .... **136-138**,180,183,184
4:7-16 175,177,178,180,
                                    181,189
4:11-13 92
4:13 178
4:30 .... **176-181**,189
5:18 .... 8,**186,187**,189,
                                    190,191
5:18,19 198
6:16 178
6:17 29

PHILIPPIANS

1:17 128
3:4,5 229
3:18,19 234

COLLOSSIANS
1:18 263
2:9 263
2:14 52
3:16 8,190,191,198
4:10 284
4:14 284

I THESSALONIANS
1:5 159,160,192,232,
233,234
5:19,20 .... **189,190**
5:21 275

II THESSALONIANS
2:1,2 280
2:9 122
2:15 279
3:14 279

I TIMOTHY
2:10-12 150
4:14 189,236,272

II TIMOTHY
1:6 .... 184,**188,189**,190,
236,237,272
1:7 188
1:14 236
3:15,16 15
3:16,17 32,92,257
4:3,4 206
4:11 284

HEBREWS
1:1,2 13,290,295
2:3,4 33,73,184,190,
244,287,288
2:15 242
6:6 66
9 54
9:8-14 17

9:9,10 228
9:13,14 218,228,231,258
9:16,17 52
9:24 311
10 54
10:1-4 240,242
10:3,4 258
10:4 17
10:22 243
10:25 66,67,167
10:30 67
10:37 67,179
10:38 258
11 262
11:7 43
12:18-21 242
12:22-24 243
12:26-29 55,67
13:9 73

JAMES
1:8 264
2:21,22 43
2:26 7
3:5,6 266
3:14,15 210,211
3:16,17 211
5:7-9 67

I PETER
1:10-12 12
1:12 192
2:2 262
2:5,9 178
2:8,9 57
2:9 309
3:12 70
3:18-21 43,243
3:19,20 37,43
4:7 67
4:17,18 51,67

II PETER
1:19	48
1:21	10,12
2:5	37,43
2:15	285

I JOHN
1:1-5	170,171,237
1:7-10	258
2:1	122
2:18-27	**166-171**
2:20	173
2:27	**146,147,239**
3:5	150
3:21	243
3:23,24	**171-173**
4:1	146,168,170,239,281
4:1-6	**172,173**
4:3	170,284
4:5	206
4:6	169,206,207
4:8	262
4:13	237
4:13,14	**171-173**
4:19	306

JUDE
3	33,113,262
10	212
11	285
19,20	167,211,212,235, 250,251

REVELATION
1:1	58,59
1:3	59,66
1:10	234,235
2:14	36
3:9	207
4:2	234,235
5:5	173
7:3	173
10:7	56,60,301
12:11	262
22:6	59
22:18	290

BY GIFT OF PROPHECY

(Eph. 3:1-6)

V. 2 Have Prophecy —
   Know: 1. Mysteries
            2. Knowledge

V. 3 Revelation —
   Made Known: 1. Mystery
                  2. I Wrote
   (Ye read . . . understanding)

V. 8 Whether there be —
   Prophecies . . . done away
   Tongues . . . cease
   Knowledge . . . done away
     (Divine Revelation through inspiration.)

V. 5 Now Revealed Unto —
   Apostles ⟩ in the Spirit
   Prophets

V 9 For (we):
1. Know in Part (Per. Knowledge)
2. Prophecy in part (Public Preaching)

V.6 To wit, that the Gentiles are:
1. Fellow heirs
2. Fellow members of the body
3. Fellow partakers of the promise

V. 10 But (contrast):
   When PERFECT come . . .
   Part done away.

Vs. 8-9 I was Made A Minister —
1. To Preach
2. To make men see . . . the Mystery.

V. 11 Illustrated:
   Child to Man

V. 12 For:
1. Now we see darkly . . . then face to face.
2. Now I know in part . . . then fully.

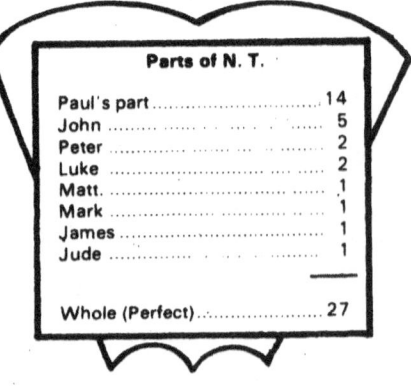

```
        Parts of N. T.
Paul's part....................14
John ...........................5
Peter ..........................2
Luke ...........................2
Matt. ..........................1
Mark ..........................1
James .........................1
Jude ..........................1
                              ___
Whole (Perfect)..............27
```

V. 13 Now Abideth:
1. Faith (Rom. 10:17) ⎫ Derived
2. Hope (Rom. 15:4) ⎬ through
3. Love (I Jn. 4:19) ⎭ SCRIPTURES

"ALL SCRIPTURE IS GIVEN BY INSPIRATION OF GOD, AND IS PROFITABLE FOR DOCTRINE FOR REPROOF, FOR CORRECTION, FOR INSTRUCTION IN RIGHTEOUSNESS: THAT THE MAN OF GOD MAY BE PERFECT, THROUGHLY FURNISHED UNTO ALL GOOD WORKS." (II Timothy 3:16-17)

THE WORK OF THE HOLY SPIRIT

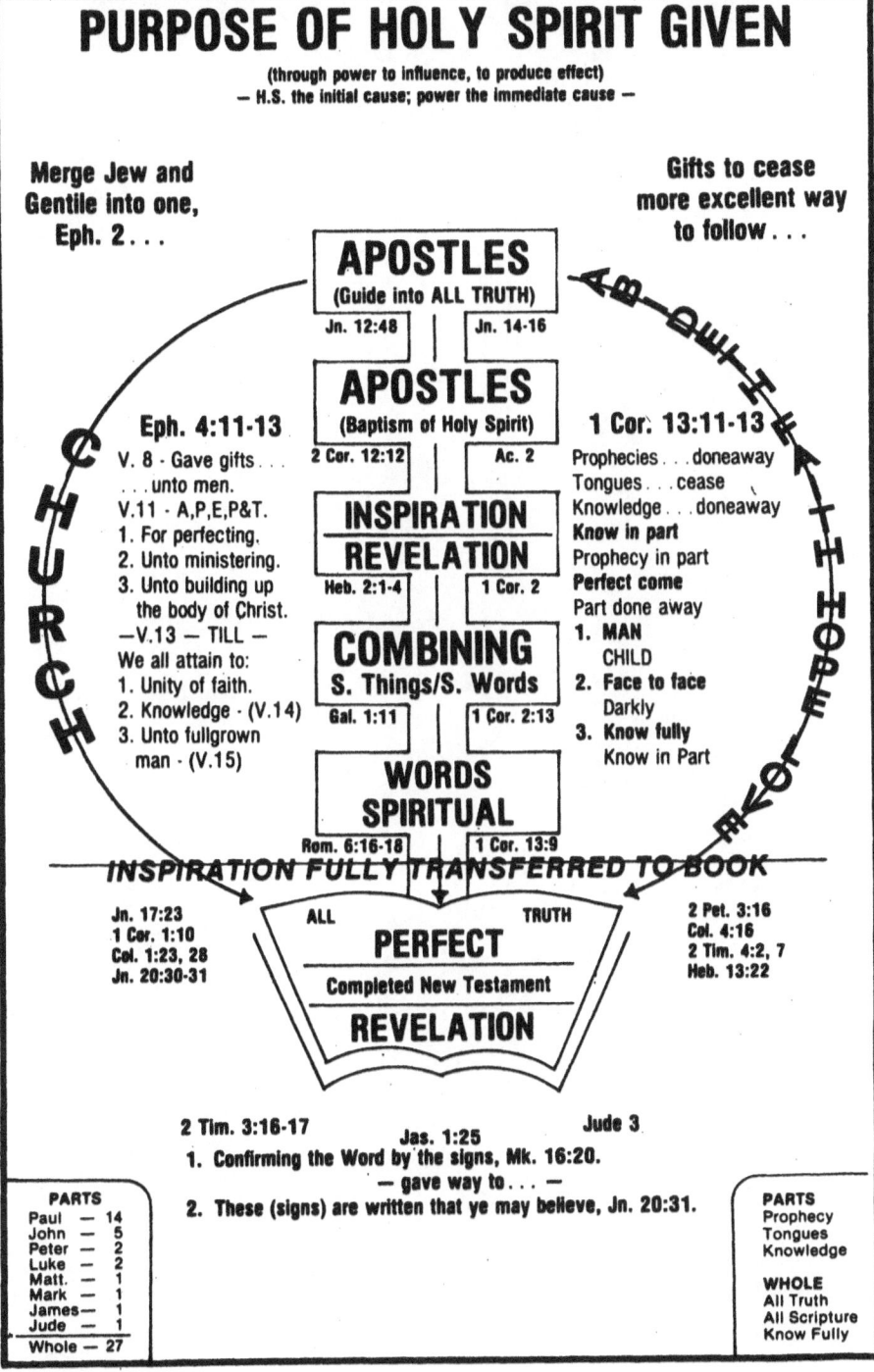

www.ingramcontent.com/pod-product-compliance
Lightning Source LLC
Chambersburg PA
CBHW030238170426
43202CB00007B/45